Legal Drafting

Legal Drafting

Susan L. Brody
Associate Professor of Law
John Marshall Law School

Jane Rutherford
Associate Professor of Law
DePaul University College of Law

Laurel A. Vietzen
Coordinator of Paralegal Studies
Elgin Community College

John C. Dernbach
Visiting Associate Professor of Law
Widener University School of Law

ASPEN
PUBLISHERS

111 Eighth Avenue, New York, NY 10011
www.aspenpublishers.com

Library of Congress Catalog Card No. 93-80291

ISBN 0-7355-1693-6

16 17 18 19 20

To all our families,
both personal and professional

Summary of Contents

Contents

Chapter Three   Write Carefully   65

Part II   *Applying the Process*   *131*

Chapter Four   **Drafting Estate Planning Documents**   **133**

Chapter Five   Drafting Contracts   **203**

Preface

Nearly 90 percent of all lawyers draft documents such as wills or contracts. However, relatively few texts exist to teach students how to write these documents, which are so commonly used in the practice of law. Nevertheless, a dramatic trend is emerging toward adding legal drafting to law school curricula so that students learn how to write documents that use law without citing it.

This book is divided into two parts. Part 1 teaches a process for legal drafting, encompassing those issues that are common to drafting all documents. Part 2 applies the process to various contexts, focusing on those drafting issues that are unique to specific types of documents.

Part 1 of this book consists of three chapters that teach a process, or strategy, for legal drafting. Chapter 1 reviews other skills students bring to the drafting process, including legal research, objective writing, and persuasive writing. The chapter explains why those skills are prerequisite to effective legal drafting and then describes the new skills necessary for the drafting process.

Chapter 2 sets out seven recursive steps of legal drafting. The seven-step process gives students a place to start and leads them through drafting an entire document. Each step is explained, illustrated with examples and diagrams, and tested with exercises. The emphasis on a consistent process teaches students how to draft new texts and how properly, carefully to adapt forms to new uses. Students move beyond the myth of merely "filling-in-the-blanks" and create customized documents. After working through the book, we hope the drafting process becomes second nature and provides a useful transition from law school to practice.

Chapter 3 focuses on the most important step: writing carefully. It reviews many principles of good writing, emphasizing concepts that are particularly important in legal drafting, for example, the difference between intentional vagueness and ambiguity. The chapter provides a detailed view of the elements of careful writing, including numerous exercises, examples, and editing tips, which can be used either as text or as reference material.

Once the process has been introduced, Part 2 of the book applies the process to four particular kinds of documents: wills and trusts (Chapter 4), contracts (Chapter 5), pleadings (Chapter 6), and legislation (Chapter 7). Unlike specialized drafting texts, these chapters are not meant to teach the underlying substantive law. Although the chapters recognize and integrate the need to research and understand the law as part of the drafting process, these chapters are designed to be used either in a legal writing course focused on drafting or to add a writing component to a doctrinal course.

Each chapter presents text, examples, sample documents, and exercises to demonstrate each of the seven steps of the drafting process. The exercises require students to draft provisions from scratch, to edit existing provisions, and to create entire documents. Each chapter includes at least one annotated document that illustrates the seven steps of legal drafting.

This book can be used straight through in a general drafting course because it sets out the rules (the seven steps) and then applies them to various contexts. But it can also be used for a drafting component in a doctrinal course such as Contracts, Civil Procedure, Business Transactions, Wills and Trusts, Estate Planning, Family Law, or Legislation. For example, a contracts professor may require students to read Chapters 1, 2, and 3, as well as Chapter 5 on Drafting Contracts.

Regardless of the course in which it is used, the skills learned in this book will provide a bridge between curriculum and practice. For those who will be drafting documents, we hope this book provides a sound drafting method that will prepare newly licensed attorneys to tackle a variety of drafting assignments. For those who may never actually draft documents, the process practiced in this book will make them better at reading and interpreting documents, tasks performed daily and continually by all those associated with the practice of law.

Susan L. Brody
Jane Rutherford
Laurel A. Vietzen
John C. Dernbach

January 1994

Acknowledgments

This book has taken so many years of work that it would be difficult, if not impossible, to mention all the people who helped us. Numerous secretaries, student research assistants, colleagues, and family members all helped shape the content and format of this book. We thank you all for your hard work and contributions. Most importantly, we wish sincerely to thank our colleagues in the field of legal writing. Many examples from their books, documents, presentations, and the like have been incorporated throughout this book. Because we reviewed so many materials on this topic, we apologize if we failed to attribute any particular example to its author. All of these examples help clarify concepts and ideas essential to the success of this book.

There are a few people we do wish to thank specifically. Professors Ralph Brill, Vincent DeLiberato, Ardath Hamann, Carol Parker, and Timothy O'Neill contributed ideas and reviewed significant portions of many drafts. Their guidance was invaluable. Ms. Kenda Jo McCrory read drafts and provided helpful comments. The adjunct professors who teach drafting at The John Marshall Law School gave us useful feedback after each draft was written, used in class, rewritten, and reused over and over again. Mr. Eugene Schiltz, one of those adjunct professors, suggested ideas and analogies so perfectly suited to the book's themes, that we have incorporated them in the final manuscript. Ms. Gwen Konigsfeld and Ms. Beth Schaeffer toiled at their computers for countless hours to insure that the final manuscript was as perfect as possible when delivered to Little, Brown. Finally, Mr. Richard Heuser was instrumental in developing this book. His knowledge about law text books seems to us unmatched by any other person who helped shape this book. Moreover, he believed in us and supported our ideas, even at a time when we questioned the book's concept. He inspired us during every step of the creative process. To all these people, we are indeed truly grateful.

Legal Drafting

PART I
A Process for Legal Drafting

CHAPTER *1*

An Introduction to Legal Drafting

A. *Introduction*

   This book has three goals. First, it will serve as a transition from law school to law practice. You will become familiar with the legal documents not typically studied during law school but that lawyers read, use, draft, and interpret daily.

   Most law school writing classes focus on writing projects that teach legal analysis, such as memoranda and briefs. They do not focus on nonanalytical documents such as wills, contracts, pleadings, and legislation. This focus is understandable, since legal analysis is an entirely new discourse for most law students and is the primary teaching tool in law school. Moreover, legal analysis is a prerequisite skill to any type of law practice — even one in which lawyers draft primarily wills or contracts. For example, when you draft a will, you need to analyze the circumstances and apply the law from the viewpoints of all the persons who will be affected by the will: persons who will receive gifts under the will, persons who have been left out of the will, the probate court, lawyers, trustees, guardians, executors, and others. Thus, when you learn legal analysis through writing briefs and memoranda, it helps prepare you to draft other documents.

   But mastery of legal analysis alone will not ensure that you effectively draft documents such as wills, contracts, pleadings, or statutes. Legal drafting requires a combination of other skills not specifically taught in most law school curricula. The absence of courses that teach such skills reinforces the myth that drafting is merely a fill-in-the-blank activity. However, the skills of legal drafting require much more than that. They are detailed and varied.

   The skills necessary to write a legal memorandum or brief are generally obvious from the document itself, for example, research, analysis, organization, and persuasion. In contrast, those necessary to draft a will, contract, pleading, or statute are not necessarily obvious from the faces of those documents. For example, when you draft a will, you should be familiar with the relevant portions of the state probate code, but you would infrequently, if ever, cite them. Thus, the skill of legal research is necessary to draft a will but is not obvious from the will itself. Similarly, to protect your client's wishes, you should anticipate a will contest by each potentially hostile person and draft the will accordingly. But you would rarely, if ever, expressly state those possibilities in the text of the will. Thus, the skills of understanding multiple audiences and anticipating future contingencies are required, but neither is necessarily evident from the document.

These are just a few examples of skills needed to draft effectively. When you finish this book, you will be familiar with all the skills necessary for legal drafting. As a result, you will be prepared to tackle the drafting of numerous documents used in a law practice.

The second goal of this book is to teach you a structure, or process, for drafting those documents. Because you probably have never drafted legal documents before, you might feel overwhelmed and find it difficult to think of a method to complete a document. In response, you might decide to cut and paste different sections of various forms. If you do so, the finished product will likely be an inaccurate hodgepodge that will confuse your readers and perhaps even undermine your client's wishes.

This book will prevent that result by teaching you a process for drafting and the requisite skills to master the process. By doing so, however, it will also teach you the proper role that forms play throughout the process. This book recognizes the widespread use of forms throughout the profession but will show you how to use forms as an integral part of the drafting process, rather than as a replacement for it.

Moreover, as you master the steps of the process, you will be able to transfer, apply, and alter forms to suit each client's particular circumstances and easily tailor each new document. In a sense, the process will teach you to be a legal architect. You will systematically create a blueprint, or master plan, for the document, carefully structure each section, and precisely build each word to satisfy your plan. The process will guide you to draft clear and accessible documents.

The third and final goal of this book is to reinforce rules of good writing and to illustrate how they apply to drafting documents. Most poorly drafted documents are traceable to lawyers' poor writing.[1] There are three general reasons for poor writing. First, lawyers are not usually well-trained in English and need to increase their mastery of the English language,[2] especially the basic principles of sentence structure.

Second, lawyers rely too heavily on forms without editing them. Because forms are written to cover every conceivable person and circumstance, by definition they are general, abstract, and sometimes even ambiguous. Because lawyers are not usually well-trained in English, they find it easier to copy a form than to alter one. Moreover, even those trained in English may find it quicker to copy a form than to edit it. The potential for lawsuits, however, including one for legal malpractice, makes it well worth while to make your documents as simple and as accessible to the reader as you can.

Third, law students and newly licensed lawyers imitate the writing of more experienced lawyers and thus perpetuate poor writing. This book will bring you back to the basics of good writing, reviewing principles you probably have not thought about since grade school and applying those principles in an entirely new context.

Thus, the three goals of this book are to (1) serve as a transition between law school and practice; (2) provide you with a process for legal drafting; and (3) reinforce principles of good writing. Before these goals can be accomplished, however, some background is necessary. The remainder of this chapter will provide a definition for legal drafting, explaining how it is different from other forms of legal writing with which you are already familiar. It then will explain all the skills necessary for legal drafting, beginning with those skills previously learned in other legal writing courses and moving on to those that need to be acquired to draft effectively.

B.   Drafting Defined

Drafting is a type of legal writing that reduces to writing clients' desires regarding legally significant transactions or events, for example, wills, contracts, pleadings, and statutes. These documents differ from legal memoranda and briefs in many significant ways.

First, drafted documents use the substantive law differently than do memoranda or briefs. Both objective and persuasive memoranda or briefs analyze the law. An objective memorandum or brief explains case law and other authorities, analyzing them from all possible viewpoints. A persuasive memorandum or brief argues those authorities, taking a position that presents one particular viewpoint.

In contrast, drafted documents are not analytical at all. In fact, the law itself is infrequently mentioned in most forms of legal drafting. Although legal drafting requires a thorough understanding of the relevant substantive law, it does not present the law.

Second, clients have much more input regarding the contents of a drafted document than they do regarding the contents of an objective or advocacy memorandum or brief. Because memoranda and briefs analyze the law, their primary sources are cases, statutes, and other authorities that the lawyer chooses. Similarly, the lawyer chooses what facts to include in a memorandum or brief because she knows which ones are legally significant.

In contrast, the client has more control over the contents of a will or contract and, although to a lesser extent, over the contents of a pleading or statute. Although a lawyer always has an obligation to counsel a client on the content of a document, the primary source will always be the client. A will, for example, tells how your client wants to dispose of property upon death. A complaint explains a wrong committed against your client and the relief your client desires. Thus, clients determine the content of such documents to a greater extent than they determine the content of a memorandum or brief.

The third difference between legal drafting and other forms of legal writing is that some documents may aim to satisfy not only your client's desires but also nonclients' as well. This is never true of a persuasive memorandum or brief. An objective memorandum may present a nonclient's position but is usually for the purpose of determining a way to defeat it, not finding a way to advance it.

In contrast, for example, a contract conveys terms that will satisfy not only your client's desires but your opponent's as well. Similarly, a statute may be drafted to reflect the desires of numerous constituencies: a state or other governing body, the public, various lobbyists representing interest groups, and legislators. The input from these various sources makes drafting very different from writing legal memoranda or briefs.

Fourth, drafted documents are multifarious. They are read by a variety of diverse audiences for whom there may be a variety of objectives and whose activities may be governed in a variety of ways. The multidimensional audiences, objectives, and activities create tensions and conflicts not present when you write memoranda and briefs.

Regarding audiences, there may be numerous audiences for every document you draft, each having a different perspective and a varying level of education. For example, a real estate sales contract for construction of a new building will be read by the parties, their lawyers, architects, accountants, loan officers, and others. In contrast, the audiences for memoranda and briefs are more unitary. Those documents are read almost exclusively by lawyers and judges who generally have the same educational background.

Regarding objectives, legal drafting sometimes requires you to satisfy inconsistent objectives through the same document. For example, when you draft a complaint, you are trying to set out your case clearly and convincingly, both to persuade a judge who never heard of your case before and to discourage the defendant from fighting. You also may anticipate a motion to dismiss either because you have tried to fit unusual facts into established law or because you have tried to make a case for expanding law. In either case, you will be trying to survive that motion. At the same time, you are trying to set out your case objectively because pleading rules generally require you to be simple[3] and, strategically, because you want to force your opponent to admit as many of the allegations as possible.

In contrast, a memorandum or brief usually has one purpose. An objective memorandum seeks to analyze all sides of a controversy and recommend a solution to a lawyer or judge. A persuasive memorandum or brief seeks to convince a judge or lawyer that its position is legally correct.

Regarding activities, legal drafting governs how a variety of people will act. The terms of a real estate sales contract, for example, affect the conduct of the buyer, the seller, the real estate broker, the lending institution, and the title company, to name a few. The terms of a will affect the beneficiaries, the executor, the probate lawyer, the probate court, and in some cases other fiduciaries, such as guardians or trustees. In contrast, memoranda and briefs do not govern conduct; they describe rather than regulate behavior. Thus, drafting requires you to perform many diverse goals through a single document.

Fifth, drafting is different because it requires you to anticipate all possible future contingencies. Because most drafted documents govern future conduct, you must ask "what if" for every term included in the document. You need not do so for legal memoranda and briefs, however, because they do not operate in the future.

Two types of contingencies may occur: (1) circumstances may change and (2) the document's form, language, or organization may be subject to multiple interpretations. You want to ensure that no matter what the future circumstances are, your client's intent is satisfied. You also want to prevent multiple, inconsistent interpretations that would defeat your client's intent.

For example, when drafting a will you must consider numerous circumstances that could change prior to the testator's death. The death of a beneficiary, the destruction or replacement of bequeathed property, and the reduction of available money are but a few such circumstances you should anticipate. To illustrate, assume that a testator wants to provide for a favorite nephew. He signs a will giving the nephew "all of my Acme, Inc., stock." He fails, however, to amend his will years later when he receives Zeta, Inc., stock to replace the Acme stock. Under those circumstances, the testator's wishes may not be realized.

You also need to consider the way a bequest is written. Consider the following examples:

> The testator intends to give her "gold watch" to her granddaughter, but you use the word "jewelry" instead. Will the testator's intent be realized?

> The testator has one sister and four nieces. You draft, "I give $100,000 in equal shares to my sister and my nieces." Do the four nieces together take half, $50,000 ($12,500 each), leaving $50,000 for the sister? Or does each person get one-fifth, $20,000 each?

> Consider the phrase, "I give $5,000 only to my grandson, John." Does the testator wish to give $5,000 to only one person — John? Or does he wish to limit the amount he gives to John to only $5,000? What if there is also a provision later in the will that says, "I give my account at Home Federal to my descendents in equal shares." Is John excluded from this gift?

The consequences of such oversights in language could indeed defeat the testator's intent as well as cause unnecessary litigation. Anticipating all conceivable contingencies and interpretations of your work will avoid those problems.

Sixth, the products of legal drafting look different from memoranda and briefs. In fact, they do not look like narrative texts; they look much more like formal but detailed outlines. Subheadings and headings may replace textual transitions. Enumeration and tabulation may replace syntax and help explain the relationship between the concepts presented. To illustrate, a memorandum or brief might describe the books and records of a partnership as follows:

> The books and records of the partnership are subject to the following rules. For each fiscal year from July 1 through June 30, the books and records shall show the condition of the partnership business and finance. In addition, the partners shall have access to the books and records during ordinary business hours and determine where the books will be kept. Finally, yearly audits will be conducted and paid for with partnership funds, although a partner may conduct an audit of the books at any other time at his own expense. Regarding the yearly audit, the auditors will generate a balance sheet and an income statement and mail copies of both to each partner. If a partner objects to any item in the balance sheet or income statement, he shall notify the partnership in writing, within 30 days of the day they were mailed. If he fails to do so, he waives any objection.

Drafted in a partnership agreement, the books and records provisions might look like this:

Books and Records
1. <u>Contents</u>: The books shall show the condition of the business and finance of the partnership.
2. <u>Fiscal Year</u>: July 1-June 30.
3. <u>Location of Books</u>:
    a. The partners shall determine where the books will be kept.
    b. The partners have access to the books during ordinary business hours.
4. <u>Yearly Audit</u>:
    a. The partners shall pay for a yearly audit.
    b. The auditors will do both of the following:
        1. generate two financial statements: a balance sheet and a statement of income and expenses; and
        2. mail to each partner copies of the financial statements
    c. If a partner objects to any items disclosed in the financial statements, he shall perform both of the following or else he waives any objections. He shall
        1. notify the partnership in writing and
        2. give the notice within 30 days of the date the statements were mailed.
5. <u>Additional Audits</u>: In addition to the yearly audit, a partner may audit the books at his own expense at any time.

Note that the headings and subheadings replace the introductory sentence as well as the transition words, "In addition," "Finally," and "Regarding the yearly audit." Enumerating and tabulating replace syntactical structure and help define the relationship between subjects and verbs. Thus, the appearance of a drafted document can be very different from a memorandum or brief.

Seventh and finally, legal drafting is different because the existence of forms may lead you into a false sense of completion. Because there is no counterpart to forms when you write a memorandum or brief, legal drafting will likely provide your first experience with forms. But do not let their mere existence trap you into using them to replace your own thinking and writing process. Allowing that to occur may be a disservice to your client. Forms can be informative and useful but they should not be used to replace the drafting process. Each client, situation, and document presents unique circumstances and deserves its own planning and drafting. There is no replacement for thoroughly thinking through each and every part of a document and how it should be completed for particular circumstances.

Thus, there are at least seven significant differences between legal drafting and other forms of legal writing. These differences generate the need for you to develop some new skills. But drafting also requires you to use skills previously developed when you learned to draft memoranda and briefs. Thus, you need to combine old and new skills to draft effectively. The remainder of this chapter will classify old skills and new skills, explaining how each is used in the drafting process.

C. *Previously Learned Skills Required for Drafting*

1. Advocacy and Objectivity

Good legal drafting requires the skills of objectivity and advocacy, which you have probably learned in previous legal writing courses. For example, one of your first legal writing experiences probably was to write an objective memorandum of law, analyzing all sides of a controversy and recommending a solution from an objective viewpoint. You may also have been asked to suggest a client's best legal position, based on your objective analysis.

You also probably have written persuasive, or advocacy, documents such as an appellate brief or a trial court brief or memorandum. These documents required you to understand all sides of a controversy but to present only one as convincingly as possible. Thus, you have learned the skills of objectivity and advocacy for the purpose of writing objective memoranda of law and persuasive documents.

Both those skills are necessary for effective legal drafting. For example, when you draft a contract, you are an advocate because you must represent your client's best interests and negotiate, on her behalf, for provisions best suited to her needs. Yet, the other parties to the contract are not really your "opponents." You need to be objective to understand the nonclients' position or positions and compromise in the drafting process because there will only be one final product. In a sense, drafting a contract is a cooperative venture, even though your primary task is, of course, to represent your client.

Drafting wills, pleadings, and legislation also requires a combination of advocacy and objectivity. When drafting a will, you remain objective in that you need to present to your client all possible options for all possible future contingencies: the death of a beneficiary or destruction of bequeathed property, for example. You are an advocate, however, in that you need to think about those persons who may contest the will and why they may do so. You also want to protect the testator's property from the Internal Revenue Service (IRS) and cut the costs of probate. You want to draft the will with these considerations in mind.

When drafting pleadings, you need to present the allegations objectively because ethical considerations[4] require you to do so and because you want to force your opponent to admit to as many allegations as possible. But you need to be an advocate, too, to persuade the court that your client should recover for the cause of action pleaded and to discourage your opponent from believing he has the winning side.

When drafting legislation, you may represent a particular lobbying group; yet, you also must consider contrary positions because legislation is meant to serve the public in general. Thus, you will use the skills of objectivity and advocacy when drafting the documents discussed in this book.

2. Legal Research

Drafting also requires yet another skill that you have probably developed already in law school: legal research. The drafting process does not exist in a vacuum apart from the law itself. You must thoroughly understand the relevant law in order to draft accurately and avoid future litigation. For example, consider an employment contract. Suppose your client, the employer, wants to include a covenant not to compete. Both you and the lawyer representing the employee must know the law in your jurisdiction concerning such covenants. Similarly, when drafting a will, you may need to learn about the rights of a surviving spouse in your jurisdiction as well as federal estate tax consequences. Likewise, a complaint for an unfamiliar cause of action would require research to discover the elements that must be pleaded. Finally, when drafting legislation, you need to be familiar with existing law related to the subject matter of the legislation. If you are familiar with all related statutes, you will avoid conflicts with existing law. Legal research is an integral and necessary element of legal drafting.

3. Principles of Effective Writing and Organization

The principles of effective writing that govern well-written legal memoranda and briefs also govern well-drafted documents. When you wrote memoranda and briefs in your other legal writing courses, you probably reviewed the rules of logical organization, paragraph and sentence structure, word choice, grammar, and so forth. When you wrote those documents, you applied those rules and edited your work to ensure the rules were followed. Even if you were not consciously aware that you were doing so, you deliberately chose and organized each word, sentence, paragraph, and section of your memoranda and briefs.

Unfortunately, however, you may easily forget such rules when you draft documents such as wills, contracts, pleadings, or statutes. The existence of forms might cause you to inadvertently ignore those rules during your drafting process. Forms may give you the impression that you have been handed a well-organized, clearly written, syntactically and grammatically correct, completed document that is satisfactory — or even perfect — for a particular situation. That impression, however, is erroneous. In fact, the organization and language used in forms can never replace clear, organized, original work. The structure and words used in forms are intended to be general and abstract, not specific and concrete. Because a form is meant to encompass so many possibilities, its organization and words can never accurately satisfy any particular set of facts without significant revision.

Because there are no forms to lean on when you draft memoranda or briefs, you necessarily follow the rules of organization, sentence structure, and grammar as a natural part of your writing process. But too often lawyers and law students use forms to replace that part of the process of legal drafting, blindly copying forms or combining several of them, without thinking about their language or structure. Often, the results can be disastrous. A document that is not logically organized will be inaccessible and frustrating to the reader. A document that has wordy or sloppy sentences will be subject to multiple interpretation and even litigation. Inaccurate word choice or misplaced punctuation can also change the entire meaning of a provision.[5] For these reasons, the fundamentals of good writing that you applied to memoranda and briefs are also crucial for effective legal drafting.

D. New Skills Required for Drafting

1. Integrating Structure and Content

The prior section of this chapter made you aware that organization, or structure, is just as important in legal drafting as it is in other forms of legal writing. But organization may be achieved in legal drafting through techniques other than traditional sentence and paragraph structure. Headings, subheadings, enumeration, and tabulation will help achieve organizational clarity. Moreover, they will also serve another purpose. They will integrate the structure with the content of the document.

In your prior writing classes, you probably learned how to use headings and subheadings to delineate sections of objective memoranda and briefs. But unless you wrote memoranda or briefs presenting complex facts and issues, you probably did not extensively use headings within the analysis section of an objective memorandum or within the argument section of a brief.

In legal drafting, headings and subheadings are used extensively to make your writing more accessible to the reader. They are not only used as an organizational technique but also as a tool to combine the "text," or substance, of a document with a mechanism for outlining it. Titles, headings, indexes, and tables of contents often serve this purpose. They not only make it visually easy for the reader to follow the document, but they also help the reader understand the relationship between the ideas presented. As you learned earlier in this chapter, for example, headings may be used to replace textual transitions.

Read the section of a partnership agreement shown in Exhibit 1-1. The section is the last one in a four-page agreement that sets forth terms for three partners to write jingles for television and radio commercials.

You were probably bored and confused reading this exhibit. There are 22 ideas grouped together without any express connection between them, other than the heading "miscellaneous." A large number of miscellaneous terms, especially when they appear in a short, simple document, usually signals that the writer did not sufficiently classify and organize the provisions before drafting. In this document, two of the four pages were presented as "miscellaneous" terms.

Unfortunately, the word "miscellaneous" does not adequately classify and organize the ideas or convey to the reader the relationship between the ideas. There are several groups of related provisions, however, as shown in Exhibit 1-2. In this version it becomes clear that the writer obviously knew that each group of paragraphs was related, or she would not have placed them in the chosen order. Simple headings can classify the groups of ideas. They adequately connect the ideas and make the document much easier to follow.

Consider another revision of this same section, as shown in Exhibit 1-3. Note that the simple headings classify the provisions and make the document much easier to follow. They also help the reader understand the relationship between

Exhibit 1-1.   Section of a Partnership Agreement

Article Six: Miscellaneous

1. The Partnership's fiscal year shall commence on July 1st of each year and shall end on June 30 of each year.

2. Full and accurate books of account shall be kept at such place as the Partners may from time to time designate, showing the condition of the business and finances of the Partnership; and each Partner shall have access to such books of account and shall be entitled to examine them at any time during ordinary business hours.

3. At the end of each fiscal year, the Partnership shall be audited at the Partnership's expense. A balance sheet shall be prepared setting forth the financial position of the Partnership as of the end of that year and a statement of income and expenses for that year. A copy of the balance sheet and statement of operations shall be delivered to each Partner as soon as possible.

4. Each Partner has the right to audit the Partnership at any other time at his own expense.

5. Each Partner shall be deemed to have waived all objections to any transaction or other facts about the operation of the Partnership disclosed in such balance sheet and/or statement of operations unless he shall have notified the Partnership in writing of his objectives within thirty days of the date on which such statement is mailed.

6. This agreement shall be effective only upon execution by all of the proposed Partners.

7. No waiver of this agreement shall be valid unless in writing and signed by the person or party against whom charged.

8. This agreement shall be binding upon and inure to the benefit of the parties hereto and their respective heirs, legal representatives, executors, administrators, successors, and assigns.

9. Upon dissolution of this Partnership, Paul Hughes has the sole right to use the Partnership name.

10. If Paul Hughes dies but the Partnership does not dissolve, the Partnership may continue to use the Partnership name.

11. Each Partner shall be required to devote 15 hours each month to sales work on behalf of the Partnership.

12. Each Partner may continue or engage in other work, in addition to Partnership work, in order to support himself.

13. Each Partner shall act in the best interests of the Partnership.

14. New Partners may be added to this Partnership by agreement.

Exhibit 1-1 (*continued*)

15. Any new Partner's contribution to this Partnership's capital shall be negotiated.

16. If any Partner leaves or dies during the pendency of a project, that Partner shall get his full share of the profits from that project upon completion.

17. Upon the death of any Partner, the Partnership shall continue.

18. The Partnership shall purchase insurance policies on all Partners' lives with Partnership funds. The policies shall be for the benefit of the Partnership. At the end of each fiscal year the Partnership shall agree as to the worth of the Partnership and purchase that amount of insurance on each Partner in proportion to his share in the Partnership. Upon the death of a Partner the Insurance proceeds shall be used by the Partnership to purchase the de-

ceased Partner's Interest from his estate.

19. Any Partner who wishes to withdraw from the Partnership must give the Partnership thirty days notice in writing.

20. If a Partner wishes to withdraw his worth in the Partnership, upon the Partner's withdrawal from the Partnership, the remaining Partners may purchase his worth.

21. As used herein, unless the context clearly indicates to the contrary, the singular number shall include the plural, the plural the singular, and the use of any gender shall be applicable to all genders.

22. In the event any parts of this agreement are found to be void, the remaining provisions of this agreement shall nevertheless be binding with the same effect as though the void parts were deleted.

Exhibit 1-2.   Categorized Section of a Partnership Agreement

*Paragraphs 1-5 Relate to the Books
and Records of the Partnership:*

1.   Each Partner has the right to audit the Partnership at any other time at his own expense.

2.   Full and accurate books of account shall be kept at such place as the Partners may from time to time designate, showing the condition of the business and finances of the Partnership; and each Partner shall have access to such books of account and shall be entitled to examine them at any time during ordinary business hours.

3.   At the end of each fiscal year the Partnership shall be audited at the Partnership's expense. A balance sheet shall be prepared setting forth the financial position of the Partnership as of the end of that year and a statement of income and expenses for that year. A copy of the balance sheet and statement of operations shall be delivered to each Partner as soon as possible.

4.   The Partnership's fiscal year shall commence on July 1st of each year and shall end on June 30 of each year.

5.   Each Partner shall be deemed to have waived all objections to any transaction or other facts about the operation of the Partnership disclosed in such balance sheet and/or statement of operations unless he shall have notified the Partnership in writing of his objection within thirty days of the date on which such statement is mailed.

*Paragraphs 6-8 Relate to the
Effectiveness of the Agreement:*

6.   This agreement shall be effective only upon execution by all of the proposed Partners.

7.   No waiver of this agreement shall be valid unless in writing and signed by the person or party against whom charged.

8.   This agreement shall be binding upon and inure to the benefit of the parties hereto and their respective heirs, legal representatives, executors, administrators, successors, and assigns.

*Paragraphs 9-10 Relate to the
Partnership Name:*

9.   Upon dissolution of this Partnership, Paul Hughes has the sole right to use the Partnership name.

10.   If Paul Hughes dies but the Partnership does not dissolve, the Partnership may continue to use the Partnership name.

*Paragraphs 11-13 Define the
Work to Be Performed by
Each of the Partners:*

11.   Each Partner shall be required to devote 15 hours each month to sales work on behalf of the Partnership.

Exhibit 1-2 (*continued*)

12. Each Partner may continue or engage in other work, in addition to Partnership work, in order to support himself.

13. Each Partner shall act in the best interests of the Partnership.

Paragraphs 14-15 Relate to the Addition of New Partners:

14. New Partners may be added to this Partnership by agreement.

15. Any new Partner's contribution to this Partnership's capital shall be negotiated.

Paragraphs 16-18 Define What Happens Upon Death of a Partner:

16. The Partnership shall purchase insurance policies on all Partners' lives with Partnership funds. The policies shall be for the benefit of the Partnership. At the end of each fiscal year the Partnership shall agree as to the worth of the Partnership and purchase that amount of insurance on each Partner in proportion to his share in the Partnership. Upon the death of a Partner the insurance proceeds shall be used by the Partnership to purchase the deceased Partner's interest from his estate.

17. Upon the death of any Partner, the Partnership shall continue.

18. If any Partner leaves or dies during the pendency of a project, that Partner shall get his full share of the profits from that project upon completion.

Paragraphs 19-20 Relate to Withdrawal from the Partnership:

19. Any Partner who wishes to withdraw from the Partnership must give the Partnership thirty days notice in writing.

20. If a Partner wishes to withdraw his worth in the Partnership, upon the Partner's withdrawal from the Partnership, the remaining Partners may purchase his worth.

Paragraphs 21-22 Relate to the Interpretation of the Agreement:

21. As used herein, unless the context clearly indicates to the contrary, the singular number shall include the plural, the plural the singular, and the use of any gender shall be applicable to all genders.

22. In the event any parts of this agreement are found to be void, the remaining provisions of this agreement shall nevertheless be binding with the same effect as though the void parts were deleted.

Exhibit 1-3.   Reorganized Section of a Partnership Agreement

A. Books and Records

1. The fiscal year shall be from July 1-June 30.

2. The Partners shall determine, from time to time, where the books will be kept. The books shall show the condition of the business and finances of the Partnership. The Partners shall have access to the books during ordinary business hours.

3. The Partnership will pay for a yearly audit of the books. The auditors will generate two financial statements: a balance sheet and a statement of income and expenses. They shall deliver copies to each Partner.

4. Each Partner may audit the books at any other time, at his own expense.

5. If a Partner objects to any item disclosed in the financial statements, he shall notify the partnership, in writing, within 30 days of the date the statements were mailed. Each Partner shall waive any objections if he does not comply with these requirements.

B. Effectiveness of the Agreement

1. This agreement shall be effective only when all the Partners execute it.

2. A Partner may waive this agreement, only if he does so in writing and all the Partners sign the waiver.

3. This agreement shall be binding on all the Partners' successors.

C. Name of the Partnership

1. If the Partnership dissolves, Paul Hughes shall own the Partnership name.

2. If Paul Hughes dies, the Partnership may continue to use the name.

D. Responsibilities of the Partners

1. Each Partner shall devote 15 hours per month to sales for the Partnership.

2. Each Partner shall act in the best interests of the Partnership.

3. Each Partner may perform work other than Partnership work.

E. Addition of New Partners

1. If the Partners agree, new Partners may be added.

2. A new Partner shall negotiate his contribution to the Partnership.

F. Death of a Partner

1. After the death of a Partner, the Partnership shall continue.

2. At the end of each fiscal year, the Partners shall agree as to the worth of the Partnership. They shall then purchase life insurance on each Partner's life for an amount equal to his share of the Partnership. If a Partner dies, the Partnership shall use the insurance proceeds to purchase the deceased Partner's interest.

3. If a Partner dies while a project is pending, his estate shall receive his full share of profits upon completion.

G. Withdrawal of a Partner

1. A Partner may withdraw if he gives the Partnership thirty days notice in writing.

2. The remaining Partners shall have first right to purchase the withdrawing Partner's share of the Partnership.

the terms under each heading and between the headings themselves. Finally, note that the provisions under each heading have been reorganized, too, also making it even easier to follow.

There are still other techniques to organize a document to integrate structure and content. If you create subheadings, enumerate, and tabulate, you will further organize the document and make it even easier for the reader to understand the relationship between the ideas presented. Enumerating means listing one by one. Tabulating means setting up words, phrases, or sentences in rows or columns. Consider this revision of the "Books and Records" section of the partnership agreement.

Books and Records
1. <u>Contents</u>: The books shall show the condition of the business and finance of the partnership.
2. <u>Fiscal Year</u>: July 1-June 30.
3. <u>Location of Books</u>:
    a. The partners shall determine where the books will be kept.
    b. The partners shall have access to the books during ordinary business hours.
4. <u>Yearly Audit</u>:
    a. The partners shall pay for a yearly audit.
    b. The auditors will do both of the following:
        1. generate two financial statements: a balance sheet and a statement of income and expenses; and
        2. mail to each partner copies of the financial statements.
    c. If a partner objects to any items disclosed in the financial statements, he shall perform both of the following or else he waives any objections. He shall
        1. notify the partnership in writing and
        2. give the notice within 30 days of the date the statements were mailed.
5. <u>Additional Audits</u>: In addition to the yearly audit, a partner may audit the books at his own expense at any time.

You have already seen this section on page 8 of this chapter for the purpose of recognizing that the products of legal drafting look different than memoranda and briefs. There is no "text" as you traditionally recognize it, and headings replace textual transitions.

This same illustration also teaches you that subheadings make it easier for the reader to find information in the document — in this example, the topics chosen for the subheadings relate to the "Books and Records." Also, enumeration and tabulation help the reader understand the relationship between the concepts presented under each subheading.

Thus, creating headings and subheadings, enumerating, and tabulating are new skills that you did not learn when you wrote memoranda or briefs. They will not only help you organize documents but will also help you integrate the structure and the content of your document to make it easier to understand.

2. Using Forms

Lawyers often use forms to assist them in drafting legal documents. But forms should be used sparingly and properly — never in lieu of your own thinking.

Recall the "miscellaneous" section of the partnership agreement in Exhibit 1-1. Recall also that the drafter of that section failed to properly classify and organize the terms. There are several possible causes of the drafter's failure to do so. He could have merely overlooked the need to organize them. Alternatively, the disorganized format could have resulted from the drafter's haphazard reliance on forms. He may have compiled various provisions from numerous form books without stopping to classify them. Or, he may have copied an entire form for all the provisions preceding the "miscellaneous" section; afterwards, he may have realized there were numerous terms that his client desired but that were excluded from the form he chose. Hence, a "miscellaneous" category seemed perfectly logical to present the terms that were not in the form he followed. In either case, the drafter erroneously used a form, or forms, to replace his own thinking about classifying and organizing information — a critical step of the drafting process.

If you use forms to replace steps necessary to draft effectively, your document will not only be defective organizationally, but its language might be sloppy, too. Forms often contain archaic language, wordy patterns, and legalese. Their language is abstract and general. Because they are designed to cover many possible situations, their language cannot be definite or precise. No one form has been prepared for your specific client in her precise situation.

As a drafter, you are like a master chef who might have 20 or 30 different recipes for beef stroganoff that he refers to from time to time for ideas.[6] He makes it a little differently each time, depending on the quality of the ingredients, the number and tastes of his customers, the time he has to prepare it, and so forth. Each time, he will think carefully about the various factors and tailor his recipe accordingly. Occasionally, he may use some premade bottled sauce or substitute one ingredient for another. But unless he had cooked the sauce from scratch several times, learned the effect of each ingredient, and tried the result on his various customers, he would not know how to revise the recipe so that it would be delectable for each customer's particular tastes.

Similarly, legal forms compile many ingredients, or ideas, with which you may be unfamiliar. You may understand the overall function of the final product, but you may not understand the effect of each provision. If you are not completely familiar with each ingredient, or term, as well as the process to create the final document, the document will be ineffective for each of your client's particular circumstances. Until you have drafted documents in their entirety, reading, understanding, evaulating, and revising forms are difficult skills to master.

For these reasons, this book favors original drafting. However, it also will teach you when to use forms to assist you. Throughout this book, references may be made to forms, practitioner's guides, checklists, and the like as an integral part of the research necessary to draft a document. But those sources never should replace your own thinking or writing.

You must specifically consider each client's particular needs. There is no single way to draft any type of document. Understanding that there is more than one correct style and format will make you flexible and enable you to tailor each document to suit the situation and client.

3. Gathering the Facts

Another skill that drafting will require you to develop is fact gathering. In writing memoranda and briefs in prior writing courses, the "facts" probably were provided by your instructors. For example, in your typical first semester legal writing course, you likely received a memorandum from a senior partner of a law firm, setting forth a situation presented by a prospective client. You may have been asked to research the law and present an objective memorandum, analyzing the situation and recommending a solution. The facts were given to you in their entirety. There were to be neither changes nor additions to them. If your research revealed a need for additional information, that information was not necessarily available to you.

Similarly, in your typical second semester legal writing course, you may have received a written opinion from a lower court (trial or reviewing court), setting forth its decision and rationale in a particular case. Based on the opinion, you were asked to research the law and write a persuasive document, for example, an appellate brief.

While both of those writing assignments forced you to concentrate solely on your research and writing skills, they did not help you develop a lawyering skill that is a prerequisite to effective legal drafting: fact gathering.

It would be wholly unrealistic to teach you how to draft wills, contracts, pleadings, and legislation based on preplanned memoranda or opinions. Therefore, this book will teach you how to gather facts, focusing on the questions to ask to ensure that you can obtain all the legally significant information. This book's approach to gathering facts can be applied to drafting any type of document.

4. Writing for Multiple Audiences

Earlier in this chapter, you learned that the products of legal drafting differ from memoranda and briefs in that they affect the conduct of and are read by multiple audiences, having numerous and varying relationships to the contents of the document. In fact, you often must satisfy conflicting audiences through one document and sometimes through a single provision. Therefore, you must consider these diverse audiences at every stage of the drafting process.

Writing for multiple audiences is a skill you did not learn when you wrote memoranda and briefs. Memoranda and briefs are generally addressed to judges and lawyers, all of whom you are trying to reach in generally the same way. Also, judges and lawyers have a similar ability to understand your documents.

In contrast, to draft wills, contracts, pleadings, and statutes, diverse goals must be met, diverse purposes must be satisfied, diverse activities must be described and governed, diverse personalities must be considered, and diverse abilities to understand the resulting document must be anticipated.

Thus, you must think about many, possibly conflicting, dimensions of a single document's audiences. You must anticipate who will read, interpret, implement, and be governed and affected by your document and draft it accordingly. This book will teach you a method for identifying the audiences and figuring out how each will dictate the way you will draft a document. The method can be applied to all kinds of documents.

5. Anticipating the Future

This chapter has already taught you that one way in which the products of legal drafting differ from memoranda and briefs is that they operate in the future. Thus, to draft effectively you must currently anticipate all possible future contingencies. Identifying audiences and anticipating their goals, activities, personalties, and abilities is really just one aspect of anticipating the future. There are a variety of others.

For example, the persons who are the subjects of your documents could die or become disabled. New persons may succeed those who were originally named in your document. The property your document addresses could become misplaced, destroyed, or relocated. New laws could change the meaning and effect of your document or require new provisions. Triggering events for contingent provisions may or may not occur. You must draft each provision to anticipate every conceivable "what if" event or circumstance.

Similarly, you must anticipate every conceivable interpretation of the format and language of your document. You want to avoid multiple interpretations, especially if they could result in litigation. This book will teach you to think about all conceivable contingencies at every step of the drafting process.

E. Conclusion

The chapters that follow will: (1) review previously learned skills needed for effective legal drafting, (2) teach you new skills needed for effective legal drafting, and (3) prepare you to draft well-written documents. In the first part of the book, Chapter 2 presents a seven-step process for legal drafting, while Chapter 3 focuses more narrowly on the step of writing carefully. Then, in the second part of the book, Chapters 4, 5, 6, and 7 apply the concepts covered in Chapters 2 and 3, addressing specific types of drafting: estate planning documents, contracts, pleadings, and legislation.

This book will serve as a transition between your legal education and career. The chapters are specifically designed so that you do not need significant drafting experience or in-depth course background in relevant substantive areas. After you have studied this book and drafted (and redrafted) several projects, you should be adequately prepared to begin many of the drafting projects typically assigned to a newly licensed practitioner of law.

Notes

1.   *See* Laymen Allen & C. Rudt Engholm, *Normalized Legal Drafting and the Query Method*, 29 J. Legal Educ. 380 (1978); James Raymond, *Legal Writing: An Obstruction to Justice*, 30 Ala. L. Rev. 1 (1978); Steven Stark, *Why Lawyers Can't Write*, 97 Harv. L. Rev. 1389 (1984); Irving Younger, *No More Ugly Legal Prose*, 72 A.B.A. J. 140 (1986).

2.   *See* Solomon Bienenfeld, *Plain English in Administrative Law*, 63 Mich. B.J. 856 (1984); Harry Haynsworth IV, *How to Draft Clear and Concise Legal Documents*, 31-No. 2 Prac. Law. 41 (1985); Maurice Kirk, *Legal Drafting: Some Elements of Technique*, 4 Tex. Tech L. Rev. 297 (1973); Kermit L. Danahoo, Note, *Avoiding Inadvertent Syntactic Ambiguity in Legal Draftmanship*, 20 Drake L. Rev. 137 (1970).

3.   *E.g.*, 735 ILCS 5/2-603 (1993) [At the time of this writing, the statutory compilations in Illinois have been changed from "Ill. Rev. Stat." to "ILCS." Since there is not yet an official Uniform System of Citation style for this new compilation, we have used "ILCS" consistently throughout this book. — EDS.]; *see generally* Note, *Has a "Kafkaesque Dream" Come True? Federal Rule of Civil Procedure 11: Time for Another Amendment?*, 67 B.U. L. Rev. 1019 (1987).

4.   Every lawyer must "represent a client zealously within the bounds of the law." Model Code of Professional Responsibility Canon 7 (1981) (hereinafter Model Code). However, a lawyer may not accept employment from a client to advance claims that are "unwarranted under existing law." Model Code DR 2-109(A)(2) and DR 7-102(A)(2); Model Rules of Professional Conduct Rules 3.1 and 3.4 (1983) (hereinafter Model Rules). A lawyer may advance claims based on a "good faith argument for extension, modification, or reversal of existing law." *Id.* He/she may not advance frivolous claims. Model Code EC 7-4; Model Rules 3.3.

The rationale for the preceding ethical guidelines is that "zealous advocacy enables the tribunal to come to the hearing with an open and neutral mind." Model Code EC 7-19 and n.33. This ethical process results in an "informal, impartial tribunal capable of administering justice promptly and efficiently. . . ." Model Code EC 7-20.

5.   For an example of the ramifications of poor draftmenship, *see* Ansvar Am. Ins. Co. v. Hallberg, 568 N.E.2d 77, 79 (Ill. App. Ct. 1991).

6.   Analogy originally created by Eugene Schiltz, Esq., adjunct instructor at The John Marshall Law School.

CHAPTER 2

The Process of
Legal Drafting

A. *The Seven Steps of Legal Drafting*

Chapter 1 taught you that to draft effectively, you must use both previously learned skills as well as newly acquired ones. It did not teach you, however, a process or method for using the skills. When you think about drafting a memorandum or brief, you may readily think of the steps necessary to complete a finished product: identify the issues, research, redefine the issues, research again, outline, draft, research again, redraft, and so on.

In contrast, when you think about drafting, you may find it difficult to think of a process to complete a finished product. You may think only of filling in blanks on a form. As Chapter 1 explained, however, drafting requires much more than that, and many skills are required even to use forms accurately.

This chapter will present a process for legal drafting[1] that you can apply to any type of document. The process consists of seven steps:

1. understand the audiences;
2. gather the facts;
3. know the law;
4. classify, organize, and outline;
5. write carefully;
6. test for consequences;
7. edit and rewrite.

Following these steps will help you draft well-organized, comprehensive, concise, and precise documents.

B.   Preliminary Instructions for Following the Seven Steps

Although the steps are numbered one through seven, the process is not strictly chronological. You may need to change the order of the steps in the process. Your decision to do so will vary with your knowledge of and experience with the subject matter. For example, rather than first thinking about the audience, you may need to research the general area of law as your first step. If you know little about partnership agreements, you will be unable to discern the audiences and unable to formulate questions to gather the facts unless you have researched the general area of the law. Similarly, if you know nothing about the negligent infliction of emotional distress, you will be unable to gather the facts needed to draft a complaint for that tort unless you are familiar with the elements of that cause of action.

When you know little about a topic, you also may want to do some research to find a similar document drafted under other circumstances. By doing so, you may be able to discover the relationship between the substantive law you have just researched and the actual language drafted in the sample document. Looking at a sample will also provide a picture of the document, which you may have never seen before. You should never, however, rely on any sample document without conducting your own research, creating your own organization, and drafting your own language, all specifically suited to your client's particular needs. Thus, knowing the law rather than understanding your audience may, in some cases, be the first step in your process.

The drafting process is also recursive. That is, the knowledge gained during one step in the process may require you to move back to an earlier step and reconsider or repeat what you did. Several examples illustrate this point. While you are researching the law, you may discover that you need additional facts. At that time, you may have to reinterview your client or witnesses or do whatever else is necessary to discover the facts that you need. Similarly, while you are outlining or writing a first draft, you may question the enforceability of some of the agreed-upon language. Therefore, you may have to perform additional research on the language and provision at issue. Yet another example is when you are finishing the final draft. Then, you may discover that a paragraph you added to the last section is more logically connected to an earlier section of the document. You therefore may need to reorganize even at that late date.

These examples illustrate that the steps required for effective drafting are interrelated and dependent upon each other. You should execute each step carefully and not hesitate to review or re-do any of them as the necessity arises.

C.   Explanation of the Seven Steps

1.   Understand the Audiences

Audience[2] is a broad concept. In order to understand your audiences, you must ascertain both who will read your document and how they will use it. Your audiences include all persons who will ever read the document. These readers may vary widely. Thus you need to identify the specific characteristics of your audiences in order to make your document accessible to your readers.

Similarly, you must identify how your audiences will use the document. Some documents, such as pleadings, wills, real estate sales contracts, or partnership agreements, initiate a transaction.[3] For example, a pleading begins a lawsuit and a partnership agreement begins a partnership. Other documents, such as trusts, condominium bylaws, or statutes are intended to regulate future conduct.[4] Still others, such as a deed or a marital separation agreement, merely reduce to writing some transaction that has already occurred.[5]

Of course, many if not all, documents may have more than one or all of these functions. Or, they may have different functions for different audiences. For example, although a real estate sales contract initiates a transaction, it also regulates the conduct of the buyer, seller, lender, broker, and perhaps others. Likewise, it may reduce to writing conduct that has already occurred, such as a deposit of earnest money. In this regard, the contract serves all three functions. Thus, it may be impossible to give any document a single label about its function. Understanding the multiple functions that legal documents perform, however, will help you understand the audiences and make your document accessible to all its readers.

Understanding your audiences is also important because the audience controls the tone of the document. Chapter 3 will explain in detail methods for changing the tone of your document, including making the document objective or adversarial.

You can identify the audiences if you think of all who will potentially read the document or whose activity it will control. When you identify your audiences you must consider your client's relationship to the readers. An audience may be friendly, that is, share interests similar to your client's, or hostile, that is, have interests that conflict or potentially conflict with those of your client.

Another factor to consider in identifying the audience is its education and experience. The readers may include members of the legal profession: the lawyers who negotiate and write the document, the lawyers who may litigate about the document, and the court that may interpret the document. Other audience members may include nonlawyers: the parties to a contract, the public whose conduct a statute may control, a nonparty affected by the document (e.g., a beneficiary under a will), or members of other professions, such as accountants and engineers. These various people may have differing abilities to read and understand your document.

Unlike memoranda and briefs whose audiences are almost exclusively lawyers, the audiences for these types of documents are frequently nonlawyers. Moreover, memoranda and briefs do not control the activity of the clients on whose behalf they are written. In contrast, the provisions of a will, contract, pleading, or statute may significantly affect the personal and business conduct of numerous people. If these people cannot understand the document, they will not be able to use it effectively.

Errors made in drafting a document may have immediate and direct results. For example, an error in a will may disinherit a child whose support depends upon the inheritance, while an ambiguity in a real estate sales contract may cause litigation and delay the closing and possession of a new home. Similarly, a broad statement of a trustee's powers may grant more discretion than the settlor intended, and an unclear statement of partnership responsibilities in a partnership agreement may set forth unfair or unequal division of labor. Likewise, inaccurate wording in a complaint will not adequately inform the defendant of her alleged wrongdoing and will make her unable to properly prepare a defense. Moreover, it may subject the lawyer who drafted the complaint to sanctions[6] or cause the case to be dismissed or delayed.[7] Unclear, imprecise legislation will confuse those governed by the legislation and will generate litigation to interpret the statute.

Therefore, you must anticipate who will read, interpret, implement, and be affected by the specific type of document. A will, for example, affects not only its executor and beneficiaries, but also influences the lawyer, the court ultimately probating it, and even a trustee if a testamentary trust is included. A contract to sell a house will be read and interpreted not only by the buyer and the seller, but also by the lawyers representing both sides, the title company issuing the title insurance and the lending institution issuing a mortgage.

Because these documents may affect so many people, anticipating who will use and read them is an important prerequisite to drafting. Think of every possible person, or audience, who will read the document. For each, ask:

1. Who is he/she/it?
2. What is the purpose for which this audience will use the document?
3. Is the audience's interest(s) friendly or hostile to those of your client?
4. How long will the audience use the document — short-term or long-term?
5. What is the audience's educational background and experience?

The answers to these questions will present the broadest possible view of the future effect of the document.

Example

Suppose you were asked to draft the partnership agreement used in the example in the preceding chapter. If you recall, it was a partnership agreement among three people in the business of writing jingles for TV and radio commercials.

Here is a list of the persons who will likely read and use the document:

1. The current and future partners to the agreement.
2. The lawyers who will negotiate for the individuals and write the agreement.
3. The lawyers who will represent the ongoing business.
4. The accountants who prepare the business books, records, and tax returns.
5. Third-party accountants or representatives.
6. Individual partner's accountants.
7. New partners and their lawyers.
8. Partners who seek to change the partnership relationship (and their lawyers).
9. Partners' estates or guardians.

Read Exhibit 2-1. It illustrates the effect on these persons by answering the five questions set forth above.

Although you need not make a chart like the one in Exhibit 2-1 for every document you draft, doing so for several drafting experiences will help you think thoroughly about your audiences. After you have completed a draft, it may even serve as a type of checklist to help you "test for consequences" (step six of the process outlined in this chapter). As you become more experienced, the process of thinking about your audiences will become second nature to you, and you will no longer need the list or chart.

Thinking about the answers to these questions for each person who will use the document will help prepare you to begin the drafting process. It will help you set the tone of the document.

Exercise 2-1

For each of the following documents, list all possible persons who will read or use it. Then, for each person, answer the five questions, set forth on page 26 of this chapter, that determine the effect of the document.

a. Petition for dissolution of marriage.
b. Residential lease.
c. Legislation regulating disposal of nuclear waste.
d. Ordinance prohibiting sale or purchase of alcoholic beverages on Sundays.
e. Physician's employment contract, containing statewide restrictive covenant for seven years.

2. Gather the Facts

Gathering all the relevant facts is also a crucial preliminary step to effective drafting. A typical law school writing assignment generally gives the students all the relevant facts. In practice, however, the facts are gathered from client interviews, meetings with other lawyers and their clients, interviews with witnesses, witnesses' statements, and various other documents.

As a new associate asked to draft a document, you may not be the lawyer who completed the interview or otherwise gathered the facts. Moreover, even if you did conduct the interview, you may later discover that you need additional facts. You may discover the need for these facts at other stages in the drafting process, for example, while outlining the document, examining form books, or researching the relevant law. Sometimes obtaining the additional facts may be as easy as phoning your client. Other times, further investigation or research may be necessary. In either case, you cannot draft an accurate document unless you know all the relevant facts. A determination of the relevant facts will always be controlled by six simple questions: who? what? where? when? why? and how?

a. Who?

Identifying the audiences is a good place to start to answer this question. Consider, as examples, a will, a partnership agreement, a complaint, and a proposed city ordinance setting a curfew for persons under 18. The primary audience for

Exhibit 2-1.   Audience Chart for Partnership Agreement

	Audience	Purpose	Interest	Duration	Education
1.	Partners involved in initial drafting of the agreement and the initial partnership	To set forth terms of the business relationship; the partners and their contribution; responsibilities; share of profits; and losses, etc.	Partnership interest: friendly Individual interest: varying degrees of friendliness	Long-term	Nonlawyer; probably little business education
2.	Lawyers who draft the agreement, negotiate for each partner, and may remain lawyer for each individual partner	To set forth clients' agreement and to represent each partner currently and in the future	Basically friendly; may be hostile	May be short-term or long-term	Lawyer
3.	Lawyer who represents the ongoing partnership	To interpret, enforce, and amend the provisions	For interpretation: friendly; for enforcement: hostile; for amendment: generally friendly	Long-term	Lawyer
4.	Partnership accountants	Keep books and records; do tax returns for partnership	Friendly	Long-term	Accounting; generally nonlawyer

5. Third-party accountants or representatives (personnel for bank, IRS, etc.)	To seek information or result for the third party	May be somewhat hostile	Generally short-term	Varies depending on circumstances
6. Individual partner's accountant	To assist individual partner in personal accounting matters — e.g., preparation of individual tax return	Generally friendly	Long-term	Accounting; generally nonlawyer
7. New partners	Compliance with agreement to become partner; take over responsibilities	Friendly; may have some potentially varying interests	Long-term	Nonlawyer; probably little business background
8. Lawyers who represent new partners	Review agreement and represent new partner's individual interest	Somewhat hostile	May be short-term or long-term	Lawyer
9. Partners who seek to change the partnership relationship (ejected partner, demoted partner, excluded partner)	Protect interest in the partnership or other individual interests	May be hostile	May be short-term or long-term, depending on circumstances	Nonlawyer
10. Partner's estate or guardian	Maximize individual financial gain	Hostile	Short-term	May be a lawyer or person educated in business

the will is the beneficiaries. Thus, you must make certain that you gather the names of all the beneficiaries. You may also want to know their ages. In the event that they are minors, you may want to include special provisions.

The primary audience for a partnership agreement is the partners themselves. Therefore, make sure that you know the names of all the partners who will be bound by the agreement. Similarly, you need to know their proportionate shares in the partnership, as well as how they will provide for adding a new partner or ejecting a current one.

The primary audiences for a complaint are the judge, the jury, and the parties. You must therefore identify them all. There may be multiple plaintiffs, defendants, and counter-claimants, each of whom may play a different role in the action.

There may be numerous audiences for a local curfew law. Certainly, people under 18 are one such audience. In addition, other people may be affected, including guardians, local proprietors, business persons, local law enforcement officials, juvenile court officers, and school personnel. You must consider the interest of each in defining the content of the ordinance.

The answer to the "who" question will also include persons other than the audiences. You may need to gather "who" facts regarding people other than those who will read the document or whose activity will be controlled by it. For example, a witness to a will may never read the will or be affected by its terms but is a necessary person to consider to complete the document. Similarly, the children whose parents are divorcing may never read their parents' settlement agreement and their own conduct may not be controlled by it; however, they must also be considered when gathering facts to draft the settlement agreement.

b. What?

The "things" to be covered by the document will answer this question. Consider the same four examples. For a will, the facts to be gathered should include all of the property the testator wants to distribute, including real property and personal property. For a partnership agreement, things to be covered include the contribution of each partner, the roles of the partners, distribution of profits and losses, withdrawal of one partner, and the effect on the partnership of death of a partner. These terms constitute the general basis for the partnership agreement. Things to be covered by a complaint include an explanation of the incident at issue, its history, and its damages. Things to be covered by a curfew ordinance would include the hours, enforcement, punishment, and supervision.

c. Where?

The basis for the answer to this question will vary with the type of document. For a will, the location of the property may be important if the property is real estate, bank accounts, property located in other jurisdictions, or any other property that will not be easily accessible after the testator's death. For a partnership agreement, the location of the headquarters of the business and location of the books and records are some "where" questions that will need to be answered and included in the agreement. The location of the parties to a complaint and of the incident itself will determine jurisdiction and venue, two important "where" facts that should be pleaded in a complaint. The exact location of people and things involved in the incident at issue will also establish causation, a requirement for pleading both civil and criminal actions. The geographical boundaries of the community as well as an explanation of where minors must be after curfew are some of the "where" questions that the ordinance would need to address.

d. When?

Again, the answers to this question will vary with the type of document and the circumstances. The same four examples illustrate the numerous possibilities.

A will is always effective upon death. However, the testator may desire to change the time for property distribution if the beneficiary is a minor or if the testator desires to make a contingent gift (e.g., a gift to be distributed only if the beneficiary completes his college education).

A partnership agreement is generally effective upon its execution. However, it may contain provisions that will not be effective unless certain triggering events occur. The death, withdrawal, or retirement of a partner; the addition of a new partner; and the dissolution of the partnership are some examples of future events that will trigger the application of certain provisions in the agreement.

The most important "when" questions for a complaint will be the timing of the event that created the cause of action. This date is important because it will determine when the complaint must be filed to comply with the statute of limitations. In addition, the timing of the specific acts at issue are also relevant to a pleading because they will establish causation.

The "when" questions for the curfew statute include the hour defining the curfew's limitation and the days during the week to which the curfew will apply.

e. Why?

"Why" includes both the purpose (or purposes) of the document and the intent of the party who is responsible for creating it. You will find it difficult to identify purpose because documents typically have multiple — even conflicting — purposes. In fact, every provision may have its own purpose. Likewise, the parties' intent may vary with each purpose.

For example, when drafting a complaint, you must comply with pleading rules that require you to allege facts objectively. Objective language may also force the defendant more readily to admit the allegations. Yet, you also want to choose language that persuades the judge and jury that the defendant is liable and that discourages the defendant from fighting you. Reconciling conflicting purposes is perhaps one of the biggest challenges you will face when drafting documents.

Whatever they are, the purposes may be express or implied. An express purpose is stated, for example, when a disinheritance clause in a will explains the reason for disinheritance. Similarly, contracts often contain "recitals," which explain why the contract was written, and many statutes also contain a statement of purpose.

Sometimes, however, the purposes may be implied. For example, the multiple purposes of a complaint — complying with pleading rules, forcing the defendant to admit to the allegations, and persuading the judge and jury — are all implicit. They are not expressly stated in the text of the complaint.

Likewise, when a parent testator has left the entire estate to her spouse and children, her intent to provide solely for them after her death is implied, although she may not have expressly said so in the will. Similarly, not all legislation will expressly state its purposes or goals, but they are often implied from the substantive provisions of the statute. For example, the implied purpose of a curfew statute is to protect minors, even though that may not be expressly stated. Whether express or implied, gathering the "why" facts is a necessary prerequisite to drafting a comprehensive, accurate document.

f. How?

The answers to "how" questions explain the mechanisms for achieving the desired results. "How," in this sense, always governs future conduct. For example, how should a trustee named in a will spend money on behalf of the beneficiaries? Should he pay expenses directly to vendors, or should he give the money to the beneficiary or to the beneficiary's guardian? How can a partnership agreement be amended? What type of vote is needed? Must the amendment be in writing? For the curfew statute, how should it be enforced? Should enforcement be by fine or injunction? The answers to these questions will help you set forth the means, not just the ends, in your documents.

As you become experienced with drafting numerous types of documents, you may develop aids to assist you in the fact gathering process. Client interview sheets and question checklists are some examples. Commercial checklists are available in some research sources that may help you formulate your questions.[8]

Exercise 2-2

Using the who?, what?, where?, when?, why?, how? method, list the facts you need to gather for each of the documents listed in Exercise 2-1. Recall that Exercise 2-1 asked you to identify the audiences for those documents. Your awareness of the audiences will now help you begin to determine the facts you need to gather.

3. Know the Law

You must know the law at all stages of the drafting process. Before beginning the process, you should research the unfamiliar areas of the law that are related to the document. Fact gathering will be virtually impossible unless you know the legally significant facts that you need to discover. As you gather the facts, you may discover you need to research a specific point of law with which you were not familiar. Knowledge of the law continues to be important during all stages of the drafting process to help you predict all conceivable future consequences and to draft the document to avoid negative consequences such as litigation or tax problems.

There are four different categories of law that you will need to know: substantive, procedural, interpretive, and ethical. The substantive law, of course, relates to the basic content of the document you are drafting. For example, you must know the general rules about partnerships in your jurisdiction before you draft a partnership agreement. Perhaps the Uniform Partnership Act,[9] or parts of it, have been adopted. Similarly, you must know the tax ramifications of dividing property upon divorce before you negotiate and draft a marital settlement agreement. If you are drafting legislation, you should be familiar with related statutes to avoid inconsistencies or conflicts. You also should be familiar with related common law to determine if your legislation would significantly change it.

You also will need to research the relevant procedural laws. For example, if you draft a complaint, you will need to consult both local and state court rules that may govern the form of the pleading. Is verification necessary? If you draft interrogatories, the number of permitted questions and subparts will generally be governed by local court rules. Similarly, if you draft a will, the state's Probate Code will govern such issues as how many witnesses are necessary. If you draft a contract, you will need to research procedural questions, such as how many officers must sign the contract in order to bind a corporation. Some statutes may even govern the way a contract looks.[10] Finally, if you draft legislation, the title, form, and presentation of the document will be governed by state constitutional or local government rules. These examples illustrate but a few of the many procedural rules that are important to know as a prerequisite to presenting a valid document.

You must also know the law that governs how your document will be interpreted. You need to research and be familiar with rules of interpretation, or construction, that may apply to the document. For example, many rules govern the construction and interpretation of wills,[11] contracts,[12] and statutes.[13] Similarly, other rules govern the specificity and clarity[14] of pleadings. You must be familiar with these interpretive rules in order to draft a thoroughly prepared document.

Finally, you must understand the relevant ethical considerations. For example, if you have negotiated and drafted a contract, make sure you have made all necessary disclosures to your opponent.[15] If you have drafted and filed a complaint, make sure it is not frivolous[16] and that the facts will support the allegations.[17] If you have answered interrogatories, make sure you have made the relevant and necessary disclosures.[18] If you have drafted a will, make sure there are no conflicts of interest (e.g., as the lawyer who drafts it, you should not be a beneficiary).[19] These examples illustrate just a few of the ethical considerations you must research in order to draft your document.

Only after you understand the relevant substantive, procedural, interpretive, and ethical law will you be able to outline and begin to draft the document. Your research, however, does not stop when you begin to outline or write. As new substantive, procedural, interpretive, or ethical issues arise, you should perform additional research.

Specific provisions of the document may require additional research. For example, if your client wants a restrictive covenant to be included in an employment contract, you must research whether such covenants are enforceable and, if so, under what conditions. You must be certain of the validity and enforceability of every provision; otherwise, your document merely invites future litigation.

Opposing counsel may also create the need for additional research. She may question the future interpretation of proposed language or ideas, thus requiring you to research further and redraft.

Thinking about the audiences and referring to the chart you made earlier will also help identify issues for further inquiry. For example, if you are unsure of the effect that one provision would have on a particular audience, further research may be required.

Finally, checking sources such as practice-oriented manuals[20] or guides geared for particular subjects[21] may reveal special problem areas that may require additional research.

Researching the law and drafting a document to prevent negative consequences are some of your major duties as a drafter of documents. Step six of the process outlined in this chapter will suggest a more detailed methodology for anticipating contingencies. Sufficient knowledge of all the relevant law, however, is a crucial step to achieve that goal.

Exercise 2-3

What type of research would you need to perform before drafting the following documents?

a. Complaint for cause of action in Federal District Court under the Americans with Disabilities Act.
b. Complaint under the Federal Equal Pay Act.
c. An antenuptial agreement.
d. Articles of incorporation for a not-for-profit corporation.
e. Cause of action based on uninhabitable conditions in a rented apartment.
f. Shareholder agreement between shareholders of a closely held corporation.
g. Statute governing wrongful death.
h. Complaint under the Federal Tort Claims Act.

Based on your research for each, what specific provisions do you think may trigger the need for further, more detailed research?

4. Classify, Organize, and Outline

This step enables you to begin actually writing. At this point, you should be well informed about your document. You met with your client, and therefore understand the type of document he desires. You gathered the facts you think are important, and you have researched the relevant law.

Now you should classify, organize, and outline the information you have obtained, before drafting the text of the document. By doing so, you will ensure that nothing is inadvertently deleted and that the information is presented in a logical order. Not only must there be a logical connection between the sections of a document, there must be a logical progression of ideas within each section.

The pages that follow illustrate one method for classifying, outlining, and organizing facts, using the partnership agreement as an example. Again, suppose you were drafting an agreement between three people to write jingles for television and radio commercials. Remember that any contingency not addressed will be controlled by the state's version of the Uniform Partnership Act. This may not always be in your client's interest; therefore, cover as many contingencies as possible.

First, list the facts you have gathered. Assume that the following is the list of facts you gathered from your client and from meetings with counsel for the other two partners.

Example

- Paul Hughes — partner
- Cynthia Marks — partner
- David Judd — partner
- business office: 2222 North Main Street, Big City, Big State 11111
- Creative Audio Visuals — name of partnership
- Hughes contributes name and logo
- partners want insurance policies on each other in event of death; parties will agree each year on the value of the business; that amount will be used as basis for insurance purchase
- no assignment to others
- Hughes will maintain books
- partners want each to devote at least 15 hours/month to sales
- partners want equal shares of profits and losses
- Marks and Judd contribute $1,000 but Hughes only has $500 to contribute; all agree that name and logo contributed by Hughes are worth at least $500 at time business begins
- want to write jingles for television and radio commercials for profit
- no partner has authority for any transaction more than $250 without agreement by all
- all to work on jingles: lyrics and music
- if Hughes withdraws, partnership can use name and logo for six months; thereafter, he gets them back
- yearly audit required; but any partner may request an additional one at any time at his own expense
- books available to each partner during regular business hours
- 90% of profits on each project available for distribution; 10% into partnership account
- no new partners without unanimous consent; unanimous agreement on new partner's contribution, too
- withdrawal — 60 days' notice in writing

Second, list categories, or classifications, for presenting sections of the document. The categories should be based on your list of facts, as well as your substantive legal research and any other research you may have performed, such as reviewing practitioner's sources for drafting particular documents. Your second list may look like this:

Example

Place
Purpose
Books and Records

        Capital Contributions
        Profits and Losses
        Death
        Withdrawal
        Name of Partnership
        Partners' Names
        Responsibilities of Partners
        Dissolution
        Assignment
        Liability/Indemnification
        Interpretation of the Agreement
        Disability
        Addition of New Partners

Note that most of the categories are based on the facts in the list. Several, however, do not relate to any of the facts elicited from interviews with your client or meetings with opposing counsel. "Dissolution," "Liability/Indemnification," and "Interpretation of the Agreement" are some examples. The drafter discovered those categories while researching the substantive area, partnerships, and by reviewing the practitioner's sources, including forms. All of the classifications will ultimately form a preliminary topic outline after you follow the next three steps.

    Third, rank the categories in an order that is logical. Moving from background or general information to more specific information is one way to present information logically. It is also logical to present information in chronological order. Thus, place provisions relating to the current operation of the partnership before the provisions that depend on future contingencies.

    The names of the partners and the partnership name, place, and purpose are background information. Therefore, they should be ranked as the first four categories, like this:

Example

      3 Place
      4 Purpose
         Books and Records
         Capital Contributions
         Profits and Losses
         Death
         Withdrawal
      2 Name of Partnership
      1 Partners' Names
         Responsibilities of Partners
         Dissolution
         Assignment
         Liability/Indemnification
         Interpretation of Contract
         Disability
         Addition of New Partners

The provisions about the current operation of the partnership should be next, rather than information about the operation based on future contingencies such as death, disability, or withdrawal. The current operation provisions include the "Responsibilities of the Partners," "Capital Contributions," "Profits and Losses," and "Books and Records." Of these, it is logical to present the "Contributions" first because there would be no partnership books and records, responsibilities, or profits and losses without the initial contribution to set up the partnership. Moving from general to specific, "Responsibilities" could be presented next, followed by "Books and Records" and "Profits and Losses." Your list would now look like this:

Example

3	Place
4	Purpose
7	Books and Records
5	Capital Contributions
8	Profits and Losses
	Death
	Withdrawal
2	Name of Partnership
1	Partners' Names
6	Responsibilities of Partners
	Dissolution
	Assignment
	Liability/Indemnification
	Interpretation of Contract
	Disability
	Addition of New Partners

The remaining provisions all depend on future events. Some relate to future events that will affect all the current partners: assignment, liability, and new partners; others depend on an event affecting one of the partners' ability or desire to remain a partner: Disability, Death, and Withdrawal. "Dissolution" depends on a desire to terminate the partnership and "Interpretation" depends on a disagreement regarding the terms. Although it is not mandatory to put them in precisely this order, this is one logical way to present the remainder of the categories. Your list would now look like this:

Example

3	Place
4	Purpose
7	Books and Records
5	Capital Contributions
8	Profits and Losses
13	Death
14	Withdrawal
2	Name of Partnership

         1   Partners' Names
         6   Responsibilities of Partners
        15   Dissolution
         9   Assignment
        10   Liability/Indemnification
        16   Interpretation of Contract
        12   Disability
        11   Addition of New Partners

Fourth, convert the ranked categories into an ordered list of headings. Your ordered list would look like this:

Example

         I.   Partners
         II.   Name of Partnership
         III.   Place of Partnership
         IV.   Purpose of Partnership
         V.   Capital Contributions
         VI.   Responsibilities of Partners
         VII.   Books and Records
         VIII.   Profits and Losses
         IX.   Assignment
         X.   Liability/Indemnification
         XI.   Addition of New Partners
         XII.   Disability
         XIII.   Death
         XIV.   Withdrawal
         XV.   Dissolution
         XVI.   Interpretation of the Agreement

Fifth, convert the ordered list of headings into a preliminary topic outline by dividing the headings into subtopics. At this time, you may be able to think of subtopics for only a few headings. You may need to repeat this step later, especially after you have integrated your facts. Once you integrate the facts, you will be able to more easily identify subtopics. Your topic outline may look like this:

Example

         I.   PARTNERS
         II.   NAME OF PARTNERSHIP
         III.   PLACE OF PARTNERSHIP
         IV.   PURPOSE OF PARTNERSHIP
         V.   CAPITAL CONTRIBUTIONS
         VI.   RESPONSIBILITIES OF PARTNERS
         VII.   BOOKS AND RECORDS
                 A. location
                 B. audits
                 C. availability to partners

```
      VIII.   PROFITS AND LOSSES
              A.   distribution to partners
              B.   distribution to partnership accounts
       IX.    ASSIGNMENT
        X.    LIABILITY/INDEMNIFICATION
       XI.    ADDITION OF NEW PARTNERS
      XII.    DISABILITY
     XIII.    DEATH
              A.   value of business
              B.   life insurance policies based on value
      XIV.    WITHDRAWAL
              A.   notice in writing
              B.   ownership of name and logo if Hughes withdraws
       XV.    DISSOLUTION
      XVI.    INTERPRETATION OF AGREEMENT
```

Sixth, now that you have a topic outline, integrate each fact into the relevant category or classification. In some situations, the document you used to gather the facts, for example, interview sheets, may already integrate the facts and general classifications. In other situations, you need to integrate all the facts into a separate outline. If you need to use each fact only once, cross out each one in your list as you use it. If you need to use a fact more than once in your document, do not cross it out but instead label it to correspond to the section in the document where you have integrated it. You may need to use facts more than once in a multi-count complaint or in complex legislation. Look carefully at Exhibit 2-2 on pages 40 through 43. It demonstrates the use of the "cross-out" method, each fact being used only once in the partnership agreement.

Now look at Exhibit 2-3 on pages 44 and 45. It summarizes the entire process thus far. The preliminary topic outline + the facts = the outline for the entire document.

Seventh, reorganize and reclassify categories to account for unintegrated facts and to discover omitted facts. You now have integrated the information you have gathered into the classifications you listed. Note, however, that there are some facts that have not been crossed out in page 43 of Exhibit 2-2, and they are not included in the summary in Exhibit 2-3 on pages 44 and 45; they did not fit into any of the headings or subtopics. You may need to reclassify your headings or subheadings or even create new ones to accommodate these facts. Or, you may discover that the facts should be deleted altogether because they are legally insignificant.

For example, Hughes's contribution of the name and the logo for the partnership and their value of $500 have not been included anywhere. Dividing "capital contributions" into two subheadings, "cash" and "name and logo" will help. Section V will now look like this:

```
        V.    Capital Contributions
              A.   Cash
                   1.   Hughes: $500
                   2.   Marks: $1,000
                   3.   Judd: $1,000
```

Exhibit 2-2.   Incorporating Facts into Topic Outline

Facts

- ~~Paul Hughes~~

- ~~Cynthia Marks~~

- ~~David Judd~~

- ~~2222 North Main Street~~
  ~~Big City, Big State 11111~~

- ~~Creative Audio Visuals~~

- Hughes contributes name and logo

- want insurance policies on each other in event of death; parties will agree each year on the value of the business; that amount will be used as basis for insurance purchase

- no assignment to others

- Hughes will maintain books

- want each to devote at least 15 hours/ month for sales

- want equal shares of profits and losses

- Marks and Judd contribute $1,000 but Hughes only has $500 to contribute

- agree that name and logo worth at least $500 at time business begins

- ~~want to write jingles for T.V. and radio commercials~~

- no authority for any transaction more than $250 without agreement by all

- all to work on jingles: lyrics and music

- if Hughes withdraws, partnership can use name and logo for six months; thereafter he gets them back

- yearly audit required; but any partner may request an additional one at any time at his/her own expense

- books available to each partner during regular business hours

- 90% of profits on each project available for distribution; 10% into partnership account

- no new partners without unanimous consent; unanimous agreement on new partner's contribution too

- withdrawal — 60 days' notice in writing

I.   Partners
   A. Paul Hughes
   B. Cynthia Marks
   C. David Judd

II.   Name of Partnership
   Creative Audio Visuals

III.   Place of Partnership
   2222 North Main Street
   Big City, Big State 11111

IV.   Purpose of Partnership
   to write jingles for T.V. and radio commercials

Exhibit 2-2. (*continued*)

Facts

- ~~Paul Hughes~~

- ~~Cynthia Marks~~

- ~~David Judd~~

- ~~2222 North Main Street~~
  ~~Big City, Big State 11111~~

- ~~Creative Audio Visuals~~

- Hughes contributes name and logo

- want insurance policies on each other in event of death; parties will agree each year on the value of the business; that amount will be used as basis for insurance purchase

- no assignment to others

- ~~Hughes will maintain books~~

- ~~want each to devote at least 15 hours/ month for sales~~

- ~~want equal shares of profits and losses~~

- ~~Marks and Judd contribute $1,000 but Hughes only has $500 to contribute~~

- agree that name and logo worth at least $500 at time business begins

- ~~want to write jingles for T.V. and radio commercials for profits~~

- no authority for any transaction more than $250 without agreement by all

- ~~all to work on jingles: lyrics and music~~

- if Hughes withdraws, partnership can use name and logo for six months; thereafter he gets them back

- ~~yearly audit required; but any partner may request an additional one at any time at his/her own expense~~

- ~~books available to each partner during regular business hours~~

- ~~90% of profits on each project available for distribution; 10% into partnership account~~

- no new partners without unanimous consent; unanimous agreement on new partner's contribution too

- withdrawal — 60 days' notice in writing

V. Capital Contributions
   A. Hughes $500
   B. Marks $1,000
   C. Judd $1,000

VI. Responsibilities of Partners
   A. 15 hours per month
   B. Each to work on jingles: lyrics and music

VII. Books and Records
   A. location: Hughes will maintain
   B. audit: yearly required; but any partner may request an additional one at his/her own expense
   C. availability: books available to each partner during regular business hours

VIII. Profits and Losses
   A. Each to share equally in profits and losses
   B. 90% of profits from each project available for distribution; 10% into a partnership account

Exhibit 2-2. (*continued*)

Facts

- ~~Paul Hughes~~

- ~~Cynthia Marks~~

- ~~David Judd~~

- ~~2222 North Main Street Big City, Big State 11111~~

- ~~Creative Audio Visuals~~

- Hughes contributes name and logo

- want insurance policies on each other in event of death; parties will agree each year on the value of the business; that amount will be used as basis for insurance purchase

- ~~no assignment to others~~

- ~~Hughes will maintain books~~

- ~~want each to devote at least 15 hours/ month for sales~~

- ~~want equal shares of profits and losses~~

- ~~Marks and Judd contribute $1,000 but Hughes only has $500 to contribute~~

- agree that name and logo worth at least $500 at time business begins

- ~~want to write jingles for T.V. and radio commercials for profits~~

- no authority for any transaction more than $250 without agreement by all

- ~~all to work on jingles: lyrics and music~~

- if Hughes withdraws, partnership can use name and logo for six months; thereafter he gets them back

- ~~yearly audit required; but any partner may request an additional one at any time at his/her own expense~~

- ~~books available to each partner during regular business hours~~

- ~~90% of profits on each project available for distribution; 10% into partnership account~~

- ~~no new partners without unanimous consent; unanimous agreement on new partner's contribution too~~

- withdrawal — 60 days' notice in writing

IX. Assignment
No assignment of partnership interest

X. Liability/Indemnification

XI. Addition of New Partners
A. unanimous consent needed for addition of new partner
B. unanimous agreement regarding amount of new partner's contribution

XII. Disability

Exhibit 2-2. (*continued*)

Facts

- ~~Paul Hughes~~

- ~~Cynthia Marks~~

- ~~David Judd~~

- ~~2222 North Main Street~~
  ~~Big City, Big State 11111~~

- ~~Creative Audio Visuals~~

- Hughes contributes name and logo

- ~~want insurance policies on each other in~~
  ~~event of death; parties will agree each~~
  ~~year on the value of the business; that~~
  ~~amount will be used as basis for insurance~~
  ~~purchase~~

- ~~no assignment to others~~

- ~~Hughes will maintain books~~

- ~~want each to devote at least 15 hours/~~
  ~~month for sales~~

- ~~want equal shares of profits and losses~~

- ~~Marks and Judd contribute $1,000 but~~
  ~~Hughes only has $500 to contribute~~

- agree that name and logo worth at least
  $500 at time business begins

- ~~want to write jingles for T.V. and radio~~
  ~~commercials for profits~~

- no authority for any transaction more than
  $250 without agreement by all

- ~~all to work on jingles: lyrics and music~~

- ~~if Hughes withdraws, partnership can use~~
  ~~name and logo for six months; thereafter~~
  ~~he gets them back~~

- ~~yearly audit required; but any partner may~~
  ~~request an additional one at any time at~~
  ~~his/her own expense~~

- ~~books available to each partner during reg-~~
  ~~ular business hours~~

- ~~90% of profits on each project available~~
  ~~for distribution; 10% into partnership ac-~~
  ~~count~~

- ~~no new partners without unanimous con-~~
  ~~sent; unanimous agreement on new part-~~
  ~~ner's contribution too~~

- ~~withdrawal = 60 days' notice in writing~~

XIII. Death
   A. value of business: Each year,
       partners agree as to value of the
       business
   B. life insurance policies
       1. Partnership will purchase in-
           surance on each partner's life
           for 1/3 of the agreed upon
           value
       2. In the event of death of a
           partner, the partnership will
           use the insurance proceeds to
           buy the deceased partner's
           interest.

XIV. Withdrawal
   A. Withdrawal — 60 days' notice in
       writing
   B. If Hughes withdraws, partnership
       can use name and logo for six
       months; thereafter, he gets them
       back.

XV. Dissolution

XVI. Interpretation of the Agreement

Exhibit 2-3.　Summary — Integrating Facts

Preliminary Topic
Outline　　　　+　　　　*Facts*　　　　=　　　　*Outline*

Preliminary Topic Outline

I. PARTNERS

II. NAME OF PARTNERSHIP

III. PLACE OF PARTNERSHIP

IV. PURPOSE OF PARTNERSHIP

V. CAPITAL CONTRIBUTIONS

VI. RESPONSIBILITIES OF PARTNERS

VII. BOOKS AND RECORDS
  A. location
  B. audits
  C. availability of partners

VIII. PROFITS AND LOSSES
  A. distribution to partners
  B. distribution to partnership accounts

IX. ASSIGNMENT

X. LIABILITY/INDEMNIFICATION

XI. ADDITION OF NEW PARTNERS

XII. DISABILITY

XIII. DEATH
  A. value of business
  B. life insurance policies based on value

XIV. WITHDRAWAL
  A. notice in writing
  B. ownership of name and logo if Hughes withdraws

XV. DISSOLUTION

Facts

- Paul Hughes
- Cynthia Marks
- David Judd
- 2222 North Main Street Big City, Big State 11111
- Creative Audio Visuals
- want insurance policies on each other in event of death; parties will agree each year on the value of the business; that amount will be used as basis for insurance purchase
- no assignment to others
- Hughes will maintain books
- want each to devote at least 15 hours/month for sales
- want equal shares of profits and losses
- Marks and Judd contribute $1,000 but Hughes only has $500 to contribute
- want to write jingles for T.V. and radio commercials for profits
- all to work on jingles: lyrics and music
- if Hughes withdraws, partnership can use name and logo for six months; thereafter he gets them back

Outline

I. Partners
  A. Paul Hughes
  B. Cynthia Marks
  C. David Judd

II. Name of Partnership
  Creative Audio Visuals

III. Place of Partnership
  2222 North Main Street
  Big City, Big State 11111

IV. Purpose of Partnership
  to write jingles for T.V. and radio commercials

V. Capital Contributions
  A. Hughes $500
  B. Marks $1,000
  C. Judd $1,000

VI. Responsibilities of Partners
  A. 15 hours per month
  B. Each to work on jingles: lyrics and music

VII. Books and Records
  A. Location: Hughes will maintain
  B. Audit: Yearly required; but any partner may request an additional one at his/her own expense.
  C. Availability: books available to each partner during regular business hours

VIII. Profits and Losses
  A. Each to share equally in profits and losses
  B. 90% of profits from each project available for distribution; 10%

XVI. INTERPRETATION OF AGREEMENT

- yearly audit required; but any partner may request an additional one at any time at his/her own expense
- books available to each partner during regular business hours
- 90% of profits on each project available for distribution; 10% into partnership account
- no new partners without unanimous consent; unanimous agreement on new partner's contribution 100
- withdrawal — 60 days' notice in writing

IX. Assignment
   no assignment of partnership interest

X. Liability/Indemnification

XI. Addition of New Partners
   A. unanimous consent needed for addition of new partner
   B. unanimous agreement regarding amount of new partner's contribution

XII. Disability

XIII. Death
   A. value of business: Each year, partners agree as to value of the business
   B. life insurance policies
      1. Partnership will purchase insurance on each partner's life for 1/3 of the agreed upon value
      2. In the event of death of a partner, the partnership will use the insurance proceeds to buy the deceased partner's interest.

XIV. Withdrawal
   A. Withdrawal — 60 days' notice in writing
   B. If Hughes withdraws, partnership can use name and logo for six months; thereafter, he gets them back.

XV. Dissolution

XVI. Interpretation of the Agreement

      B.   Name and Logo
         1.   Hughes contributes both
         2.   Value $500 at time business begins

Similarly, the $250 limitation on all transactions without partner approval also has not been included. Relabeling the "Responsibilities" section, to "Partners' Responsibilities and Limitations" will help classify the $250 limitation. Section VI will now look like this:

    VI.   Partners' Responsibilities and Limitations
       A.   Each Partner contributes 15 hours per month
       B.   Each Partner shall work on jingles: lyrics and music
       C.   No Partner shall have authority for any transaction costing more than $250 unless all partners agree

You now have reorganized and reclassified to account for unintegrated facts. But you also need to discover any omitted facts. Review your outline, re-read your research, and consult your client to ensure you have not deleted any important facts. Although you will do this again when you test for consequences (step six) and edit (step seven), the drafting process is recursive, and it is never too early to begin checking your work.

Eighth, correct any empty or omitted categories by consulting your client and researching. Note that there are several empty categories, that is, those with no facts underneath them: "Liability/Indemnification," "Disability," "Dissolution," and "Interpretation of the Agreement." You will want to determine why they are empty. They may be empty for several reasons: The pertinent facts may have been omitted, the category may merely be a legal principle that does not necessarily require supporting facts, or the category may be altogether unnecessary.

For example, the Liability/Indemnification section is empty but is necessary because unless otherwise indicated, partners are jointly and severally liable for all liability incurred on behalf of the partnership. Thus, you will need to explain this to your client and discuss whether to exclude or include such a provision.

If your client wishes the liability to be joint and several, you have two choices. You can either exclude the term altogether, since the law will read such a rule into the agreement. Or, you may want to expressly include the provision. If you exclude the term and the rule should change, then your client's intent would not be satisfied. In either case, no supporting facts would be necessary; you would merely be reciting a legal principle.

If, however, your client wishes to alter the joint and several liability rule, you will then need to discuss the alternatives and how to negotiate them, especially if you think the other partners will oppose the alternative your client desires. In this situation, you may need some supporting facts or you may again merely recite a legal principle that redefines the liability and indemnification of the partners.

Similarly, the categories about disability of a partner and dissolution of the partnership are empty. If a partner becomes disabled, you will need to know how to distribute profits, allocate losses, and redefine job responsibilities. Likewise, if one or more of the partners wants to dissolve the partnership, terms governing dissolution should already be determined. Regarding both categories, supporting facts may be necessary.

Finally, the "Interpretation of the Agreement" category is also empty. It is merely a heading for several legal principles. Perhaps experience with other contracts and your research has taught you to include provisions that dictate the interpretation of the agreement. For example if one provision is adjudicated invalid or unenforceable, you want to ensure that the remainder of the agreement remains valid. Thus, this is one principle you would include in the "Interpretation of the Agreement" section.

You should check your outline not only for empty categories but for omitted ones as well. To ensure that you have not omitted provisions that may be helpful or necessary, you may want to research the law and consult additional forms or checklists that other attorneys have prepared or that are in research books. Using forms at this stage of the drafting process serves a useful purpose: It helps ensure that you have not overlooked any important provisions. Had you used them sooner in lieu of your own classifying, organizing, and outlining, you would have failed to tailor the document for your client's particular, unique circumstances.

Ninth, convert the outline into a draft of the document. Once you have classified, organized, and outlined your agreement, the next logical step is to draft it. Although you may have consulted commercial forms or form books and used them as a checklist for classifying and organizing, you should not rely on them for exact language because they are generally filled with archaic language, legalese, and wordy patterns. They are tailored to cover every conceivable situation, not your specific one. Thus, their language will not help you draft your particular document. Step five of the process will cover careful writing. Because the techniques of that step of the drafting process are detailed and varied, they are set forth separately in Chapter 3.

After you complete a preliminary draft of your document, you may need to reoutline, reclassify, or further subclassify the terms of your document. Doing so will be especially important if the document is complex or detailed. Because a well-drafted document should also be visually easy for the reader to follow, additional headings and subheadings, enumeration, and tabulation may make the document easier to read. Step five of the drafting process on writing carefully will also detail techniques for creating documents that are visually easy to follow.

Exercise 2-4

Here is a list of facts gathered from a client interview. The client, Linda Smith, wants you to draft a will for her. Research any reference sources necessary and then classify the facts in appropriate categories for drafting the will.

FACTS:

1. Linda Smith
2. 1303 South Big Tree, Big City, Little State 12345
3. husband: Ralph A. Smith
4. 3 children:
    (1) Andrea, born 1/30/54, married to Michael Gabriel
    (2) Paul, born 7/3/56, unmarried

           (3)   Elizabeth, born 4/11/58, married to David Jones, with whom she has two children: Jennifer, born 4/22/80, Jerry, born 1/26/86

5.   wants to be cremated
6.   one life insurance policy for $400,000; husband is beneficiary
7.   Assets:
        Residence: home in joint tenancy
        Current value of home: $350,000; no mortgage
        Certificate of deposit currently containing $50,000
8.   taxes, if any, not to be paid by beneficiaries except pro rata by those who receive life insurance proceeds
9.   all property to husband
10. if he does not survive her, property to be divided as follows:
      a. $10,000 to each living grandchild to be used for college education. If any of the grandchildren are under 30 years old, the money should be held in trust. The trustee: First National Bank of Big City. If any grandchild dies before 30, his/her share should be divided equally between remaining grandchildren. Any portion of a grandchild's share not used by age 30 should be disbursed to that grandchild. If none of the grandchildren live to age 30, the money should be distributed like the residue of the estate.
      b.   Mrs. Smith's mother's diamond engagement ring to Andrea; to Elizabeth, if Andrea is deceased; if both are deceased, Mrs. Smith wants the ring to remain in the family.
      c.   All other property to be divided equally among the children; if any of the children are deceased, their share(s) to be divided equally among the deceased child's children. If any such grandchild is less than 30, his/her share to be put in trust. If all children predecease the Smiths, property to be shared equally by the surviving grandchildren.
      d.   if husband and all children and grandchildren predecease Mrs. Smith, all property to her sister, Catherine Black
      e.   Executor: Richard Banks
      f.   household goods and personal effects to surviving children

Questions:

1.   What classifications do you need?
2.   How should the classifications be organized?
3.   Do you need additional facts? What are they?
4.   Are there any irrelevant facts that you should delete? List them.

5. Write Carefully

Even if your document is well organized, it may not achieve your purposes if it is poorly written. Moreover, poorly drafted documents may engender a lawsuit. For these reasons, step five in the drafting process, write carefully, is critical.

The techniques of writing carefully are so detailed and varied that the topic requires an entire chapter. Thus, Chapter 3 of this book will detail methods to create a document that is complete, consistent, and accessible to the reader. Specifically, it will teach you three fundamental goals: be clear, use the proper tone, and be concise.

The first goal, clarity, requires that your document be both well focused and well ordered. A document too narrowly focused will be incomplete. If the focus is scattered, the document will be inconsistent. Even a well-focused document, however, may be inaccessible to the reader. Thus, documents are more accessible if they follow a clear order. A well-ordered document has parallel structure, moves from familiar material to unfamiliar material, and is visually easy to read.

Second, documents will also be more accessible if you carefully choose your tone. You need to identify the perspective of each of your audiences so that you can balance their conflicting needs. Once you have identified their perspectives, you will be able to decide how sophisticated to make your language. For example, for consumers, you should write documents in plain English. In contrast, for a more technical audience you may sometimes need to use terms of art, which are necessary and accepted in many industries. Whatever the perspective or language you use, you must emphasize important information at every level of your document.

Third, it will be easier for your reader to find important information if your document is concise. You should use as few words as possible to convey all the ideas necessary to complete your document.

6. Test for Consequences

Anticipating all possible future contingencies is a major part of legal drafting. Recall that Chapter 1 listed two types of contingencies you should anticipate: (1) circumstances and events regarding persons or property named in the document and (2) consequences of the form, language, and organization of the document itself.

The prior five steps in this chapter have already required you to consider some of those contingencies before completing your first draft. For example, recall that when you considered the audiences, you were required to anticipate whether they would be hostile or friendly and their ability to easily read the document. You also were required to think of every possible person who ever would read or use the document. Gathering the facts by the "who-what-where-when-why-how" method also required that you think about future possibilities and the effect of the document. Similarly, you considered the future legal ramifications when you researched the substantive, procedural, interpretive, and ethical rules pertaining to the document. You also considered future contingencies when you organized and classified the terms of the document: You tried to ensure that all facts, current and anticipated, were included; you tried to anticipate all necessary provisions and terms. Finally, you considered the possible future effects of your word choice, word placement, number of words, sentence structure, and visual format in striving to communicate as clearly as possible, to avoid ambiguities or inconsistencies in the document. Thus, you have already considered some contingencies.

Anticipating future consequences, however, is such a critical element of effective and thorough legal drafting that it is important now to review each step and test the document for its efficacy. "Testing" for consequences requires that you play the "what if" game for each step in the process.

Review the audiences and facts, altering them, one by one, to predict outcomes. Determine then, whether the document has been prepared to cover every conceivable situation. Take an imaginary, step-by-step walk through the transactions or events contained in the document. Determine then, whether the document will work, that is, whether it will be legally valid by complying with all relevant substantive, procedural, interpretive, and ethical laws; compare sections and sentences to make sure there are no substantive inconsistencies. Next, recheck the classifications and organization to make sure the document is logically presented. Finally, review your language for clarity, tone, and conciseness. Errors in language can create substantive errors that alter the intended meaning. Also check the document for its pictorial clarity. A visually unpleasing and difficult-to-follow document will be frustrating to the reader and will not be carefully read. It also may create ambiguities. Chapter 3 will present, in more detail, principles of clear writing and format that you will want to consider in testing the document.

7.   Edit and Rewrite

After you have tested the document, three types of editing and rewriting will be necessary. First, you will want to rewrite and reorganize the document to correct any substantive, organizational, or language errors that you may have discovered when you tested for consequences. Second, you will want to proofread the document thoroughly, correcting any grammar, punctuation, or spelling errors. Correct grammar, punctuation, and spelling are an integral part of all good writing, including legal drafting. The improper placement of one comma or one word can change entirely the meaning of a sentence or alter the legal ramifications of a particular clause or provision.[22]

After you have corrected any errors, the third and final editing technique is to re-read the document several additional times, rechecking each time for a different step in the process. In this way, you will be able to identify and correct the errors you have made in the document. Also, you will be able to recognize at what step in the process you made the errors, hopefully learning how to avoid similar errors in drafting future documents.

The following will-drafting project illustrates the way you may edit a document, using the seven steps to identify its errors. First, a brief summary of some facts is presented. Then, a student draft of the will is presented, containing errors that are labeled and explained to correspond with the steps in the drafting process.

SAMPLE DOCUMENT: Will of Michael Porter

FACT SUMMARY:

Testator:	Michael Porter
Age:	55
DOB:	_____
Profession:	Partner with Peat, Moss & Co., large accounting firm
Children:	1. Steven, age 29, DOB _____, C.P.A. Steven's wife: Margaret O'Brien, attorney child of Steven & Margaret: Andrea, 3 years DOB _____.
	2. Robert, age 23, DOB _____, in his first year of medical school; father pays.
Testator's Wife:	Laura, age 40, DOB _____. Laura has 1 daughter from a prior marriage: Cynthia, 11 years, DOB _____.
Testator's Desires:	1. Provide for wife for rest of her life but principal of his estate to go to his sons or their children after Laura's death.
	2. Laura to live in their house after his death but also wants house to go to his sons after Laura's death.
	3. If Robert does not complete medical school by the time Michael dies, Michael wants Robert to receive $30,000 to pay for his education.
	4. Wants to leave Cynthia $20,000; if he dies before Cynthia is 25 years old, the money is to be held in trust.

```
Assets:              1. Residence at 1910 Washing-
                     ton, Hinsdale, Illinois; val-
                     ue: $275,000; $215,000 mort-
                     gage.
                     2. $225,000 in securities in a
                     brokerage account at E.F. Hut-
                     ton.
                     3. $25,000 in a money market
                     account at First National Bank
                     of Chicago.
                     4. $5,000 in a joint checking
                     account at First National Bank
                     of Hinsdale.
                     5. $100,000 life insurance;
                     beneficiary: ex-wife, Martha.
```

LAST WILL AND TESTAMENT
OF
MICHAEL PORTER [1]

I, Michael Porter, of Hinsdale, Illinois, being of sound mind and body, [2] declare this to be my last will and testament, and I revoke all other wills and codicils that I may have made. [3]

Article I

I direct my executor to pay all my just debts, [4] all expenses incurred from my funeral, my last illness and the administration of my estate from[5] my residuary estate. [6]

[1] *Organization and Clarity:* Whole document needs more exact headings

[2] *Know Law:* "Sound mind and body." Does claiming "sound mind" make it so?
Write Carefully: Conciseness

[3] *Edit:* Break into 2 Sentences

[4] *Test for Consequences:* Include mortgage?

[5] *Edit:* Grammar. What does "from my residuary estate" modify?

[6] *Write Carefully:* Pictorial Clarity. Enumerate? Tabulate?

Article II

I direct that all estate, inheritance or other succession taxes incurred by reason of my death[7] shall be paid by my Executor[8] out of the principal of my residuary estate without contribution or reimbursement from any person.

Article III

No person named in this will shall be deemed to have survived me unless he or she is living thirty-one (31) days after the day of my death.

Article IV

1. I direct that my wife, Laura Porter, of Hinsdale, Illinois, receive my house [9] located at 1910 Washington, Hinsdale, Illinois (or any insurance settlement for this house if applicable). If my wife predeceases me or upon her death, I direct the executor to sell my house (or place any insurance settlement for this house if applicable) [10] and add the proceeds into Trust C, established in Article V, section 2(c).

2. I direct that my son, Robert Porter, is to receive $30,000.00. These funds are to be used by Robert to complete medical school. If my son does not continue medical school or withdraws from medical school, then no funds are to be allotted, or any remaining funds are to be forfeited. [11]

---

[7] *Test for Consequences:* Who pays tax on insurance proceeds?

[8] *Write Carefully:* Actor, passive

[9] *Know the Facts:* Testator wanted wife to get life estate in house, not fee simple.

[10] *Write Carefully:* Clarity, parentheticals.

[11] *Write Carefully:* Clarity
Facts: Is this a contingent gift? i.e., Does Robert get the money only if he has not yet completed medical school? What is intent of Testator if son has already graduated or if he quits after Testator's death?

Article V

I give all my residuary estate, being all real and personal property, wherever situated, in which I may have any interest at the time of my death not otherwise effectively disposed of to FIRST NATIONAL BANK OF HINSDALE as trustee. My residuary estate, which includes the proceeds of the insurance policy on my life, ⑫ securities, a money market account at First National Bank of Chicago, and a checking account at First National Bank of Hinsdale⑬ ⑭ shall be held and disposed of in the following trusts:

    1. For Cynthia Kraft: ⑮

      A. If Cynthia Kraft of Hinsdale, Illinois, survives me then the trustee shall as of the day of my death place $20,000.00 into "Trust A." ⑯

      B. Cynthia Kraft shall not be allowed access to Trust A until she turns twenty-five (25) years of age. At age 25⑰ Cynthia Kraft is to receive all the income and the principal from Trust A, and, subsequently, Trust A shall terminate.

    2. For Laura Porter:

      A. If my wife, Laura Porter, survives me (and for the purposes of this Article she shall be considered to survive me if the order of our deaths cannot be determined), the trustee shall as of the date of my death place my residuary estate and the proceeds of my life insurance policy (making my wife, Laura Porter, the new beneficiary and excluding

---

⑫ *Know the Facts:* Insurance policy is payable to ex-wife; therefore, proceeds are not part of the residuary estate.

⑬ *Test for Consequences:* What if accounts are moved to different banks?

⑭ *Write Carefully:* Clarity, conciseness; pictorial clarity: Enumerate? Tabulate?

⑮ *Organization and Know the Law:* Sec. 1 and 2 don't belong in same article just because they are both trusts. Gift to Kraft is a general bequest in trust, not part of residuary.

⑯ *Edit:* Commas

⑰ *Test for Consequences:* What if Cynthia dies before 25? *Edit:* Comma

the old beneficiary, Martha Porter, my ex-
wife) into ''Trust B.'' [18]
     B. The trustee shall pay to my wife, for
her life, all the interest from Trust B, even
if she remarries.
     C. My primary concern after my wife's
death is that the income and the principal of
Trust B is given to my sons, Steven Porter and
Robert Porter, in equal shares. [19] If one of
my sons predeceases my wife then his share is
to be split equally among or between his
children. If both my sons predecease my wife
then the entire sum is to be split in equal
shares among or between all their children.
If any of the receiving children are under
the age of twenty-five (25) then a Trust is to
be established. [20] Under this trust, when
each child reaches the age of 25 the trustee
shall distribute to him or her his or her portion of the income and the principal from
that Trust. If, however, upon wife's death,
I do not have any living descendants then the
income and the principal from Trust B is to be
given to the International Planned Parent-
hood Federation or any organization it might
subsequently become. [21]
     3. Notwithstanding anything to the con-
trary, the trust[22] under this instrument shall
terminate not later than twenty-one years after the death of the last survivor of my descendants living on the date of my death, at
the end of which period the trustee shall distribute each remaining portion of the trust

[18] *Test for Consequences:* Conflicts with Article III of will; cannot change insurance beneficiary in will.
Write Carefully: Conciseness.

[19] *Test for Consequences:* Does Trust B terminate or continue after wife's death?

[20] *Write Carefully:* Clarity: Is this a new trust? Are the "receiving children" the testator's grandchildren?

[21] *Organize:* Mixes descent w/terms of the trust.
Write Carefully: Pictorial clarity: distinguish descent from trust; Enumerate? Tabulate?
Edit: Commas

[22] *Organize:* Does this relate to all "trusts?"

---

property according to the proportions established in this Article, section 3(c). [23]

Article VI

1. I direct that the trustee of my estate,
FIRST NATIONAL BANK OF HINSDALE, shall have
full, complete and absolute possession and
control of all the trust property, including
all income derived from the trust property to
promote the best interest of the trust. [24] The
only limitation placed on the trustee's power
is that no money shall be invested in commodities futures.

2. No trustee shall be required to do the
following: to provide bond as a trustee; to obtain the order or approval of any court in the
exercise of any power or discretion; or to
qualify before, be appointed by or account to
any court.

Article VII

I direct that my wife, Laura Porter, receive
all of my personal and household effects which
have not yet been disposed of, [25] such as furniture, furnishings, jewelry, automobiles
and clothing (including any insurance). [26] If
my wife predecease me[27] then the executor is to
sell all my personal and household effects and
add the proceeds to Trust C, established in Article V, section 2(c).

Article VIII

1. I appoint my son, Steven Porter, as executor of this will. The executor shall have
all the powers and discretion over my estate
during administration that the trustee is giv-

---

[23] *Write Carefully:* Standard form language?
Pictorial Clarity: subheading

[24] *Know the Audiences:* How will Trustee know what to do?
Write Carefully: Clarity; conciseness

[25] *Organization:* Already disposed of entire residue in Article V.

[26] *Write Carefully:* Precision: What does "including any insurance" modify?

[27] *Edit:* Comma

en regarding the trust property in Article VI. [28]

2. In the event my son, Steven Porter, dies, resigns, refuses or is unable to act as executor of this will, I then appoint FIRST NATIONAL BANK OF HINSDALE to act as executor of this will, and having all title, rights, powers, duties, and obligations conferred upon the executor of my will. [29]

3. No executor shall be required to do the following: give any bond as executor of the will; or obtain the order or approval of any court in the exercise of any power or discretion. [30]

I have signed this will[31] on this tenth (10th) day of February, 1987.

_____
Michael Porter

We saw Michael Porter, in our presence, sign this instrument at its end; he then declared it to be his will and requested us to act as witnesses to it; we believe him to be of sound mind and body[32] and not under duress or constraint of any kind; and then we, in his presence and in the presence of each other, signed our names as attesting witnesses; all of which was done on the date of this instrument. [33]

NAME   ADDRESS

_____   _____

_____   _____

_____   _____

[28] *Know the Audiences and Clarity:* Will executor know what his powers are?

[29] *Write Carefully:* Clarity and conciseness. One sentence?

[30] *Write Carefully:* Conciseness

[31] *Edit and Test for Consequences:* (. . . "consisting of 5 pages, this page included") What if a page is lost?

[32] *Know the Law:* Sound body does not matter.

[33] *Write Carefully:* Pictorial clarity: Break up sentence? Enumerate? Tabulate?

Labeling and identifying the errors in this way will make it easy for you to correct them.

The editing and rewriting step in the process is not merely a detail. It is an integral and critical step to drafting effective and legally valid documents. No document, no matter what its form, style, or content, can satisfy even minimal standards of competence unless it is drafted and redrafted several times.

D. *Conclusion*

The seven steps of legal drafting presented in this chapter can be summarized as follows:

SEVEN STEPS OF LEGAL DRAFTING

1. Understand the multiple audiences
    a. nature: friendly/hostile
    b. education and experience
    c. use of the document
2. Gather the facts
    a. who?
    b. what?
    c. where?
    d. when?
    e. why?
    f. how?
3. Know the law
    a. substantive
    b. procedural
    c. interpretive
    d. ethical
4. Classify, organize, and outline
    a. list facts
    b. list categories
    c. rank categories
    d. convert the ranked categories into an ordered list of headings
    e. convert the ordered list of headings into a preliminary topic outline
    f. integrate facts into the outline
    g. reorganize and reclassify categories to account for unintegrated facts and to discover omitted facts
    h. consult client and review law and form books to discover omitted categories and correct empty ones
    i. convert the outline into draft of document
5. Write carefully
    a. be clear
    b. use the proper tone
    c. be concise

6. Test for consequences (play the "what if" game)
    a. review audience and facts, altering them one by one to predict outcomes
    b. take an imaginary walk through the transaction, step by step, to see if the document works
        (i) is it legally valid in substance, procedure, interpretation, and ethics?
        (ii) is it internally consistent substantively?
    c. recheck the classification and organization to see if it is logically presented
    d. check the language for precision, tone, and conciseness
    e. check the document for visual clarity
7. Edit and rewrite
    a. rewrite and reorganize substance and language
    b. edit for spelling, punctuation, and grammar
    c. review the document as a whole, reading it several times, each time to identify and correct errors made in a different step in the process

Chapter 3 will present step five of the process, "write carefully," in detail; Chapters 4, 5, 6, and 7 will illustrate how the process can be applied to drafting wills, contracts, pleadings, and legislation.

Notes

1. *See generally* Michael L. Goldblatt, *Well-drafted Contracts Keep Client and You Out of Court. Here's How,* 7 Preventive L. Rep., June 1988, 14-15; Harry J. Haynsworth, *How to Draft Clear and Concise Legal Documents,* 31 Prac. Law. 41 (1985).

2. For an additional discussion of audience, *see* Stephen V. Armstrong & Timothy P. Terrell, Thinking Like A Writer, 2-1–2-11 (1992); Richard H. Weisberg, When Lawyers Write 85 (1987); Veda Charrow & Myra Erhardt, Clear and Effective Legal Writing 38-57 (1986).

3. Reed Dickerson, Materials on Legal Drafting 81-82 (1981). Dickerson calls these "achieving documents" because their purpose is to realize the expectations of the participating individuals. *Id.*

4. *See id.* at 82. "Regulating documents" are those agreements that contain policy statements and mechanisms available to resolve audience differences. *Id.* The result of a successfully drafted "regulating document" is that the participating individuals can " 'live together' " amicably throughout the transaction period. *Id.*

5. *Id.* at 80-81. A "fulfilling document" will either complete or confirm transactions or "stage[s] in human relations." *Id.* Therefore, the purpose of a "fulfilling document" is primarily evidentiary because its future effect depends upon the fact that it exists. *Id.*

6. Fed. R. Civ. P. 11. *See also* Cal. Civ. Proc. Code §447 (West 1973 & Supp. 1993); Ill. S. Ct. Rule 137 (1993) (signing of pleadings, motions, and other papers — sanctions); Mass. Gen. Laws Ann., R. Civ. P. 11(a) (West 1992); Minn. Stat. Ann., R. Civ. Proc. 11 (West Supp. 1993); N.Y. Jud. Law §487 (McKinney 1983 & Supp. 1993); Ohio Rev. Code Ann., Ohio Rules Civ. Proc. 11 (Page 1988); Tex. R. Civ. P. Ann. r. 13 (West 1990).

7. Fed. R. Civ. P. 12(e). Several states have enacted statutes that allow the court to order a more particular statement and, thus, allow for delay. *See also* Cal. Civ. Proc. Code §430.10(g) (West 1973 & Supp. 1993); 735 ILCS 5/2-612 (1993); Mass. Gen. Laws Ann., R. Civ. Proc. 12(e) (1990); Minn. Stat. Ann., R. Civ. P. 12.05 (West Supp. 1993); N.Y. Civ. Prac. L. & R. §3024 (McKinney 1991); Ohio Rev. Code Ann., Ohio R. Civ. P. 12(e) (Page 1988 & Supp. 1992).

8. *See, e.g.,* Am. Jur. Legal Forms 2d (1992); Louis R. Frumer & Marvin Waxner, Bender's Federal Practice Forms (1992); Federal Procedure Forms, Lawyer's Ed. (1975); 2 Nichols Cyclopedia of Legal Forms Ann. (1978); Jacob Rabkin & Mark H. Johnson, Current Legal Forms with Tax Analysis (1993); West's Legal Forms (1986).

9. Uniform Partnership Act, 6 U.L.A. §§1-45 (1969). All states but Louisiana have adopted the Uniform Partnership Act or the Revised Uniform Partnership Act of 1976. *See also* Marlin M. Volz et al., The Drafting of Partnership Agreements (7th ed. 1986); Selected Corporation and Partnerships Statutes, Rules and Forms 417-439 (1989).

10. The Uniform Commercial Code provides how a sales contract should look where it includes a provision disclaiming implied warranties. The provision must mention "merchantability," and in the case of a writing the provision must be "conspicuous." U.C.C. §2-316(2) (1990). "Conspicuous" has been interpreted to include typeface that is bold, larger sized, or in all caps. Glenn Dick Equip. Co. v. Galey Constr. Co., 541 P.2d 1184 (Idaho 1975). However, provisions that have failed due to "inconspicuousness" include the placing of terms in italics only, placing terms on the reverse side, or burying terms in the fine print. Office Supply Co. v. Basic/Four Corp., 538 F. Supp. 776 (E.D. Wis. 1982); Rudy's Glass Constr. Co. v. E. F. Johnson Co., 404 So. 2d 1087 (Fla. Dist. Ct. App. 1981); Blankenship v. Northtown Ford, Inc., 420 N.E.2d 167 (Ill. App. Ct. 1981).

Similarly, other statutes and regulations dealing with financial contracts demand a specific form in disclosing such terms. Under the Truth in Lending Regulations, banks and lending institutions are required to disclose the terms of credit agreements. *See* 12 C.F.R. §226.1(b) (1992). The information given must be given "clearly and conspicuously in writing, in a form that the consumer may keep" for her records. 12 C.F.R. §226.17(a)(1). Specifically, the terms "finance charge" and "annual percentage" shall be disclosed *more* conspicuously than any other disclosure. 12 C.F.R. §226.17(a)(2). This would include the amount charged, all of which would be segregated from other disclosed information to ensure its prominence. *See also* 15 U.S.C. §1632(a) (1988). The U.S. Code mirrors the above Truth in Lending Regulations by requiring the financial terms in leases or credit arrangements to be written "clearly and conspicuously." *Id.* Also, annual percentage rates and financial charge terms must be "more conspicuous" than other terms. *Id.* Such information that is required to be disclosed must be grouped together and "conspicuously segregated." 15 U.S.C. §1637(b)(2)(B), §1638(b)(1). *See also* William H. Danne, Jr., Annotation, *Construction & Effect of U.C.C. §2-316(2) Providing That Implied Warranty Disclaimer Must Be "Conspicuous,"* 73 A.L.R.3d 248 (1976).

11.   William J. Bowe & Douglas H. Parker, 4 Page on the Law of Wills §30 (1961) (hereinafter Page on Wills). Knowing when and if certain rules of construction apply to a will is crucial in determining if the will as drafted will fulfill the desires of the testator. Lichter v. Bletcher, 123 N.W.2d 612 (Minn. 1963); Prince v. Nugent, 172 A.2d 743 (R.I. 1961); In re Burns' Estate, 100 N.W.2d 399 (S.D. 1960).

Several states even use different rules of construction that apply simply because the will was drafted by an attorney. In re Buckner's Estate, 348 P.2d 818 (Kan. 1960); Succession of Jones, 172 So. 2d 312 (La. Ct. App. 1965); Estate of Carroll, 764 S.W.2d 736 (Mo. Ct. App. 1989); Matter of Will of Schieder, 436 N.Y.S.2d 591 (App. Div. 1981); In re Falvey's Will, 224 N.Y.S.2d 899 (App. Div. 1962); In re Estate of Ginter, 158 A.2d 789 (Pa. 1960).

12.   John H. Jackson & Lee C. Bollinger, Contract Law in Modern Society: Cases & Materials 1003-1035 (1980); Walter H. E. Jaeger, 4 Williston on Contracts §§600-630 (3d ed. 1961); 4 Page on the Law of Contracts §§2020-2065 (1920); Thomas Thacher, *Construction,* 6 Yale L.J. 59 (1896); *See also* Hensler v. City of Los Angeles, 268 P.2d 12 (Cal. Dist. Ct. App. 1954); Stevens v. Fanning, 207 N.E.2d 136 (Ill. App. Ct. 1965); Oldfield v. Stoeco Homes, Inc., 139 A.2d 291 (N.J. 1958); John F. Davis Co. v. Shepard Co., 47 A.2d 635 (R.I. 1946).

13.   4 Page on Wills §30.27. *See generally* Norman J. Singer, 2A Statutes & Statutory Construction (5th ed. 1992) (hereinafter Sutherland Statutory Construction); Karl N. Llewellyn, *Remarks on the Theory of Appellate Decision and the Rules of Canons about How Statutes Are to Be Construed,* 3 Vand. L. Rev. 395 (1950). One such rule on the placement of words and phrases is *ejusdem generis.* 4 Page on Wills §47.17. Usually applied to statutes, this doctrine of construction states that where general words follow specific words, the general words are construed to include only those things that are included in the same class, or are of like kind, as the preceding specific words. *Id.* Likewise, when specific words follow general words, the doctrine restricts application of the general terms to things that are similar to the specific words. *Id.* This rule exists to give purpose to both phrases, with one indicating a class and the other illustrating it. *Id.* State v. One Hundred and Fifty-Eight Gaming Devices, 499 A.2d 940 (Md. 1985); Martin v. Commonwealth, 295 S.E.2d 890 (Va. 1982); Winner v. Marion County Commn., 415 So. 2d 1061 (Ala. 1982); Kostecki v. Pavlis, 488 N.E.2d 644 (Ill. App. Ct. 1986); State v. Williams, 449 So. 2d 744 (La. Ct. App. 1984).

An illustration might be "dollars, yen, kroner, and other currencies." While rubles would be interpreted to be included in the general term, "other currencies," Monopoly money would not because it has no value and would not be considered "of like kind." Similarly, a "no vehicles, such as trucks, vans, or cars, are allowed" ordinance may not encompass a bicycle. While still a "vehicle," a bicycle is not in the same class as the larger, motorized vehicles and thus is not a member of the restricted, general class.

Modern commentators have tended to be critical of the rule of *ejusdem generis,* treating it as extreme legalism to the detriment of the common law. Sutherland Statutory Construction, §47.18. In an effort to avoid the harsh results of strict construction, states have developed exceptions and modifications to the rule. *See* F.H. v. K.L.M., 740 P.2d 1006 (Colo. Ct. App. 1987). When the specific terms given do not imply a class, the rule does not apply to the general terms. Burke v. Sullivan, 265 P.2d 203 (Mont. 1954); Thompson v. Railroad Commission, 232 S.W.2d 139 (Tex. Civ. App. 1950); State v. Williams, 627 P.2d 581 (Wash. Ct. App. 1981). Also, if the list of specific words embraces and exhausts all of the class, the general terms take on meaning beyond the class. In re Special Educ. Placement of Walker, 520 N.E.2d 777 (Ill. App. Ct. 1987); National Bank of Commerce v. Estate of Ripley, 61 S.W. 587 (Mo. 1901). Finally, the rule of ejusdem generis will not apply if there is a clear manifestation of contrary intent. Scudder v. Annapolis Hosp., 341 N.W.2d 504 (Mich. Ct. App. 1983); Madison County Bd. of Educ. v. Miles, 173 So. 2d 425 (Miss. 1965); State, Div. of Wildlife v. Barker, 457 N.E.2d 312 (Ohio 1983).

The doctrine of *ejusdem generis* has been applied to contracts as well. Keller v. Ely, 391 P.2d 132 (Kan. 1964); Cronkhite v. Falkenstein, 352 P.2d 396 (Okla. 1960); Southland Royalty Co. v. Pan Am. Petro. Corp., 378 S.W.2d 50 (Tex. 1964); W. F. Magann Corp. v. Virginia-Carolina Elec. Works, Inc., 123 S.E.2d 377 (Va. 1962). *See* 4 Williston on Contracts, §619.

Ejusdem generis also applies to the construction of wills. Brink's, Inc. v. Illinois Commerce Commn., 439 N.E.2d 1 (Ill. App. Ct. 1982); In re Grainger's Estate, 38 N.W.2d 435 (Neb. 1949); In re Armour's Estate, 94 A.2d 286 (N.J. 1953).

14. *See* 1 Moore's Federal Practice Rules Pamphlet 127-142 (1990); 5A Charles A. Wright & Arthur R. Miller, Federal Practice and Procedure §§1341-1397 (1990).

15. A lawyer may not "knowingly make a false statement of law or fact." Model Code of Professional Responsibility DR 7-102(A)(5) (1981) (hereinafter Model Code). The lawyer may also not "counsel or assist his client in conduct that the lawyer knows to be illegal or fraudulent." *Id.* DR 7-102-(A)(7). If your client is attempting to defraud someone, you should insist she rectify the situation. *Id.* DR 7-102-(B)(1). If she doesn't, the lawyer should disclose the fraud to "the affected person or tribunal." *Id.*

16. A lawyer may not advance frivolous claims. *Id.* DR 2-109-(A)(2), DR 7-102(A)(2); EC 7-4, EC 7-5; Model Rules of Professional Conduct §3.1 (1983) (hereinafter Model Rules).

17. Model Code DR 7-102(A)(2); Model Rules §3.1.

18. Model Code EC 7-4 n.12.

19. *Id.* EC 5-5, EC 5-6; Model Rules §1.5(d)(1).

20. *See generally, e.g.,* Elliott L. Biskind, Legal Writing Simplified 126-156 (1971); Frank E. Cooper, Writing in Law Practice 271-370 (1963); Reed Dickerson, The Fundamentals of Legal Drafting 36-54 (1965).

Form books may also be helpful in discovering what other information may be needed to draft an effective document. *See also* Illinois Forms Legal and Business (1986); Institute of Continuing Legal Education, Michigan Basic Practice Handbook (Fred S. Steingold ed., 1981); New Jersey Forms: Legal and Business (1975); West's McKinney's Forms (1986).

21. *See, e.g.,* Gilbert G. Cantor, The Lawyer's Complete Guide to the Perfect Will (1984); National Conference on Federal Legislative Drafting in the Executive Branch, Professionalizing Legislative Drafting, the Federal Experience (Reed Dickerson ed., 1971); Valera Grapp, Portfolio of Business Forms, Agreements and Contracts (1985); Ludwig Mandel, The Preparation of Commercial Agreements (7th ed. 1978); Tax Law & Estate Planning Series, Practising Law Institute, Ser. No. 182, Basic Will Drafting (1988); Thomas L. Shaffer, The Planning and Drafting of Wills and Trusts (2d ed. 1979); Robert P. Wilkins,

Drafting Wills and Trust Agreements: A Systems Approach (2d ed. 1989); Charles K. Plotnick, *How to Handle the Will Interview,* 23 Prac. Law., July 15, 1977, at 81-86.

Sources that are state specific are also available as guides for drafting specific documents. Angela G. Carlin & Richard W. Schwartz, Merrick-Rippner Ohio Probate Law (4th ed. 1989); Oregon State Bar Committee on Continuing Legal Education, Workman Compensation Practice in Oregon (1968); C. Darrell Sooy, California Real Property Sales Transactions (Supp. June 1991). *See* Jane S. Whitman, *Probate and Trust Questions,* 48 Ill. B.J. 380 (1960).

22.   For the importance of word choice and punctuation, *see, e.g.,* Colorado Milling & Elev. Co. v. Chicago, Rock Island & Pac. R.R. Co., 382 F.2d 834 (10th Cir. 1967); Plymouth Mut. Life Ins. Co. v. Illinois Mid-Continent Life Ins. Co., 378 F.2d 389 (3d Cir. 1967); Beverly Hills Oil Co. v. Beverly Hills Unified School Dist., 70 Cal. Rptr. 640 (Ct. App. 1968). *See* In re Fisk's Estate, 187 P. 958 (Cal. 1920); Randolph v. Fireman's Fund Ins. Co., 124 N.W.2d 528 (Iowa 1963). *See also* Lowery v. Wilson, 200 S.E. 861 (N.C. 1939); Dorman v. Goodman, 196 S.E. 352 (N.C. 1938); Baker v. McDel Corp., 191 N.W.2d 846 (Wis. 1971).

See generally Biskind, Legal Writing Simplified, *supra* note 20, at 51-71; Gertrude Block, Effective Legal Writing: For Law Students and Lawyers 1-13 (3d ed. 1986); Dickerson, The Fundamentals of Legal Drafting, *supra* note 20, at 112-132; Morton S. Freeman, The Grammatical Lawyer 1-326 (1979); Ronald L. Goldfarb & James C. Raymond, Clear Understandings: A Guide to Legal Writing 42-57 (1982); Henry Weihofen, Legal Writing Style 255-280 (1961).

Write Carefully

As explained in the first two chapters of this book, legal drafting is a multi-step process. You must have evaluated your audiences, gathered your facts, researched the law, and organized your material before you are ready to write. Although completing these steps will give you a fairly good idea of what you want to say, you will still need to be careful about the way you actually write the document.

There are two reasons this chapter focuses in a more detailed way on how to write. First, students often take the writing process for granted. They have been writing for years and assume that all writing is the same. Drafting documents, however, requires the writer to be very precise. Second, poor writing turns documents into lawsuits. The language of the document must speak for itself. The parties bound by the document must be able to determine their obligations from the document. Otherwise disputes must be resolved by litigation.

Generally, good writing is achieved by striving for three fundamental goals: be clear, use the proper tone, and be concise. In order to fulfill these goals you need to concentrate on six different levels: the transaction, which includes other related documents; the document as a whole; the section; the paragraph; the sentence; and the word. This chapter will help you write a clear, concise, integrated document by providing a set of guidelines that operate on all six of these levels.

A. Be Clear

Clarity is crucial. Others will be referring to the document you draft in order to evaluate their legal rights. For example, your client may need to refer to a contract to see what her rights are if the other party is late in performing. If the contract is unclear, the result may be unnecessary litigation and possibly even a legal malpractice claim.

A document is clear if it is 1) complete, 2) consistent, and 3) accessible to the reader. You can create complete, consistent, and accessible documents if you choose the correct focus and order for your document.

The focus of the document is the most important key to clarity. If the document is focused too narrowly, it omits necessary information. If the focus is scattered, the document may be inconsistent. A reader cannot supply missing information or reconcile inconsistencies. Accordingly, if you focus your document well, it will be complete and consistent.

However, a well-focused document is not necessarily accessible to the reader. Readers find it easiest to read documents that follow a predictable order and integrate that structure into a readable format. Accordingly, this section will concentrate on two techniques for achieving clarity: focus and order.

1. Focus Accurately

A photographer controls the way we see a subject by changing the focus. He can focus on an overview or a particular detail. He can make the picture clear or fuzzy, distinct or ethereal. The focus he chooses will depend on the purpose of the picture. Thus, a photo for an anatomy text would need to be much more distinct and detailed than a picture of a sunset.

Similarly, you must choose how to focus your document. You must decide whether to be precise or intentionally vague. Vague documents provide flexibility, while precise documents provide firmness. Drafted documents must be flexible enough to meet changing needs, but firm enough to protect the client's interests. Accordingly, you must adjust the focus of your document to meet your purposes.

Although you may intentionally draft a vague document to achieve flexibility, you do not want your document to be ambiguous. The first part of this section describes intentional vagueness and the two ways you can create it: through generality and abstraction. The second part of the section describes ambiguity and its causes: inconsistencies and omissions.

a. Choose How Vague or Precise to Be

You must decide how vague or precise to make your document. Many lawyers have been taught to view vagueness as a villain to be avoided. For example, constitutional law courses discuss statutes that are void for vagueness.[1] Thus, many young lawyers think that an ironclad document is one that spells out every conceivable detail. On the contrary, many of the best documents are intentionally vague because vague documents are flexible enough to adjust to changing circumstances. For example, a contract may require that a party "act in good faith" rather than merely comply with a technical rule.

Many lawyers believe that vague language is simply nebulous or empty. However, vague language is more like a piece of elastic waistband. Readers know generally what it is, even if they can't be sure exactly how far it will stretch. Thus vague language carries a core meaning with undefined limits. Precise language, on the other hand, has sharper limits, like a leather belt that won't stretch to cover unexpected changes.

For example, if you were drafting a will for someone who wanted to leave property to her grandchildren, you could choose varying levels of precision:

> VAGUE: I give my grandchildren . . .
> PRECISE: I give John Rogers and Sally Smith . . .

The vague word, "grandchildren," will stretch to include grandchildren born after the will is signed. The technically more precise "John Rogers and Sally Smith" will exclude after-born grandchildren.

Of course, no word can be absolutely exact. Vagueness is a matter of degree. For instance, "car" is more precise than "motor vehicle." However, "car" also is vague. Does it include railroad cars as well as automobiles? You must choose how far you want the language of your document to stretch. You have two mechanisms to adjust the fit: generality and abstraction.

i.   Choose How General or Specific to Be

The Internal Revenue Code of 1913 was only a few pages long. It set forth certain general principles to govern income taxation.[2] The current code is volumes long and quite detailed. Thus, there is an enormous range of specificity available for every document.

At the transaction level, in determining how specific to be, you must consider whether your document should be designed to cover a single transaction or multiple transactions. For example, assume that a bank asked you to draft the documents for a car loan. You could draft documents for the particular car loan: forms that covered a loan for $10,387.00, and a blue, 1990 Chevrolet Celebrity. You also could draft broader documents, which could be used for any car loan, with spaces for bank employees to fill in the details about the amount of the loan and the make and model of the car. You also could draft even broader documents, which covered any loan in which the bank had the right to repossess property. Of course, your client, the bank, would have to help make this decision.

Similarly, if you were drafting legislation, you might have a fair amount of discretion as to the scope of the new statute. For example, a legislator might be concerned about the level of mercury in a lake where he fishes. If he asks you to draft proposed legislation to correct the problem, you have to decide the scope of the legislation. You might want to create an entire environmental plan to regulate water pollution in the state. You might limit the legislation to water that drains into lakes or rivers. You could prohibit all water pollutants, or limit the legislation to toxic chemicals, toxic metals, or only mercury. You could aim the statute to regulate the conduct of everyone, or limit it to industry, or cities, or individuals who dump more than a certain quantity of pollutants.

Once you have established the scope of the document itself, you must consider how general or specific to make the language within the document. Consider a drunk driving statute. When you think of drunk driving, you may think of drunks driving cars:

> It is a felony for any drunk person to drive a car.

Because this language is specific, it is easy to apply. The state only needs to prove that the person was drunk and was driving a car. However, this statute is too specific. It would be legal for a drunk to drive a truck, tractor, or trailer. Thus, you may be tempted to list all the examples you can envision:

> It is a felony for any drunk person to drive a car, truck, trailer, or tractor.

Although adding a list to the provision broadens it, the statute still suffers from over-specificity. If you name a specific item in a document, but fail to name other similar items, a court may presume that you meant to exclude the unnamed items.[3] Thus, a drunk on a motorcycle might not be covered.

It is extremely difficult to dream up every possible future contingency. Thus, documents that provide detailed lists almost inevitably omit something. One solution is to move to a broader category. Instead of trying to list everything a drunk could drive, describe the category of things that are driven:

> It is a felony for any drunk person to drive a motor vehicle.

Even if you forgot motorcycles when you wrote this statute, they would be covered. Thus, general language provides more flexibility for the document. It will adapt more easily to unforeseen future circumstances.

Broader categories, however, are harder to apply to specific situations. Consider the drunk homeowner who cuts figure eights in the lawn with a riding lawn mower. Arguably the drunk homeowner is driving a "motor vehicle." However, unlike cars, trucks, trailers, tractors, and motorcycles, riding lawn mowers are neither fast enough, nor large enough to create serious risks unless they are driven on highways. Thus, "motor vehicles" may be overly broad.

One solution might be to combine the general category with the specific list:

> It is a felony for any drunk person to drive a car, truck, tractor, trailer, motorcycle, or other motor vehicle.

Now, however, the reader may be confused. Because the general term "motor vehicles" includes all the items on the list, the list seems unnecessary. Courts construe documents so that each word in the document has meaning.[4] Accordingly, courts limit the general term to the class created by the specific lists.[5]

The problem with this limitation is that the specific list may describe different classes. In our example, the list could be interpreted to describe vehicles with wheels. If so, the statute would include lawn mowers. The list also might define a class of vehicles meant to operate on highways. If so, the statute would not include lawn mowers. Nevertheless, attaching the list somewhat narrows the term motor vehicle. For instance, since the entire list operates on land, a motorboat would be excluded.[6]

EDITING TIP: If you list specific items, ask yourself how all those items are similar. The similarity may suggest a general term that will make your document more flexible.

You need to think about how general or specific to be at the word level too. Some words describe an entire class of items, while others describe specific items. For example, "appliances" is a general term that refers to an array of mechanical devices, while "toaster" is quite specific. The choice depends largely on what your client wants. Thus, when you draft a will, the client must decide whether she wants to give all the "jewelry" or only a "ring."

Remember, however, that changes occur as time passes. The ring may be sold or traded for a bracelet. Child support that seemed generous in 1980 may seem minuscule in 1990. Thus, your client may prefer to agree to "30 percent of gross income" as child support, rather than "$500 per month." General terms may more flexibly account for changing circumstances.

However, do not make your terms so general that they leave your meaning unclear. For example, although "jewelry" is a general term, the parties will understand it. However, they may not understand "heirlooms." If terms get too broad, they eventually lose their meaning altogether.

Exercise 3-1

a. Identify the general and specific language in the following. Change any language that is too general or too specific.

A person commits a theft if he intentionally embezzles, steals, purloins, knowingly converts, obtains unauthorized control over, obtains by deception, obtains by threat, retains longer than authorized, or otherwise interferes with property so as to permanently deprive the owner of possession.

b. You are the attorney for a school district that has had problems with students bringing dangerous items to school and using them as weapons. Draft a regulation that allows the school district to expel such students.

ii. Choose How Abstract or Concrete to Be

Just as you have a range of choices about how general or specific to make your document, you must choose how abstract or concrete to make it. Concrete items conjure up real physical images, while abstractions elicit more mental images. For example a "ball" is more concrete, while a "sphere" is more abstract. Abstractions are removed from the real world and are, hence, theoretical. Concrete items are tangible and rooted in the real world. Lawyers are paid to think for a living; therefore, they are more comfortable with abstractions than many readers. Abstractions can confuse some readers.

For example, in the Marx Brothers' movie, *A Night at the Opera,* Groucho and Chico discuss a contract:

Groucho: "The party of the first part shall be known in this contract as the party of the first part."
Chico: It sounds a little better this time.
Groucho: Well it grows on you. Want to hear it once more?
Chico: Only the first part.
Groucho: Well, it says: "The first part of the party of the first part shall be

known in this contract" — look: Why should we quarrel about a thing like
that? (*He tears off the offending clause.*)

Chico (tearing the same clause out of his contract):   Sure, it's too long
anyhow. Now what have we got left?

Groucho: Well I've got about a foot and a half. . . . Now, then: "The party
of the second part shall be known in this contract as the party of the
second part."

Chico: Well, I don't know. I don't like the second party.

Groucho: You should have come to the first party. We didn't get home till
around four in the morning.[7]

The "party of the first part" that Groucho and Chico are parodying, is an abstraction. It is used in some forms to take the place of the name of the contracting party. Similarly, "name" is an abstraction for "Jane Doe," and "Jane Doe" is an abstraction for a particular woman.

Don't confuse abstraction with generality. Although "party of the first part" is an abstraction, it is not general. It refers to one specific person, not a category or class of people. A general category is larger than the specific items it includes, but an abstraction is merely another name for the same item. "Party of the first part" merely is another more abstract name for the same person. An abstraction could, of course, also be general. Accordingly, abstractions may be either general or specific. The following chart helps to explain how these concepts overlap:

	ABSTRACT	*CONCRETE*
GENERAL	Water going vessel	Boat
SPECIFIC	Small water going vessel propelled by oars	Dinghy

Abstractions inherently distance items from their real world contexts. Accordingly, if you use abstract terms, readers will need to work harder to understand them. Hence, you should not use abstractions without a good reason.

However, sometimes abstractions help you focus on more important issues. Recall the example of drafting a drunk driving statute. The term "motor vehicle" seemed to apply to riding lawn mowers, even when they were driven on front lawns. Instead of thinking concretely about the kinds of vehicles that should not be driven while drunk, try to think about the more abstract purpose of the statute. Is the purpose to keep highways safe? If so, then the lawn mower should be included only if it is driven on the highway. In fact, if your concern is drunks meandering around highways, you may even want to include pedestrians. Thus, it might improve the statute to phrase it in terms of its purpose, safety.

Safety is an abstraction because it is theoretical, more of a concept than a concrete item. However, safety may be too general a category. If the statute makes it a felony for any drunk to be unsafe on a highway, a drunk passenger could be prosecuted for failing to wear a seatbelt. The real purpose is not merely to protect the drunk, but to discourage behavior that poses risks to others. The statute needs a narrower abstract term:

It is a felony for any drunk person to behave in a reckless manner on a
highway.

This improved statute would include lawn mowers only if they were driven on a highway. Thus, abstract language ("reckless") helps express the purpose of a document ("safety").

However, because the abstract language has changed the focus of the statute to recklessness, some of the original meaning is changed. If a drunk drives a car carefully on the highway, has the drunk committed a felony? Arguably not. It is only a felony for the drunk to be reckless. Thus, the statute must be improved with some more concrete language:

> It is a felony for any drunk person to behave in a reckless manner on a highway. Recklessness includes, but is not limited to, driving a motor vehicle or walking on a highway.

EDITING TIP: If you use abstract language, think about whether you need to add concrete language to make it clear.

Abstract language also is distancing. It can make a document sound more objective than it really is. For example, in Illinois, a number of statutes apply to "cities with populations in excess of 1,000,000."[8] In reality, this phrase is a general abstraction for "Chicago." Similarly, abstract language can be used in a will to explain favoritism. For instance:

> CONCRETE: I give to Jane Godfrey . . .
> ABSTRACT: I give to my eldest daughter who has been a faithful caretaker in my old age . . .

Unfortunately, the abstract language omits important information. What if Jane dies, and ungrateful Gail Smith is now the eldest daughter? Combining abstract and concrete language helps:

> COMBINED: I give to my eldest daughter, Jane Godfrey, who has been a faithful caretaker in my old age . . .

EDITING TIP: Whenever you decide to use abstractions, you should think about whether you want to add any concrete language to serve as an illustration or explanation. If you add concrete language, make it clear how it relates to the abstract ideas. Is it an illustration, an explanation, or an exclusive list?

Although abstractions are useful tools to shift the focus to more important issues, they are dangerous because they frequently omit or obscure important information. Accordingly, you should use them sparingly. Unfortunately, many writers use abstract language out of laziness. You should take the time to think about whether abstract or concrete language will serve your purposes. One way to double check whether you have used language that is too abstract is to look for frequently used abstractions.

EDITING TIP: Watch for the following abstract words:

aspect	consideration	function
basis	degree	matter
characteristic	facet	situation
circumstance	factor	way
concept	foundation	

These words are abstract, but they do not shift the focus to more important issues. Thus, they are empty words. Edit them out of your prose.

When you decide how to focus your document, you must think about your goals and the best way to achieve them. Different parts of the same document may require different degrees of precision. It is less important to characterize language as general or abstract than to be sure it meets your needs.

Exercise 3-2

a.   You represent a college that has had a number of unfortunate racist and sexist incidents on campus. The university wants you to draft a policy for the student handbook that gives the university flexibility in dealing with these problems, but also lets students know when they have gone too far. Draft the policy.

b.   Identify the abstract language in the following provision. Which abstractions help? Which abstractions should be changed? Should any of the concrete language be made more abstract? Rewrite the provision to be clear and have the proper focus:

SUBSTITUTED PERFORMANCE

(a) Where without fault of either party the agreed berthing, loading, or unloading facilities fail or an agreed type of carrier becomes unavailable or the agreed manner of delivery otherwise becomes commercially impracticable but a commercially reasonable substitute is available, such substitute performance must be tendered and accepted.

(b) If the agreed means or manner of payment fails because of domestic or foreign governmental regulation, the seller may withhold or stop delivery unless the buyer provides a means or manner of payment which is commercially a substantial equivalent. If delivery has already been taken, payment by the means or in the manner provided by the regulation discharges the buyer's obligation unless the regulation is discriminatory, oppressive or predatory.

b.   Avoid Ambiguity

Although you may sometimes want to adopt a more general focus by being intentionally vague, you never want to be ambiguous. Vague language may allow a number of alternatives within a defined general class. However, if a provision can be interpreted to mean two different and inconsistent things, it is ambiguous. Because ambiguity incorporates inconsistency it is dangerous. Ambiguity arises from either omissions or inconsistencies.

i. Avoid Omissions

When you omit necessary items, the reader must supply them from the context of the document or transactions. Different readers may make different assumptions about the missing information. Thus, you create ambiguity if you omit necessary items at any level.

At the transaction level, omitted documents create ambiguity. For example, a will might provide that personal property will be distributed according to a list attached to the will. Without the list, the will is ambiguous. Similarly, a complaint that incorporates attached exhibits is ambiguous if the exhibits are omitted.

It is relatively easy to create a checklist to follow to be sure you draft all the necessary documents for a transaction. Similarly, it is easy to double-check that all the documents are included within the appropriate packet. Sometimes, however, it is the client who misplaces a necessary document.

EDITING TIP: Watch for cross references to other documents. Have you prepared all the necessary documents? Can you combine or eliminate any?

When you need multiple documents, physically attach them to each other. The more complex the transaction is, the more important it is to keep all the necessary documents together. Use large clips or binders to create document files with indices and tabs so you can find necessary items quickly.

Omissions are more common within a document. Omitted provisions are more difficult to spot. When you gather your facts, you discover some of the necessary provisions, and when you research the law, you discover more. Forms can help here. Although they, too, may be incomplete, they will give you a start on creating a checklist of the kinds of provisions that should be included. However, if you simply copy an old form for a new use, you are likely to omit crucial provisions. No two transactions are identical, so no two documents should be either.

The best way to discover omissions is to test your first draft carefully. Ask yourself the following questions about each section or provision: (1) who? (2) what? (3) when? (4) where? (5) why? and (6) how? If you test your provisions carefully, you are likely to find most of your omissions. Most lawyers, either consciously or unconsciously, do some testing. Unfortunately, the testing process becomes tedious at the sentence level and many drafters get sloppy. As a result many sentences fail to communicate *who* must act.

BAD: The marital home shall be sold.[9] (by whom?)

Omissions are particularly insidious because the reader usually cannot supply the missing terms from the context.

ii. Avoid Inconsistencies

Readers may find it hard to resolve inconsistencies. Accordingly inconsistencies create ambiguity at many levels. Sometimes the document you draft is inconsistent with other documents.[10] For instance, a new statute might be inconsistent with an existing statute. If you are drafting legislation, you can prevent statutory conflicts with careful legal research.[11]

Similarly, two documents that are both part of the same transaction may conflict. For example, an individual selling her house might sign both a real estate sales contract and a real estate agent's listing agreement. If the two documents conflict about who pays the commission, an ambiguity arises. You can prevent these transactional ambiguities in one of two ways. If possible, you can draft all the documents yourself,[12] in which case you can be sure they are consistent. If, however, your client already has signed a necessary document, you can prevent transactional ambiguities by gathering your facts carefully. For example, if you get a copy of the listing agreement and read it carefully before you draft the sales contract, you can be sure the documents are consistent.

At the document or section level, ambiguities arise when different parts of the document seem to contradict each other.[13] For example, consider a marital settlement agreement that contains these provisions:

Example

Child Support

The husband agrees to pay to the wife each month support in an amount equal to:

1. 1/2 the total annual cost of parochial education,
2. 1/2 the total monthly cost of child care, and
3. 1/2 the monthly mortgage expenses, but
4. the total amount of support to be paid in any given month, shall not exceed 25% of the husband's net income.

Rehabilitative Support

The husband agrees to pay support of $1,000 each month to the wife for a period of 3 years to enable her to become fully self-supporting.

The agreement is ambiguous. Is the $1,000 rehabilitative support covered by the limit in paragraph 4? The husband will argue that when paragraph 4 limited the "*total* amount of support," it included the rehabilitative "support." The wife will argue that the limit applies only to child support. She will point to the fact that paragraph 4 is a subpart of the section entitled "Child Support." In doing so, the wife is arguing that the context of the document makes the meaning clear.

Although context often helps to resolve apparent ambiguities, you should not rely on context alone to make your document clear. In order to avoid inconsistent provisions, you must draft your document as a whole, rather than as a collection of unrelated provisions. Indeed, omissions and inconsistencies are almost inevitable if you simply copy sections from other documents and insert them in your new document. Lawyers are paid to exercise legal judgment, not merely to "cut and paste." Of course, you need not reinvent every provision each time you draft a document. However, you must scrutinize every provision to be sure that it suits your purposes and is consistent with the rest of the document.

Ambiguities also arise at the sentence level. Typically, sentences have multiple meanings because the words are in a confusing order.[14] For example:

> BAD: No employee shall inspect the furnace *while smoking*.

Which one is smoking: the employee or the furnace? "Smoking" is a descriptive word, or modifier. Sentence ambiguities frequently arise from misplaced modifiers. Hence, you can clarify the sentence by placing the modifier near the word it modifies:

> BETTER: 1. *While smoking,* no employee shall inspect the furnace.
>
> OR
>
> 2. No employee shall inspect a *smoking* furnace.

EDITING TIP: Watch for words ending in "-ing."[15] Frequently these words modify other words or phrases. Place a modifier ending in "-ing" directly next to the word or phrase it modifies.

In the previous example, the modifier ("while smoking") was tacked on to the end of the sentence. Merely moving a modifier to the middle of the sentence will not clarify it. For example:

> BAD: Employees *only* may use this restroom.

It is unclear whether this sentence means that customers cannot use the restroom, or that employees cannot use other restrooms. The modifier seems to modify both the word before it ("employees") and the words after it ("may use this restroom").[16] Again, moving the modifier solves the problem:

> BETTER: 1. *Only* employees may use this restroom.
>
> OR
>
> 2. Employees may use *only* this restroom.

EDITING TIP: Watch for these words:

almost	hardly	nearly
even	just	only
exactly	merely	simply

Always place these modifiers *immediately before* (not after) the word they modify.

Sometimes, however, the modifier should be placed *after* the words it modifies. Otherwise, confusion results:

BAD: No checks may be cashed by cashiers *without prior approval.*

Which needs to be approved: the cashier or the check? Readers expect prepositional phrases to immediately follow the words they modify. Because "without prior approval" is a prepositional phrase, readers might expect that the "cashier" must receive prior approval before she can cash checks.

BETTER: No checks *without prior approval* may be cashed by cashiers.

This sentence could be further improved by phrasing it in the positive and making "cashier" the subject of the sentence:

BEST: Cashiers may cash only previously approved checks.[17]

EDITING TIP: Watch for prepositions like:

between	during	regarding
by	except	to
concerning	for	upon
despite	in	with

Always place prepositional phrases immediately *after* (not before) the words they modify. Readers are confused when prepositions are misplaced because prepositional phrases help explain how ideas in the sentence relate to each other.

Similarly, conjunctions such as "or" and "and" also tell readers how ideas relate to one another. Unfortunately, each of these words is ambiguous itself. For example, if a parent tells a child that she may have "ice cream *or* cake," the parent probably means that the child may have only one of the two, not both. In this instance, "or" is used as an exclusive alternative: X or Y, *but not both.* Sometimes, however, "or" is used to suggest multiple alternatives: X or Y, *or both.* For example, a parent might suggest that children go outside to "roller-skate *or* ride bikes." In that instance, the children are free to do either, or both. The meaning of "or" is not always clear from the context. For example, consider this provision from a bank loan:

If a debtor fails to make a payment when due, the bank may:

1. sell the collateral *or*
2. assess late fees of 5% of the amount missed.

If the bank sells the collateral, may it charge a late fee also? The debtor will argue that the bank must choose between the two remedies. The bank, on the other hand, will argue that it may do both. Nothing in either the language or the context can resolve the dispute.

Courts have split on the correct interpretation of "or." In fact, one court has interpreted the same provision of a forfeiture statute to mean two different things. The statute referred to "knowledge *or* consent. . . ." The first time the court considered the issue, it ruled that either knowledge *or* consent was sufficient.[18] Approximately a year later, the same court interpreted the identical language to mean that *both* knowledge *and* consent were required.[19]

Accordingly, when you use the word, "or" you should always add language that clarifies your meaning. For example, you could clarify the bank loan:

OPTION 1 (Bank must choose between 2 remedies):

If a debtor fails to make a payment when due, the bank may *either:*

1. sell the collateral *or*
2. assess late fees of 5% of the amount missed,

but not both.

OPTION 2 (Bank retains both remedies):

If a debtor fails to make a payment when due, the bank may:

1. sell the collateral,
2. assess late fees of 5% of the amount missed, *or*
3. *both.*

You can add similar language when "or" joins a series with more than two options. For example:

OPTION 1 (Bank must choose a single remedy from many):

If a debtor fails to make a payment when due, the bank may *only* pursue *one* of the following options:

1. sell the collateral,
2. assess late fees of 5% of the amount missed, *or*
3. declare the full amount of the indebtedness due and payable immediately.

OPTION 2 (Bank retains all remedies):

If a debtor fails to make a payment when due, the bank may *exercise one or more of the following options:*

1. sell the collateral,
2. assess late fees of 5% of the amount missed, *or*
3. declare the full amount of the indebtedness due and payable immediately.

In contrast, "and" signifies that the items in a list are in addition to one another, or cumulative. However, the conjunction "and" is also ambiguous. Sometimes "and" means that all of the items must be kept *together*. For instance, when a parent tells a child to put on her "socks *and* shoes," the child will not have complied if she only puts on her shoes. However, sometimes "and" means any or all of the items listed:

If a debtor fails to make a payment when due, the bank may:

1. sell the collateral,
2. assess late fees of 5% of the amount missed, *and*
3. declare the full amount of the indebtedness due and payable immediately.

Since the bank has the right to exercise all three options together, it should also have the right to exercise a single option. The debtor is hardly likely to complain that the bank only charged a late fee and failed to sell the collateral. In these instances the reader could discern what "and" meant from the context. However, the context does not always help. For example:

Retired and disabled people are entitled to government surplus food.

In order to qualify for surplus food, must an individual be

1. *both* retired *and* disabled, or

2. *either* retired *or* disabled?

Once again the solution is to add words to clarify the meaning:

OPTION 1 (Must be *both* retired *and* disabled):

Only people who are *both* retired and disabled are entitled to government surplus food.

OPTION 2 (May be *either* retired *or* disabled):

Either retired people *or* disabled people are entitled to government surplus food.

EDITING TIP: Watch for the conjunctions "and" and "or." When you use one, ask yourself:

1. Are the items listed mutually exclusive: That is, does one alternative eliminate the others? If so, then use words that specify exclusivity like "one" or "only" to clarify the conjunction.
2. Are all the items all part of a single unit: That is, if one item applies, must they all apply? If so, use words like "all" or "together" to clarify the conjunction.

EDITING TIP: Avoid "and/or." Each of the words has a dual meaning and at least some of the meanings are inconsistent. Instead use words that exactly describe the connection: "one or more of . . ."; "any or all of. . . ."

Because "or" and "and" tell readers how ideas relate to each other, they are very important transition words. Later in this chapter when you study the use of precise transitions, remember that "or" and "and" can be ambiguous. Consider carefully how you use each of those words.

Ambiguities also arise at the word level.[20] Many words have multiple meanings. For example, "poker" means both a card game and a metal rod used for stirring a fire. Usually, however, the meaning is clear from the context:

> The butler bludgeoned her with the poker.
>
> The butler lost $500 playing poker.

Sometimes, however, multiple meanings cause genuine ambiguities. For example, a federal statute defines a career criminal to be a person who repeatedly has committed "burglary."[21] Unfortunately, however, "burglary" has many different meanings. It may be limited to a nighttime forced entry of a home with the intent to commit a felony,[22] or it may mean merely entering any private structure to commit any crime.[23] This ambiguity had to be resolved by the United States Supreme Court.[24] It is relatively easy, though, to avoid the problem of words with multiple meanings by simply defining the term in your document.[25]

Word level ambiguities also arise when a drafter misuses a word. Inexperienced lawyers seem most confused by "shall," "will," and "may." These words are confusing because they are used for two different purposes. They express the future tense:

> The sun *will* shine. (later — in the future)

However, these terms also are directives:

> You *shall* give back the ring. (an order)
>
> You *will* give back the ring. (a statement)
>
> You *may* give back the ring. (a prediction, giving permission)

You can eliminate the confusion by using the present tense whenever possible:

> NOT: The wife *shall* retain title to the car.

(This is unclear for two reasons: 1. Does she have title now? 2. Is she compelled to retain title, or may she dispose of the car?)

> BUT: The wife *retains* title to the car.

(This version is clear: She has title now, and she is permitted, but not compelled, to keep it.)

The present tense addresses your readers whenever they use the document. The important time is not when you are writing it, but when your readers use it. Moreover, if you use the present tense, your document makes statements instead of predictions. For example:

> NOT: All men *will* be created equal.

> BUT: All men *are* created equal.

If you keep your document in the present tense, you can use "shall," "will," and "may" as directives. Remember that they have distinct meanings. The following chart may help you use the words appropriately:

WORD:	*IMPACT:*	*EXAMPLE:*
Shall	Issues an order (must)	Seller *shall* furnish a title insurance policy.
May	Grants discretion (may, but need not)	Buyer *may* inspect the property.
Will	States agreement (agrees to)	Seller *will* keep the property in good repair.

If you follow the rules of this section, you will avoid ambiguities.

Exercise 3-3

Find the ambiguities in this document. Rectify inconsistencies and supply necessary information to make the documents unambiguous. Remember to test for omissions.

MARITAL SETTLEMENT AGREEMENT

DATED: July 12, 1991.

Recitals:

A. The parties were married on March 26, 1975 in Chicago, Illinois.
B. Two children were born to the parties, Erica Jane and Steven Timothy. No children were adopted.
C. The parties agree that each will be a fit parent.

In consideration of the mutual promises, the parties agree:

1. Wife shall have the right to prosecute any action for dissolution she has brought or may bring against her husband.

2. Husband and wife shall be deemed to be fit parents. Wife shall have custody of the children, subject to husband's liberal rights of visitation.

3. Husband shall pay child support only in the amount of $625 per month.

> 4.   Husband shall pay necessary religious and educational expenses for single children.
> 5.   Wife shall retain the house and household and personal effects except for the personal property of the husband that was inherited.
> 6.   Husband only shall retain the right to the tax deductions and exemptions for the children.
> 7.   Husband shall maintain health insurance, life insurance, and disability insurance, which shall not be discontinued, for the benefit of the children, without wife's consent.
> 8.   The proceeds of the sale of the house will be divided equally.
> 9.   Husband in equal installments will pay a lump sum settlement in lieu of maintenance in the amount of $12,000.

2. Order Carefully

In order to be clear, the first fundamental goal, the document must be both focused and accessible to the reader. Readers expect documents to follow a logical order. Chapter 2 discussed how to outline. To create the outline in Chapter 2 you classified various information, sorted it into categories, and placed those categories into a hierarchy. In creating the outline you focused on substance, not clarity.

Now you need to reconsider the order in which you discuss various provisions to be sure that the document is clear. Otherwise the reader will not be able to follow and use the document. Three basic rules will enable you to create clearly ordered documents:

1.   Use parallel structure.
2.   Move from familiar material to unfamiliar material.
3.   Integrate structure and content to create pictorial clarity.

a.   Use Parallel Structure

As a general rule, you should express similar ideas in similar language. When you do so your structures are parallel. Parallelism helps the reader see similarities within your document, making the document clearer. Your structure should be parallel both grammatically and functionally. A brief review of grammatical parallelism will help you understand functional parallelism as well.

i.   Use Parallel Grammatical Structure

When each related idea is expressed in the same grammatical structure (for example, verb, noun, dependent clause), the text is grammatically parallel. Because readers may be confused by nonparallelism, you should express related ideas in the same grammatical form. For example, consider this example listing the rights of a lender:

> BAD: If the debtor fails to make a payment, the lender has the following options:

    (1)   *require* that the debtor pay the full amount immediately,
    (2)   *liquidation* of the collateral, or
    (3)   the *right of set off* against any deposit.

This example is nonparallel because the lender's options are described by a verb (require) in subsection (1), by a noun made out of a verb[26] (liquidation) in subsection (2), and by a simple noun (right) in subsection (3). Since the first option is expressed as a verb, the reader expects each succeeding option to be expressed as a verb. Thus, different grammatical structures, as shown above, may confuse the reader. You can clarify this provision by using parallel grammatical structures:

BETTER: If the debtor fails to make a payment, the lender may:

    (1)   *require* that the debtor pay the full amount immediately,
    (2)   *sell* the collateral, or
    (3)   *seize* any deposit.

This example is better because each of the options is described by a verb (require, sell, and seize). Using parallel language to describe the options underscores that each is the option of the lender.

ii. Use Parallel Functional Structure

Merely keeping your grammar parallel is not sufficient, however. A document is functionally nonparallel if the structure alters your meaning. If you use similar language to express different ideas, the reader may miss the contrast. Consider this example:

1.   *The seller agrees to*[27] furnish the purchaser with a warranty deed to the property at the closing.
2.   *The purchaser agrees to* apply for financing immediately, and to use her best efforts to procure such financing.
3.   *The parties agree to* reprorate the taxes when the next tax bill is issued.
4.   *The parties agree to* include all personal property in the seller's bill of sale.

In the above example, the grammar is quite parallel. Each sentence begins with "The (noun) agrees to. . . ." However, the provisions are not functionally parallel as the following chart illustrates:

Who agrees:	*What agreed:*	*Who Performs:*
1. **Seller**	furnish deed	**Seller**
2. **Purchaser**	apply for financing	**Purchaser**
3. **Parties**	reprorate taxes	**Parties** jointly
4. **Parties**	include in bill of sale	**Seller**

In the first three sentences, the individuals who agree are the ones who must perform. The seller must furnish the deed; the purchaser must apply for financing; and both parties must reprorate the taxes. In the fourth sentence, however, both parties agree, but only the seller must furnish the bill of sale.

After reading the first three sentences, the reader would expect that all of the seller's obligations would begin with, "The seller agrees to. . . ." Accordingly, the reader may be confused by the fourth sentence and fail to see that it creates an obligation on the seller. Because the faulty parallelism in this example affects the meaning of the document, it is functional rather than grammatical.

You may find it much harder to identify prose that is functionally nonparallel than prose that is grammatically nonparallel. You can only spot it if you consciously think about the logical structure of your document. Logically, if:

> "Seller agrees to . . ." creates Seller's obligation, and

> "Purchaser agrees to . . ." creates Purchaser's obligation,

then,

> "Parties agree to . . ." creates Parties' (joint) obligation.

You create such logical structures by choosing to repeat and vary certain phrases. In the example, the language "The _____ agrees to . . ."[28] was repeated to create structure, but words were varied to reflect differences (seller, purchaser, and parties). If you keep your document parallel grammatically and functionally, it will force you to consciously consider both word choice and structure. If you lift language from different forms, you are likely to find that different words are used to express the same idea. Such unnecessary variation will confuse your reader because it results in a random structure rather than a logical one.

Parallel structure also helps you communicate the document's organization to your reader. When you outlined your document, you divided it into major categories of equal importance. Each of these major categories were subdivided into subcategories. Parallel structure helps convey this hierarchy to your reader. Thus all the major categories should be parallel both grammatically and functionally. Similarly, all items within a given classification should be expressed in parallel terms. You can emphasize such parallel organization by using visual cues. Thus, you might use capital letters for your main headings but indent your subheadings in lower case letters.

Whenever various parts of a whole have the same weight, they should be expressed in parallel terms. This rule applies to the document as a whole, to each section, each paragraph, each sentence, and each phrase.[29]

Exercise 3-4

A trust agreement is a document that authorizes someone (a trustee) to hold or manage certain property for another (the beneficiary). Revise the following provisions of a trust agreement to be both functionally and grammatically parallel. How is the current document unclear?

THE TRUSTEE

Powers

The trustee shall have the power to buy and sell any property, invest in real estate, borrow money, vote all corporate stock, hold assets, purchase any insurance, and collect debts.

Duties

The trustee shall pay out such amounts as in her discretion are necessary for the support and education of the beneficiaries.

Rights

The trustee shall provide an annual audited account of all transactions involving the trust to the beneficiaries as a matter of right.

Recall that to create a well-ordered document you must use parallel structure, move from familiar to unfamiliar material, and integrate structure and content pictorially. The second rule is the most comprehensive, if not the most important:

b. Move from Familiar Material to Unfamiliar Material

Many legal documents consist of a complicated set of directions, which tell the reader what to do in various circumstances. For example, a contract may provide what to do in the event of default, or a will may tell how to dispose of certain property. Whenever the reader is unfamiliar with a necessary step, he will become lost and unable to follow the rest of the directions.

This problem is best illustrated by an old joke. A stranger came into town and asked for directions. The old-timer explained, "That's simple. You just turn right where the old school house used to be." Unfortunately, all too many legal documents make the old-timer's mistake of assuming that information familiar to the writer is familiar to the reader.

In order to avoid this problem you should be sure that you establish a common ground of understanding with your reader and that you always move from familiar material to new and unfamiliar material. Accordingly, many legal documents start by identifying the necessary parties. For example, a complaint may start with a section entitled "Parties," which identifies the plaintiff and defendant. Similarly, a real estate contract may begin by identifying the buyer and the seller, or by describing the property.

Once you have established a familiar starting place, you must be sure that you continue to introduce each new step by connecting it to a familiar one. Thus, once you have identified the buyer, you can provide that the buyer must make a down payment of earnest money. Then you can require that the earnest money be kept in an interest bearing account. This order will be quite clear to the reader. If, however, you simply begin by announcing that any earnest money must be kept in an interest bearing account, the reader might well be lost.

You should keep your reader moving from familiar material to unfamiliar material with five different techniques:

1. identify your topics;
2. define your terms;
3. use the defined terms to avoid unnecessary variation;
4. link familiar and unfamiliar material with transitions that precisely describe how the ideas relate to each other; and
5. order your sentences carefully.

i. Identify Topics

Readers are less likely to become lost or confused if you clearly identify your topics in advance. You should identify your topics at four levels: the document, the section, the paragraph, and the sentence. At the document level, you may use an index, a table of contents, or an introduction. An index lists key topics alphabetically and identifies the page or section in which they may be found. A table of contents outlines the document using the various section headings and sub-headings and identifies where each section begins by page number. An introduction generally identifies the purpose of the document. It may also give a short organizational list of the topics to follow.

At the section level, you identify your topics in headings. For example, a real estate contract might have sections called "Parties" and "Earnest Money." Your headings should be descriptive so the reader knows what to expect and where to find important information. If you use headings like "Article One" or "Count I" to identify your organization, add descriptions to help your reader identify the topic, for example, "Article One: Specific Bequests," or "Count I: Breach of Contract." Your headings should describe the general category of ideas contained in the section.

Think about the scope of your headings. Your section headings should be neither too narrow nor too broad. If your headings are too narrow, the reader may be unable to find crucial information. If the headings are too broad, they may become meaningless. If you find that you cannot write an appropriate heading for a given section, that indicates that the section may contain either too many different ideas or unfamiliar material.

You also should identify your topic at the paragraph level. If you have a standard prose paragraph, you should use a topic sentence that tells the reader what the paragraph is about. Such a paragraph develops a single idea and the topic sentence identifies that idea.

Not all paragraphs in a document are full standard prose paragraphs however. Sometimes a single sentence adequately conveys all the information necessary on a given point. For example a real estate contract might provide:

(3) *Closing date:* This sale shall be closed on July 10, 1995.

Although a lawyer might refer to this provision as, "paragraph 3," it is merely a sentence and should therefore follow the topic rules for sentences.

At the sentence level, you should identify the topic in the grammatical subject of the sentence. If the topic is buried elsewhere in the sentence, readers may be confused:

BAD: Considering the subject of great judicial writers, it is apparent that among the greatest in the history of the United States was Oliver Wendell Holmes.

Subject = "it"   Topic = Oliver Wendell Holmes

BETTER: Oliver Wendell Holmes was one of the greatest judicial writers in the history of the United States.

Subject = "Oliver Wendell Holmes"   Topic = Oliver Wendell Holmes

The subject of the sentence should either tell the reader what the sentence is about or identify the actor. Frequently, sentences identify irrelevant actors:

BAD: *It* is agreed that the bank need not proceed against the debtor before enforcing this guarantee against the guarantor.

Subject = "It"   Actor = bank

BETTER: The *bank* may enforce this guarantee against the guarantor without proceeding against the debtor.

Subject = "bank"   Actor = bank

EDITING TIP: Watch for sentences which begin with "it is . . ." or "there are. . . ." Usually, such sentences do not make the actor the subject.

In other sentences, the subjects focus the sentence on the narrator instead of the principal actor. The focus should remain on items familiar to the reader, not the writer. Indeed, one common mistake is to make the narrator the actor:

BAD: *I* desire that the trustee's powers should be as broad as permitted by Illinois law.

Subject = "I"   Actor = trustee

BETTER: The *trustee* shall have powers as broad as permitted by Illinois law.

Subject = "trustee"   Actor = trustee

Sometimes, however, the narrator is the actor. In those instances it is perfectly acceptable to make the narrator the subject:

ACCEPTABLE: I give $10,000 to my son, John.

EDITING TIP: Watch for the word "that" early in a sentence. It may be a signal that you have used an improper subject. In each of the bad sentences above, "that" appears shortly after the subject of the sentence. If you overuse "that," your sentences may also be wordy.[30]

When you select your topics remember to consider how they fit in the document as a whole, both in terms of structure[31] and tone.[32] If you identify your topics early, you prepare the reader for the information that follows. Readers cannot understand that information, however, unless they understand the terms you use. For that reason, definition is the second technique for moving from familiar to unfamiliar material.

ii. Define Terms

You want all your readers to be able to understand what you mean. Readers may be confused by unfamiliar terms like "escrow."[33] Readers may also be confused by familiar terms used in an unfamiliar way. For example, although most consumers know what the word "accelerate" means, they may not know what it means when a "debt is accelerated."[34]

Even familiar terms used in a familiar way can cause problems. For example, both parties may think they know what an employment contract means that provides that the employee will be reimbursed for her "expenses." If "expenses" are not defined, however, a later dispute may develop over whether expenses include personal entertainment costs. Whenever you use a term that may be interpreted in different ways, you should define it.

Define your terms carefully. You cannot create a familiar shared vocabulary if the reader cannot understand your definition. Some definitions are so confusing, that the document would be clearer without them. For example, consider the Internal Revenue Code's definition of "husband" and "wife":

> As used in sections 152(b)(4), 682, and 2516, . . . if the payments described in such sections are made by or on behalf of the wife or former wife to the husband or former husband instead of vice versa, wherever appropriate to the meaning of such sections, the term "husband" shall be read "wife" and the term "wife" shall be read "husband."[35]

In this section, Congress was struggling with a common problem: gendered definitions. The code had been written assuming that men pay alimony to their former wives. However, Congress also wanted to be sure to tax the alimony received by former husbands. Congress solved the problem with a definition that seems ludicrous: wives are husbands and husbands are wives. It would have been much better if Congress had selected gender-neutral terms in the first place:

> Both husbands and wives are spouses. The spouse who pays alimony is the payor spouse, and the spouse who receives alimony is the recipient spouse.

Congress was silly to define a word to mean its opposite. Similarly, it is just as useless to define a word in terms of itself. For example, another provision of the

Internal Revenue Code provides: "The term 'stock' means stock other than stock described in section 1504(a)(4)."[36] Such a circular definition merely frustrates readers.

A definition only helps readers if it translates the defined term into familiar language. Do not assume that the reader is familiar with your own jargon or terms of art:

> BAD: "The term 'excess parachute payment' means an amount equal to the excess of any parachute payment over the portion of the base amount allocated to such payment."[37]

Indeed, whenever you define a term, think about whether you even need to use the term you are defining. Could you substitute a clear, familiar word? If not, then define the term in familiar language.

Although you may use previously defined terms in your definitions, remember that few readers memorize prior sections of a document. Hence, a definition that merely cross references the reader to a distant provision is not very helpful. For example:

> For purposes of paragraph (3), an organization described in paragraph (2) shall be deemed to include an organization described in section 501(c)(4), (5), or (6) which would be described in paragraph (2) if it were an organization described in section 501 (c)(3).[38]

Cross referencing is not an unmitigated evil however. Although you do not want your definition to consist solely of a cross reference, such references can be useful additions to an adequate definition. For example:

> A "demand loan" is one that is payable at the request of the lender. For a list of those authorized to issue demand loans, see §_____, Authorized Lenders. For a list of those authorized to incur demand loans, see §_____, Approved Borrowers.

Here, the cross reference is not a substitute for the definition. Rather, it helps a reader find relevant, related provisions.

Similarly, you should not substitute an example for a definition:

> BAD: A "secured" loan is one in which a debtor gives the lender the right to seize and sell the debtor's car if the debtor does not repay the loan on time.

This definition is inaccurate because a car loan is only one example of a secured loan.[39] Loans may be secured by many different kinds of property: houses, stocks, bonds, inventory, and so forth.

> BETTER: A "secured" loan is one in which a debtor gives the lender the right to seize and sell some of the debtor's property if the debtor does not repay the loan on time.

Although you do not want to substitute an example for a definition, examples can be useful additions to an adequate definition. Clearly labeled examples following a definition can make the definition clearer:

> BETTER: A "secured" loan is one in which a debtor gives the lender the right to seize and sell some of the debtor's property if the debtor does not repay the loan on time. For example, the typical car loan is a secured loan. The debtor gives the lender the title to the car to hold until the car is paid for. If the debtor does not repay the loan on time, the lender may seize the car, sell it, and apply the proceeds to the balance due.

Be careful how you use examples, however, because they may be interpreted to limit your definition.[40] Consider this statute:

> A person commits a theft when he/she knowingly fails to return leased property to the owner within 30 days after the owner's written demand for its return. *A notice in writing, given after the expiration of the lease, by registered mail shall constitute a demand.*

Does the owner's written demand have to be sent by registered mail in order to trigger the statute? The answer depends on whether the emphasized language is an example or a limitation. If it is merely an example, then the owner could hand deliver a demand. If, however, the emphasized language limits the prior definition, then the owner must send the demand by registered mail.

Accordingly, if you intend to merely give an explanatory example, you must use transitional words,[41] which identify it as an example: "for example," "for instance," "including, but not limited to," and the like. In the case of the theft statute, a definition followed by an example might read:

> A person commits a theft when he/she knowingly fails to return leased property to the owner within 30 days after the owner's written demand for its return. A written demand *includes, but is not limited to,* a notice in writing given after the expiration of the lease by registered mail.

Similarly, if you mean to limit your prior definition you should use words of limitation such as "only if" or "provided that." Thus, the theft statute could be rewritten to limit the nature of the demand:

> A person commits a theft when he/she knowingly fails to return leased property to the owner within 30 days after the owner's written demand for its return. A written demand is sufficient *only if* it is a notice in writing given after the expiration of the lease by registered mail.

As you can see, you want to define your terms very carefully.

You also have to think about where to place your definitions within the document. Sometimes you will want to define a term in the text as you use it so the reader need not stop to find the definition. For example, in a contract for the sale of real estate you might define "earnest money" the first time you use the term.

Thereafter the reader would be familiar with the term. This technique works well in short documents or in longer documents that use the defined term in a single section. Then the reader can read the definition and remember it long enough to make sense of the document.

Longer, more technical documents present a different problem. You may define a term in the text when you first use it and find that you do not use the term again for another several pages. By that time, the reader may have forgotten what the term means. That is particularly likely if you have defined many other new terms in the interim. Now, when the reader goes back to find the original definition, she will have a difficult time finding it since it is buried in the text. In these situations, you may want to create a separate definition section early in the document. Then when the reader needs to look up a definition, either for the first time or as a refresher, she knows exactly where to find it.

iii. Use Defined Terms to Avoid Unnecessary Variation

When you define terms, you create a familiar shared vocabulary for the reader. But creating a familiar vocabulary will not help the reader if you fail to use that vocabulary. Therefore, once you have defined a term, you should continue to use the term rather than using a confusing synonym. For example, once you have defined "earnest money," you should always call it "earnest money," and not a "deposit" or "down payment." If you always use the same words to describe the same things, your reader will understand what you mean. Unnecessary variation is confusing. Indeed, the rules courts use to construe documents assume that each word has a particular meaning and that different words refer to different things.

Similarly, courts assume that the same words always mean the same thing. Thus, if you want to convey a different meaning you should use a different word. If you use defined words consistently, you create a familiar vocabulary for your reader. Once you have a common vocabulary, you are ready to apply the fourth technique for moving from familiar material to unfamiliar material.

iv. Link Familiar and Unfamiliar Material with Precise Transitions

When you move from one part of the document to another, you must continue to move from familiar material to unfamiliar material. One useful way to do that is to use transitions that help the reader understand how the new material relates to familiar information.

If the New Information:	Use These Transitions:
1. continues familiar material	1. in addition, and, also, moreover, next, besides, furthermore, too, again
2. provides an exception to familiar material	2. however, although, nevertheless, but, still, nonetheless, despite, even though, instead
3. analogizes to familiar material	3. similarly, likewise

4. expresses a causal relationship to familiar material

4. because, consequently, as a result, therefore, hence, so, thus, accordingly

5. exemplifies familiar material

5. for example, for instance, that is, including but not limited to

6. is included in familiar material

6. including

7. concedes to familiar material

7. although, granted that, nevertheless, even if, admittedly

8. distinguishes familiar material

8. however, differs, on the contrary, in contrast, but

9. is temporally related to familiar material

9. before, after, then, subsequently, at first, soon, earlier, later, during, simultaneously, now, as soon as, meanwhile, immediately

10. shares a series with familiar material

10. first . . . second . . . third . . . , finally, former, latter, next

11. follows from familiar material

11. therefore, thus, hence, accordingly

12. is conditioned on familiar material

12. if . . . then

13. limits familiar material

13. only if, provided that

These transitions are not mutually exclusive (for example: "However, because . . ." or "If . . . then, accordingly . . ."). You can use these kinds of transitions to move from familiar to unfamiliar material within paragraphs and sentences too.

When you make your transitions from sentence to sentence be sure that you move from familiar material to unfamiliar material. Begin your new sentence with familiar material. You can do so in one of three possible patterns:

Sequential pattern: A → B
                              B → C

Centered pattern: A → B
                              A → C
                              A → D

Mixed pattern: A → B
                              A → C
                              C → D
                              D → E

In the sequential pattern, the unfamiliar material from the first sentence becomes the familiar material in the second sentence:

1. *I* give MY SON, Steven Jones, $40,000 if he SURVIVES me.

2. If my <u>son</u> does not <u>survive</u> me, then I give his DESCENDANTS $40,000 per <u>capita</u>.

In the first sentence the narrator is familiar, while the son and survival are not. Once the son and survival have been introduced, they become familiar ideas in the second sentence.

The second sentence then introduces a new concept: descendants.

	Familiar	→	UNFAMILIAR
Sentence 1:	<u>I</u>	→	SON, SURVIVES
Sentence 2:	<u>son, survives</u>	→	DESCENDANTS

The sequential pattern helps the reader understand how one idea leads to the next:

$$\text{A is to B}$$
$$\text{as}$$
$$\text{B is to C}$$

Accordingly, the sequential pattern is good for conveying sequence, causation, and conditions.

In the centered pattern, the original familiar material is the same for each succeeding sentence:

1. <u>I give my</u> CAR to my SON, CHARLES.

2. <u>I give my</u> BOAT to my DAUGHTER, SUSAN.

3. <u>I give my</u> WATCH to my NEPHEW, RALPH.

In this pattern, the same narrator gives different items to different relatives. Although the sentences do not expressly say so, they imply that the giver owns the car, owns the boat, and owns the watch. Thus, all the unfamiliar items listed bear the same relationship with the familiar topic: ownership. Accordingly, a centered pattern is more than a mere list. It suggests that the new material in each succeeding sentence relates in the same way to the shared old material.[42] Schematically you can visualize it:

A owns B		A is to B
		as
A owns C	or	A is to C
		as
A owns D		A is to D

Sometimes, however, writers use the centered pattern because they have not figured out how the sentences relate to each other:

1. I give my SON, Steven Jones, $40,000 if he SURVIVES me.

2. I give my DESCENDANTS $40,000 per capita if my son does not survive me.

	Familiar	→	UNFAMILIAR
Sentence 1:	I	→	SON
Sentence 2:	I	→	DESCENDANTS

This pattern is confusing because the gift to the son is inconsistent with the gift to the descendants. The son receives if he lives, but the descendants only receive if he dies. If the writer thought carefully about how the son's gift related to the descendant's gift, she would have either used the sequential pattern[43] or she would have enumerated it to make it clearer.[44]

The centered pattern focuses on a single topic, around which all the new information revolves:

```
        B
    I↖  ↑  ↗C
H←——A——→D
    G↙  ↓  ↘E
        F
```

This pattern can be a very powerful way to emphasize and communicate a central topic. You will learn more about emphasis when you consider the section on tone, below. Because the centered pattern focuses on a single topic, it is a useful device to guide a reader through a section that shares a single topic. For example, the sentences in a section that lists the powers of a trustee might all begin, "The trustee may. . . ." Thus, the centered pattern helps you indicate both shared topics and shared relationships.

The mixed pattern merely blends the sequential pattern and the centered pattern. Thus you might begin a section with the centered pattern to express shared relationships, but switch to the sequential pattern to indicate a sequence:

$$A \rightarrow B$$
$$A \rightarrow C$$
$$A \rightarrow D$$
$$D \rightarrow E$$

1. I give my NEPHEW, CHARLES ROBERTS, my car.

2. I give my NIECE, SUSAN GOODMAN, my boat.

3. I give my SON, STEVEN JONES, $40,000 if he SURVIVES me.

4. If my son does not survive me, then I give his DESCENDANTS $40,000 per capita.

Similarly, you might want to begin a section with the sequential pattern and switch to the centered pattern. You can create and adapt your own patterns to help your reader move from familiar to unfamiliar material.

Exercise 3-5

Revise the following portion of a real estate contract so that it moves from familiar material to unfamiliar material. Also correct any errors in parallelism.

    1.   Buyer agrees that the earnest money placed with the agent is to be deposited in the Agent's trust account.

    2.   It is further agreed that Seller shall obtain a title insurance policy at Seller's expense, insuring clear title to the property for the Buyer.

    3.   The property is to be conveyed by warranty deed.

    4.   If the Buyer fails to complete the purchase, for any other reason than inability to get financing, then the earnest money may be forfeited to the Seller as liquidated damages.

    5.   If the Buyer fails to obtain the necessary financing in the time specified, the contract shall be null and void and all unspent portions of the earnest money shall be refunded.

    6.   Time is the essence of this contract.

    7.   Seller and Buyer agree to prorate taxes based on the most recently available tax bill.

    8.   Seller shall deliver possession to the Buyer at closing, which shall be held on March 3, 1994.

    9.   The parties agree that the earnest money may be used to pay for an appraisal report and a credit report so the Buyer can obtain financing.

    10.   If the Seller fails to convey the property to the Buyer, then the Buyer has a right of specific performance.

    11.   Buyer has 45 days within which to acquire a 30-year mortgage for $100,000, charging an interest rate not to exceed 10 1/4% per annum.

v.   Order Sentences Carefully

You need to move from familiar to unfamiliar material at the sentence level too. At the sentence level, readers subconsciously expect certain familiar structures. If you make your sentences accessible to your readers, they will be free to concentrate on content rather than decoding the sentence structure.

Your document can only be as clear as the individual sentences you write. Although there are many different kinds of sentences, the basic sentence is comprised of a subject, a verb, and an object:

(subject)	(verb)	(object)
The defendant	struck	the plaintiff.

The subject of the sentence is usually a noun that answers the question who or what acted? The *defendant* acted. The verb expresses the action in the sentence. The verb usually answers the question, what did the subject do? The defendant *struck*. The object receives the action. Who or what was acted upon? The defendant struck the *plaintiff*.

The way you manipulate the subject, verb, and object of a sentence will determine how accessible the sentence is to your reader. The following rules will help you create well-ordered sentences:

1. Identify the actors.
2. Make the actors the subject of the sentence.
3. Make the topic the grammatical subject of the sentence.
4. Express action as a verb.
5. Keep the subject and verb together.
6. Keep the subject and verb close to the beginning of the sentence.
7. Keep modifiers close to the words they modify.

Identify the Actors.   A sentence that describes an action without identifying the actor omits crucial information. Compare these two sentences:

(a) BAD: The plaintiff was struck.

(b) BETTER: The defendant struck the plaintiff.

Sentence (a) omits crucial information and can confuse the reader. Who struck the plaintiff? Sentence (b) supplies the missing information and is clearer.

The actors are particularly crucial in legal documents. In a battery complaint, sentence (a) would not be sufficient. The court needs to know who struck the plaintiff. Similar problems arise in contracts. For example, consider this sentence from a sales contract:

The property shall be insured.

Both the buyer and the seller may assume that the other has the duty to insure the property. Thus, even though they agree the property should be insured, it may remain uninsured. One way to correct this problem is to use the active voice. Verbs can be in either the active or the passive voice. A verb is active when the subject of the verb does something; it acts:

Active: The defendant *struck* the plaintiff.

When the verb is active, the subject must do something; by definition there must be an actor.

A verb is passive when the subject of the verb receives the action; it is acted upon:

Passive: The plaintiff *was struck* by the defendant.

As the sentence above illustrates, not all passives omit the actor. If a verb is passive, the only way to identify the actor is to add a clause beginning with "by. . . ." If this clause is omitted, you get a truncated passive:

Truncated passive: The plaintiff *was struck*.

A truncated passive will necessarily omit the actor.

EDITING TIP: Passives have a form of the verb "to be" as part of the verb, and either are or could be followed by a clause beginning "by . . . ," which identifies the actor. For example:

>   Active: The seller *breached* the contract.

>   Passive: The contract *was breached.* (by the seller)

Merely having a form of "to be" as part of the verb, however, does not mean that the verb is passive:

>   Active: The seller *has breached* the contract.

Although the verb includes a form of "to be," the actor cannot be identified by adding a phrase beginning "by. . . ."

___

Passives are not the only kind of verbs that omit the actor. Some verbs do not express action at all. These verbs are called "linking verbs"[45] because they link the subject to some characteristic. For example:

>   Battery *is* a tort.

Common linking verbs include:

appears	exists	seems
approximates	feels	smells
becomes	grows	sounds
believes	is	tastes
deems	remains	turns
equals		

These verbs merely link two parts of the sentence. Since there is no action, there can be no actor.

The problems caused by linking verbs are exacerbated by generalized subjects like "it," "there," and "basis." These words have little independent meaning:

>   BAD: *There* is a *basis* for objection.

>   BAD: *It* is a breach of contract.

___

EDITING TIP: Look for generalized subjects,[46] like "it" and "there," coupled with linking verbs: "It is . . . ," "There are. . . ."

___

As a general rule, you should identify the actor in the beginning of your sentence. Sometimes, however, you can't identify the actor. For example, in a complaint to recover from an insurance company for a hit and run accident, you may not know who acted. A passive that omits the actor would be perfectly acceptable then: "Plaintiff's car was demolished."

Sometimes you will not want to identify a known actor. Consider, for example, a judge who must write a decision imposing the death penalty. If she includes the actor, she will say:

> *I* have decided that you should be executed.

For obvious reasons she may prefer a passive construction that omits the actor:

> The death penalty shall be imposed.[47]

Other times, the actor is irrelevant. For example, in drafting a complaint alleging that a company polluted a river, it may be irrelevant who found the toxins:

> Toxins were found in the river.

Nevertheless, as a general rule most legal documents must identify the actor to be complete and accurate. You should omit an actor only if you have a good reason for doing so.

Exercise 3-6

Change this provision to identify the actor where appropriate. You may have to supply missing information to do so. Identify all passives and linking verbs. Consider why the actor has been omitted. Supply the actor if it is helpful. Otherwise note why the actor has been omitted and identify the technique that was used to omit the actor.

PROVISION TO INSURE PAYMENT OF COMPENSATION UNDER THE WORKERS' COMPENSATION ACT

An application for approval must be filed, which shall include a current financial statement. The application shall be signed and sworn to and three copies must be submitted.

If the application and financial statement are not deemed satisfactory, (1) a bond shall be furnished guaranteeing payment or (2) evidence of liability insurance shall be furnished demonstrating that liability to pay compensation is insured by some insurance carrier licensed to do such insurance business in this State. A certificate of compliance with either (1) or (2) shall be delivered within five days after the effective date of the bond of liability insurance, whichever is applicable.

If the application and financial statement are deemed satisfactory, written notice of approval shall be sent to the employer.

Make the Actors the Subject of the Sentence.   Readers instinctively look for the actor when they read a sentence. Thus, you may frustrate readers if you bury the actor between clauses or at the very end of the sentence. Accordingly, you should make the actor the subject of the sentence:

> NOT: The child was struck in the head by the defendant with a steel base-ball bat.

> BUT: The defendant struck the child in the head with a steel baseball bat.

Even though the first sentence identified the defendant as the actor, it buried that information between two clauses near the end of the sentence. Making the actor the subject of the sentence made the sentence clearer and more forceful.[48]

EDITING TIP: Look for the word "by" in a sentence. It may be a clue that you have hidden the actor in a clause rather than making the actor the subject of the sentence. Avoid the passive voice if possible because the subject of a passive verb is never the actor.[49]

Make the Topic of the Sentence the Grammatical Subject of the Sentence. Recall the previous sentence examples:

> 1: The child was struck in the head by the defendant with a steel baseball bat.

> 2: The defendant struck the child in the head with a steel baseball bat.

One of the reasons the second sentence is clearer is that the sentence is really about the defendant, not the child. Hence the defendant is the "topic" of both sentences, but the grammatical "subject" of only the second sentence. Readers expect the topic of the sentence to be expressed in the grammatical subject of the sentence. Thus, when the reader sees a sentence begin "The plaintiff . . . ," the reader expects the sentence to be about the plaintiff. Consider these sentences:

> (a) The property shall be divided by the executor.
> (b) The executor shall divide the property.

Although both sentences convey the same information, they have different topics. The topic of sentence (a) is "property," while the topic of sentence (b) is "executor." You must decide from the context what the appropriate topic should be and make that topic the subject of the sentence. Accordingly, you might choose sentence (a) for a section that describes property and how it can be managed. However, you might choose sentence (b) for a section that describes the duties of the executor. When you make the topic of your sentence the grammatical subject, you make the sentence clearer and fit the sentence into its context. For example:

> BAD: Regarding the contract, I am confident that the partnership agreement is accurate.
>
> (topic: partnership agreement)
> (subject: I)

BETTER: The partnership agreement accurately reflects the terms of the contract.[50]

(topic: partnership agreement)
(subject: partnership agreement)

Express Action as a Verb.   Readers also expect the action of a sentence to be
expressed in the verb.

GOOD: The executor *divided* the property.

EDITING TIP: You can find a verb in a sentence by changing the time sequence.
Thus, if the sentence is in the past, move it to the future. The words you change
are the verbs. For example:

The executor *will divide* the property.

Unfortunately, all too many legal documents use an empty verb and change the
crucial action into a noun instead:

BAD: The executor effectuated a *division* of the property.

"Effectuated" is an empty verb that carries little meaning to the reader. The real
action is in the noun "division."

EDITING TIP: Watch for these endings:

-al	-ity	-sion
-ance	-ment	-tion
-ence	-ness	-ture
-ing		

These suffixes change verbs into nouns.

When verbs are changed into nouns, they become verbal "vampires,"[51] which
suck all the action out of the sentence. Such vampires weaken the sentence and
pitch it at too abstract a level.[52] Compare the following:

BAD: The amend*ment* of any part of this contract may not be a valid
modifica*tion* unless supportable by express written documenta*tion*
bear*ing* the signa*tures* of both parties.

BETTER: The parties may *amend* any part of this contract only if they both
sign a written document that expressly *modifies* the contract.

As this example illustrates, vampires don't always work alone. Often they team up with prepositional phrases and passive verbs or linking verbs to suck the action dry. Don't create vampires by turning your verbs into nouns.

Similarly, you shouldn't turn verbs into modifiers (adjectives or adverbs). These too are vampires. A vampire is any verb that has been transformed into a noun, adjective, or adverb.

EDITING TIP: Watch for these endings, which turn verbs into modifiers:

-able	-ing	-ize
-al	-ity	-ly
-cy		

BAD: It shall be deemed a viola*tion* of the contractu*al* obliga*tions* for any party to cause the disclos*ure* of unauthor*ized* knowing*ly* confidential information to anyone.

BETTER: A party *violates* the contract if she *discloses* information:

1.   which she *knows* is confidential,
2.   if she *is not authorized* to do so.

In this example, "knowingly" is an adjective. Nevertheless, it is a vampire, which sucks the action out of the sentence. Like all vampires, it weakens the sentence by focusing the action in an empty verb: "deemed." Vampire modifiers also have all the problems of modifiers in general: They may have unclear antecedents and they may sacrifice clarity to extravagance.

Indeed, writers often create vampires to lend a mysterious aura to their writing: They want to "sound like lawyers." Mystery, however, has no place in legal documents. Above all else you want your document to be clear so it can be used and enforced appropriately.

EDITING TIP: Look for prepositional phrases as a hint that you have too many vampires.

It is simple to banish vampires. Often, you can spot vampires by the endings listed above. Once you find one, transform it into a verb, as shown here:

amend<u>ment</u>	→	amend
modific<u>ation</u>	→	modify
signa<u>ture</u>	→	sign
viol<u>ation</u>	→	violate
contractu<u>al</u>	→	contract
knowing<u>ly</u>	→	know

When you change the vampire back into a verb, you may have to supply missing subjects for the new verb. For example:

> It is a violation of the contract to disclose trade secrets.
>
> A party violates the contract if he discloses trade secrets.

Unfortunately, not all vampires share these endings. For example, "sale" is a vampire made from the verb "to sell." Moreover, not all words that share these endings are vampires. For example, "fragrance" ends in "-ance" but does not come from a verb. Thus, you must think about the sentence carefully to spot all the vampires.

Wicked as it may seem, you may sometimes want to use a vampire for your own purposes. Sometimes a vampire is the best way to move from familiar material to unfamiliar material. For example, a contract might specify:

> These *provisions* are not mutually exclusive.

"Provisions" is a vampire created from the verb "provide." Nevertheless, "provisions" serves two useful functions in the sentence. First, it refers back to prior information and, hence, helps the reader move from familiar to unfamiliar material. Second, it focuses the sentence on a more appropriately abstract level. The content of the provisions is irrelevant. What matters is that the provisions are not mutually exclusive. Thus, replacing the vampire with a verb would not improve the sentence:

> The paragraphs that have been provided are not mutually exclusive.

Indeed using the word "provisions" enables you to make the topic of the sentence the grammatical subject.

Even more deviously, you may want to use vampires to distance yourself or your client from the action. Reconsider the example of the judge announcing the death penalty. She can use vampires to distance herself from her decision:

> It is the decision of this court that the imposition of the death penalty is appropriate in this instance.

Or she can use forceful, direct verbs that make the actors clear:

> I have decided that you should die.

Because judges often want to distance themselves from their decisions, they frequently use vampires.[53] Accordingly, most of the cases you read will be loaded with vampires. If you read enough of these cases, vampires will infiltrate even the language of your thoughts. Rather than trying to edit the way you think, edit your prose after you have written it. You must be very vigilant to protect your writing from vampires. Although you may choose on occasion to use one for your own purposes, remember that vampires are dangerous.

Exercise 3-7

Find the vampires in the following document and correct them. Be sure to determine whether the vampire has been used purposely. If so, explain why the vampire is helpful. You may have to change passives and linking verbs, or supply missing material to improve the document.

MARITAL SETTLEMENT AGREEMENT

Recitals:

A. The parties entered into marriage on August 11, 1978.

B. The birth of three children occurred during the marriage, Toby Augustus, Arthur John, and Kimberly Ann.

C. Without any collusion as to any dissolution proceedings between the parties and without prejudice to a right of action for dissolution, which either may have, the parties consider it in their best interest to enter a settlement between themselves on or concerning the questions of the custody and support of the children, other rights growing out of the marital relationship now or previously existing, and all rights of every description to property.

NOW THEREFORE, in consideration of the mutual promises and undertakings, and for good and valuable consideration, the receipt and sufficiency of which is hereby acknowledged, the parties do freely and voluntarily agree:

1. Husband reserves the right of prosecution of any action for dissolution of the marriage. Wife reserves the right of prosecution of any action for dissolution of the marriage.

2. The fitness of both husband and wife to the custody, control, and education of their children is deemed adequate. The children shall maintain their residence with the husband who shall have their custody. Wife shall have reasonable visitation rights.

3. Wife shall support the children with payments equal to 25% of her net income, payable monthly.

4. This agreement constitutes an acknowledgment that neither husband nor wife have any entitlement to maintenance or alimony.

5. Exclusive possession and ownership of the 1988 Honda Civic is vested in wife. Exclusive possession and ownership of the 1989 Dodge Aries is vested in husband.

6. The furnishings and personal property contained in the marital home shall be divided according to the agreement of the husband and wife.

7. This agreement constitutes consent on behalf of both the husband and wife to the contribution toward college and graduate education for the children. Such contributions shall be proportionate to their respective earnings.

8. The payment of attorneys' fees for both husband and wife shall be the responsibility of each individually.

9. It is mutually understood that all property acquired by husband

and wife has been divided between them, and that each of them has in his or her possession his or her rightful property.

10.   Both parties have had the benefit of complete disclosure and investigation with regard to the property, assets, and liabilities of the parties. Each party understands all the provisions of this agreement.

11.   In the event that any court holds any part of this agreement invalid, it is the intention of the parties that the remainder of the agreement shall be considered enforceable.

12.   This agreement constitutes the entire understanding of the parties. It supersedes all prior agreements. There are no representations or agreements other than those expressly set forth here.

13.   Modification of this agreement can only be achieved by means of a written agreement signed by both husband and wife or by a court of competent jurisdiction.

Keep the Subject and the Verb Together.   As you know, readers look first for the subject and then for the action or verb.[54] Accordingly, you should keep your subject and verb close together in the sentence. Do not separate them with intrusive phrases:

> BAD: The superior court of the proper county may, at the suit of shareholders holding at least 10 percent of the number of outstanding shares of any class, remove from office any director in case of fraudulent acts with reference to the corporation and may bar from re-election any director so removed for a period prescribed by the court.

When you find a sentence with an intrusive clause you have three options. You can: (1) delete the clause entirely, (2) delete the clause from the sentence and transform it into a new sentence, or (3) move the clause within the sentence. Consider this sentence:

> BAD: The claimant's *response,* in whatever form, *must be filed* with the hearing officer.

If the clause is meaningless, you can simply delete it. You have to exercise your legal judgment in determining whether or not the clause is meaningless. For example, you might decide that the phrase "in whatever form" adds little to the sentence. If so, you should delete it.

> BETTER: The claimant's *response must be filed* with the hearing officer.

However, you may decide that the clause is important because it entitles the claimant to respond in any form. If the clause expresses important limitations, you should not delete it entirely. If you omit important legal conditions, you do not make your document clear, you merely make it empty. Instead you should move the clause either to a new sentence or elsewhere within the sentence:

> BETTER (elsewhere within the sentence):

In whatever form, the claimant's *response must be filed* with the hearing officer.[55]

BETTER (separate sentence):

The claimant's response must be filed with the hearing officer. However, the response need not be in any particular form.

All of the improved sentences keep the subject and the verb close together: ". . . response must be filed. . . ."

It is not sufficient merely to keep the subject close to part of the verb:

BAD: Claimant's *response must be,* in whatever form, *filed* with the hearing officer.

(Verb = *must be filed,* separated by phrase)

Keep the entire verb together.

Lawyers are paid to think of every possible contingency, so you cannot simply omit all limiting clauses from your documents. Instead, you need to learn to manage multiple clauses in a way that enables you to retain the substance and still be clear. If you separate the subject and the verb by a long string of clauses, your reader will be lost. For example:

BAD: The court, upon motion made by a party before responding to a pleading or, if no responsive pleading is permitted by these rules, upon motion made by a party within 20 days after the service of the pleading upon the party, or upon the court's own initiative at any time, may order stricken from any pleading any insufficient defense.

The first step is to reunite the subject and the verb: "the court may order. . . ." However, that alone will not be sufficient:

BETTER: Upon motion made by a party before responding to a pleading or, if no responsive pleading is permitted by these rules, upon motion made by a party within 20 days after the service of the pleading upon the party or upon the court's own initiative at any time, the *court may order* stricken from any pleading any insufficient defense.[56]

The reader still has to wade through twelve prepositional phrases to get to the subject and verb! Few readers are so patient.

Keep the Subject and the Verb Close to the Beginning of the Sentence. The provision will read much more smoothly if it begins with the subject and the verb:

BEST: The *court may strike* any insufficient defense from any pleading
        (i)   on its own initiative at any time; or
        (ii) on the motion of a party if:
           (a) the party moves to strike it before responding to the pleading; or

(b)   if these rules do not permit the party to respond, then if the party moves to strike it within 20 days after the party was served.[57]

When a sentence starts with a string of clauses, the reader has to remember them while he searches for the subject and the verb. Thus, it is easier to read long sentences if the subject and verb come first.

Even in short sentences you should generally place your subject and verb close to the beginning of the sentence:

NOT: At any time during the course of employment, including vacations, an *employee may not work* for any other agency.

BUT: An *employee may not work* for any other agency at any time during the course of employment, including vacations.

You begin with the subject and the verb in order to provide a familiar context for your reader.

Sometimes you can establish that context more effectively with a short transition or introductory phrase. For example, assume a bank asked you to draft a brochure for customers who wanted loans. You are ready to write the first sentence of the text. Which of these would you choose?

1.   The borrower must apply in person.

2.   In order to qualify for a loan, the borrower must apply in person.

The second sentence is smoother because it establishes the context of the loan. It is appropriate to begin a sentence with a phrase that establishes time, place, duration, condition, or causation. Otherwise, begin the sentence with the subject and the verb.

Keep Modifiers Close to the Words They Modify.   Lawyers need to use modifying clauses in order to be precise. Misplaced modifiers make a sentence unclear:

BAD: This regulation will limit toxic waste, which will improve the environment.

BETTER: By limiting toxic waste, this regulation will improve the environment.

The toxic waste will not improve the environment; the regulation will. When you use a modifier, keep similar ideas together by placing the modifier close to the word it modifies. Readers expect to find modifiers either right before or right after the words they modify.

EDITING TIP: Watch for prepositions (by, which, with, for, on, into, that, to, from, among, as, upon); they usually introduce modifying phrases. Similarly, watch for adverbs (typically words ending in "-ly" like "only," "slowly," and so forth). Adverbs introduce modifying phrases too.

Note that the improved sentence did not begin with the subject and verb. You could accommodate both rules:

> BETTER: This regulation will improve the environment by limiting toxic waste.[58]

If the rules conflict, follow the more important rule. If you fail to identify a necessary actor, you have made an important omission. If you misplace your modifier, you may have created an inconsistency. Persistent readers may be able to struggle through an inaccessible document to make sense of it. Even the most diligent of readers, however, cannot clarify incomplete or inconsistent documents. Accordingly, it is most important to identify your actors and keep your modifiers next to the words they modify.

Thus a well ordered document moves from familiar to unfamiliar material at all levels. It identifies and defines topics, avoids unnecessary variation, uses accurate transitions, and follows the rules for ordered sentences. However, a well-ordered document must not only be parallel, and move from familiar to unfamiliar material. It also must integrate structure and content. Accordingly, we move on to the third rule for ordering your document.

c. Integrate Structure and Content to Create Pictorial Clarity

You can make your writing even more accessible and comprehensible by altering the way it appears on the paper. Three techniques may be used to do so: headings and subheadings, enumeration, and tabulation.

You already have learned that headings and subheadings are used to organize a document. They are also used to delineate sections to assist the reader in locating the document's parts and subparts. Highlighting sections is especially important in lengthy documents or documents that contain detailed subparts. For example, a will may contain a trust for grandchildren. The trust's heading may look like this:

> ARTICLE VI — Grandchildren's Trust

You may want to highlight subparts of the trust, however, with subheadings such as: Trust Purpose, Trustee's Powers, Distribution, and Termination. These subheadings will enable the reader to locate needed information by providing general categories.

Within each category you must decide whether to use general or specific terms. For example, in granting a trustee powers, you might choose to say:

> The trustee shall have the broadest powers allowable under state law.

If, however, you want to limit the trustee's powers, you may prefer to specify or "enumerate" them. Enumerating means naming one by one, or listing. For example:

> The trustee shall have the powers to invest, manage, dispose, or commingle any trust property.

Here, the powers are named one by one, or enumerated.

Drafted documents naturally lend themselves to enumeration because they often contain triggering events that result in a series of activities, rules, exceptions, or alternatives. For this reason, enumerating is a useful technique for drafting because it visually clarifies the relationships between the ideas presented.

The trustee's powers may also be enumerated like this:

> The trustee shall have all the following powers over the Trust property:
>
> 1.   investing,
> 2.   managing,
> 3.   disposing, and
> 4.   commingling.

In this sentence, the powers are not only enumerated, but also are presented in a column, or tabulated. Tabulation means arranging systematically in rows or columns. When you tabulate, the reader can visually see the relationship between the ideas, as well as locate needed information.

In some instances, tabulating may prevent ambiguity. Recall in the section on clarity, you learned that ambiguity can result not only from numerous meanings for a single word but also from the way words are arranged in a sentence or sentences. For example:

> An employee shall be reimbursed for the costs of travel, professional memberships, and professional conferences, which previously have been approved.

Do all three types of costs need to be previously approved? Or, is previous approval required only for professional conferences?

Tabulating will clarify the meaning. If all three of the costs need to be previously approved, the tabulated rewrite will look like this:

> An employee shall be reimbursed for the costs of any one or more of the following:
>
> 1.   travel,
> 2.   professional memberships, and
> 3.   professional conferences,
>
> which previously have been approved.

If previous approval is required only for professional conferences, the tabulated rewrite will look like this:

> An employee shall be reimbursed for the costs of any one or more of the following:
>
> 1.   travel;
> 2.   professional memberships; and
> 3.   professional conferences, which previously have been approved.[59]

The tabulated revisions integrate structure and content to clarify the ideas and how they relate to each other.

When tabulating you should carefully plan the spacing of your words because the spacing is crucial in visually illustrating the relationship between ideas. You need to leave white space to separate different ideas. You can do so either by skipping lines or indenting:

> Employee shall be reimbursed for the costs of:
>
> 1. travel;
> 2. professional memberships; and
> 3. professional conferences, which previously have been approved.

The drafter skipped a line to separate the introduction from the list. The drafter indented to show that the broad category, "costs," includes the list of narrower items. Thus, skipped lines indicate that ideas are separate; indentations indicate subcategories.

EDITING TIP: Whenever you use a heading or a subheading, you will probably need some white space because headings indicate separate ideas, and subheadings indicate separate subcategories.

You should also use white space to make it easier on the reader's eyes. Therefore avoid small print, small margins, large blocks of print, and long single-spaced sections.

When tabulating you also should make sure that the items in the lists are grammatically and functionally parallel in order to be clear. For example:

> BAD: Employee shall be reimbursed for the costs of:
>
> 1. travel;
> 2. professional memberships; and
> 3. when she attends professional conferences, which previously have been approved.

"Travel" and "memberships" are nouns, but "attends" is a verb. Thus this tabulation is grammatically nonparallel.

> BETTER: Employee shall be reimbursed for the costs of:
>
> 1. travel,
> 2. professional memberships, and
> 3. professional conferences, which previously have been approved.

This tabulation is grammatically parallel because all costs are nouns.[60]

When you tabulate you should think carefully about how the items in your tabulation are connected and choose your connectors (conjunctions) accordingly. Remember that "or" and "and" can be ambiguous.[61]

EDITING TIP: Other connectors you should watch for include: but, nor, for, so, yet, if, unless, since, when, neither, although, provided, while, when, before, and after. When you use such connectors be sure they precisely describe the relationship between the items in your tabulation.

Finally, when you tabulate sentences, you need to clarify the relationship between ideas with punctuation. Commas, semicolons, colons, and periods each signify a different relationship. Colons separate general matters from their subparts. Commas or semicolons separate equal items within a list. Use semicolons to separate equal items when any item is internally punctuated:

> The scheduling order may include:
>
> 1. time limits;
> 2. dates for pretrial, trial, and post-trial conferences; and
> 3. page limits for briefs.

Because item 2 is internally punctuated with commas, the drafter used semicolons to separate the other items in the list. Use commas to separate equal items where there is no internal punctuation:

> The scheduling order may include:
>
> 1. time limits,
> 2. dates for conferences, and
> 3. page limits for briefs.[62]

The above examples have illustrated how enumeration and tabulation create pictorial clarity at the sentence level. They are even more effective when applied to larger parts of a document. Consider the following portion of a loan agreement:

> The debtor defaults when he fails to pay any installment when due or sells the collateral before repaying the loan in full. If the debtor defaults, then the bank may declare the debt and all accrued interest immediately due and payable.
>
> If the debtor defaults, the bank may exercise all the rights provided by the Uniform Commercial Code, including, but not limited to, the right to sell the collateral at public or private sale and the right to seize any bank accounts up to the amount of the indebtedness.
>
> If the debtor defaults, the bank may accept a late payment. If it chooses to do so, then the debtor must pay a late fee equal to 5% of the missed installment or $50, whichever is less. If the bank accepts a late payment, it may demand additional collateral.

Although the topics flow logically, they are not visually easy to locate. Thus, headings and subheadings would help the reader:

DEFAULT

Definition: The debtor defaults when he fails to pay any installment when due or sells the collateral before repaying the loan in full. *Remedies: Accelerate the Debt:* If the debtor defaults, then the bank may declare the debt and all accrued interest immediately due and payable.

Exercise U.C.C. Remedies: If the debtor defaults, the bank may exercise all the rights provided by the Uniform Commercial Code, including, but not limited to, the right to sell the collateral at public or private sale and the right to seize any bank accounts up to the amount of the indebtedness.

Accept Late Payments: If the debtor defaults, the bank may accept a late payment. If it chooses to do so, then the debtor must pay a late fee equal to 5% of the missed installment or $50, whichever is less. If the bank accepts a late payment, it may demand additional collateral.

Note now, however, that even though the subtopics are easy to find, the reader must still trudge through a lot of words in each subpart to discover the relationship between the ideas presented. Enumerating and tabulating will help clarify the relationship between the ideas.

DEFAULT

A. *Definition:* The debtor defaults when he:
   1. fails to pay any installment when due or
   2. sells the collateral before repaying the loan in full.

B. *Remedies:* If the debtor defaults, then the bank may do any one or more of the following:
   1. accelerate the debt, declaring the debt and all accrued interest immediately due and payable;
   2. exercise all the rights provided by the Uniform Commercial Code, including, but not limited to the right to:
      a. sell the collateral at public or private sale, and
      b. seize any bank accounts up to the amount of the indebtedness; or
   3. accept a late payment. If the bank accepts such a late payment it may pursue either or both of the following remedies:
      a. demand additional collateral, or
      b. charge the debtor a late fee equal to 5% of the missed installment or $50, whichever is less.

In the final tabulation it made more sense to delete some of the subheadings and change some of the wording. Thus, tabulation is more than merely inserting headings and spaces. When you tabulate, you must scrutinize your organization. You will frequently have to reclassify information and change your language. Accordingly, tabulation helps the reader understand how the ideas in a provision relate to each other.

EDITING TIP: If you cannot tabulate a section, it probably has a flaw in organization. Ask yourself, what doesn't fit in the tabulation? Where else might it belong?

Exercise 3-8

a. Rewrite the following provision using headings and subheadings, enumeration, and tabulation to organize the provisions; help the reader locate the parts and subparts; clarify the relationship between ideas; and prevent ambiguity:

INADVERTENT DISCLOSURE

If the producing party inadvertently discloses any confidential information, the producing party shall promptly, upon discovery of such inadvertent disclosure, advise the recipient(s) in writing and the recipient(s) shall thereafter treat the information as confidential information and to the extent such confidential information may have been disclosed to persons other than the recipient(s), the recipient shall make every reasonable effort to promptly retrieve the confidential information from such persons and to limit any further disclosure of the confidential information to persons other than recipients thereafter.

b. Rewrite the following provision using headings and subheadings, enumeration, and tabulation to organize the provisions; help the reader locate the parts and subparts; clarify the relationship between ideas; and prevent ambiguity:

The trustee shall have full power and authority to manage and control the trust estate, and to sell, exchange, lease (for terms that may extend beyond the termination of the trust), rent, assign, transfer or otherwise dispose of all or any part thereof, including real property, upon such terms and conditions as she may in her discretion deem proper, and may invest and reinvest all or any part of the trust estate, in such common or preferred stocks, futures options, precious metals, bonds, debentures, mortgages, deeds of trust, notes, or other securities, investments or property that the Trustee in her absolute discretion may select or determine, including the right to co-mingle funds in common funds maintained by the trustee, it being my express desire and intention that the Trustee shall have the broadest powers allowable.

B. Use the Proper Tone

Recall that to write well you need to achieve three goals: be clear, be concise, and use the proper tone. So far this chapter has concentrated on clarity. This section will focus on tone. Even if your document is clear, your readers may find it difficult to read unless you choose your tone carefully. Your tone should reflect your readers' perspective. Thus, you have to think about how your audiences will use a document and draft the document to be efficient in those contexts. Similarly, you must adjust the tone to reflect the sophistication of your audiences. Many documents should be drafted in plain English. Nevertheless, sometimes, you may need to use the terms of art of a specific industry. Whatever language you use, your tone should reflect your content to provide the appropriate emphasis.

1. Choose the Proper Perspective

You write your document for specific audiences. In Chapter 2, you learned to identify the important audiences. For example, a contract must be written for the lawyers who negotiate it, for the parties who sign it, for the third parties who may benefit from it, for the lawyers who litigate it, and for the courts that may construe it. The initial parties are beginning a venture together and want the document to be conciliatory: to facilitate the deal rather than kill it. They see the contract as an instrument that sets out general rules for a developing relationship.[63] Accordingly, these parties want the tone to be cooperative and want to downplay rights and conflicts. Future litigants, however, may want the document to be either a sword or a shield, filled with adversary rights.

Many lawyers try to ignore these conflicting perspectives. They convince themselves that they can be neutral or objective. However, all perspectives are rooted in some particular context or viewpoint.[64] Thus, you must consciously try to balance these conflicts with language that will serve multiple uses.

Unfortunately, there are no magic rules for striking this difficult balance. The best you can do is identify the multiple perspectives and then make an informed choice. Consider, for example, the Internal Revenue Code. Its organization reflects how Congress viewed taxation: as a random collection of things to be taxed.[65] This organization is not very helpful to either of the primary audiences: the IRS and taxpayers. If a taxpayer wants to find out the tax implications of her divorce, she has to go to a secondary source to find out the relevant Code provisions, which are widely scattered throughout the Code. Similarly, the IRS might prefer an organization based on its powers and duties. Either way, the drafter should have organized it from the perspective of the people who will use the document, rather than the perspective of the people who wrote it.[66] A useful technique is to try to envision an actual consumer using the document, rather than organizing the document according to abstract ideas.

When you identify your audiences, you may find wide disparities. For example, with the Internal Revenue Code, you could expect IRS agents to be much more knowledgeable than individual taxpayers. Such disparities are common. You should draft your document so it can be understood by your least sophisticated readers. Simple language is always wise. If it is a consumer contract or an insurance policy, such "plain English" may be statutorily required.[67]

a.   Use "Plain English" for Consumer Documents

Although most of the rules of plain English[68] are included elsewhere in this chapter, it may be helpful to collect them in a single location for those instances in which you are editing a document specifically for plain English. To a large extent, drafting contracts in plain English simply means writing well.

Try to anticipate the consumer's questions. Answer those questions clearly. One of the most frequent questions will be, "What do I do next?" Accordingly, the document should follow chronological order. For example, provisions for paying installments should come before the instructions on how to renew the note. The document must explain the general scheme before it gets caught up in the details.

Questions of how, when, and where will irritate consumers if they have to keep flipping back and forth to various sections. Therefore, avoid cross-referencing by keeping related provisions close to each other.

Use clear section headings that help the consumer find information. These headings must be carefully worded. If the heading is misleading, a court may render the contract unenforceable:

> Here, the paragraph signed by defendant bore a heading totally unrelated to the sentence on which the plaintiff now relies. . . . Defendant would have been entirely justified in concluding from the heading that he was agreeing only to have his union insurance pay for his wife's hospital bills. This is a far cry from agreeing to assume personal liability.[69]

To make the document less threatening to consumers, consider making it less formal and more conversational. You can make your documents more conversational by using personal pronouns such as "I" and "you." Be consistent however. Vast confusion can result by using the same pronoun to refer to different parties.

Plain English is succinct English. The longer a provision is, the less likely it is to be read. Some statutory tests specifically require short sentences.[70] Compare these two ways of saying the same thing:

> BAD: If the proposed Insured has or acquires actual knowledge of any defect, lien, encumbrance, adverse claim or other matter affecting the estate or interest or mortgage thereon covered by this Commitment other than those shown on Schedule B hereof, and shall fail to disclose such knowledge to the Company in writing, the Company shall be relieved from liability for any loss or damage resulting from any act of reliance hereon to the extent the Company is prejudiced by failure to so disclose such knowledge. If the proposed Insured shall disclose such knowledge to the Company, or if the Company otherwise acquires actual knowledge of any such defect, lien, encumbrance adverse claim or other matter, the Company at its option may amend Schedule B of this Commitment accordingly, but such amendment shall not relieve the Company from liability previously incurred pursuant to Paragraph 3 of these Conditions and Stipulations.

BETTER: If you know of any legal defects (including liens) affecting the title to your property, you must tell us in writing. If you tell us about a defect, we cannot pay you for a loss that the defect causes, but we will still pay you for any other covered loss you have. If you do not tell us, we will not pay you for any loss you have that we could have avoided if we had known about the defect.

The 84 word opening sentence from the commitment purports to tell consumers what to do if they know of any title defects. Few consumers will ever wade through that language to discover what their obligations are. Indeed nothing is as impenetrable to the average consumer as excessively long sentences. When a sentence gets gargantuan, pare it down by eliminating the unnecessary language. Then break the sentence up into its constituent ideas and put them into a meaningful sequence of sentences.

Limiting the number of adjectives and adverbs helps. When an adjective or adverb is essential, be sure to put it next to the word it modifies. This avoids unclear references and prevents the reader from getting lost. Similarly, keep subjects close to their verbs and verbs close to their objects.

One reason that first sentence was so long is that it used a 16-word phrase to describe title defects. Lawyers love to string nearly synonymous words together.[71] Wordiness may cause other problems too. Sometimes the paired expressions have slightly different meanings. Then it is unclear which of the two words controls. Consider the phrase "authorize or direct." To authorize is to empower. To direct is to require. Which is meant? The best course is to decide which one word is best and to use it.[72]

The same lawyers who like to string synonyms together also compile long lists of examples. These lists have three distinct disadvantages. They are verbose, they are necessarily incomplete, and they end up limiting the general category they were meant to describe. Intentional vagueness[73] solves the problem.

Verbose lawyers also love archaic language. Their favorite words have not been spoken in daily conversations for centuries. Since most of these words are meaningless, it is easy to avoid them. The few that have any meaning should be translated into modern language that a consumer can understand.

EDITING TIP: Avoid these archaic words:

aforementioned	heretofore	thereon
aforesaid	hereunder	thereto
forthwith	herewith	theretofore
hereafter	notwithstanding	thereupon
hereby	pursuant to	undersigned
herein	so as	whereas
hereinafter	thereafter	wherefore
hereinabove	thereas	whereto
hereinbefore	thereby	whereupon
hereof	thereof	witnesseth
hereto		

A related but more difficult problem arises with the use of modern language. Complying with plain English statutes may mean appealing to the linguistic lowest common denominator. Words quite acceptable in modern usage may be well beyond the comprehension of some of the people who will need to understand consumer contracts.

Since most lawyers think in complex language, it is very difficult for them to simplify it. Some of the plain English statutes, however, judge contracts on the basis of a formula that considers the length of sentences and the number of syllables used.[74]

EDITING TIP: Avoid these words in consumer contracts:

acquire	indebtedness	procure
amendment	indemnity	promisee
commence	institute	promisor
deem	liability	promulgate
determine	mortgagee	purport
discharge	mortgagor	reside
execute	preceding	resolve
holder	prejudice	sole
in arrears	proceed	subsequent

Lawyers should create their own private lists adapted to their own vocabulary habits.

Because some statutes consider word size in judging the readability of a document, try to use the base or root word whenever possible. For example, say "concept" instead of "conceptualization." Often the root word will be a verb. Use verbs instead of vampires to create sentences that are much more direct and informal: "Buyer may inspect . . . ," rather than "Seller shall allow inspection. . . ."

The passive voice is another villain. It makes sentences awkward and long:

BAD: This agreement may be terminated by either party by thirty days' written notice being given to the other party.

BETTER: Either party may terminate this agreement by giving thirty days' written notice to the other.

Some of the plain English statutes also require specific sizes of print.[75] For example, federal regulations require specified terms in loans to be printed in 12-point type. Similarly, the Uniform Commercial Code requires that disclaimers of warranties be "conspicuous."[76] Thus, you must carefully research the requirements for plain language for the kind of document you are drafting.

To summarize the plain English rules:

1. organize chronologically,
2. avoid cross-referencing,
3. use clear headings,
4. use personal pronouns,
5. be concise,
6. limit modifiers,
7. avoid strings of synonyms,
8. replace lists of examples with descriptions,
9. avoid archaic legalisms,
10. simplify vocabulary,
11. avoid vampires and passives,
12. comply with statutory requirements.

Even when your audience is more sophisticated, you should keep your language as simple and direct as possible. No one wants to read legal documents. The stuffier the document sounds, the less likely it is to be read. Allow your readers to concentrate on substance rather than wading through your vocabulary.

EDITING TIP: Replace stuffy language with simple words:

NOT:	BUT:
cease	stop
commence	begin
contiguous	next
donate	give
effectuate	cause or carry out
elucidate	explain
endeavor	try
evince	show
expedite	hurry
expenditure	spend
expire	end or die
feasible	possible
indicate	show
peruse	read
prior to	before
procure	get or obtain
renumerate	pay
subsequent to	after
terminate	end
utilize	use

b. Avoid Jargon and Terms of Art

The rules of plain English require lawyers to avoid jargon. Jargon is the technical terminology that operates like shorthand within professions. You must guard against both legal jargon and your clients' jargon.

Legal jargon is easier to spot because it is frequently in Latin. You can presume that most of your audiences are not fluent in ancient languages. Thus, you should scrutinize Latin phrases to be sure that they could not be expressed more clearly in English. Of course, not all legal jargon is in Latin. Many of the redundant phrases that lawyers use are English, for example, "null and void." Thus, the real tests for legal jargon are whether your audience can understand the words, and whether the words are absolutely necessary.

Certain legal terms of art express ideas more fully and succinctly than any explanation you could write. For instance, it is far simpler and more precise to say that assets are to be distributed "per stirpes," than to use the full legal definition.[77] Other terms of art have legal significance that simply cannot be explained any other way. For example, you may be required to use the term "life estate"[78] in a deed. However, you should only use legal terms of art when absolutely necessary. Too many lawyers use legal language because they are too lazy to explain what they mean in simpler terms.

You must make the same sorts of decisions about your clients' jargon. This jargon is even more dangerous because you are less likely to understand exactly what it means. If you misuse a term, you may not know it. Accordingly, you should never use unfamiliar jargon.

However, other industries have terms of art that are necessary. For example, in providing for an audit, you may need to use terms of art like, "accrual basis,"[79] or "generally accepted accounting principles."[80] Once again, the test is whether the unfamiliar language is absolutely necessary. If you do use nonlegal terms of art, you should be sure that you know exactly what they mean.

2. Emphasize Important Information

Tone is more than merely a matter of adjusting the language of your document to your readers. You want your readers to understand which items you think are most important. Thus, you must structure your document to achieve the proper emphasis. At the document level, important material should come either first or last. Readers are fresh at the beginning of a document. Therefore, you want to take advantage of this energy and catch their attention so they will continue reading. Accordingly, begin with information you want to stress. You can bury less important or damaging matter in the middle the document, but you want to end the document strongly.

Sometimes, the order suggested for clarity (familiar to unfamiliar) may clash with the order suggested for emphasis (strong, weak, strong). You cannot emphasize material that your reader cannot understand. Accordingly, clarity is more important.

As you move through your document, you will find that you repeat certain words. For example, in a contract you may repeat the word "agree" over and over. The repeated words are frequently the ones your readers will remember. Although agreement is certainly the essence of any contract, it may not be what you want to emphasize. Instead of repeating "agree," tabulate the contract. For example:

BAD:

1.   *The seller agrees to furnish the purchaser with* a warranty deed to the property at the closing.

2.   *The seller agrees to furnish the purchaser with* a title insurance policy.

3.   *The seller agrees to furnish the purchaser with* a bill of sale.

BETTER: The parties agree:

1.   The seller will furnish the purchaser with:

    a.   a warranty deed to the property at closing,
    b.   a title insurance policy, and
    c.   a bill of sale.

In the improved example, the readers do not waste their time rereading the same preliminary information. Instead their attention is focused on the substantive requirements.

At the sentence level, you should also concentrate on emphasis. If your subject and verb come first, your reader will be able to find the familiar topic and action immediately. That frees the reader to concentrate on the new information at the end of the sentence. Thus the end of the sentence gets special emphasis.

Accordingly, a well-written sentence is like a joke. The beginning of the sentence operates like a straight line to set up the joke. The end of the sentence is the real focus of attention or the punch line. For example:

Straight line: Why did the chicken cross the road?

Punch line: To get to the other side.

If the punch line comes too soon, the joke loses meaning:

Why did the chicken get to the other side?

The same principle operates in sentences. You should put the familiar topic and action at the beginning so the reader can focus on the important information at the end:

BAD: Without a doubt, a thorough understanding of grammar and syntax is invaluable to the aspiring attorney.

The writer wants the reader to think about "grammar and syntax," but the emphasis falls on the "aspiring attorney."

> BETTER: Without a doubt, the aspiring attorney will profit from a thorough understanding of grammar and syntax.

This sentence is better because it moves the important material to the end of the sentence in the stress position.

Because the end of the sentence carries the stress, you should not finish your sentence on an unimportant word or phrase. Hence, you should scrutinize your final words. Some words are stronger than others. The hierarchy is:

Verbs = strongest   (kill)

Nouns = weaker   (killing)

Prepositions = weakest   (with)

Accordingly, you should not end sentences with prepositions.[81] Indeed, your sentences should end with a punch. Thus, instead of using a modifier to intensify the final word, choose a more forceful word.

> BAD: . . . read carefully.
>
> BETTER: . . . scrutinize.

Thus, in tone as in clarity, the key to successful writing is to focus on the reader.

C.   Be Concise

Writing carefully requires more than writing clearly in the right tone. You must also be concise, or succinct. You should use as few words as possible to express the ideas you wish to convey. However, you should not delete necessary words or ideas. If being concise conflicts with being accurate, always opt for accuracy.

Unfortunately, when students try to be concise, they frequently eliminate necessary ideas. They also eliminate important words that show the relationship between ideas. In either case, the result is an inaccurate document.

Examples

Wordy:

> The trustee shall have full power over the trust estate, including but not limited to, the right to invest the trust property, even commingling funds in common funds, upon such terms and conditions that he in his sole discretion shall determine as appropriate to fulfill the purpose of the trust, it being my express desire that the trustee have the broadest powers allowable to manage and control the trust estate.

Student Rewrite:

The trustee shall have the broadest powers to invest trust property.

Missing ideas:

1. discretion to determine terms and conditions of investments appropriate to satisfy purpose of trust
2. right to commingle funds

Misstated relationships between ideas:

broadest possible powers not limited to investing

Better:

The trustee shall have the broadest possible powers allowable to manage and control the trust estate. These powers shall include but not be limited to the power to invest the trust property. In investing the property, the trustee shall have the sole discretion to determine any terms and conditions that are appropriate to satisfy the purpose of the trust. In investing the property, the trustee shall also have the right to commingle funds in common funds.

In the above examples, the better rewrite retains all necessary ideas. Even though it is long, it is nevertheless concisely written.

This section of the chapter will set forth a number of rules that will help you identify and eliminate unnecessary words, phrases, sentences, paragraphs, or even entire provisions in a document to help you be concise.

1. Eliminate Burdensome Redundancy; Retain Beneficial Repetition

You should eliminate redundant words, concepts, and even entire paragraphs if they serve no purpose. Each word you use should be in your document for a reason. At the document level, you need not repeat the same introductory clause over and over again. For example:

NOT: 1. The buyer and seller agree that the sales price shall be $157,937.00.
      2. The buyer and seller agree that the earnest money of $15,000 will be held in an interest bearing account.
      3. The buyer and seller agree that the seller will execute a warranty deed.
      4. The buyer and seller agree that time is the essence of this contract. . . .

BUT: The buyer and seller agree as follows:
      1. The sales price shall be $157,937.00

2. The earnest money of $15,000 will be held in an interest bearing account
3. The seller will execute a warranty deed.
4. Time is the essence of this contract. . . .

Similarly you should eliminate redundant words. Many forms use unnecessary words that serve no purpose. Redundancies commonly found in forms have some historical or customary[82] value, but no substantive benefit; they merely burden the reader.

EDITING TIP: Watch for word combinations like the following:

- null and void
- make, declare, and publish
- free and clear
- true and correct
- part and parcel
- vacate, surrender, and deliver possession
- sell and transfer
- sole and exclusive
- residue and remainder
- right, title, and interest
- fair and reasonable
- loss or damage

One word will suffice. The others are redundant.

In contrast, sometimes repetition can be helpful to the reader. Repeating an idea in several relevant places will remind the reader of a fact or concept that is necessary to remember at several places in the document. For example, assume that a testator has created a trust for her grandchildren in her will, to be effective only if any of her grandchildren are under 25 years of age at the time of her death. This condition may be stated in an article of her will in which the gifts are set forth. The same condition may be repeated as the introduction to the later article that sets forth all the terms of the trust.

Repeating the condition would aid the reader, especially if the grandchildren's trust is presented several pages after the initial gift. The repetition would also help if there are several different contingent trusts in the will. Reminding the reader of the condition will help put the trust in context and keep the reader from needing to flip back several pages to refresh his memory as to the particular contingency. Thus, in some situations, repetition can be helpful to the reader.

Sometimes the same group of ideas may be repeated in entire paragraphs or provisions located in different sections of a document. You will need to assess whether the repetition is necessary. For example, many car loans provide that if a debtor misses an installment, the lender may seize the car. A provision covering details about the seizure of the car may appear in two different sections in the document: "1. Lender's Rights," and "2. Debtor's Failure to Pay."

EDITING TIP: Watch for repeated language. Assess whether it is necessary in both places. Is it burdensome and confusing to the reader, or is it helpful to have the provision repeated?

---

2. Evaluate Each Word in a List to Determine Its Necessity

Often lawyers use lists of words to express an idea, fearing that one or two words would exclude all others. They believe such a list will be flexible and prevent litigation. In fact, quite the opposite may be true. When you use long lists, courts presume you have listed everything. Therefore if you inadvertently exclude one item, a court may rule that you purposely omitted it.[83]

For example, consider the following:

> . . . wife requests that this court enjoin husband from selling, transferring, disposing, pledging, or hypothecating any of the marital properties . . .

Are all of the words necessary? Why aren't the words "assigning" or "using" included? Would either of those excluded words be encompassed by the meaning of the words included in the list? You must decide whether a single word or phrase can be used and is sufficiently broad to encompass your meaning. If so, it may be wise to omit the specific terms.

EDITING TIP: When you see a list remember this danger: A list may not exhaust all possibilities. Evaluate the need for each word.

---

3. Eliminate Unnecessary Descriptions

Sometimes detailed descriptions are necessary. For example, in a complaint, if you want to request punitive damages, you must allege "willful misconduct." Hence, the modifier, "willful," is necessary. If a testator wishes to leave her ring to her granddaughter, you need words that sufficiently describe the exact ring and granddaughter. In contrast, modifiers sometimes cause wordiness because they are unnecessary.

EDITING TIP: Watch for adjectives and adverbs like these:

certain	certainly
clear	clearly
complete	completely
definite	definitely
essential	essentially
excessive	excessively
extreme	extremely
great	greatly
intense	intensely
obvious	obviously
reasonable	reasonably
severe	severely
significant	significantly
substantial	substantially
true	truly
very	

Readers may view such embellishing language as a replacement for substance. Rather than describing a thing or action with a modifier, use a more precise and forceful noun or verb:

Use of modifier	Substitute
clearly see	focus
extreme pain	agony
specific purpose	reason
think very carefully	scrutinize

Readers may also view such modifiers as a mask for imprecision. For example, the words "obviously" and "clearly" often indicate that the statement is not so obvious or clear to the writer. Similarly, consider these phrases:

closely related
appropriate authorization

Their use may indicate that the writer himself is uncertain of his meaning. He may not know whether the ideas presented are "closely related." He may not know what constitutes an "appropriate authorization." These words may hide the writer's own uncertainty.

4.   Eliminate Unnecessary Clauses

Frequently, a word will suffice instead of a phrase. Vampires sometimes cause this type of wordiness. For example:

Use	Instead of
continue	further the continuation of
modify	create modification of
terminate	effect termination of

EDITING TIP: Other wordy clauses include:

due to the fact that	because
in all likelihood	probably
in order to	to
in regards to	regarding
notwithstanding the fact that	although
provided, however that	if
the time at which	when
until such time as	until

In many instances these phrases can be replaced with a single word, and your drafting will be more concise.

5.   Avoid Long Sentences

Too many words in a sentence burden the reader and make your writing difficult to understand. Long sentences also increase the possibility for misplaced clauses and multiple meaning. When possible, break a long sentence into two or more sentences:

BAD (one wordy sentence):

Following years of erosion by juries and courts, almost unanimous criticism by legal scholars, and, perhaps most influential, the rise of alternative no-fault systems for dealing with injuries, the common law doctrine of contributory negligence has been abandoned in a large number of jurisdictions.

BETTER (four concise sentences):

The common law doctrine of contributory negligence has been abandoned in a large number of jurisdictions. The doctrine had been eroded by courts, juries, and the almost unanimous criticism of legal scholars. The most important influence, however, may have been the rise of no-fault systems. These systems provided an alternative for dealing with injuries.

Exercise 3-9

Edit the following provision to make it concise:

> Upon refusal of a lawful demand for inspection, the superior court of the proper county, may assure the enforcement of the right of inspection with just and proper conditions or may, for good cause shown, appoint one or more competent inspectors or accountants to manage the auditing of the books and records kept in this state and the investigation of the property, funds and affairs of any domestic corporation, or any foreign corporation keeping records in this state and of any subsidiary corporation thereof, domestic or foreign, keeping records in this state and to report thereon in such manner as the court may direct.

D. *Conclusion*

This chapter has provided detailed rules to help you achieve the three fundamental goals of good writing: to be clear, to use the proper tone, and to be concise. You will draft effective documents if you remember your readers. They need clear documents that they can interpret themselves. Readers also need a document they can read easily. Hence, your document must have the proper tone and must be concise. Of course, clear, focused, concise language only works if it conveys substance. The second part of this book will apply the process of legal drafting as well as the rules of this chapter to drafting contracts, wills, pleadings, and legislation.

Notes

1. Gerald Gunther, Constitutional Law 1418-1419 (12th ed. 1991).

2. Pub. L. No. 16, 38 Stat. 114 (1913).

3. This doctrine is referred to as *expressio unis est exclusio alterius* (the expression of one is the exclusion of the others). For a fuller discussion of the doctrine, *see* Norman J. Singer, Sutherland Statutory Construction §47.23 *et seq.* This doctrine is also mentioned in the section on conciseness, *infra*.

4. Singer, *supra* note 3, at §47.17; *e.g.,* District of Columbia v. Acme Reporting Co., 530 A.2d 708 (D.C. 1987).

5. This doctrine is called *ejusdem generis* and means "of the same kind." For a fuller discussion of *ejusdem generis, see* Singer, *supra* note 3, at §47.17. *See also* Chapter 2, note 13.

6. *Cf.* Williams v. State, 698 S.W.2d 266 (Tex. Ct. App. 1985) (holding that a motorboat was not a motor vehicle; the statute only contained the general term, however).

7. Groucho Marx & Richard Anobile, The Marx Brothers Scrapbook 222 (1973).

8. *See, e.g.,* 20 ILCS 610/4 (1993); 30 ILCS 360/1-3 (1993). [At the time of this writing, the statutory compilations in Illinois have been changed from "Ill. Rev. Stat." to "ILCS." Since there is not yet an official Uniform System of Citation style for this new compilation, we have used "ILCS" consistently throughout this book. — EDS.]

9. For a fuller discussion of the rules on omitting the actor from a sentence, *see* the clear sentence rules *infra* pages 94-106.

10. Professor Dickerson calls these conflicts "external contextual ambiguities." Reed Dickerson, Materials on Legal Drafting 56 (1981). Such terms are omitted from this book purposely because they shift the focus of drafting to a more abstract level. However, these labels are included in footnotes so that you can comfortably use other reference sources on drafting.

11. New techniques of computerized research make it much easier to discover whether other statutes have used similar language. For a fuller discussion of legal research methods, *see generally* J. Myron Jacobstein & Roy M. Mersky, Fundamentals of Legal Research (5th ed. 1990); Christina L. Kunz, *et al.,* The Process of Legal Research (3d ed. 1992); Christopher G. Wren & Jill Robinson Wren, The Legal Research Manual (2d ed. 1986).

12. For a discussion of how drafting relates to the way lawyers negotiate and structure transactions, *see* Chapter 5.

13. Professor Dickerson calls these "internal contextual ambiguities." *See* Dickerson, *supra* note 10, at 56. Professor Child simply calls them "contextual ambiguities." Barbara Child, Drafting Legal Documents, Materials and Problems 338 (2d ed. 1992).

14. Ambiguity that arises from word order is sometimes called "syntactic ambiguity." *See* Child, *supra* note 13, at 323; Dickerson, *supra* note 10, at 55.

15. Such words are either nouns made out of verbs (gerunds) or participles. For a fuller discussion of the important differences in drafting legislation, *see* Dickerson, *supra* note 10, at 241 (quoting Elmer A. Driedger, The Composition of Legislation 16, 23 (2d ed. 1976)).

16. Such modifiers sometimes are called "squinting" modifiers. Child, *supra* note 13, at 329; Dickerson, *supra* note 10, at 56; Laurie G. Kirszner & Stephen R. Mandell, The Holt Handbook 236 (2d ed. 1989) (hereinafter Holt Handbook).

17.   For further rules on sentence clarity, *see infra* pages 94-106.

18.   United States v. Certain Real Property, 710 F. Supp. 46 (E.D.N.Y. 1989).

19.   United States v. Certain Real Property, 739 F. Supp. 111 (E.D.N.Y. 1990).

20.   Word level ambiguity is called "semantic" ambiguity. *See* Child, *supra* note 13, at 172-174; Dickerson, *supra* note 10, at 55.

21.   18 U.S.C. §924(e) (1992).

22.   Black's Law Dictionary 197 (6th ed. 1990).

23.   Model Penal Code §221.1.

24.   United States v. Taylor, 495 U.S. 575 (1990).

25.   For a fuller discussion of definitions, *see infra* pages 87-90.

26.   A nominalization is a verb that is changed into a noun. For a complete description of nominalizations, *see infra* pages 99-103.

27.   In addition to the problem of parallelism addressed in the text, some problems may arise from the use of the term "agree."

28.   This language is not a good choice because it is ambiguous in two ways: 1) Who is obligated to fulfill the agreement? and 2) is it a current obligation, or merely an agreement to agree? For a further discussion of ambiguity of word choice, *see supra* pages 79-80.

29.   For a full description of grammatical parallelism, *see* Holt Handbook, *supra* note 17, at 249-257.

30.   *See infra* section C.

31.   *See supra* pages 81-84.

32.   *See infra* section B.

33.   "Escrow" is an arrangement to have a third party hold given items such as a deed or money, pending certain specified conditions. Black's Law Dictionary 545 (6th ed. 1990). For example, an attorney might hold a portion of the purchase price in escrow until the seller repairs an item.

34.   A debt is accelerated if the debtor must pay the full balance early if he is late on a payment or otherwise defaults. For a more complete definition of acceleration, *see* Black's Law Dictionary 12 (6th ed. 1990).

35.   I.R.C. §7701(a)(17) (1988).

36.   I.R.C. §133(1993).

37.   I.R.C. §280G(b) (1986).

38.   I.R.C. §509(a) (1986).

39.   *See supra* section A.1 for a discussion of the breadth of focus.

40.   *See supra* page 68, notes 3-6 for the discussion of *ejusdem generis* and *expressio unis est exclusio alterius. See also* Chapter 2, note 13.

41.   For a list of transition words *see infra* pages 90-91.

42.   *See supra* pages 82-84 on functional parallel structure.

43.   *See* example *supra* page 92.

44.   For a discussion of enumeration, *see infra* pages 106-107.

45.   Holt Handbook, *supra* note 16, at 350.

46.   For a more detailed discussion of the nature of the subject of the sentence, *see infra* pages 97-99. For a more detailed discussion of the appropriate level of generality of a document, *see supra* pages 67-69 on focus.

47.   For a more detailed discussion of tone, *see infra* section B, pages 111-119.

48. Occasionally you may want to hide the actor for strategic reasons. Thus a defense lawyer might state the fact: "The child was struck with a bat." In contrast, the prosecutor might want to make the actor very clear: "The defendant struck the child with a bat."

49. For a more detailed discussion of the passive voice, *see supra* pages 95-97.

50. For a discussion of how to order sentences within a paragraph or section according to topic, *see supra* pages 90-94.

51. This principle can be explained many different ways: Use "base verbs," Richard Wydick, Plain English for Lawyers (2d ed. 1985); avoid "nominalizations," Joseph M. Williams, Style: Ten Lessons in Clarity and Grace (2d ed. 1985); Veda R. Charrow & Myra K. Erhardt, Clear and Effective Legal Writing 109 (1986).

52. For a discussion of abstraction, *see supra* pages 69-72.

53. *See infra* section B on tone, pages 111-119.

54. Readers hold their breath once they identify the subject, and only breathe again when they find the verb. Various presentations of Joseph M. Williams; various presentations of George Gopen.

55. Of course, this sentence violates the rule of familiar to unfamiliar because the reader does not know yet to what "form" refers. Thus, the next example is better.

56. Fed. R. Civ. P. 12(f).

57. Tabulation also improved this sentence. *See infra* pages 107-111. Similarly, some of the vampires have been eliminated. *See supra* pages 99-102.

58. However, this revision changes the emphasis of the sentence. The first two sentences stress that the regulation will improve the environment. The new revision stresses limiting toxic waste. For a further discussion of emphasis, *see infra* section B on tone, pages 111-119.

59. This paragraph could be improved further by eliminating the clause "which previously have been approved":

Employee shall be reimbursed for the costs of:

1. travel;
2. professional memberships; and
3. previously approved professional conferences. . . .

60. For examples of grammatical parallelism, *see supra* pages 81-82.

61. For a fuller discussion of the ambiguities of "and" and "or," *see supra* pages 76-79.

62. Semicolons are generally overused. In this example, many drafters would replace the commas with semicolons. The use of a semicolon is technically incorrect in this instance. Holt Handbook, *supra* note 16, at 440. However, since both semicolons and commas signify that the items in the series are of equal value, using a semicolon instead of a comma does not change the meaning.

63. Thus, contracts, wills, pleadings, and legislation are somewhat analogous to constitutions. The documents create new relationships that have to develop more particularly over time. For example, a sales contract establishes a relationship between a buyer and a seller; a will establishes relationships between a testator, executor, and beneficiaries; a pleading establishes relationships between litigants; and legislation establishes relationships between government and individuals. For a further discussion of these ideas, *see* David A. Funk, Group Dynamic Law: Integrating Constitutive Contract Institutions (1982); Ian R. Macneil, *Relational Contracts: What We Do and Do Not Know,* 1985 Wis.

L. Rev. 483. *Cf.* Jane Rutherford, *Duty in Divorce: Shared Income as a Path to Equality,* 58 Fordham L. Rev. 539, 549 (1990) (arguing that marriages are like constitutions).

64.   Stanley E. Fish, Doing What Comes Naturally (1989); Martha Minow, *Forward: Justice Engendered,* 101 Harv. L. Rev. 10 (1987).

65.   Income tax is divided into six categories in the Code: "normal taxes" and a variety of specialized taxes.

66.   Professor Felsenfeld calls this the "scenario" method of organization. Carl Felsenfeld & Alan Siegel, Writing Contracts in Plain English (1981).

67.   Several states now require plain language in either consumer contracts or insurance contracts. For a list of states with plain language statutes, *see* Michael Axline & John Bonine, *Plain Talk: Making NEPA Work,* 25 Land & Water L. Rev. 61, 77-82 (1990).

68.   For a fuller discussion of plain English, *see* Wydick, *supra* note 51.

69.   Saint John's Hosp. v. McAdoo, 94 Misc. 2d 967, 405 N.Y.S.2d 935 (Cir. Ct. 1978).

70.   *E.g.,* Conn. Gen. Stat. Ann. §§42-152 (West 1992) ("A consumer contract is written in plain language if it . . . uses short sentences and paragraphs . . .").

71.   For a discussion of redundancy and necessity, *see infra* pages 120-122.

72.   Dickerson, *supra* note 10, at 176-177.

73.   *See supra* pages 66-67 for a fuller discussion of intentional vagueness.

74.   Conn. Gen. Stat. Ann. §§42-152 (West 1992).

75.   *Id. See also* Chapter 2, note 10.

76.   U.C.C. §2-316(2) (1992). *See also* Chapter 2, note 10.

77.   "This term, derived from the civil law, is much used in the law of descents and distribution, and denotes that method of dividing an intestate estate where a class or group of distributees take the share which their deceased would have been entitled to, had he or she lived, taking thus by their right of representing such ancestor, and not as so many individuals." Black's Law Dictionary 1144 (6th ed. 1990).

78.   "A legal arrangement whereby the beneficiary (i.e., the life tenant) is entitled to the income from the property for his or her life." *Id.* at 924.

79.   "A method of accounting that reflects the expenses incurred and income earned for any one tax year. . . . Expenses do not have to be paid to be deductible nor does income have to be received to be taxable." *Id.* at 20.

80.   "The standards and conventions that guide accountants in the preparation of financial statements. . . ." Ralph Estes, Dictionary of Accounting 60 (2d ed. 1985).

81.   For a full discussion of emphasis, *see* Henry Weihofen, Legal Writing Style 105-134 (2d ed. 1980).

82.   Sometimes word pairs were used to bridge ancient language barriers. Thus, after the Norman conquest, many legal phrases included a native Celtic word like "bequeath" as well as a Latin or French synonym like "devise." The use of such synonyms may have continued long past their usefulness both because of tradition and the fact that for many years lawyers were paid by the word. Reed Dickerson, The Fundamentals of Legal Drafting 51 (1965).

83.   The rule of construction is often referred to as expressio unis est exclusio alterius. Literally, it means "the expression of one is the exclusion of others." Thus "when certain persons or things are specified in a law, contract, or will, an intention to exclude all others from its operation may be inferred." Black's Law Dictionary 581 (6th ed. 1990). *See, e.g.,* Iowa v. Estrella, 133 N.W.2d 97, 104 (Iowa 1965) (holding that by instructing the jury to "determine the facts when they are disputed," the trial court had impliedly instructed the jury not to determine the accuracy of undisputed facts).

PART II
Applying the Process

CHAPTER 4

Drafting Estate Planning Documents

A. *Introduction*

Although you may not plan to practice estate planning, it is likely that at some point in your career you will have to draft a will, even if it is just a simple one for a relative. It is also likely that you will have to give an opinion on or litigate some aspect of a will or a trust agreement, or do business with an executor or a trustee acting under such documents. Therefore, you should have some basic understanding of the concepts and terminology associated with estate planning documents. For purposes of studying legal drafting it is important that you learn the skills required to draft such documents because they present challenges not found in other types of drafting. The documents are unique because they may not become effective for many years; they may deal with things and people that do not yet exist; they must speak clearly to an audience that ranges from a judge to your client's least intelligent relative; and they deal with two highly emotional topics, death and family.

If you have never drafted a will before, you may need to start with step three of the drafting process — know the law — for background information. You will need to learn the law within each of the four categories discussed in Chapter 2: substantive law, procedural law, interpretive law, and ethical law. This chapter should leave you with an idea of what you need to learn about the law of your state. Although some state legislatures have attempted to make the substantive law uniform among the states,[1] the law still varies greatly from jurisdiction to jurisdiction. The following should help you get started.

B. Definitions

1. Will

A will is a document by which a person, the "testator,"[2] disposes of her property, effective at the testator's death, and expresses her wishes on other matters. Regarding property, the testator can indicate who should receive the property, how and when it should be distributed, and what conditions apply. The testator can also express other wishes. For example, she can state her preferences regarding the care of children; name a person, or executor, to manage the estate during probate; and give instructions regarding probate.

Most wills contain some or all of the following provisions:

1.	Declarations	Testator:
		a. name
		b. condition
		Impact on prior wills:
		a. revokes them, or
		b. adds to or modifies them
		Family members
2.	Definitions	
3.	Disposition of property	Specific gifts
		General gifts
		Residual gifts
4.	Trusts	Trust property
		Trustee's appointment
		Trustee's powers
5.	Appointments and Powers	Executor
		Guardian for children or incompetents
6.	Details of Administration	Direction to pay debts and taxes
		Survival clause
		Rules of interpretation of the will
7.	Execution and Witnessing	Signatures
		Affidavits of witnesses

This is not a complete list of every provision in a will but gives you a general idea of the broad topics wills may cover. A will does not have to include all of these topics. The list also does not represent the only way you can organize these topics. When you get to step four of the drafting process — classify, organize, and outline — you will reconsider how you might organize these provisions.

2.   Probate

When a person dies leaving a will, an individual who is aware of the existence of the will, such as a member of the family, the executor, or a lawyer, generally files the will with the probate court. That person, or some other interested party, may initiate probate proceedings. In very simple terms, probate is the process by which a court determines whether a will is valid and complies with statutory requirements. The process is defined by state statute.

Interested persons may challenge provisions of the will during the probate period, and the court may be called upon to interpret the will. The court also creates an estate, which holds the deceased person's property and pays his debts. The court appoints a representative of the estate, usually called an executor.[3] The executor identifies the property of the estate and brings any claims the estate might have. For example, property that belongs to the estate might be in the possession of a person who does not want to surrender it, or the estate might have the right to bring a lawsuit. The executor also handles claims against the estate, including paying bills and taxes and defending lawsuits. When these matters have been taken care of, the executor distributes the remaining property, according to the valid provisions of the will, and the estate is closed.

An estate can also be created to manage the affairs of an individual who dies intestate, that is, without a will. State laws of intestate succession govern the distribution of property when a person dies without a will.

It is not always necessary to open an estate when someone dies. A person might die owning no property, or all of her property may change ownership without judicial action because it is held in joint tenancy or in someone else's name. In addition, some jurisdictions have simplified procedures for small estates, when there are no complications.[4]

3.   Codicil

A codicil is a supplement to a will, used to "explain, modify, add to, subtract from, qualify, alter, restrain or revoke provisions" of a will.[5] To be valid, a codicil must be executed with the same formalities required for a will.

A testator can execute a codicil or a new will or revoke a will at any time if he meets all legal requirements. Under the laws of some states, the terms of the last will executed may be "blended" with the terms of earlier wills that have not been revoked.[6]

4.   Trust

A trust is an arrangement by which a person, the "trustor" or "settlor," conveys property to a "trustee" to be held, managed, and distributed for the benefit of a third party, called a "beneficiary" or "beneficiaries." A trust can be created either in a will or independently of a will.

The principal or "corpus" of a trust is the property placed in the trust, which may or may not generate income. A trust may be set up so that a beneficiary is entitled to both principal and income or so that one beneficiary is to receive income and another will be entitled to the principal at a later date.

There are many types of trusts, including: (1) testamentary, (2) inter vivos, (3) contingent, (4) noncontingent, (5) revocable, (6) irrevocable, (7) short term, or (8) long term. A trust that comes into existence at the testator's death is called a testamentary trust. A trust created to be effective during the settlor's lifetime is called an inter vivos, or living, trust. A contingent trust is one that is created only if certain events occur. For example, a parent might create a contingent trust, which will only come into being if she dies before her children reach a specified age. Such a trust is included in the Sample Will of Robert Kenneth at the end of this chapter on pages 162-176. Trusts may also be revocable or irrevocable, and short term or long term. These different types of trusts may be joined in different combinations. The Sample Trust of Marie King, at the end of this chapter on pages 176-199, is a revocable, inter vivos trust, also known as a "living trust."

Just as there are many types of trusts, there are many possible reasons for creating a trust. In order to avoid probate a settlor might establish a trust that names himself as both the initial trustee and the initial beneficiary. The settlor names a trustee to take his place upon his death or incompetency. The person so named is called a successor trustee. The settlor will also name a successor beneficiary to receive the property upon his death. The trust actually owns the property that the settlor has conveyed to it, so that when the settlor dies, he, personally, does not have assets that require creation of an estate. The trust does not die but continues in existence despite the death of the settlor/trustee/initial beneficiary. A settlor might also create a trust for a number of other purposes: to attempt to reduce tax liability,[7] to protect the privacy of his investments, to assuage his concern that he will be unable to manage the property, or to provide for the care of some person or thing during and beyond the settlor's lifetime.

5. Fiduciary

A fiduciary is one to whom power or property is entrusted for the benefit of another. If a testator has minor children, as many as four fiduciaries might be named in a will: an executor, a trustee, a guardian of the person, and a guardian of the estate. All four functions can be served by one person. Every will should name an *executor* (and an alternate choice) to administer the estate during the probate period. This is a relatively short-term job, compared to the other positions. The position of *trustee* will come into being only if a trust is created. The trustee will hold legal title to and control and distribute trust assets according to the trust directions given in the will. A trustee's powers can be very flexible. The *guardian of the person* will have actual physical custody of the children. The testator may nominate a guardian, but the choice is subject to review by the court. A *guardian of the estate* manages property for a minor or incompetent person. The position does not have the flexibility that can be given a trustee but may be necessary if a child has assets outside the trust created by the will or other law, for example, Social Security benefits.[8]

There are many considerations that go into drafting provisions relating to fiduciaries. You should check state law for age and residency requirements for fiduciaries and familiarize yourself with the powers and duties given fiduciaries by your state's statute. You may want to expand or limit the powers and duties to fit your client's situation. Normally you will give fiduciaries broad powers to save time and money. Further, outsiders may be more willing to deal with fiduciaries who have broad powers. For example, if an estate must sell a house, the transaction will be easier if the executor can list the house with a realtor, negotiate and sign a sales contract, perhaps provide financing, and execute closing documents without having to get court approval for each action.

The fiduciaries should also have flexibility to make the best of economic circumstances and the client's assets. For example, assume a testator owned gold that, pursuant to his will, became a trust asset upon his death. Gold is not normally considered an appropriate trust asset because it does not produce income. If the trustee does not have broad powers to choose or maintain assets, he therefore may be compelled to sell the gold even if economic circumstances will cause a loss. Accordingly, you must carefully consider the nature of the trust assets and the testator's goals when you define fiduciary powers.

If you name a corporate fiduciary, be sure that the estate can afford the fee and that the fiduciary is willing to act under your documents. It is possible to name co-fiduciaries, but it can lead to problems. You must indicate what should happen if the fiduciaries disagree and whether one fiduciary may perform ministerial functions alone, to avoid a situation in which an out-of-town co-trustee must be present to open a safe deposit box or sign checks. Some wills authorize a named fiduciary to appoint successor fiduciaries or to appoint co-fiduciaries (sometimes from a list).

Although the preceding overview may give you some general idea of the law, you will need to research specific issues that arise with each will you draft. The information provided in section C.3 of this chapter and in the notes in the sample wills at the end of this chapter present more details about the law governing wills. The notes reflect the particular issues raised by the samples. Other issues will arise in other wills you draft. Simply reading this chapter will not resolve all legal questions that may arise. Ultimately, there is no substitute for your own research.

C.   *The Drafting Process for Wills*

Now that you are familiar with some of the basic terminology associated with estate planning documents, you are ready to begin the general drafting process.

1.   **Understand the Audiences**

The audiences for estate planning documents are varied and include: your client, your client's family, potential beneficiaries, fiduciaries, lawyers, judges, accountants, and creditors. These audiences each have their own particular perspective. You must evaluate each audience specifically to assess how knowledgeable it is and how hostile or friendly it is.

Although your client is probably friendly, you must be sure your client understands the documents. Your client should read the documents to verify that all of his wishes have been addressed. It is in the best interest of the lawyer to draft the documents so that they can be easily understood by the client, particularly if complicated family relationships or tax issues are involved. If the client cannot understand a will or a trust, the client will not be able to say whether it reflects his wishes and circumstances. Such a situation may result in a lawsuit.

Overblown language may give clients the impression that the lawyer is trying to inflate the value of legal counsel in estate planning. This is particularly true as clients become more educated and less willing to blindly trust a lawyer. Most lawyers now view their role as that of counselor and technician. Rather than projecting the impression that some kind of "voodoo" is involved, a modern lawyer is likely to inform the client of the options available and implement the client's wishes in the simplest, most efficient way possible. A client expects to be able to read and understand the documents and appreciates seeing that her concerns have been addressed in a logical way. She also expects to be able to explain the documents to other audiences like family members.

Family members or other potential beneficiaries may be slightly more hostile audiences. Both those who are included and those who had hoped to be included may criticize the document. They may be displeased with their exclusion, or with the amount of their gifts, or with conditions attached to the gifts. These individuals and their lawyers may read the document in an effort to find faults that would persuade a court to declare the document, or a particular provision, invalid or ambiguous.

You may deflect some hostility by softening the tone of your documents. For example, assume a client wants to disinherit one child to provide more money for a handicapped child. Compare the following examples:

> BAD: I give nothing to my daughter, Roberta, under this will. I give the entire residue of my estate to my son, John.

> BETTER: Because my son, John, is permanently disabled, I give John the entire residue of my estate. Regretfully I give my daughter, Roberta, nothing under this will.

Although a disinherited party probably will be disappointed, an explanation not only deflects anger, it also may preclude a successful will contest. An explanation may be particularly important if the client wants to disinherit a child or children.[9]

Fiduciaries are more likely to be friendly but will have varying degrees of knowledge. For example, executors are frequently spouses who have little or no knowledge of probate procedures. In contrast, professional fiduciaries, such as banks, usually are very knowledgeable both about procedures and investments. A knowledgeable professional fiduciary is likely to recognize risks created by poorly drafted documents and may be unwilling to act when such risks exist. You should draft your documents so that they can be understood by unsophisticated fiduciaries and will be acceptable to professional fiduciaries.

Lawyers and accountants are usually knowledgeable. However, these experts may be more or less hostile depending on the interests they represent. For example, a lawyer or an accountant may represent a client who intends to challenge the will. These experts are specially trained to scrutinize documents for ambiguities and technical errors. You must draft your document carefully enough to satisfy even the most hostile audiences.

Although judges are theoretically objective, they will be scrutinizing your documents to be sure they comply with relevant law. Even if no one objects, a judge may refuse to enforce a sloppily drafted provision. For example, even if all parties agree that the executor need not post a bond, if the document does not waive the bond properly, the judge may require a bond. Generally judges are irritated by sloppy documents.

Consider the will of Marie H. King and the Marie H. King Revocable Trust at the end of this chapter. Make a list of the members of the audiences for the documents and their unique interests. Identify potential conflicts. Pay particular attention to Article One of the will and Article Six of the trust.

Exercise 4-1

Consider the will of Marie H. King and the Marie H. King Revocable Trust at the end of this chapter. Make a list of the members of the audiences for the documents and their unique interests. Identify potential conflicts. Pay particular attention to Article One of the will and Article Six of the trust.

2. Gather the Facts

The next step in writing a will or trust is to gather the facts. This step is very important and may be time consuming because accurate and complete facts are necessary to carry out your client's wishes.

The basic factual questions described in Chapter 2 dictate the type of information you will need. You should use these basic questions either to develop a client interview form or checklist, or to revise an existing one.

Example

The Basic Questions

WHO: Client: name
                               address
                               previous name
                               date of birth
                               place of birth
                               marital status
                               earlier wills, codicils, trusts

	Relatives:	names and addresses of all relatives entitled to notice under relevant state probate code
		events that affect family relationships: deaths, divorces, adoptions, guardianships, incompetencies, other legal proceedings
	Fiduciaries:	executors, trustees, guardians (including second choices): names, addresses, relationships
	Beneficiaries:	those to receive gifts (including second choices)
WHAT:	Property:	types of property the client owns location how title is held special handling or management requirements encumbrances: mortgages, liens, etc. expectancies: inheritances, lawsuits, etc. debts owed to client
	Liabilities:	possibility of federal or state taxes debts support obligations
	Other:	involvement in existing trusts other formal/informal financial relationships
WHERE:	Client:	other residences likelihood of moving
	Property:	any subject to jurisdiction of other states
	Fiduciaries:	any problems created by their locations
WHEN:	Conditions:	triggering events, e.g., when trust should be created, distributed; any conditions on gifts, powers of fiduciaries, etc.
WHY:		under what circumstances client would want to change provisions
		assumptions being made about: current facts future facts law gifts

HOW:	Property:	specific gifts
		general gifts
		conditional gifts
		residuary clause
		trusts
	Fiduciaries:	care of children
		relationship with other fiduciaries
		desired degree of discretion
		desire to waive bond
		other personal concerns

Your will interview form may not provide all the information you need. Also, you should not rely solely on what your client tells you; you may have to investigate outside the interview to clarify matters or to verify the client's understanding of facts. For example, the client may not know how the title to property is held or understand his rights in a business or under an existing trust. Or, the client may not correctly identify his relationship to certain people and may not know whether he is obligated to provide for those individuals.

Exercise 4-2

a.   Examine the sample will of Robert Kenneth at the end of the chapter and identify legal matters and assumptions that should be discussed with the client.

b.   In order to obtain thorough information for preparation of estate planning documents, you may need to ask personal questions. Identify the kinds of questions that might upset a client. Why are these questions necessary and how might they be asked without offending the client? What particular problems might arise if a husband and wife arrive together for an interview? Are there ethical considerations?

c.   Your client wants to create a trust for her niece's education. Make a list of the information you will need in order to draft appropriate provisions.

d.   Your client wants to leave vacation property to his church. Make a list of information you will need in order to draft this provision for his will.

e.   Your client tells you that she wants to leave everything to her spouse, except for items listed on a piece of paper she hands you. What additional information will you need, assuming that the list states:

Camera and equipment to grandson, Joe Waldin
Turquoise to brother, Jeff Waldin
Family bible to Joe at age 21
Insurance policy provided by my employer to daughter, Elise Andrews.

f.   Using samples you find in form books and the wills at the end of this chapter as guides, develop a client interview form.

3. Know the Law

Although the definitions at the beginning of this chapter provided some general background, if you have completed the exercises in the previous section you know that a lawyer must know some detailed law in order to adequately interview clients. Even more knowledge is required to draft the documents. In addition to knowing substantive law, you need to know the procedural law, ethical requirements, and rules of interpretation.

a. Know the Procedural Law

Procedural law differs from state to state. You will need to do research to determine which state's law is likely to govern and whether you can select the applicable law.[10] Then you will need to research the formalities required to create a valid will under the applicable law. If you fail to follow the proper formalities, the will is invalid and the laws of intestate succession will govern how the property is distributed. These laws may not reflect the testator's intent.

Most states require that a will be in writing, signed by the testator, and witnessed by two or three people. Many lawyers use more witnesses than are required by state law, in case a witness is disqualified or the law of another state governs. Generally, the testator must intend to sign a will and must sign it at the end, and the witnesses must sign it in the presence of the testator. Witnesses must be competent, as defined by state law, and should not be beneficiaries under the will. In some states the testator must sign in the presence of the witnesses; in some states the testator must sign before the witnesses sign. Some states require that the testator "publish" the will, or identify it as his will, to the witnesses. Because testamentary intent is required, most wills contain a declaration of intent to make a will, whether publication is required or not. States also have different presumptions concerning integration, such as a requirement that the entire will be physically present during execution.[11] Some states recognize holographic wills, which are in the handwriting of and signed by the testator but are not witnessed.[12] A few states recognize "nuncupative" or oral wills under limited circumstances.[13]

Because the required formalities differ from state to state and because your client might die in another jurisdiction, it may be wise to draft your documents to comply with the strictest formalities. Not all states will admit to probate a will that complies with the laws of the state where it was executed if it does not comply with the laws of the state of probate.[14]

In addition, you must be familiar with the relevant probate procedures and rules regarding trust administration so that you can draft documents that are easy to administer and that secure every possible advantage for your client. For example, it may be possible to include language with the witnesses' signatures that will make a will "self-proving" so that the witnesses need not be located after the death of the testator unless the will is challenged.[15] You may also be able to waive a requirement that an executor or trustee post a bond and, by waiving the requirement, save the estate a substantial sum of money.[16] You will also want to consider whether it is possible and desirable to draft documents that will allow your fiduciaries to act without court order or to avoid periodic accountings to the court.

Exercise 4-3

a. Your client wants to refer to a list, which is currently in her safe deposit box and which she changes from time to time, to describe the distribution of her personal property. This is called incorporation by reference. Will a court enforce such a provision?

b. Your client brings along a neighbor to act as a witness to the execution of his will. You fail to notice that the neighbor is to receive all of the client's fishing gear under the will. You do not use extra witnesses. Is the will invalid under the laws of your state? If not, will the neighbor be able to take the gift?

c. Your client wants to make a "pour-over" gift in her will, which would give a substantial sum to a living trust that the client created several years ago for the benefit of her sisters. Again, this is a matter of incorporation by reference. States differ as to whether this is permissible. Is such a gift valid? Will the gift remain valid if the trust is amended after the will is executed? Are there any special requirements for describing the trust in the will?

b. Know the Ethical Requirements

Ethical concerns in drafting estate planning documents tend to fall into two categories: whether the lawyer can serve functions in addition to drafter — for example, executor, trustee, beneficiary — and whether the document reflects the testator's wishes untainted by conflicts of interest.

The rules of your jurisdiction may prohibit a lawyer from drafting an instrument if the lawyer is a beneficiary.[17] Because you may be called upon to draft wills for family members, you may have to determine whether such a prohibition applies when the lawyer is related to the testator. You may also have to determine whether it applies when the beneficiary is another member of the firm, the lawyer's spouse or child, or an entity in which the lawyer has a substantial interest. You should also determine whether you should act as a witness, remembering that if the will is challenged, witnesses may be required to testify. In considering whether to witness the will, you must also consider other roles you may play: executor, trustee, or attorney for either. Remember that normally executors and trustees who are not family members are compensated.[18] It is certainly possible to imagine a number of possible conflicts; many of these situations could at least cause an appearance of impropriety.

You must always remember who your client is and ask yourself whether you can serve that client's interests, given your relationship to others. For example, it is common for an adult child to bring an elderly parent to a lawyer to make a will. Often the lawyer will have previously represented the child. The lawyer must carefully consider whether the will truly reflects the wishes of the parent, rather than those of the child, and whether the parent is competent. Similarly, a husband and wife may meet with you together for wills. One of the spouses may take the lead and tell the lawyer what "they" want. The lawyer must be careful to determine that the other spouse's wishes are not being ignored. Moreover, even if they agree at the time the wills are originally executed, several years later a conflict may develop if one spouse wants to make changes without notifying the other. Thus, the lawyer must disclose, at the time of the meeting, the potential for conflicts.

Finally, you must consider your own competence. A client's family or financial situation may indicate that his will or trust should be drafted by someone with greater expertise. One important consideration in making this determination is whether there are any federal estate tax or state estate or inheritance tax implications. Federal estate tax law is very complicated and applies to larger estates. Not all states have an estate or inheritance tax.

Exercise 4-4

a. Twelve years ago your long-time client, Susan Schein, had you draft a will in which she gave $5,000 to each of five of her employees and the balance of her estate to her spouse. She also executed powers of attorney, giving her spouse total control of her property and all financial and health decisions in the event of her incompetence. Shortly after executing the documents, Susan began to have serious problems. Her health failed, and her business went into bankruptcy. She is now totally incompetent and does not even recognize her spouse. She has not heard from her former employees in ten years. She and her spouse have very little money and her spouse is concerned that when she dies, much of what they have left will go to the former employees. He wants to know whether he can destroy Susan's will and effectively revoke it, under the power of attorney. Can he? If he decides to do so, can you assist him?

b. Two years ago you drafted wills for Mr. and Mrs. Andrews. They stated that they wanted to leave everything to each other because, although it was a second marriage for each of them, they trusted each other to take care of both sets of children. Now Mrs. Andrews has asked that you draft a new will in which she will give every thing to her natural children. This would mean that Mr. Andrews's children would take nothing if he died first. What are your obligations, if any?

c. Know the Rules of Interpretation

A well-drafted document should be self-explanatory and require no interpretation, but you must know enough about the interpretive law of your state to recognize potential problems. The courts have developed rules for construing ambiguous wills and trusts and for dealing with mistakes in the contents and in the execution. These rules may not reflect the real intentions of the testator and can be quite harsh. Rules of construction may result in a distribution of property that all of the parties agree is not what the testator would have wanted. In some cases introduction of extrinsic evidence concerning a testator's intentions, including the testimony of the attorney who drafted the document, has been excluded.[19]

In order to avoid such consequences for your client you must write carefully (as discussed in Chapter 3 and later in this chapter), but you must also be aware of how the courts in your jurisdiction deal with ambiguities and what types of provisions have been considered ambiguous. For example, do the courts of your state make presumptions in favor of upholding a gift to avoid intestacy? Does the presumption depend on whether the beneficiary and testator were related? Do the courts permit introduction of extrinsic evidence regarding the testator's intentions? Does it matter whether the mistake or ambiguity is obvious on the face of the document or apparent only in light of outside facts? How do the courts deal with apparent inconsistencies within a document and with partially inaccurate descriptions of property? No lawyer intentionally drafts a document that will require judicial interpretation, but familiarity with precedent may help you avoid overlooking a potential problem.

Exercise 4-5

a. Your client wishes to leave everything to his wife. He has two young children and wants to leave only small, token gifts to them. Does your jurisdiction permit children born after the execution of the will to claim a share of the estate? Would it make a difference if "afterborn children" are mentioned in some way in the will?

b. Your client wants to leave her estate to her descendants. Your client's son is in the process of adopting a boy who is 15 years old. Your client wishes to exclude her adopted grandson from sharing her estate. She would prefer to avoid specifically noting the exclusion to avoid unnecessarily insulting the boy, in the likely event that her son survives her. Is a specific exclusion necessary or will the use of certain terminology accomplish the same result without direct reference?

c. Will the court treat a statement that "it is my desire that the trustee pay for my son's education" the same as a statement that "the trustee shall pay for my son's education"?

d. Your client leaves a substantial gift to be divided among his "sisters," but fails to mention that two of his sisters are actually half sisters. You do not define the term "sisters" in the will, nor do you name the individuals. Can the full sisters successfully argue that they should receive more?

e. At the request of a client, you include a "no contest" or "in terrorem" clause in a will, providing that if any of the beneficiaries contest the will they forfeit all interests they may have under the will. The client dies and his daughter, in good faith and based on good evidence, challenges the will, claiming that her father was the victim of a fraudulent scheme perpetrated by his sister. What is the effect of the clause? Does it matter whether the challenge is successful?

f. In drafting a will you include a seemingly harmless direction, found in many forms, that the executor should "pay all just debts." (i) The client dies during a time of extremely high interest rates. The lender who holds a low-interest-rate mortgage on the client's house claims that the direction means that the executor must pay off the mortgage. The client left the house to her disabled brother, who was not a party to the mortgage. The estate has few other assets, so payoff is possible only if a new, high-interest-rate mortgage can be obtained. Is the lender correct under the law of your state? (ii) Also, might the direction be interpreted as requiring payment of a debt that could be considered "just" but is no longer enforceable, perhaps because of the statute of limitations?

d. Know the Substantive Law

The beginning of this chapter introduced you to some general concepts and terminology relating to estate planning documents. As you learned in the preceding sections, it is also necessary to learn the specific probate laws of your state. The following material is intended to help you identify and understand the additional substantive research you will need to conduct.

Every state has laws that govern how property is distributed on the death of its owner. Even among the community property states, there are many variations. Different rules apply when the decedent dies leaving a valid will (called "testate") and when the decedent dies without a will (called "intestate").

Under the laws of intestate succession, a married person's property is typically divided between the surviving spouse and any children, even if the children are young and the estate is small. Many state probate codes provide that a surviving spouse receives one-half of the estate and the children receive one-half of the estate.[20] If the decedent has no spouse or children, the property is divided among other relatives, even if they had no relationship with the decedent. Without a will a person cannot make gifts of specific property or state a preference regarding a guardian for children. The absence of a will can also cost the estate money because the representative of the estate may have to purchase a bond to insure his performance and may have to submit to court supervision that could have been waived by will. If minors are entitled to property, the person managing that property may incur costs in accounting for the property to the court.

The application of some rules may be avoided by the terms of a valid will. Others cannot be avoided. For example, many states provide a forced share for a surviving spouse,[21] regardless of the terms of the will. If the terms of a will disinherit a spouse or give the spouse less than the statutory entitlement, the spouse can renounce the will and claim a share of the estate, even if the will was properly executed. If the client wants to divest a spouse of inheritance rights, she must change the underlying facts by getting a divorce, or executing a valid prenuptial agreement, waiving the spousal forced share. She cannot avoid the forced share rule simply by changing her will.

In other circumstances, the facts cannot be changed. For example, your client must be legally capable of making a will. This is commonly referred to as having testamentary capacity. Because you cannot change your client's abilities, you must research the law of your jurisdiction to determine whether your client has such testamentary capacity. Testamentary capacity generally depends on the testator's awareness of his property and of family, traditionally called the "objects of his bounty." Although a testator may be too young to execute a will, testamentary capacity does not otherwise depend on age, physical health, or education.[22] The first paragraph of a will, called a "declaration," often recites that the testator is competent. Such declarations do not bind the court and are not necessary, but many wills include them.

Because some legal rules and assumptions can be avoided or changed by a will or trust, you must research substantive law so that you can counsel your client about available options. For example, the client may say that she wants to leave all of her money to her three children and that if she outlives any of her children she wants the deceased child's share of the money to go to her grandchildren or great grandchildren, descended from the deceased child. Most likely, the client has not thought about how the shares will be calculated if a child or children have predeceased her. The two terms used to describe the distribution options are "per stirpes" and "per capita with representation."

Per Stirpes.   The shares are divided by the number of children, with each surviving child taking a share and each grandchild who is the child of a deceased child taking a portion of his parent's share. The portion is determined by the number of siblings that the grandchild has.[23]

Per Capita with Representation.   The shares are determined at the first level (e.g., child or grandchild) at which there are survivors. Each living person at that level takes an equal share, and the descendants of each nonsurvivor at that level divide their ancestor's share.[24]

The following diagrams may help you understand the differences. For each diagram, assume that a will states a gift is to "my surviving children and the descendants of any children who do not survive me."

The first diagram assumes that the testator has outlived child A, but not children B and C. The result will be the same under either per stirpes or per capita with representation:

DIAGRAM 1

THREE CHILDREN:
ONE PREDECEASED THE TESTOR;
TWO SURVIVED THE TESTATOR

Result Under Either Per Stirpes
or Per Capita with Representation

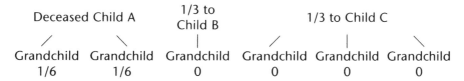

If the grandchildren take the money under per stirpes, each will share her parent's portion equally with her siblings (not all other grandchildren). In this case, the result seems reasonable and would be the same under allocation per capita with representation because there are survivors in the first level — children.

The second diagram assumes that all the children predecease the testator. In these diagrams, the result under per stirpes allocation is different from that under per capita with representation allocation:

DIAGRAM 2

THREE CHILDREN:
NONE SURVIVE THE TESTATOR

Result Under Per Stirpes

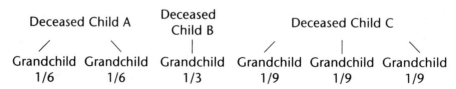

Result Under Per Capita
with Representation

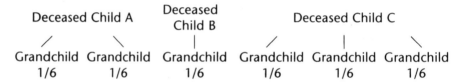

Per Capita with representation appears more reasonable and is the trend of the law.[25]

The terms "per stirpes" and "per capita" are very commonly used in estate planning documents. In fact, different courts define these terms differently. Some courts may use "per stirpes" when they mean "per capita with representation." Other courts may use "per capita" when they mean "per capita with representation." The preceding explanations and diagrams illustrate the generally accepted academic definitions. For these reasons, it is not essential that you use these terms, and in fact it is probably more desirable to describe the desired distribution in your own words. If you do want to use the terms of art, be sure you fully understand your state's definitions of them and at which level the division into shares is made. In some cases the client may want something that does not fit neatly within the definitions.

In addition, a client may want to avoid or change legal assumptions about gifts of different types of property. Gifts made in wills and trusts can be classified into one or more categories: specific gifts, general gifts, gifts to be paid from a specified source, residuary gifts, and contingent gifts.

A specific gift identifies a particular item, such as "my antique desk" or "my emerald ring." General gifts are gifts of a specified amount of money. Sometimes a testator will specify that a gift of money is to be paid from a particular source. For example, your client might want to give his son "Five Thousand Dollars to be paid from the proceeds of the sale of my IBM stock." A residuary gift disposes of all of the remaining property of a particular type, for example, "all of my remaining personal property" or "all of the rest of my property, of all types." Although the term "residue" might bring to mind "leftovers," the gift of the residuary estate is often the largest gift and may be intended to provide for the support of a surviving spouse and children.[26] A contingent gift depends on the happening of a specified event. For example, "If John is married at the time of my death, I give him my car."

Classification is important because different assumptions apply concerning the order of distribution and abatement. Abatement is the reduction of gifts because the estate is not sufficient to pay all claims and satisfy all gifts. The client can specify the order of abatement or can make certain gifts conditional. This might be desirable because, unless the will states otherwise, residuary gifts generally abate before specific and general gifts. In practice, however, most clients make specific and general gifts as tokens and intend that the residuary estate will support surviving relatives. A wealthy client might leave $10,000 to the animal shelter and the rest of her estate to her son. Would the client want her son to get nothing if circumstances changed and her estate had only $10,000 remaining after payment of debts? To avoid such a result she could make the specific gift conditional on an estate of a certain size.

In addition, you need to consider the possibility of ademption, which can occur when property that was the subject of a specific gift is not part of the estate. For example, the testator may have given his son an antique car that was destroyed in an accident immediately before the testator's death. Would the testator want his son to receive insurance proceeds? Property may also have been sold, traded, given away prior to death, lost, or otherwise disposed of.

The doctrine of satisfaction may apply when the testator executes a will and then, during her life, makes a gift to a beneficiary. Does the lifetime gift "satisfy," or cancel the gift in the will? The answer depends on the classification of the gift and varies from state to state. Again, your client may want to change the result that would otherwise follow from your state's law.

Some wills separate gifts of real estate from gifts of other kinds of property. Inheritance of real property was treated differently at common law, and, under some states' laws, title and possession of real estate vested in the beneficiary immediately. Real estate may also be treated differently for purposes of exoneration, which concerns the estate's obligation to pay any debts secured by the property. In addition, while the law of the state where the decedent was domiciled generally governs personal property, the law of the state where the property is located is likely to govern distribution of real property.[27] Finally, the value of real property, the need for particular management, or complications concerning how title is held may indicate that separate treatment is appropriate.

Your client may come in with firm ideas about what he wants in his will or trust. You must research those wishes to be sure they can be carried out under relevant substantive law. Even if permitted, some choices may be unwise. For example, clients may request a joint will. A joint will is a single instrument signed by two or more testators. Courts generally construe joint wills as creating a contractual relationship. You should avoid joint wills because of problems that will arise if one of the testators wants to change the terms. Generally a joint will cannot be changed after the first testator dies.

Reciprocal wills are two separate wills that have provisions that mirror each other.[28] Courts generally hold that no contract is created by the mere executions of reciprocal wills; consequently, a reciprocal[29] will can be revoked or changed even after the death of the first testator. These are very typical for spouses. If two testators want to bind each other to agreed schemes of distribution, they should make that intention clear by means of contractual terms.

Knowledge of substantive law is relevant to each step in the process of drafting estate planning documents. Each new client may present new questions. No single text can attempt to answer, or even anticipate, all of those questions. As a lawyer you must look for those questions and research the answers thoroughly when they do arise.

Exercise 4-6

a.   Your client wants to name as executor or trustee her brother, who lives about 75 miles away but in another state. Will your state law allow him to act as executor or as trustee?

b.   Your client previously executed a will and, later, a codicil. He did not tell you about them because he thought the will was no longer valid and did not understand the legal significance of the codicil. You draft a new will that does not specifically revoke the earlier documents, which still exist. How will a court in your state treat the earlier documents?

c.   Your client wants to leave her spouse about 90 percent of her estate, but in a trust, so that the spouse will receive all income from the property but can only receive distributions of principal for his "needs" as determined by the trustee. At the spouse's death the property is to be distributed to the client's relatives. The spouse has never liked the relatives and will try to prevent them from receiving anything. May the spouse renounce the will and, if so, what effect does the renunciation have on the gift to the relatives? Does the will continue to have any validity? Will the spouse improve or worsen his financial position by renouncing?

d.   Does your state have a "mortmain" statute that restricts testamentary gifts to charity?

4.   Classify, Organize, and Outline

Now that you have gathered the facts and researched the law, you must combine them into a coherent will. First, list the facts you have gathered. Second, list the broad categories you discovered in researching the law. You can identify the necessary categories by thinking about the goals of the will:

- it must comply with statutory requirements
- it should address the client's legal obligations
- it should describe the distribution of property desired by the client
- it should appoint an executor and other necessary fiduciaries and describe their duties
- it may provide instructions for administration of the estate

These goals bring to mind many provisions that might be included in a will:

Goal	Category
Statutory requirements:	identification of testator declaration of intent to make a will attestation (signature) witness statements and signatures
Legal obligations:	identification of family members provision for spouse provisions for guardianship of children payment of debts and taxes
Distribution:	specific gifts general gifts contingent gifts residuary gifts trusts
Administration:	revocation of earlier wills name fiduciaries fiduciary powers definitions

Although these categories are commonly found in wills, not every will contains all of them. A particular client's situation may involve other goals and categories that must be considered, for example, disinheritance. Once you have a list of general categories, you are ready to put them in a logical order.

Estate planning documents can be ordered in different ways. The order you choose for your categories is important because order may affect meaning. The reader expects the categories to be ordered according to some logical principle and may interpret its provisions according to what appears to be logical. For example, assume a will contains several specific gifts, followed by the residuary clause giving "all the remaining property to Ellen." After the residuary clause, a specific gift of "my emerald ring to Nancy," is thrown in at the end of the will. Might Ellen argue that she is entitled to the ring? The very words "remaining property" indicate a particular order. Similarly, assume a will creates a trust for a grandchild in article 3, lists the trustee's powers in article 4, provides for the payment of debts and defines terms in article 5, and creates a second trust, for another grandchild, in article 6. Might a reader conclude that two trustees do not have the same powers or that the trusts are to be treated differently in other respects (e.g., payment of debts)?

The organization of the will as a whole may reflect either client priorities or the chronology of the probate process that you learned about when you researched the procedural law. Many modern wills use client-oriented organization, which deals first with those matters unique to the individual client, such as identification of family, appointment of fiduciaries, and gifts. Matters that are common to most wills or that are covered by statute, such as a payment of debts clause, are dealt with toward the end. This organization tends to please the client and directs his focus to matters within his expertise, such as his family and wishes.

A will oriented to the chronology of the probate process may first identify the testator, appoint the executor, and direct payment of debts. This traditional format is comfortable for some clients and lawyers. Other orders are also possible. You may create a form oriented to some other priority or decide that a particular client's situation dictates a different format.

In organizing estate planning documents, you should identify your categories with headings. Headings help the reader anticipate your topics and put them in perspective. Although you may find that the forms of wills and trusts you examine while doing your research do not use headings, or use them only for large categories, identifying each topic with a heading is a good practice. Compare the sample wills of Robert Kenneth and Marie H. King at the end of this chapter on pages 162-199.

Your headings should reflect your organizing principle and should be helpful to the reader. Imagine acting as trustee, with powers described in a 30-page will, and having to respond to various questions and requests from beneficiaries on a regular basis. Would traditional headings, "Article I," "Article II," help you perform efficiently? You would probably prefer headings oriented to the client's wishes, such as "My Family," "Gifts," and "Trust." If the client has a large or complicated estate, you might prefer even more specific headings, oriented to the chronology of probate and trust administration, such as "Payment of Debts," "Gifts Outside Trust," "Distributions Under Trust," and "Trustee Powers."

Once you have identified and organized your general categories, you should create and organize subtopics where necessary. Subtopics are generally organized so that the reader is first given general information and then specific details. Obviously it would be confusing to read that the trustee has authority to distribute principal to pay for a grandchild's education before reading that a trust is being established for the testator's grandchildren. You must also consider what is most important or most likely. For example, if the client is 40 years old, married, and the mother of children 15, 17, and 19 years old, it is likely that at her death she will be survived by either a spouse or adult children. Those situations should be dealt with first. It is less likely that she will die, not survived by a spouse, while she still has a minor child. That possibility calls for creation of a trust and should be described next. It is not likely that a spouse and all descendants will predecease her, so you should deal with that possibility last.

Organizing the dispositive provisions of estate planning documents requires special consideration. It is a mistake to simply list the gifts in the order in which the client states them. Doing so may create confusion about distribution and whether the gifts are conditional.

Although most documents, like contracts or legislation, move from broad categories to specific details, the gift provisions in estate planning documents usually move from specific to broad categories. This type of organization reflects the substantive law concerning distribution and abatement. Obviously, a specific gift of "my antique desk to Joan" and a general gift of "ten thousand dollars to Fred" reduce what is available for distribution of "all of the rest of my property to Rebecca." Therefore, gifts of identified items or specified amounts are usually stated before gifts of broad categories of property.

In addition, contingent gifts, which are distributed only if certain conditions have been met, should be separated from noncontingent gifts to avoid confusion. Conditional gifts, like specific gifts, are identified before gifts of broad categories. This helps clarify the disposition of the gift if the condition is not met. For example, if a client gives "my collection of law books to Jim, if he is a practicing lawyer" and subsequently gives "all of the rest of my property to Bob" it is clear that Bob gets the books if Jim is not a practicing lawyer.

When you have finished organizing your general categories and subtopics, you will have an outline and you can begin to integrate the facts you have gathered into that outline. Refer back to your fact list, and note in the margin where the fact fits in your topic outline. Then transfer your facts to an expanded outline, checking off each fact as you use it. A section of that expanded outline might look like this:

I.   Specific Gifts
     A.   Contingent gifts:
          1.   If John graduates from college before his 25th birthday — gold pocket watch.
          2.   If not, gold pocket watch to nephew, Peter Krump.
     B.   Noncontingent gifts:
          1.   antique Dresden finger bowl to daughter, Sarah.
          2.   parrot, Polly, to granddaughter, Patricia.
II. General Gifts
     A. $5,000 to Church
     B. $5,000 to ASPCA
III. Residuary Gifts
     A.   Personal Effects and Household Goods
          1.   to wife if surviving
          2.   to Sarah if wife not surviving
     B.   All Other Property: cash, stocks, real property, etc.
          1.   to wife if surviving
          2.   if wife not surviving, in trust for . . .
IV. Trust
     A.   Trustee-Sarah . . . etc.

It will not always be clear where a given fact belongs. For example, assume that your outline contains categories dealing with the care of the client's children and the powers of fiduciaries. Into which of these categories would you place the client's wish that her children attend private schools? You must use your judgment. Sometimes, you may even decide to include it in both places, to be sure that both the trustee and the guardian are aware of your client's preference for private schools. However, repeated provisions must be consistent. Avoid repeating facts unless you have a reason to do so.

After you have created an outline, re-read your client interview form to make sure that you have not overlooked any of the client's wishes. You may find that some information does not easily fit into your categories. You may have to change your outline to account for such facts. You may need to add headings or subtopics, or you may need to change existing topics to include those facts. For example, assume that your client stated that he wants to leave his personal property, including some valuable pieces of art, to his wife, but that if his wife does not survive him, he wants his nieces and nephews to "bid" on the items. This is unusual and you might forget to include in your outline until you re-examine your fact sheet. You could include this with the gift of personal property to the wife, but if you do so you should be sure that your headings and organization of subtopics are appropriate. You do not want to "bury" this so that it might be overlooked or hard to find, and you do not want to create confusion about whether there should be bidding if the wife survives. You may decide to create a new topic.

You should also express your client's wishes regarding alternate beneficiaries. Assume in the preceding outline, for example, that Sarah predeceases the testator. Without an alternate beneficiary named, the Dresden finger bowl will pass to the residuary beneficiary. Therefore, your client may want to include an alternate beneficiary for each gift. For similar reasons, you should always include alternate fiduciaries, for example, executors, trustees, and guardians. In the event the person named fails to act in the appointed capacity, you want to express the testator's alternate choices.

Just as your outline may have missed known facts, your outline may contain categories for which you are missing facts. Those categories were generated from your legal research. Review that research to determine what, if any, additional facts you need from your client. For example, you may have a survival clause in your outline, as a result of earlier research. Does the client want to name an alternate beneficiary in case a beneficiary dies soon after the client, as might happen if they were in an auto accident together? If so, you should include a clause requiring that the beneficiary survive the testator by a certain amount of time in order to take the gift. Otherwise, the gift may have to pass through two estates and may be given to a person your client would not have chosen.[30]

Finally, double-check to be sure that you have not omitted any necessary categories. One useful source to help you identify missing categories is form books. The use of forms and form books is discussed at the end of this chapter.

At long last, you are now ready to convert your expanded outline into a draft of the document. When you do so, be sure to write carefully.

Exercise 4-7

a. Develop a short outline of the "Gifts" category of a will for a client who says the following:

> My main concern is for my wife and kids. Of course my wife will take care of the kids, so I want to leave her everything. My oldest son, Pete, is my first wife's child, so I do want to leave him $35,000 separately because it came from his mother's family. Other than that, I want to leave each of my kids $5,000 as a nest egg, but only if I can do it without the estate having to sell any of the stock or real estate. If I get an inheritance from my uncle I'd like to leave $10,000 to his church. If my brother is still alive, I'd like to leave him my Rolex watch and $5,000, but again, only if it doesn't require selling the stock or real estate.

b. You have been retained by Marie King's daughter, who is named as executor and trustee under the documents at the end of this chapter. Your client asks you what she should do with her mother's stock certificates. Try to locate the relevant provisions. What could you do to improve the organization of these documents to make such instructions easier to locate?

5. Write Carefully

Careful writing is particularly important in drafting estate planning documents because such documents are essentially sets of instructions. By the time the instructions in a will are to be implemented, it is no longer possible to go to the client for clarification. As previously discussed, the states have developed rules for resolving ambiguities and mistakes, but these rules may not reflect the wishes of the testator. In writing estate planning documents, you will have to consider all of the steps described in Chapter 3, giving special attention to clarity, as achieved by proper focus and tone of your documents.

a.   Focus

The correct balance of intentional vagueness and precise description is essential to drafting wills and trusts. You must identify your client's goals and consider possible changes in circumstances to achieve that balance.

Estate planning documents deal with a broad range of transactions, people, and property that will exist in the future, so vagueness can be essential. For example, a will that states, "I leave my house at 325 Diane Avenue to Marie" is not appropriately vague if the testator's goal is simply to provide Marie with a residence. The testator may not own that particular house at his death. Clients often do not consider possible changes in circumstances, but wills and trusts should anticipate even unlikely changes. A 60-year-old widow may adopt her orphaned niece; a client so wealthy that he wants to make substantial gifts to charity may be almost destitute when he dies; a client who has no assets may become a rich landlord.

Examine the dispositive provisions of the will of Robert Kenneth at the end of this chapter. Note the use of vague language to deal with possible changes in circumstances. Also consider how definitions and other "boilerplate" create flexibility. For example, the testator has four children, but the will states that the term "children" includes children born or adopted in the future.

Vagueness is not ambiguity, however. For example, a gift of "a car to Jennifer" can be interpreted in a number of ways. A gift of "any car I may own at my death" or "a new car of her choosing" is intentionally vague, but not ambiguous because, while no particular car is identified when the will is written, it will be easy to identify the gift when the testator dies. Similarly, the will of Robert Kenneth at the end of this chapter leaves a gift to "children who survive me and who do not receive the Rolex." It is impossible to positively identify those people when drafting the will, but who they are will be clear at the time of distribution. When vagueness is required, you must find language that does not tie you to circumstances that exist at any particular time, but that avoids ambiguity because it permits only one interpretation at any given time.

Intentional vagueness is not accomplished by sloppy word choices, either. For example, stating that a trustee "shall pay the reasonable costs of a college education" is vague in that it is flexible with regard to amount. On the other hand, stating that the trustee "may" make such payments, or that "it is my desire that the trustee provide an education," may be ambiguous because such language could be interpreted as allowing the trustee discretion not to make any payments.

There will be times when vagueness is inappropriate. For example, your client may want to give Marie the house at 325 Diane Avenue because her father built that house. In such cases a high degree of precision may be necessary. If your client wants to give "the Hendry painting, known as 'Winter Pond,' to Gail," describing the same gift as "the oil painting in my hall to my niece" could create a number of problems. Does it refer to the entry room or the corridor? What if there are two paintings? What if the painting is in the closet because the area is being painted? What if Gail is a godchild, whom the client has always referred to as his niece, although she is not a blood relative?

In using intentional vagueness, be careful that you are not creating a situation that enables the testator to change his will without observing the formalities of executing a will. For example, if you draft a provision that leaves $10,000 to a person "identified in a letter that will be found with this will," the testator can change the beneficiary without observing the formalities of execution. This may be allowable, if the testator is incorporating by reference an existing list or a trust that might be amended, or if the determinative act or event has independent legal significance.[31] The law varies from state to state and has many exceptions, so do not include such a provision without researching the law of your state.

A common error in attempting to find the correct balance of vagueness and precision is to list examples. If you are attempting to identify or include a specific item or person as part of a general category, it may be appropriate to state that inclusion. For example, if a client owns unusual property, you may want to refer to "all of my personal property, including my art collection and my airplane." On the other hand, if you are simply trying to clarify your description by naming items or people that might be included in a category, you may create ambiguity. People reading the document, and courts interpreting the document, may conclude that the general description is limited by the examples. For example, if a will directs payment from the estate of "all of my debts, including U.S., state, and local taxes," might there be an argument that the recipient of an investment taxable in Canada must pay the tax herself? Ask yourself whether a list is necessary. Often a general description is adequate by itself. Does it matter whether the named executor "does not survive, is not competent, declines, or ceases to act"? Would such language cover the situation if the named executor were in prison, willing, but unable, to act? You could simply name an alternate executor in the event that the named executor "fails to act."

You must also avoid omissions that create ambiguity. Again, you must create documents that do not permit inconsistent interpretations. For example, your client may tell you that he wants his personal property divided by a bidding process among his children. The client may not have considered how this should be accomplished or may believe that the children will readily agree on a procedure, but you should anticipate conflicts and resolve them by addressing the essential questions: who?, what?, when?, where?, why?, and how?

b. Tone

You must be sure that you have written documents that your client can understand. Only your client can tell you whether you have properly communicated her intentions. To accomplish this, you must use plain English, avoid terms of art, and avoid the passive voice. Imagine a client confronted with a statement that "the corpus of the trust shall be distributed to my descendants." It is likely that the client cannot determine who is going to implement the distribution, what is going to be distributed, who is going to get it, or how much they will get.

Many forms and form books in use for drafting wills and trusts contain archaic language and redundancies. Inexperienced students and lawyers may think it is easier to state that "I give, devise, and bequeath all the rest and residue of my estate, wherever situated, and including realty, personalty, and other property in which I may have an interest at my death" than to determine whether that language serves any purpose. It is generally adequate to state "I give the rest of my estate." The simpler wording can be understood by virtually any person who is part of your audience.

Exercise 4-8

Identify the ambiguity in the following statements and suggest clarifications:

1. I give, devise, and bequeath my watch to my son-in-law, Bob, to use and possess for his lifetime.

2. I leave Mary $10,000 for taking care of my dog.

3. I give to my nephew my money and coin collection.

4. I give the residue of my estate to my nieces and my brother Harold, equally. (The testator has eight nieces at the time of his death.)

5. If my wife does not survive me, I give the residue to my nieces and nephews.

6. I give my jewelry to my daughters, to be divided as they agree, with Linda to have first choice.

7. I give my stocks and bonds to my brother and sister equally, but if either predeceases me, then all to the survivor.

8. To my daughters, or their survivors, I give the residue of my estate.

9. I leave my home to my son. (The testator lived on a large farm.)

10. I give to my brother and my nephew, in equal proportions, my real estate, upon which is situated the Acme factory, together with a one-third interest in my partnership in Acme. I leave to each of my partners in Acme, Matthew and Paul, a one-sixth interest in my partnership in Acme.

6.   Test for Consequences

By the time you have reached this step, you have already spent a substantial amount of time considering possible changes in circumstances and the consequences of your word choices as you drafted each part of the document. Now you must examine the document as a whole and reconsider each of the steps in the drafting process.

First, reconsider your *audiences*. Put yourself in the position of the person who will have to follow those instructions — the executor or trustee — and imagine how you would proceed under various circumstances. Imagine that you are a beneficiary, or that you had expected to be a beneficiary. Consider the position of creditors. Use the basic questions identified in step two of the drafting process (gather the facts) to organize your thoughts. Following those questions, change the facts. Would the document remain valid, considering what you learned when you researched the substantive, procedural, interpretive, and ethical law:

1. (*who?*) What if any party died, divorced, married, had children, or became incompetent or if an identified class did not exist?

example: imagine that the named trustee has died or become incompetent; imagine that the client's spouse has died or become incompetent; imagine that there are no surviving children.

2. (*what?*) What if the nature of the client's property has changed drastically?

    example: imagine that the client has become very wealthy and now owns investments in real estate and in businesses; imagine the client's estate has shrunk so that there are not sufficient assets to distribute all gifts or to pay a corporate fiduciary.

3. (*where?*) What if the location of important people or property changes?

    example: imagine that the testator has died after retiring to another state; that the named executor or trustee has moved to another state; that the testator now owns land in a state other than the state of his residence.

4. (*when?*) What if the testator either dies very soon or lives a very long life, or conditions described in the document do not occur at expected time?

    example: imagine that the client lives 70 years after executing the document or dies the next day; imagine that the client's spouse outlives the client and all of their children, but is survived by grandchildren.

5. (*why?*) What if the client's motives change?

    example: imagine that the situation that motivated the client to execute the document changes: an incompetent beneficiary dies or is restored to competence; the client divorces or gets married; children become adults; the family business is sold. Will the document still serve some purpose or might it become detrimental?

6. (*how?*) What if the client's wishes cannot be implemented?

    example: imagine that the subject of a specific gift has been destroyed; imagine that a fiduciary refuses to act.

As you imagine that you are the executor or the trustee, going through the probate process or the administration of a trust, do not simply identify steps in the process. Fill in the precise details that are unique to this client. For example, do not simply think "if the named trustee resigned, the successor trustee would be entitled to act." Look through the document, find the actual spot where the successor trustee is named and the location of the provision giving her authority to act. This will help you determine whether the document is well *organized* and visually easy to follow and, most importantly, whether you accidentally omitted any provisions or included inconsistent provisions.

Finally, examine your *writing.* As you consider the various audiences, consider whether they will understand the document. More importantly, consider whether your writing will give them a basis for arguing that the document is ambiguous.

Exercise 4-9

Read the introduction to Marie King's will on page 161 and then read Marie King's will and trust at the end of this chapter. "Test for consequences," and identify potential problems. Use your imagination and consider big picture changes, such as the possibility that Matt is rehabilitated and is no longer disabled, as well as less significant changes, such as the possibility that Marie King does not keep her list of personal property up to date.

7. Edit and Rewrite

When you have completed a draft of a will or trust, set it aside for a time so that you can "step back from it" and read it with fresh eyes. You may discover that the document should be reorganized. For example, although many estate planning documents do not have separate sections for definitions, the inclusion of definitions and explanations within the substantive provisions may be distracting and make your sentences long and hard to follow. In rewriting the trust provisions, for example, you may decide to simplify your descriptions of distributions so that the trustee is directed to "pay all income to the children" and create a separate section to define that "pay to" means to "pay directly to, expend for the benefit of." You would also define "children" and "income" in that separate section.

Once you have organized the will in the most readable fashion, go back again and look at the tone of individual sentences. Eliminate "lawyerisms," archaic phrases, and self-dealing expressions; use defined terms to eliminate distracting explanations; use the active voice; and shorten sentences and paragraphs whenever possible.

Finally, proofread very carefully. Most problems in interpreting estate planning documents result from carelessness. Typographical and spelling errors are inexcusable in a will or trust. The consequences of dropped words or inaccurate punctuation can be disastrous. Furthermore, clients become very angry when they see that one of their wishes has been overlooked or that the name of a favorite sister was misspelled. Imagine that the testator wanted to leave his cousin 100 shares of IBM stock and you overlooked a typographical error that made the gift 1,000 shares. In many jurisdictions you would not be allowed to testify concerning the mistake; the estate would have to give the cousin 1,000 shares.

Exercise 4-10

Re-read the introduction to Marie King's will on page 161 and then edit the will and the trust of Marie King using the guidelines described in this chapter.

SAMPLE DOCUMENTS

The sample documents that follow are not sample forms for you to follow. They are not "good" documents. Many flaws were included for teaching purposes.

Use the following sample documents to evaluate other forms you examine while doing your research as well as your own drafting. Examining these samples should help you understand some of the options available to your clients and some estate administration problems and solutions. The samples may also help you develop some ideas about how to communicate clearly and about whether particular language is necessary or simply "legalese." You will also see alternate methods of organization and learn what you need to ask your client and what legal questions you will have to research.

If your practice involves estate planning, you will eventually develop your own forms. In doing so, do not simply copy a form that you find in a book or that is in use in your area. Using the principles set forth in this chapter, and your own research, draft documents that you fully understand and that reflect your best professional judgment. Then use them only as a starting point. Remember that each client is an individual, with unique circumstances and concerns. As you work with each client, run through the seven-step drafting process presented in this book. As you become accustomed to doing this, you will be able to do it quickly, and you will find that you are able to prepare an appropriately "customized" product for each client.

Introduction to the First Sample Document:
Will of Robert Kenneth

The first sample document presented here is a will that was written for a married man, about 40 years old, with four minor children. The client has no unusual problems such as an incompetent beneficiary, a family-run business, or children by more than one mother. His estate, while of respectable size (about $200,000), is not large enough, nor is it likely to become large enough, to produce any federal estate tax or state inheritance tax concerns. Much of the client's property consists of joint tenancy property and insurance, which will pass outside the will. His main concern is that his children be taken care of according to his instructions, should he and his wife both die while the children are young. He is also very concerned about making life easier for his wife if he should die before she does. He knows that if he dies without a will, his children may inherit part of his estate, which could result in financial hardship for his wife or in her having to account for spending the children's money on their behalf. He wants to make certain specific gifts. He is well educated and expects to be able to read the will and understand it.

Most of the first will has been written using short sentences and paragraphs and plain English so that the client will not be confused by it. The will has been organized according to the testator's priorities. A number of fairly important details concerning administration of his estate are, therefore, at the end of the will. Note the use of headings that identify the priorities.

Although not all wills contain a trust, the Robert Kenneth will includes a contingent trust, in case the testator dies while he still has a minor child and his wife does not survive him. Two sets of trust provisions are included in the will, to show you how trusts can be structured to fit the client's needs. If Robert Kenneth were your client, you would explain the alternatives to him and include only one set of provisions, appropriate to his situation. The first Article Six would be appropriate for a client who is most concerned about having his children cared for while they are young and less concerned about distributing equal amounts to them when they become adults. The second Article Six reflects a desire to have the beneficiaries receive equal shares and would be more likely to be chosen by a very wealthy client or to set up a trust for people who are not depending on the settlor for support while they are young.

There is one other way in which the Robert Kenneth Will is unlike a will you would actually draft for a client. It contains an extremely long list of powers for the fiduciaries. Some of the powers are even inconsistent with others. Furthermore, they are not organized and do not include headings. They are included simply to give you an idea of what is possible and what you must consider in drafting a will for an actual client. In preparing a will for a real client you must consider the client's situation, the powers available under state law, and the fiduciaries in deciding which powers to include and whether it is necessary to include powers at all.

Introduction to the Second Sample Document: Will of Marie H. King

The second sample document presented here, the Will of Marie H. King, is intended to coexist with an inter vivos trust, which is the final sample document and which is created outside the will. The Marie King documents reflect different factual situations and goals than existed for Robert Kenneth and a different method of organization is appropriate.

The Marie King will is a "pour-over will" prepared for a widow who has a disabled, adult son. It is called a "pour-over will" because, after dealing with personal effects and details concerning debts, it "pours" the residuary into the already-existing inter vivos trust. Two documents were used because the trust is created while Marie King is alive; the will becomes effective only at her death and deals with concerns that will not arise until that time, including the disposition of property that did not become part of the trust. Research state law before using a pour-over arrangement. Because the trust can be amended without observing testamentary formalities, such an arrangement allows the testator to change the effect of her will without observing those formalities. Most states permit a pour-over will, but some have special requirements concerning whether the trust must be in existence before the will, how it must be described, and whether it must be funded.[32]

Remember that while it is important to know the law of your jurisdiction, it is often more important to know the questions than it is to know the answers. A well-written will should not require construction or interpretation. For example, the law of the jurisdiction might define the term "descendants" as not including children adopted by a child of the testator. If the will specifically includes those children in its definition of the term, however, the testator's intent will govern. A well-written will that does not depend on state law for definitions will also survive if the testator moves to a different state.

Review these two samples, studying the editorial comments. Are there any errors you can identify that have not been noted? There may be more, especially in the trust section of the second sample document, which is sloppily drafted and very tedious to read. Note how you respond, as a reader, to its language and organization. Do you respond positively? Do you want to read the entire document? Or are your discouraged from doing so?

WILL OF
ROBERT KENNETH

I, Robert Kenneth, of City, State, declare this to be my will and revoke any other wills I may have made.

Article One
My Family

I am now married to Leslie J. Kenneth (my spouse). We have four children: Carol, April, Peter, and John, all of whom are minors and live with my spouse and me. Any reference to my children includes my four named children and any children born to or adopted by me in the future. [1] The term descendants shall include all children, grandchildren, or great-grandchildren born to or adopted by the named ancestor. [2]

Article Two
Appointment of Fiduciaries

1. *Executor.* I appoint my spouse as executor of my estate. If my spouse does not act as executor, I appoint the oldest of my children then qualified to act as executor. If neither my spouse nor any child of mine acts as executor, I appoint my sister, Laura Cobb ("Laura"), of City, State, as executor. [3]

2. *Trustee.* I appoint Laura as trustee of any trust or trusts created pursuant to this will. If Laura does not act as Trustee, I appoint the Acme Bank & Trust Co. of City, State, as Trustee.

3. *Guardian.* I nominate Laura as guardian of the person of any of my children who require a guardian. If Laura does not act as guardian, I nominate my spouse's brother, Mark Edwards

[1] *Classify, Organize, Outline:* Do definitions belong here?

[2] *Write Carefully:* Is a definition of "descendants" necessary? Does it preclude gifts to great-great-grandchildren?

[3] *Write Carefully:* Note the description of alternate executor.

("Mark"), of City, State, as guardian. If a guardian of the estate of any child of mine is required, I nominate as guardian of the estate the person then acting as guardian of the person of the child.

4. *Powers*. The fiduciaries named in this article④ shall have the powers specified in Articles Six and Seven of this will⑤.

5. *Bond*. I direct that no fiduciary named in this article be required to furnish security on any performance bond required. Any fiduciary named in this article may act independently of court supervision and without court order, to the fullest extent permitted by law.

<u>Article Three</u>
<u>Gifts</u>

1. *Conditional Gifts*. If the value of all my property passing under this will is at least fifty thousand dollars ($50,000), I make the following gifts, otherwise the named property shall become part of my residuary estate: ⑥

a. *Kenneth Corp. Stock*. I give any stock I may own⑦ in the Kenneth Corp., or in any entity into which the Kenneth Corp. has merged, reorganized, or otherwise consolidated, to Laura if she survives me. If she does not survive me, I give the stock to her children who survive me, in equal shares.

b. *Rolex watch*. I give the Rolex watch I inherited from my father to my son, Peter, if he survives me. If he does not survive me, I give the watch to my son, John, if he survives me.

----

④ *Test for Consequences:* Only "named" fiduciaries?

⑤ *Edit and Rewrite:* Check the accuracy of references to other sections.

⑥ *Edit and Rewrite:* Punctuation.

⑦ *Test for Consequences and Write Carefully:* Note the description of the amount of stock. If a specific amount were named, would there be problems if there were a split?

---

      c. *Cash for Children*. I give to each of my children who survive me and who do not receive the Rolex watch, the sum of two thousand dollars ($2,000).

      d. *Books*. If Mark survives me and is married at the time of my death, I give him my collection of books.

      e. *Cash for Animal Shelter*. I give two thousand dollars ($200) 8 to the Brady Animal Shelter, located in City, State.

      f. *Cash for Brother's Children*. I give five thousand dollars ($5,000) to the children of my late brother, Richard. 9

2. *Unconditional Gifts*. 10 Regardless of the value of my property passing under this will, I make the following gifts:

      a. *Cash for Cancer Society*. I give two thousand dollars ($2,000) to the American Cancer Society, 11 State Branch.

      b. *Fishing Equipment*. I give all of my fishing equipment, excluding any boat I may own to my friend, Robert Warski, of City, State.

      c. *Personal Effects*. I give the rest of my personal effects to my spouse, if my spouse survives me. If my spouse does not survive me, I give my personal effects in substantially equal shares to my children who survive me.

        i. My children shall determine, among themselves, how the personal property shall be divided. 12 If my children fail to agree on a division of all the property

---

8 *Edit and Rewrite:* If the mistake is not corrected, which amount governs?

9 *Know the Law and Test for Consequences:* Contains a "class gift" —when does class close? How will shares be determined?

10 *Write Carefully:* Could distinction between conditional and unconditional gifts be made clearer (pictorial clarity)?

11 *Know the Law:* What is the result if the charity's name is not correctly stated?

12 *Test for Consequences:* Is this likely to cause family problems? Will it be easy to implement?

within six months after my death, my executor shall sell any property as to which the
children have not agreed. The executor may
use the proceeds of such a sale to substantially equalize the value of the shares received by my children, if the executor
believes it desirable to do so, and shall
add any remaining proceeds to my residuary
estate.

ii. If any of my children are minors at
the time of the division of my personal
property, the guardian of any child may select property for that child, as that child
could have done if not a minor, and the executor may distribute the chosen property
to the guardian without further responsibility.

Article Four
My Residence

I give my residence, whether at 1234 Main
Street, City, State, or elsewhere, to my
spouse, if my spouse survives me, subject to
all encumbrances. [13]

Article Five
Residuary Estate

1. *Gift of Residue.* [14]
a. I give all the rest of my property of
all kinds, wherever situated, but excluding
any property over which I may have a power of
appointment[15] (my residuary estate) to my
spouse if my spouse survives me.
b. If my spouse does not survive me, and
I have no surviving children or all of my
children who survive me are at least 21 years

---

[13] *Test for Consequences:* Is this consistent with the debt payment clause?
Write Carefully: What does "subject to all encumbrances" modify?

[14] *Classify, Organize, and Outline:* Arranged from likely to unlikely.

[15] *Know the Law:* What is a power of appointment? (*See* endnote 33.) Why exclude it here? (*See* endnote 26: You don't want to ruin careful tax planning.)

old, I give my residuary estate to my descendants, [16] per stirpes. [17]

c. If my spouse does not survive me and I
am survived by a child not yet 21 years old I
give my residuary estate to the Trustee to be
administered as described in Article Six. [18]

d. If I am not survived by my spouse or by
any descendants, I give my residuary estate
one-half to those people who would be entitled to my estate under the laws of intestate
succession and one-half to those people who
would have been entitled to take my spouse's
estate under the laws of intestate succession, if my spouse had died at the moment of
my death. [19]

2. *Powers of Appointment.* I do not exercise
any power of appointment[20] in this will.

Article Six
Children's Trust

1. *Payments.* Until termination of the
Children's Trust, the Trustee shall pay to
each child of mine, in equal or unequal shares,
any part or all of the net income and principal
of the Trust as the Trustee determines from
time to time to be necessary. In determining
what is necessary, the Trustee shall consider
each child's health, need for support and education, and other resources. The trustee
shall give preference to the needs of each
child who is not yet 21 years old and has not
completed his or her college education. The

[16] *Test for Consequences:* A minor grandchild may be entitled to distribution —how would the money be handled? See powers of fiduciaries.

[17] *Write Carefully:* The words "children" and "descendants" are both used. Is the use of both words confusing? Also, note the use of "per stirpes," — at what generation does division into shares occur?

[18] *Edit and Rewrite:* Punctuation.

[19] *Test for Consequences:* Would testator want this if he survived his wife by many years? *Write Carefully:* Pictorial clarity?

[20] *Know the Law:* What is a power of appointment?[33]

Trustee shall add any undistributed net income to principal annually.

2. *Termination.* The Children's Trust shall terminate when there is no living child of mine under age 21. At termination the Trustee shall distribute the remaining principal and any accrued, undistributed net income of the Trust to my then-living descendants, per stirpes. If I have no living descendants at the termination of the Trust, the Trustee shall distribute according to Article Five, Paragraph 2. [21]

3. *Charges Against Distributive Share.* No payment of income or principal to a child prior to termination shall be charged against the share distributed to the child or the child's descendants upon termination.

Alternate Article Six
Children's Trust

1. *Division into Shares.* Upon my death the Trustee shall divide my residuary estate into equal shares, one share for each of my children who survive me and one share for the collective descendants of each child of mine who did not survive me.

2. *Distribution.* The Trustee shall immediately distribute to the beneficiary of the share, directly or according to the provisions of Article Seven paragraph — , [22] the shares of my surviving children who are at least 25 years old and the shares created for the descendants of any children who did not survive me shall be distributed per stirpes. [23]

3. *Trust Administration.* The Trustee shall hold the remaining shares in separate trusts, as follows:

a. *Periodic Payments.* The Trustee shall distribute to or for the beneficiary of each trust any part or all of the net income and principal of the trust as the Trustee deter-

---

[21] *Edit and Rewrite:* Check the reference to another section.

[22] *Edit and Rewrite:* The reference is missing.

[23] *Write Carefully:* Is the tone of this section appropriate? Could it be made easier to read?

mines from time to time to be necessary. In determining what is necessary the Trustee shall consider the beneficiary's health, need for support and education, and other resources. Any net income not distributed shall be added to principal annually.

b. *First Distribution.* When the beneficiary reaches age 21, the Trustee shall distribute to the beneficiary one-half of the then-existing principal of the trust and shall retain the rest of the trust assets.

c. *Termination.* Each trust shall terminate when the beneficiary reaches age 25 or dies before reaching age 25. At termination the Trustee shall distribute all remaining principal and income to the beneficiary or to the descendants of a deceased beneficiary, per stirpes. If a deceased beneficiary has no descendants, the Trustee shall distribute to my descendants, per stirpes. [24]

Article Seven
Powers of Fiduciaries

I give my executor and the Trustee (the "fiduciaries") [25] the following powers in addition to those granted by law:

a. To take possession of property, retain, invest in, and reinvest in any kind or amount of property even though investment in such property might violate principles of sound investment and diversification. [26]

[24] *Test for Consequences:* Who would get the money if a beneficiary died without descendants? Consider the definition of "descendants"— *see* Article One.

[25] *Know the Law:* Should the powers of both fiduciaries be in one section? Do these powers add to what is available under state law?

[26] *Test for Consequences:* This means that the fiduciary does not have to sell property that has sentimental value or that should not be sold because of market conditions.

b. [27]To deal with the estate or trust on
a fair, arm's length basis, keeping in mind
that any potential benefit from the transaction should inure to my estate or the trust
and not to the fiduciary. This includes the
right of a corporate fiduciary to deal with
its own stock and to borrow from itself. [28] If
a corporate fiduciary's own stock is part of
the trust or estate, the corporate fiduciary
shall delegate to its co-fiduciary the power
to vote such stock, or, if it is acting as
sole fiduciary, it shall vote the stock pursuant to the direction of _____. [29]

c. To enter into transactions with other fiduciaries, including executors or
trustees of estates and trusts in which the
beneficiaries have an interest and including himself as fiduciary for other estates
and trusts.

d. To sell (at public or private sale),
give options on, mortgage, exchange, lease,
dedicate, grant easements upon, and contract with respect to any real or personal
property, in any manner and for such consideration and on such terms as to cash, credit,
or otherwise, as the fiduciary believes advisable. [30]

e. To employ attorneys, appraisers,
auditors, depositories, and agents, with or
without discretionary powers, and to compensate them from principal, income, or
both. [30]

f. To exercise in person or by proxy all
voting and other rights with respect to
stocks or other securities.

g. To bring, collect, pay, contest,
compromise, settle, or abandon claims in favor of or against the estate or trust.

[27] *Classify, Organize, and Outline:* Headings would make administration easier.

[28] *Gather the Facts:* Are these powers appropriate to the client's situation? Is a cofiduciary possible?

[29] *Edit and Rewrite:* The name is missing.

[30] *Write Carefully:* Pictorial clarity; also, are all the words in the lists necessary?

     h. To make any distribution or division in cash or in kind or both (including in undivided interests in property) at values to be determined by the fiduciary. Any determination made in good faith by the fiduciary shall be final and binding on all parties even though the distributive shares may, as a result, be composed differently. [31]

     i. To borrow money for the purpose of paying any taxes or expenses of the estate or trust or for any other purpose the fiduciary deems advisable, and to encumber assets of the trust or estate to secure such debt.

     j. To repair, improve, remodel, demolish, or abandon any real or personal property. [32]

     k. To make loans or advances, to renew or extend loans and advances, and to reduce interest rates on obligations held by the trust or estate.

     l. To obtain and maintain any insurance.

     m. To establish and maintain accounting reserves for taxes, insurance, repairs, etc.

     n. To apportion and allocate receipts and expenses between principal and income.

     o. To execute and deliver any deeds, contracts, mortgages, bills of sale, or other instruments necessary or desirable for the exercise of the fiduciary's powers.

     p. To pay himself reasonable compensation for his services.

     q. To pay all packing, shipping, insurance, and other charges relative to the distribution of personal property.

     r. [33]To join with my spouse in filing

---

[31] *Test for Consequences:* This means that the fiduciary does not have to sell property that has sentimental value or that should not be sold because of market conditions. The fiduciary may also consider the tax positions of the beneficiaries in distributing assets.

[32] *Write Carefully:* Would "exchange" be included? What do the rules of interpretation say?

[33] *Write Carefully:* One sentence?

joint federal income tax returns, and to consent to have any gifts reported on any federal gift tax return filed by my spouse reported as made one-half by me to the extent permitted by the Internal Revenue Code, and to pay any part or all of the tax shown due on such returns (including deficiencies, interest, and penalties subsequently determined to be due) without reimbursement.

s. [34]The fiduciaries shall not be liable for any action or failure to act or for any loss or depreciation in value, whether due to an error in judgment or otherwise, if the fiduciary has exercised good faith and ordinary diligence in exercising his duties.

t. Except in instances of bad faith, no fiduciary shall be liable for the acts of another fiduciary.

u. Any fiduciary may from time to time delegate any or all of its powers to a successor fiduciary named in this will. Such a delegation must be in writing.

v. Any fiduciary may employ any bank or trust company, custodian, or agent, and may register or dispose of property in the name of a custodian, agent, or nominee as a fiduciary, and may pay all associated expenses.

w. Any fiduciary may accept additional property from any source and administer it as a part of a trust created by this will.

x. If at any time the value of any trust created hereunder is less than $_____ [35] the fiduciary may terminate the trust and distribute the principal and undistributed income of the trust to the beneficiary then entitled to income.

y. Any fiduciary may consolidate any trust with any other trust having the same beneficiary and substantially identical terms by terminating the trust created under this will and transferring all of its property to the other trust.

[34] *Write Carefully:* One sentence?

[35] *Test for Consequences:* Institutional fiduciaries may be unwilling to handle small amounts, or the cost may be prohibitive.

---

     z. The trustee may at any time distribute from the principal to the beneficiary any amount the trustee deems advisable to enable the beneficiary to make an unusual or nonrecurring expenditure, such as the purchase of a home or a business, or payment for a wedding or trip. [36]

     aa. [37]The "education" of a beneficiary shall include primary, secondary, and trade schools, college, university, and graduate schools, technical or other schools, and special courses of study, any or all of which may be either public or private, together with the cost of room, board, tuition, textbooks, laboratory and other fees, travel and other expenses reasonably incurred by students at the level of the beneficiary.

     bb. [38]If any property in my estate or in any trust created pursuant to this will becomes distributable to a beneficiary who is under a legal disability or under the age of 21, or if, in the sole judgment of the fiduciary, payment to a particular beneficiary is unwise or undesirable because the beneficiary may not be able to apply the distribution to the beneficiary's own best interest and advantage, then the fiduciary may make all or any part of the payment or distribution in any one or more of the following ways:

    1. to the legal representative of the beneficiary;
    2. directly to the beneficiary;
    3. to a custodian for the beneficiary under

---

[36] *Gather the Facts:* Is this consistent with client's goals?

[37] *Write Carefully:* Pictorial clarity; one sentence? Rules of interpretation: Was anything inadvertently excluded?

[38] *Test for Consequences:* Note that paragraphs bb and cc are inconsistent; both deal with distribution to a grandchild (not covered by the trust); paragraph bb also deals with distribution to an adult who, though not covered by Article Six, may not be able to manage his assets. *Write Carefully:* One sentence? Pictorial clarity? Subheadings?

the applicable Uniform Gifts to Minors
Act;

4. to an adult relative of the beneficiary;
5. by paying and applying the property for
    the benefit of the beneficiary.

The decision of a fiduciary as to the method
of distribution shall be final and binding on
all beneficiaries, and the receipt of the payee shall be sufficient discharge so that the
fiduciary need not see to the further application of the payment.

    cc. Whenever the fiduciary is directed
to distribute any money or property to a person who is then under 21 years old, the fiduciary shall hold that money or property in
trust for that person until he or she reaches
age 21. In the meantime the fiduciary shall
use part of the income and the principal of
that person's share, as the fiduciary deems
necessary, to provide for the support and education of that person. If the beneficiary
dies before reaching age 21, the property
shall be distributed to the beneficiary's
estate.

<u>Article Eight</u>
<u>Details of Administration</u>

1. *Debts and Taxes.* I direct the executor to
pay, from my residuary estate, without apportionment or reimbursement, all expenses of my
last illness and funeral, expenses of the
administration of my estate, all my just
debts, [39] and all estate, inheritance, transfer, and succession taxes (other than generation—skipping transfer taxes, which are not a
liability of my estate) including interest and
penalties, which become due because of my
death. [40]

---

[39] *Write Carefully:* "All" my "just" debts?

[40] *Test for Consequences:* Is this inconsistent with gift of real estate?

Know the Law: Would the estate otherwise be liable for all of these payments?
Write carefully: One sentence? Pictorial clarity?

2. *Survival.* No person named or described in this will shall be considered to have survived me unless he or she is living on the thirtieth (30th) day after the day of my death. [41]

3. *Insurance.* Each gift under this will shall include any prepaid existing insurance insuring against loss of the item given and any proceeds of such policies that are unpaid at my death.

4. *Spendthrift Clause.* [42] No interest under this will or under any trust created pursuant to this will shall be assignable by any beneficiary, or be subject to the claims of a beneficiary's creditors, including claims for alimony or separate maintenance.

5. *Advances.* No gift made by me during my lifetime to any beneficiary under this will shall be considered an advance against any gift under this will.

6. *Rule Against Perpetuities.* [43] Notwithstanding any other provision of this will, all trusts created pursuant to this will shall terminate, and the Trustee shall distribute each trust to the then-beneficiary, no later than 21 years after the death of my last descendant who was alive at the time of my death. [44]

7. *Challenges.* If any person takes any action to prevent the admission to probate or to contest the validity of this will, that person shall take nothing under this will. [45]

---

[41] *Write Carefully:* What are the possible problems if stated as "is living one month after my death"?

[42] *Know the Law:* What is the legal effect of a spendthrift clause in your state?

[43] *Know the Law:* Do you know what this means?

[44] *Write Carefully:* Standard form book almost always used. Why?

[45] *Know the Law:* Are "in terrorem" clauses effective in your state? May the testator choose applicable law?

8. *Choice of Law.* I direct that this will be construed and interpreted under the laws of the state of _____ in effect at my death.

I have signed this will, consisting of _____ pages, including this page, and have initialed the first _____ pages in the presence of the undersigned witnesses and have requested that the undersigned witness my signature on November 5, 19_____.

_____

Robert Kenneth

[46] We certify that in our presence on November 5, 19_____, Robert Kenneth signed the foregoing instrument and acknowledged it to be his will. We certify that in the presence of and at the request of the testator and in the presence of each other we have signed below as witnesses. We certify that we believe the testator to be of sound mind and memory and not acting under duress or constraint of any kind.

_____

_____

_____

_____

Affidavit of Witnesses [47]

We the attesting witnesses to the will of Robert Kenneth, state under oath that each of us was present and saw Robert Kenneth sign and declare as his will the instrument of which this

---

[46] *Know the Law:* Check the language under state law.

[47] *Know the Law:* Are affidavits of witnesses necessary?

affidavit is a part and that each of us believes the testator to be of sound mind and
memory and not under duress or constraint of
any kind; and that each of us attested the will
at the testator's request and in the presence
of the testator and each other.

_____

_____

_____

Subscribed and sworn to
before me this November 5, 19____

_____

notary public

WILL
OF
MARIE H. KING

[1] I, MARIE H. KING, of Springfield, Mystate,
hereby revoke all wills and codicils that I may
heretofore have made and make and declare this
to be my Last Will and Testament.
   1. I give and bequeath all my tangible personal property, including, but not limited to
my automobiles, clothing, jewelry, household
furnishings, personal effects, club memberships, books, and pictures, pursuant to an
itemized list that I have prepared and attached to this will therein designating the
distribution of said personal property. [2]

---

[1] *Classify, Organize, and Outline;*
Write Carefully: This entire
document lacks clear headings
and subheadings. Is there any
logical order to all introductory
material that precedes Article 1?

[2] *Write Carefully:* Eliminate redundancies and legalese. Should
examples be listed? *Know the
Law:* Is the list provision valid?
It attempts incorporation by
reference.

2. I have three children on the date hereof: my sons, Paul Jeffrey King and Matthew Charles King, and my daughter, Amber Leigh Dolanga.

3. Any insurance policies that provide indemnity for the loss of or damage to any of my property, and any claim that I may have at the time of my death under such policies, I bequeath, respectively to those persons who shall or would have become the owners of such property by reason of my death under the provisions of this Article or otherwise. ③

Article One

1. My executor shall pay out of that portion of my probate estate not required to satisfy any residuary④ bequests and devises under this will, without apportionment or claim for reimbursement:

(a) the expenses of my last illness and funeral, of delivering and safeguarding bequests, and the administration of my estate, including fees and expenses attributable to assets includable in my gross estate.

(b) all my enforceable debts, except any debts secured by life insurance or any real or personal property whether owned by me jointly or individually. To the extent that my executor is required to pay any such debts, my executor shall seek reimbursement from the devisee, legatee, joint owner or beneficiary of the property or life insurance, which is security for the debt.

(c) all inheritance and estate taxes (and any interest and penalties) payable by reason of my death, except for any such taxes attributable to (1) property over which I may have a power of appointment, and (2) qualified terminable interest property. ⑤

---

③ *Write Carefully:* One sentence?

④ *Test for Consequences:* Is this possible? Is it a typo? Should it be "nonresiduary"?

⑤ *Know the Law:* What is qualified terminable interest property? (*See* endnote 26, relating to federal estate tax.)

```
    2.  The foregoing provisions to the con-
trary notwithstanding, my executor shall re-
quest the trustee under the MARIE H. KING
REVOCABLE TRUST to pay any expenses, debts,
and taxes that cannot be paid out of my probate
estate without necessitating (1) the abate-
ment of any nonresiduary devise or legacy, or
(2) the sale of assets that are not readily
marketable. In any event, U.S. Treasury Bonds 6
redeemable at par in payment of Federal estate
taxes (whether held by the trustee or the ex-
ecutor) shall be used first in payment of such
tax. Any such bonds held by my executor shall
be used for the payment of the Federal estate
tax before any such bonds held by the Trustee
are used for that purpose. 7
    3.  Nothing in this will shall be deemed to
exercise any power of appointment 8 I may
have.

                   Article Two 9

    I devise and bequeath the residue of my es-
tate, excluding any property over which I have
power of appointment 10 and specifically ex-
cluding joint tenancy property, which I hold
at the time of my death with my daughter, Am-
ber, which property shall become her sole
property upon my death, to the trustee acting
at the time of my death under the trust exe-
cuted on _____, 11 prior to the execution of
this will, by me as settlor and accepted by me
as trustee and known as the MARIE H. KING
TRUST. 12 My residuary estate shall be added to
```

[6] *Know the Law:* Why are bonds mentioned?

[7] *Test for Consequences:* Check for consistency with the rest of the article.

[8] *Know the Law:* What is a power of appointment? (*See* endnote 33.) Why include this provision?

[9] *Classify, Organize, and Outline:* Pictorial clarity.

[10] *Know the Law:* Why exclude power of appointment here?

[11] *Edit and Rewrite:* Be sure that the date is inserted and that the trust is correctly identified.

[12] *Write Carefully:* Long sentences; pictorial clarity.

such trust and administered and distributed under the provisions thereof, including any amendments made pursuant to its terms at any time prior to my death. [13] To the extent that this bequest is ineffective, I hereby give and bequeath such residuary estate to Amber as trustee, to be held, administered and distributed pursuant to the terms and provisions of the said trust agreement as it exists on the date hereof, which is hereby expressly incorporated herein by reference.

Article Three [14]

1. [15]I nominate and appoint my daughter, Amber, as executor of this will.

2. My executor shall appoint an ancillary executor to act in any state where ancillary administration is necessary and where my executor for any reason fails to qualify. Any ancillary executor shall, with respect to such property subject to ancillary administration, have all the powers conferred upon my executor, which however, shall be exercised only with the approval of my executor.

3. No surety or other security shall be required on any bond furnished by my executor or ancillary executor in any jurisdiction for any purpose.

[16]4. My executor shall have, during the period of administration of my estate, the powers granted to the trustee of the trust previously described and, in addition, the following administrative and investment powers, and any others granted by law, to be exercised without order of any court as my

---

[13] *Know the Law:* Are there any state law limitations on pour-over into a trust amended between execution and death?

[14] *Classify, Organize, and Outline:* Add headings to make more visually accessible.

[15] *Gather the Facts:* Alternate choice.

[16] *Write Carefully:* Conciseness? Pictorial clarity.

---

executor determines to be in the interests of
my estate:

(a) to invest in and retain any property
as provided by the laws of Mystate relating
to investments by trustees and in force from
time to time. [17]

(b) to sell any [18], for cash or on credit, at public or private sale; to exchange
any property for any property; and to grant
options to purchase.

(c) to collect, pay, contest, compromise, or abandon claims of any kind.

(d) [19] unless otherwise provided in this
instrument, to make payments, distributions, and divisions of property in cash or
in kind on the basis of fair market values at
the time of payment, distribution, or division; in so doing, to allot undivided interests in property and to allocate different
kinds or disproportionate shares of property or interests therein; to make these and
other elections, including elections under
the tax laws, as the executor deems proper
without adjustment between principal and
income, and the executor's exercise of any
such power shall be binding on all beneficiaries.

(e) to enter into any transaction authorized by this article with fiduciaries of
trusts or estates in which any beneficiary of
my estate has any interest even though such
fiduciary is also executor hereunder.

(f) to vote all shares of stock in person
or by proxy.

5. If any property would upon receipt by the
trustee of the previously described trust be
immediately distributable to a beneficiary of
such trust, my executor may distribute such
property directly to such beneficiary. [20]

---

[17] *Test for Consequences:*
Paragraph a limits investments
to what is permitted by statute.

[18] *Edit and Rewrite:* "Property" is
the missing word.

[19] *Write Carefully:* Conciseness?
Pictorial clarity?

[20] *Write Carefully:* Is this a clear
sentence?

6. Whichever valuation date my executor elects for purposes of the Federal Estate Tax, [21] or if my executor elects to claim as a deduction for federal income tax purposes any expenditures made from my estate, no adjustment shall be made by reason of such election between the beneficiaries of my estate or of any such trust. [22]

7. Any corporate executor, if acting, shall receive compensation in accordance with its published schedule of fees in effect at the time or times its services are rendered. [Signature and witness signatures intentionally omitted. – EDS.]

MARIE H. KING REVOCABLE TRUST

I, MARIE H. KING, of Springfield, Mystate, hereby make this Declaration of Trust, which shall be known as the MARIE H. KING REVOCABLE TRUST. By acceptance of this instrument, the trustee hereinafter named agrees to administer the trust created herein according to its terms. [23]

Article One

1. I hereby transfer the property listed in Exhibit A, attached hereto and by this reference made a part hereof, to the trustee. [24]

2. I, or any other person, may transfer, by will or otherwise, any property to the trustee, to be administered as provided in this in-

---

[21] *Know the Law:* Never include a provision you do not understand.

[22] *Write Carefully:* Is this a clear sentence? Pictorial clarity.

[23] *Write Carefully:* Legalese? Are clearer headings needed throughout the entire document?

[24] *Write Carefully:* Sentence structure: What does "to the trustee" modify? Legalese. *Edit and Rewrite and Know the Law:* Check for exhibit A. Is it attached? What else needs to be done if real estate, certificates of deposit, and bank accounts appear on the list? What does it mean to "incorporate by reference" another document?

strument, and may subject the proceeds of any insurance policies to the terms of this instrument by designating the trustee as beneficiary thereof.

Article Two

I may, from time to time, revoke or amend this instrument, in whole or in part, but only by an instrument in writing (other than a will) signed and delivered to the trustee during my life.

Article Three

This instrument and the trusts created hereby shall be construed and governed by the laws of Mystate in force from time to time. [25]

Article Four [26]

The trustee shall pay to me in convenient installments during my life the income of the trust, and such portion of the principal as I may request from time to time; provided, however, that if I become incapacitated, the trustee shall, as long as such incapacity continues, pay such amounts from the income and from principal as the trustee may deem necessary and proper for the support of the group consisting of myself and my son, Matt. Any sums advanced for my son Matt shall be solely for the purposes set forth in Article 8 [27] and shall be subject to the same restrictions. The trustee may make unequal payments, which shall not be considered advancements. Any income not thus paid shall be added to the principal of the trust.

[25] *Write Carefully:* Legalese.

[26] *Classify, Organize, and Outline:* Make this more visually

accessible; work on sentence structure.

[27] *Edit and Rewrite:* Check all references to other sections.

Article Five

1. I reserve during my lifetime all rights under any insurance policies held hereunder, including[28] the rights to change[29] the beneficiary, to pledge or collect the cash surrender values, and to receive all dividends. If any policy is surrendered, or if the beneficiary of any policy is changed, this trust shall be revoked with respect to such policy upon acceptance of such surrender or change of beneficiary by the insurance company. During my lifetime, the trustee shall have no responsibility with respect to any policies except to hold any policies received in safekeeping and to deliver them upon my written request.

2. Upon being advised of my death, the trustee shall collect the proceeds of any policy on my life payable to the trustee and may exercise any available optional method of settlement. [30]

3. Payment to the trustee shall discharge the liability of the insurance company so paying, which need not see to the application of any payments. The trustee may compromise claims arising in connection with any policy, and need not engage in litigation to enforce payment without indemnification for any resulting expenses. [31]

Article Six

1. After my death, the trustee shall pay such amounts as my personal representative may request in writing for the purpose of paying all or part of the expenses of my funeral, the

---

[28] *Write Carefully:* Should this read "including" or "including but not limited to?"

[29] *Know the Law:* Under your state law, does this affect the validity of the pour-over provisions of the will?

[30] *Classify, Organize, and Outline:* This trust deals with two distinct situations: during settlor's life, and after settlor's death. Would a different organization or the use of headings make that distinction more evident?

[31] *Edit and Rewrite:* Punctuation.

administration of my estate, my debts, and federal and state death taxes. In any event, U.S. treasury bonds redeemable at par in payment of federal estate tax (whether held by the trustee or the personal representative) shall be used first in payment of such tax. [32] Any such bonds held by my personal representative shall be used for the payment of the federal estate tax before any such bonds held by the trustee are used for that purpose. The trustee may make such payments either directly or to my personal representative, without any duty to see to their application.

2. In making the payments required under this article the trustee may use proceeds of insurance on my life to the extent other assets are not available, but it shall in no event use assets otherwise excludable from my gross estate for federal estate tax purposes. [33]

Article Seven

After my death, for purposes of Article Eight, [34] the "trust estate" shall consist of the principal and any accrued and undistributed income of the trust at the time of my death plus any property added thereto by my will, or payable to the trustee by reason of my death, reduced by the payment of debts and administration expenses as provided by Article Six. [35]

---

[32] *Edit and Rewrite:* Check for consistency with the will. *Write Carefully:* Is the list of items too limiting? Would a mortgage be included as a debt? What does the parenthetical modify? Where does it belong in the sentence?

[33] *Write Carefully:* Make into two sentences?
Know the Law: Were paragraphs 1 and 2 blindly copied from a not-so-recent form? The purpose of these paragraphs is to limit estate taxes. Always check the most recent tax laws.

[34] *Edit and Rewrite:* Check references to other sections.

[35] *Write Carefully:* One sentence? Legalese?

Article Eight

1. Upon my death, the trustee shall distribute my stock in Big Chicken Corp., ElectroLaw, Inc., and LMM Corporation, and 300 shares of Midland Motors, [36] whether already in the trust or received by the trustee pursuant to my will, to my son PAUL J. KING.

2. I record that I have made no specific provisions hereunder for my daughter, AMBER, because certain property held in joint tenancy with her during my life shall constitute her share of my estate. I further record[37] that the joint tenancy property was specifically titled with her to accomplish my wish that the property transfer to her upon my death and was not titled in joint tenancy merely for convenience's sake.

3. [38]All of the remainder of the estate, after the payment of expenses under Article Seven (which expenses shall be paid out of this portion of the trust estate) shall be held in trust as the MATTHEW CHARLES KING TRUST upon the terms and conditions as follow[39]:

  (a) all funds shall be held in trust throughout Matthew's lifetime and be administered pursuant to the terms and conditions hereof.

  (b) all funds allocated to the trust are to be administered by the trustee solely for the benefit of my son, Matthew, except as provided in subparagraph (e).

[36] *Test for Consequences:* What if the names changed? What if there is no Midland Motors stock in the trust or estate when King dies?

[37] *Write Carefully:* Watch word choice —"record" — is it necessary at all?

[38] *Edit and Rewrite:* Check reference. Is it clear that paragraph 3 is to occur after the settlor dies? Why create a new trust with a new name? Is it unnecessarily confusing? *Write Carefully:* Break this into several sentences.

[39] *Classify, Organize, and Outline:* Make this visually accessible.

Matthew is a disabled veteran and the express purpose of this trust is to provide for his extra and supplemental needs, over and above the benefits he otherwise receives as a result of his disability from any governmental source or private agency that provides services or benefits to disabled people. For example, the trustee may purchase those goods or services that would enhance Matthew's comfort and happiness, including, but not limited to: entertainment items (such as a television, VCR, or the like); evaluations of supplementary therapy programs or services; transportation to visit relatives; and the like — all to the extent not otherwise provided. Anything to the contrary herein notwithstanding, no income or principal shall be paid to or expended for the benefit of Matthew as long as there are sufficient monies available to him for his care, comfort, and welfare from federal, state, and local governmental agencies and departments. The trustee shall consider such governmental funds in determining whether there are other funds available to the beneficiary from sources other than the trust estate and shall use trust assets only to supplement and never to substitute for such funds. In no event may trust income or principal be paid to or for the benefit of a governmental agency or department, and the trust estate shall at all times be free of the claims of such governmental bodies. 40

(c) Because of Matthew's disability, the trustee is directed to purchase goods and services on his behalf and not to distribute cash to him. In purchasing goods and services for Matthew the trustee is to avoid duplication of benefits provided for him by governmental entities and to limit expenditures to supplemental goods and services.

40 *Classify, Organize, and Outline:*
How does this paragraph fit into
the scheme of subparagraphs
3(a) and 3(b)?

Write Carefully: Legalese;
pictorial clarity; parallelism.

[41](d) Until the termination of this trust, the trustee shall expend for the benefit of Matthew so much or all of the net income and principal as the trustee determines from time to time to be necessary for Matthew's supplemental needs, evaluated after considering the other benefits Matthew receives from governmental sources. Any undistributed net income shall be added to principal. At no time and under no circumstances shall Matthew have the right to demand income or principal from this trust.

(e) If, at the time that my grandchildren reach college age, the trust principal exceeds its initial value either by virtue of appreciation or by additions from undistributed income, the trustee is authorized to spray net income not needed for Matthew's care to pay for any grandchild's college expenses and to invade principal[42] if necessary for such purposes. [43]

(f) Upon Matthew's death, the trustee shall distribute the remaining principal equally to my grandchildren. [44]

4. Except as otherwise provided in this instrument, if any person entitled to distribution has not attained the age of twenty one years or is incapacitated, his or her share shall vest[45] in him or her but the trustee may

[41] *Know the Audiences:*
Think about who is to act
as successor trustee. Who are
the grandchildren? Might this
create a conflict? (Amber, *see*
Article Ten; Amber's children,
see Article Nine; *compare* d.
and e. of this Article.)

[42] *Test for Consequences:* Should
there be limits on invading
principal?

[43] *Write Carefully:* Must all
grandchildren be college age?

Word choice —"spray"?
Break this into more than one
sentence? Enumerate? Tabulate?

[44] *Test for Consequences:* If
a grandchild predeceased
Matthew, leaving children,
should those children be entitled
to shares?

[45] *Know the Law:* What does it
mean that the share shall
"vest"?

distribute the share to a custodian under any
Uniform Transfer to Minors Act, or, in the
trustee's discretion, the trustee may retain
the share in trust until he or she reaches such
age or such incapacity is removed. In the meantime, the trustee shall pay to or for the benefit of such person as much or all of the net
income and principal of the retained trust as
the trustee considers necessary for his or her
support and education, and may add to principal any income not so expended. If the person
dies prior to final distribution, the entire
trust shall be distributed to his or her estate. [46]

Article Nine [47]

1. For all purposes under this instrument:
   (a) adoption of a child shall have the
same effect as if such child had been born to
the adopting parents, but only if such child
was a minor at the time of the adoption.
   (b) the word "spouse" includes a widow
or widower.
   (c) except where distribution is directed to the "descendants per stirpes" of
a person, the word "descendants" includes
descendants of every degree, whenever born,
whether or not a parent or more remote ancestor of such descendant is living. Where distribution is directed to any person's
descendants per stirpes who are living at a
designated point of time, the stirpes shall
begin with the children of such person,
whether or not any child of his is then living. [48]

---

[46] *Write Carefully:* Break into several sentences? Pictorial clarity.

Write Carefully: Check each provision for sentence structure and pictorial clarity.

[47] *Classify, Organize, and Outline:* Would subheadings help Article Nine? Do all provisions under this article really belong together?

[48] *Know the Audiences:* Can beneficiaries and trustee understand this? Is it necessary?

(d) a person shall be considered "incapacitated" (1) if and as long as he is adjudicated disabled because he is unable to manage his estate or financial matters or (2) if two doctors familiar with his condition certify to the trustee in writing that the person is unable to transact ordinary business, and until there is a like certification to the trustee that such incapacity has ended.

(e) where appropriate, words of the masculine gender include the feminine and words used in a plural or collective sense include the singular and vice versa.

(f) the word "trustee" includes any successor trustee or trustees.

(g) except as otherwise provided in this instrument, income accrued or collected but not distributed at the termination of any beneficial interest hereunder shall be treated as if it had accrued or been collected after the termination of such interest. The trustee may charge any such income with any accrued taxes, expenses, or compensation that it considers proper.

(h) in determining what amounts are necessary for the support of any person, the trustee shall take into account (1) the standard of living to which such person is accustomed; (2) his obligation, if any, to support others; (3) the obligation, if any, and the ability of others to support him; and (4) other income available for his support so far as is known to the trustee.

49 (i) whenever the trustee deems it to be in the best interests of a beneficiary to whom the trustee is directed or authorized to pay income or principal, the trustee may distribute such income or principal in any one or more of the following ways, and the

---

49 *Edit and Rewrite:* Check for consistency or redundancy — *see* Article Eight, paragraph 4.

trustee shall not be required to see to the
application of any distribution made: directly to the beneficiary; to a legally appointed guardian or conservator of the
beneficiary; to a custodian for the beneficiary under any Uniform Transfers to Minors
Act; to an adult relative; to anyone with
whom the beneficiary is residing; to any person acting as the beneficiary's attorney in
fact under a durable power of attorney.

(j) in determining whether any testamentary power of appointment has been exercised, the trustee may rely on an instrument
admitted to probate in any jurisdiction as
the Will of the donee of the power. If the
trustee has no written notice of the existence of such a will within three (3) months
after the death of the donee of the power, the
trustee may assume that the donee died intestate. This paragraph shall not limit any
right of any person against anyone to whom
the trustee has distributed property in reliance thereon. [50]

(k) the terms "gross estate" and "taxable estate" refer to the amounts described
by these terms in the Internal Revenue Code
in force from time to time.

(l) the word "persons" includes corporations.

(m) if any distribution, other than a
distribution made pursuant to a power of
withdrawal or appointment, is a taxable distribution for generation-skipping tax purposes, the trustee may, out of the principal
of the trust from which the distribution is
made, either pay any tax attributable to the
distribution or increase the distribution
to the extent determined by the trustee to be
sufficient to enable the distributee to pay
any such tax. In the event of a taxable ter-

[50] *Write Carefully:* Is the last
sentence of subparagraph j
clear?

mination for generation–skipping purposes,
the trustee shall, out of the principal of
the trust or share to which such termination
relates, pay any tax attributable to the
termination without compensating adjust-
ments. [51]

2. No interest in income or principal in any
trust under this instrument shall be assignable by any voluntary or involuntary act of a
beneficiary or by operation of law, nor shall
any such interest be liable to be taken for any
obligation, including any obligation to pay
alimony, of any beneficiary.

3. Anything in this instrument to the contrary notwithstanding, each trust under this
instrument which is still in existence twenty-
one (21) years after the death of the last to
die of myself and all the beneficiaries hereunder living at the date this instrument becomes irrevocable shall terminate and the
trustee shall distribute the trust to the
then–beneficiary or beneficiaries.

4. I have three children now living, Paul
Jeffrey King, Matthew Charles King, and Amber
Leigh Dolanga. I have one grandchild now liv-
ing, Kyla Jessica Dolanga.

Article Ten

1. I shall act as trustee under this instrument. Upon my death or if I resign or become incapacitated, I name my daughter, Amber, as
successor trustee. I give my daughter the
right to designate in writing persons or corporations to act as successor trustee in the
event that she is, at any time, unable or unwilling to serve.

[52]2. Any trustee may resign or release any
powers conferred by this instrument by giving
thirty (30) days' written notice to all adult
income beneficiaries. For purposes of this Article, any person who is 18 years of age or over

---

[51] *Know the Law:* Do you fully understand this provision? Do not blindly copy form language.

[52] *Classify, Organize, and Outline:* Make this more visually accessible.

---

and is not incapacitated and to whom the trustee is then directed or authorized to pay income is an adult income beneficiary. [53] If there is no such beneficiary, written notice shall be given to the legal guardian or conservator, if any, or if none, to a near adult relative of each minor or incapacitated income beneficiary. A majority of the persons entitled to such notice may remove a corporate trustee upon giving thirty days' written notice to such corporate trustee, fill any vacancy caused by the resignation or removal of a corporate trustee, and, without liability to themselves, approve the accounts of and release any trustee ceasing to act for any reason. Such approval and release shall be binding upon all persons with the same effect as though such accounts were approved by a court of competent jurisdiction, but shall not enlarge or shift the beneficial interest of any beneficiary. Each successor trustee appointed to fill a vacancy caused by the resignation or removal of a corporate trustee shall be another corporation, organized under the laws of the United States or any state thereof, having a capital and surplus of not less than $2,000,000.

3. Without any conveyance or order of court, any successor trustee shall have all the powers granted to the original trustee and shall assume all the duties imposed upon the original trustee. No successor trustee shall have any responsibility to inquire into the acts of any predecessor trustee. Any person may, without liability, rely on the written certification of a successor trustee that such successor trustee has been duly appointed and has power to act.

[54]4. Except as otherwise provided in this

---

[53] *Write Carefully:* Check the sentence structure.

[54] *Write Carefully:* Check sentence structure and pictorial clarity for all of paragraph 4.

Classify, Organize, and Outline: Headings and subheadings for all of paragraph 4.
Know the Law: Is there any Uniform Trustees Act in your jurisdiction that affects paragraph 4?

instrument, the trustee shall have the following administrative and investment powers, and any others granted by law, with respect to each trust created by this instrument, to be exercised without order of any court as the trustee determines to be in the best interests of the beneficiaries:

(a) to invest in any property or interest in property, foreign or domestic, without being limited by any statute or rule of law concerning investments by trustees, including, without limiting the generality of the foregoing, bonds, debentures, mortgages, notes (secured or unsecured), common or preferred stock, interests in common trust funds, interests in mutual funds, partnerships, limited partnerships, joint venture, oil, gas, or other mineral interests, commodities, commodity futures, financial instrument futures, and real estate;

(b) to sell any property, for cash or on credit, at public or private sale; to exchange any property for other property; and to grant options to purchase;

(c) to make loans to any person, including any beneficiary;

(d) to borrow money, either from the banking department of the named corporate trustee or from others, and to mortgage or pledge any property, even though the obligation incurred may extend beyond the termination of any trust;

[55](e) to vote any corporate stock, either in person or by proxy, with or without power of substitution, except that if the possession of this power as to any security would adversely affect the issuing company or the trustee's ability to retain or vote such security, the trustee shall vote such

[55] *Know the Law:* What does the paragraph mean?

security as directed by the income beneficiary or beneficiaries of the trust in which
such security is held;

(f) to unite with the owners of other securities in carrying out any plan for the reorganization of any corporation; to deposit
securities in accordance with any such plan;
and to pay any expenses that may be required
with reference to any such plan;

(g) to hold any asset in the name of a
nominee, in bearer form or otherwise, without disclosure of any fiduciary relationship;

(h) to purchase liability and casualty
insurance of any kind for the protection of
the trust estate, including comprehensive
liability insurance;

(i) to determine in a fair and equitable
manner, in cases not covered by statute in
force at the time of the determination, how
receipts and disbursements shall be cred-
ited or charged between income and principal; and to set aside reasonable reserves for
depreciation and depletion;

(j) to collect, pay, contest, compromise, or abandon claims of any kind, and to
execute instruments containing covenants
and warranties creating a charge against any
assets held by, and excluding any personal
liability of, the trustee;

(k) unless otherwise provided in this
instrument, to make payments, distributions
and divisions of property in cash or in kind
on the basis of fair market values at the time
of payment, distribution, or division; in so
doing, to allot undivided interests in property and to allocate different kinds or
disproportionate shares of property or interests therein; to make these and other
elections, including elections that the
trustee may make under the tax law as the
trustee deems proper without adjustment between principal and income or with respect to
depreciation in the value of property; the
trustee's exercise of any such power shall be
binding on all beneficiaries;

(l) to terminate any trust under this
instrument having a value of less than Twen-

ty-Five Thousand Dollars ($25,000) and dis-
tribute the trust to the income beneficiary,
or, if there is more than one, to my descendants, per stirpes, living at the date of
termination, or, if no descendant of mine is
then living, to the income beneficiaries in
equal shares; [56]

(m) to make joint investments for any
two or more trusts hereunder;

(n) to consolidate into a single trust
any trust arising out of this instrument with
any other trust, arising under this or any
other instrument, which has the same provisions, beneficiaries, and trustee;

(o) to pay all reasonable expenses of
administration, including compensation to
the trustee and to the persons employed by
the trustee, including agents, auditors,
accountants, and attorneys. Any corporate
trustee, if at any time acting, is authorized
to receive compensation in accordance with
its published schedule of fees in effect at
the time or times its services are rendered;

(p) to enter into any transaction authorized by this Article with fiduciaries of
trusts or estates in which any beneficiary
hereunder has an interest, even though such
fiduciary is also a fiduciary hereunder.

(q) to transfer the situs of the trust
estate to some other place; and in so doing,
to resign and appoint a substitute trustee
who may delegate any or all trustee powers to
the appointing trustee as agent, and to remove any substitute trustee appointed pursuant to this subparagraph at any time and
appoint another, including the appointing
trustee;

(r) to reduce the interest rate on any
mortgage; to consent to the modification or
release of any guaranty of any mortgage; to
continue mortgages upon and after maturity
with or without renewal or extension, and to

[56] *Test for Consequences:* What results are possible given Marie King's situation? How might I. affect Matthew's disability benefits. (*See* Article 8, paragraph 3.)

foreclose any mortgage and to purchase the mortgaged property or acquire it by deed from the mortgagor without foreclosure;

(s) with respect to real estate: to make leases and to grant options to lease for terms of any length, even though the terms may extend beyond the termination of any trust; to grant or release easements and other interests; to enter into party wall agreements, to develop and subdivide; to dedicate parks, streets, and alleys; to vacate any subdivision or alley; to construct, repair, alter, remodel, demolish, or abandon improvements; and to take any other action reasonably necessary for the preservation of the property or the income therefrom;

[57] (t) with respect to real and tangible personal property not located in the state of administration: if the trustee is unable or unwilling to act, to appoint an individual or another corporation as trustee who (1) shall have all of the powers of the appointing trustee, (2) shall not, unless required by law, make periodic judicial accounting, but shall furnish the appointing trustee with semi-annual statements, and (3) may delegate any or all trust powers, to the appointing trustee; to require any trustee so appointed to remit to the appointing trustee the income and net proceeds of any sale of any property; and to remove any trustee appointed pursuant to this paragraph at any time and to appoint another, including the appointing trustee;

(u) with respect to farm property: to lease on shares; to purchase and sell farm equipment and produce of all kinds; to engage agents, managers, and employees and delegate power to them; and to perform such acts

[57] *Know the Law and Write Carefully:* If there is a statutory requirement of accounting, which can be waived, does this language clearly waive it, or could it be considered ambiguous?

as the trustee deems appropriate, using such methods as are commonly employed by other farm owners in the community in which the farm property is located;

(v) with respect to interests in oil, gas, and other minerals: to drill, mine, and otherwise operate for the development of oil, gas, and other minerals; to enter into contracts relating to the installation and operation of absorption and repressuring plants; to enter into utilization or pooling agreements for any purpose including primary or secondary recovery; to place and maintain pipe lines and telephone and telegraph lines; to execute oil, gas, and mineral leases, division and transfer orders, grants, and other instruments; and to perform such other acts as the trustee deems appropriate, using such methods as are commonly employed by owners of such interests in the community in which the interests are located;

(w) with respect to proprietorship interests: to continue the business and participate in its management by having the trustee or one or more agents of the trustee act as a manager with appropriate compensation from the business; to incorporate the business, and to make secured or unsecured loans to the business or to pledge property for the debts of the business;

(x) with respect to partnership interests: to continue in the business and participate in its management by having the trustee or one or more agents of the trustee act as a general partner, limited partner, or employee with appropriate compensation from the business; to enter into new partnership agreements or to incorporate the business; to increase the investment in the business and to make secured or unsecured loans to the partnership or to pledge property for the debts of the business; and to waive the filing by the surviving partners of any partnership inventory, appraisal, account, bond, or security — in no event shall the trustee individual be subject to any liability of the partnership;

(y) with respect to closely held stock:
to retain any closely held stock even though
it may constitute all or a large proportion
of the trust estate; to participate in the
conduct of any business of the corporation by
which such stock was issued; to vote any such
stock in person or by proxy for the election
of directors of the corporation, including
voting for persons who may be agents or employees of the trustee; to permit any directors who are agents or employees of the
trustee to act as officers of the corporation
and, as directors, to vote for the payment of
reasonable compensation to themselves as
directors or officers and concerning all
matters relating to the policies or management of the corporation; to participate in
any reorganization, merger, consolidation,
recapitalization, liquidation, or dissolution of the corporation or any change in the
nature of the business of the corporation; to
invest additional capital from the trust estate in the corporation; to make secured or
unsecured loans from the trust estate to the
corporation; to guarantee loans to the corporation; to pledge trust property for the
payment of its debts; to extend credit to the
corporation in the trustee's corporate capacity; to make any decision or exercise any
discretion that the trustee believes to be in
the corporation's best interest, and in any
case where the trustee determines that there
may be a possible conflict between the interests of the trust beneficiaries and the corporate interests of the business and its
stockholders or other owners, the interest
of the trust beneficiaries should be considered subordinate; and in the exercise of any
power granted in this subparagraph, to be
held to such standards as are common in the
general business community. [58]

[58] *Classify, Organize, and Outline:*
Add headings and subheadings.

5. The foregoing powers may be exercised for a reasonable period after the termination of any trust.

6. No person paying money or delivering any property to the trustee need see to its application, and no person dealing with the trustee shall be obligated to inquire into the terms of this instrument or the necessity of expediency of any act of the trustee. 59

7. No surety or other security shall be required on any bond furnished by any trustee in any jurisdiction for any purpose.

IN WITNESS WHEREOF, the Settlor and Trustee have hereunto signed their respective names and affixed their respective seals 60 this _____ day of _____, 19___. 61

_____
MARIE H. KING, SETTLOR

ACCEPTED BY:

_____
MARIE H. KING, TRUSTEE

Sworn to and subscribed before me by MARIE H. KING this _____ day of _____ 19___.

_____
Notary Public

---

59 *Write Carefully:* Sentence structure.

60 *Know the Law:* Seals?

61 *Write Carefully:* Legalese.

Notes

1. *E.g.*, fourteen states adopted the Uniform Trustees' Powers Act, *see, e.g.*, Ariz. Rev. Stat. Ann. §§14-7231–14-7237 (1991). Fifteen states adopted the Uniform Probate Code, in some cases with substantial changes, *e.g.*, Me. Rev. Stat. Ann. tit. 18-A, §§1-101–8-401 (West 1979). Six states adopted the Uniform Trusts Act, *e.g.*, N.M. Stat. Ann. §46-2-1 (Michie 1978). Two states adopted the Uniform Statutory Will Act. Uniform Statutory Will Act, 8A U.L.A. 385 (1984); *see, e.g.*, Mass. Gen. L. ch. 191B, §1-15 (1987).

2. A testator is "one who makes or has made a testament or will; one who dies having a will." Black's Law Dictionary 1475 (6th ed. 1990). The terms "testator" and "executor" are used in this chapter to refer to either a man or a woman acting in those capacities. Although no longer favored, some lawyers use the terms testatrix and executrix to refer to women.

3. If the will identifies the person who will perform these functions, the person is generally called an executor. If the court appoints a person not named in the instrument, the person may be called an administrator. The Uniform Probate Code uses the term "personal representative." The term executrix, once used to refer to a female executor, is no longer favored.

4. *See, e.g.*, Uniform Probate Code §§3-502–3-504, 8 U.L.A. 1 (1975) (supervised administration of the estate under the authority of the court) (hereinafter U.P.C.).

5. Black's Law Dictionary 258 (6th ed. 1990).

6. *E.g.*, 755 ILCS 5/4-7 (1993) [At the time of this writing, the statutory compilations in Illinois have been changed from "Ill. Rev. Stat." to "ILCS." Since there is not yet an official Uniform System of Citation style for this new compilation, we have used "ILCS" consistently throughout this book. — Eds.]; Cal. Prob. Code §6120 (West 1991).

7. For a discussion of federal estate tax, *see infra* note 26.

8. For a discussion of the functions of a guardian, *see* Jerome A. Manning, Estate Planning 169-172 (1988).

9. An explanation of an omission may, at least, establish that the omission was not accidental, based on incorrect assumptions, or that the testator was not the victim of undue influence. In some states, under "pretermitted child" statutes, a child born after execution of a will may claim a share of the estate unless the will states that the exclusion was intended, even if nothing was left to other children. *See, e.g.*, U.P.C. §2-302(a). In some states even children alive when the will was executed must be specifically mentioned to avoid an assumption of accidental oversight. Okla. Stat. tit. 84, §132 (1990).

10. The U.P.C. allows the testator to select the applicable law. U.P.C. §2-506. The Uniform Probate of Foreign Wills Act provides that a will may be valid if it complies with the law of the jurisdiction where probate proceedings are to occur, the law of the jurisdiction where it was executed, or the law of the testator's domicile at the time of her death. Uniform Probate of Foreign Wills Act §§1, 5, 8A U.L.A. 543, 551 (1950).

11. For a general discussion of types of wills and formal requirements, *see* Dan E. McConaughey, Wills: The Truth About Probate 16-23, 34-43 (1984).

12. *Id.* at 17-19.

13. *Id.* at 20-22.

14. Many, but not all, states have adopted the Uniform Probate of Foreign Wills Act or an equivalent law, which states that a will is admissible to probate if the will complies with the laws of: the state where it was executed, the state of testator's domicile at the

time of execution, the state of testator's domicile at death, or the state of probate. *See* U.P.C. §2-506.

15. U.P.C. §2-504.

16. U.P.C. §3-605.

17. *See, e.g.,* Model Code of Professional Responsibility EC 5-5, 5-6 (1981); Model Rules of Professional Conduct Rule 1.5(d)(1) (1983); Illinois Rules of Professional Conduct Rule 1.8(c) (1993).

18. U.P.C. §3-719.

19. *E.g.,* Estate of Blacksill, 602 P.2d 511 (Ariz. Ct. App. 1979); Estate of Barker, 448 So. 2d 28 (Fla. Dist. Ct. App. 1984); Gustafson v. Svenson, 366 N.E.2d 761 (Mass. 1977); State, Fish & Game Commn. v. Keller, 568 P.2d 166 (Mont. 1977); Matter of Rutherford, 508 N.Y.S.2d 596 (App. Div. 1986). *But see,* In re Will of Goldstein, 363 N.Y.S.2d 147 (App. Div. 1975); In re Estate of Gibbs, 111 N.W.2d 413 (Wis. 1961).

20. *See, e.g.,* 755 ILCS 5/2-1(a). *Compare* U.P.C. §2-102 (spouse receives entire estate if children of decedent are also children of spouse; different rules apply if there are children from prior marriages).

21. U.P.C. §2-301; Wanda Ellen Wakefield, Annotation, *What Constitutes Transfer Outside the Will Precluding Surviving Spouse from Electing Statutory Share Under Uniform Probate Code §2-301,* 11 A.L.R.4th 1213 (1982). Community property states do not provide for a forced share because the surviving spouse has a one-half interest in all of the community property. At least one state provides for a statutory forced share for children under 23 and handicapped adult children. *E.g.,* La. Civ. Code Ann. art. 1493 (West Supp. 1993).

22. For a general discussion of persons who can make a will, *see* McConaughey, *supra* note 11, at 30-33.

23. "Per stirpes" means that living descendants represent a deceased ancestor and divide the share of that ancestor. *See* John Ritchie, Neill H. Alford & Richard W. Effland, Cases and Materials on Decedent's Estates and Trusts 88-111 (6th ed. 1982).

24. The majority of intestacy statutes adopt this rule. *See, e.g.,* U.P.C. §2-106.

25. William M. McGovern, Sheldon F. Kurtz & Jan Ellen Rein, Wills, Trusts and Estates (1988). Historically, the term, "per capita," when used alone, referred to a scheme of distribution in which all takers were treated equally regardless of generation. More recently, this scheme of distribution is infrequently used and the term, even when used alone, is often read to mean per capita with representation.

26. In some will forms the residuary estate is divided into two trusts, with no outright distribution to the surviving spouse, to avoid federal estate tax. Assets left to a surviving spouse are exempt from taxation under the marital deduction. There is also a $600,000 exemption for assets left to persons other than a spouse (the unified credit). If assets are left to the spouse outright, they avoid taxation in the first estate but may be taxed (to the extent that they exceed $600,000) as part of the estate of the second spouse to die. If the surviving spouse leaves the assets to a new spouse, taxation is avoided, but the assets may leave the family.

The two-trust scheme takes advantage of both exemptions while maximizing the probability that assets will stay in the family. One trust is funded with an amount that takes advantage of the unified credit. Normally, the surviving spouse is given the right to income for life and a right to principal under defined circumstances. Upon the death of the second spouse, the trust is distributed to descendants. Although the second spouse to die has had the benefit of the assets until death, the assets do not go through the second estate and stay in the family. The second trust, containing the balance of the assets, takes advantage of the marital deduction by giving the surviving spouse more extensive rights in the assets.

One of the rights the spouse is given is a power of appointment, which is a right to determine who will receive the trust assets upon the second spouse's death. If the spouse does not exercise that power, the assets never become part of his estate and pass directly to those named in the will of the first spouse, generally descendants, thereby taking advantage of the second spouse's unified credit. In this way, the assets stay in the family while avoiding a layer of taxation. The property given to the spouse is called "qualified terminable interest property." Consider the possible implications of a survival clause or of a statutory assumption that if there is no proof that the spouses did not die simultaneously, each survived his/her spouse for purposes of his/her own will. Because these assumptions could destroy the tax scheme, some marital trust wills contain provisions reversing the simultaneous death presumption. *See* I.R.C. §§2010, 2523f (1988).

27.   Restatement (Second) of Conflicts §§240, 263 (1971).

28.   Reciprocal wills are occasionally called "mutual wills." But a joint will is also sometimes called a "joint and *mutual* will." The term "mutual" has a different meaning in each of these two contexts. Only in the second context does "mutual" mean mutuality of contract as typified by a joint will.

29.   McConaughey, *supra* note 11, at 16-17.

30.   If a will does not provide for an alternate disposition in the event that a beneficiary dies before the testator or does not live for the required survival period, the gift may "lapse" and become part of the residuary estate. Whether the gift will lapse or go to the descendants of the named recipient may depend on the relationship between the testator and the named recipient. State laws vary.

For some testators, for tax reasons, use of a survival clause is inappropriate for some gifts. *See supra* note 26. If a survival clause is not included, consider the possibility of simultaneous death. Examine your state's law and determine what impact it would have on property ownership and on tax liability.

Another consideration is how to define "survival." If you do not define the term, state law will govern. Some states define the term in its ordinary sense; others state time requirements. The Uniform Probate Code requires survival for 120 hours. U.P.C. §2-104. A testator may want a longer period, to avoid allowing the named recipient's will to govern disposition or to provide for desired tax consequences. If you include a survival clause, be precise in defining how the time will be calculated, be sure you understand the tax implications, and think about its impact on the probate process.

31.   U.P.C. §2-512.

32.   *See* Uniform Testamentary Additions to Trusts Act §§1-6, 8A U.L.A. 603 (1960, 1983); *see also* U.P.C. §2-511.

33.   A power of appointment "is a power created or reserved by a person (the donor) having property subject to his disposition, enabling the donee of the power to designate, within such limits as the donor may prescribe, the transferees of the property or the shares in which it [will] be received." Restatement of Property §318-(1) (1940); *see generally* 5 William J. Bowe & Douglas H. Parker, Page on the Law of Wills §§45.1-45.25 (1962). If a client does wish to exercise a power of appointment, consult state law and the document that created the power. Very specific language may be necessary. For an example of why a person might be given a power of appointment and why many wills specify that no power is exercised, *see supra* note 26.

CHAPTER **5**

Drafting Contracts

A. *Introduction*

Contracts are like people. No two are alike. Each one serves different functions for different parties. The variety partly arises from the fact that many contracts are negotiated, unlike pleadings or wills.[1] As a result, contracts tend to be collaborative ventures in which one attorney submits a draft, and the other attorney then reviews the draft to suggest changes. Successive drafts may be exchanged repeatedly until both parties are satisfied. Of course, the parties may not have equal bargaining power, or time may limit this negotiation process. However, in theory at least, contracts are negotiable.

As a result of this process of negotiation, you may find yourself constrained by your opponent's views and your client's desire to make the deal. Lawyers who insist on creating an entirely one-sided contract often risk losing the deal altogether. On the other hand, lawyers who capitulate on every issue leave their clients unprotected. Hence, when you draft a contract you must be both an adversary and a mediator at the same time. In contrast, when you draft pleadings and wills, you act primarily as an advocate, so you and your client are free to exercise your joint judgment to pursue the client's interests free from contrary views of how the document should be drafted.

Nevertheless, drafting contracts is similar to drafting other kinds of documents. Contracts, like wills and legislation, are flexible and relatively unconstrained. Although a number of statutes and common law rules limit the extent of contracts, many of the rules can be varied by agreement. Indeed, many legal rules merely operate as default provisions that establish the result if the parties fail to agree. For example, the Uniform Partnership Act provides that if the partnership dissolves, the partners split the remaining profits equally.[2] That result can be changed, however, by the partnership agreement. In the contract, the partners can agree that the senior partner gets 60 percent of the profits on dissolution and that all junior partners then share the remaining 40 percent equally. Therefore, flexible contracts enable the parties to be creative in fashioning results tailored to their particular needs.

In addressing those needs, you can choose among a variety of different ways to structure a deal. For example, if your client is starting a new venture, she might want to choose a general partnership, a limited partnership, a joint venture, a not-for-profit corporation, a closely held corporation, or a publicly traded corporation. You need to know your client's needs as well as the advantages and disadvantages of each legal structure in order to advise your client. You should not focus on a single kind of transaction until you have considered all the options.

Frequently, you need to draft several different documents for a single transaction. For instance, for a simple real estate sale, you might need a broker's listing agreement, a real estate sales contract, a deed, a title policy, an affidavit of title, a bill of sale, and a closing statement. Part of your job is to determine what needs to be done to complete the transaction. Accordingly, drafting contracts requires you to exercise a great deal of initiative in finding out about the various options and requirements.

When drafting most contracts, like wills and legislation, you must look to the future to try to predict unforeseen consequences and adapt the document to meet them. Other contracts, however, are more like pleadings in that they memorialize a transaction that already has occurred.

B.   Parts of a Contract

Because contracts are so varied, no two look exactly alike. Despite this variation, there is a common organization to most contracts, regardless of content. Although you usually will not begin to organize your document until later in the drafting process, it may be helpful to begin with step 4 and to consider the parts of a contract now. Even though contracts need not be organized in any particular form, contracts typically are divided into six parts: the identification, the recitals, the statement of consideration, the body, the signatures, and the acknowledgments.

1.   Identification

The identification section gives the crucial background information necessary to identify the contract, including the date,[3] the names and possibly the addresses of the parties, and a description of the contract topic. For example, the identification section of an employment contract might read:

EMPLOYMENT AGREEMENT

This agreement is made August 29, 1992, between The Inventive Company, Inc. ("TIC") and Imogene B. Smart ("Smart").

Properly identifying the parties is crucial. It must be clear from the outset who is bound to do what for whom. Remember that "party of the first part" and "party of the second part" are appropriate only in Marx Brothers' movies. There is no need for any confusing titles. The best way to identify the parties is by name. Indicate how the party will be identified throughout the rest of the contract in parentheses following the name: Charles Chaplin, ("Chaplin"). If two or more of the parties have the same last name, or if it is a form contract, use a brief description instead of the name: Charles Chaplin ("Seller") and Oona Chaplin ("Buyer"). For a corporation, use either an acronym or a significant word from the formal business name: International Business Machines, Inc. ("IBM") and McDonald's, Inc. ("McDonald's"). Once the parties have been identified, be consistent. Always refer to the same party the same way to avoid confusion.

2.   Recitals

The recitals come next. These are the preliminary statements that briefly define the purposes of the contract, the intent of the parties, or the assumed facts. In older documents, the recitals were introduced by the word "whereas," but most modern contracts omit this meaningless term. Recitals in an employment contract might read:

> TIC invents and manufactures kitchen equipment. Employees have access to a number of inventions prior to patenting and to other trade secrets, which TIC wishes to protect. Smart is a designer who wishes to become a TIC employee.

Officially, recitals are not part of the contract. Accordingly, anything crucial should be restated in the body of the agreement. Be especially careful to examine recitals of fact. If factual statements amount to warranties or conditions, they should be made expressly in the body of the document.[4] Although recitals may be contractual second-class citizens, they serve a useful purpose. Frequently, a court will examine the recitals to determine the intent of the parties.[5] Consequently, recitals should help resolve ambiguities, not create them. So be sure your recitals are consistent with the primary contract provisions. If the terms vary, the main contract will control,[6] even when the recitals are broader in scope.[7]

3.   Consideration

After the recitals, most contracts recite the consideration. All contracts must be supported by adequate consideration in order to be enforceable.[8] Although clients sometimes want the amount of consideration to be kept private, especially in publicly recorded documents, in most instances it is wise to state the full, actual consideration. If a client does request confidentiality, do not state a fictitious amount. In many states mutual promises are sufficient.[9] A statement of consideration might read simply:

> Accordingly, TIC and Smart mutually agree: . . .

4. Body

The body of the contract comes next, setting forth the actual terms of the contract. These terms are usually divided into various headings and subheadings to make the agreement clear.

5. Signatures

The signatures immediately follow the body of the contract. Do not place them on a separate page. Otherwise it may appear that the parties never read the contract. In order to guard against accusations of later amendments, you may want to have the parties initial the bottom of each page when they sign the contract. If any changes are made at the time of execution, the changes should be initialed by both parties. Individuals should sign their names as they are written in the identification section. Corporate signatures should comply with appropriate state law and may require a corporate seal, attestation by more than one officer, or other formalities.

6. Acknowledgments

For most purposes, your broad sketch of the contract is now complete. Occasionally, you need to add an acknowledgment. An acknowledgment is a statement to the effect that the parties have read the contract and voluntarily signed it. Usually the acknowledgment is notarized.

Recorded documents must be acknowledged.[10] For example, when a purchaser buys land under articles of agreement, he will want to ensure that the seller does not convey the property during the course of the contract. So the purchaser records the contract in the same way deeds are recorded. Such a document would have to be acknowledged.

In some jurisdictions, acknowledged contracts are self-proving.[11] That means that in any litigation, the contract can be admitted into evidence without calling the individual who signed the contract to the stand to testify about the signing. In long-term contracts, where the executing individual may change jobs, move, or die before any litigation arises, it may be wise to add an acknowledgment.

Now that you have an overview of the parts of most contracts, you are ready to begin the drafting process.

C. The Drafting Process for Contracts

Whatever the nature of the contract, you once again follow the same familiar steps in drafting the agreement:

1.   understand the audiences;
2.   gather the facts;

3. know the law;
4. classify, organize, and outline;
5. write carefully;
6. test for consequences; and
7. edit and rewrite.

1. Understand the Audiences

First you must decide who will read and use your contract. Obviously, your primary audiences are the contracting parties themselves. At the drafting stage, usually your audience will include the attorneys for the contracting parties as well. At the beginning of the transaction, these parties are quite friendly because they are trying to make a deal. They look forward to mutual benefits and do not see themselves as direct adversaries, although they are keenly aware of their own interests. In the future, however, these parties may become much more adversarial. One party may try to evade the contract if a better deal comes along or if performance becomes too onerous. One party may breach the contract. One party may try to terminate the contract. In each of these situations, a currently friendly audience is transformed into an openly hostile audience. To make matters even more complex, you cannot know for sure which party is likely to want to evade the contract. A contract written to protect your client when the other side breaches may hurt your client if she becomes the breaching party. Your goal is to draft a contract that does not alienate your current friendly audiences, but that protects your client in the event that the parties become more hostile.

If litigation results, your audience will include the court, possibly a jury, and the litigating attorneys. Opposing counsel will be openly hostile and try to demonstrate either that the contract clearly favors his client, or that it is ambiguous and should be interpreted to favor his client. In either event, the contract must stand up to careful scrutiny from a hostile audience.

Even if the deal progresses smoothly, future audiences may look at the contract differently from the currently contracting parties. The current parties frequently focus on the most important elements of the deal, such as price, and gloss over details that might cause disagreement. Future readers, however, may look to the contract to provide detailed mechanics for how to proceed. For example, when negotiating a contract for the sale of goods, the parties may be more concerned with the price and date of delivery than with the procedures for collecting the funds. However, when the seller receives an out-of-state check that takes ten days to clear, she may be reluctant to deliver the goods until the check clears. Both parties will then look back to the contract to see if the seller can demand payment by cashier's check or money transfer, or if she has the right to withhold delivery until the check clears. If the contract is silent, then both parties may be angry. If, however, the issue had been raised and resolved in the negotiation phase, then the parties may have been able to agree on a mutually satisfactory way to solve the problem. For example, a wire transfer that has been planned in advance is less onerous than one that must be arranged at the last moment with little or no notice. Consequently, your first task is to identify who the audiences are and how their perspectives might change over time.

The parties who negotiate the contract may also differ from the parties who use it. For example, a collective bargaining agreement may be negotiated by teams that include top union and management leaders and their counsel. However, when the contract is applied to resolve a particular grievance for a particular employee, the union representative may be a union steward while the company may be represented by a shop supervisor or personnel worker. These new individuals trying to use the contract probably will not have been present when it was negotiated and written. Moreover, they may have different levels of expertise than the original negotiators. They will not necessarily have an institutional memory of the negotiation process or informal understandings of the terms and procedures provided for in the contract. Accordingly, you must draft contracts to be accessible to a variety of audiences with different perspectives and levels of expertise.

As a general rule, you should make your contract accessible to the least sophisticated audience you can foresee. In order to be accessible, it must be clearly organized with useful headings and easily understood language. Moreover, you should not assume knowledge of information not contained within the document itself. If additional information is required, you can attach it as exhibits. Be sure to specify whether any attached exhibits are part of the contract itself, or merely illustrative examples or references.

You should consider not only who will use your contract, but how they will use it. For example, when you draft a real estate sales contract, you know that it will be used by the buyer, the seller, their attorneys, the lender, the real estate brokers, the closing officer, and the title company that insures the title. Each of these parties will use the contract differently.

The buyer and seller use the contract in three different ways. First, the contract records the deal the parties have struck. Second, the contract regulates the steps that lead up to closing (for example, when a home inspection must be completed). Finally, the contract may resolve any disputes that may arise. The lender on the other hand, will use the contract to establish that there is a firm deal and to verify the sales price. Hence, the lender may look first to be sure that the contract has been properly signed by the parties and that the sales price fits within the lending structure. The title company also is concerned with the sales price because it may base its fees on the amount of insurance purchased. It may be even more interested in any description of the property that can help locate the correct title documents. At the very least the title company needs the address, but often it would prefer a complete legal description. The brokers will want to know which party is responsible for paying their commissions. Finally, the closing officer will want to check all prerequisites to closing to make sure that they have been complied with before funds can be disbursed and the deed recorded. Accordingly, you need to draft the contract so each of these parties can find correct and clear information.

Sometimes your client brings you a draft of a contract for you to review. The draft may have been prepared by your client, by the other contracting party, or by a third party such as another lawyer or a real estate broker. One of the things you should look for in reviewing the contract is whether the contract has anticipated all future audiences. You know that audiences are likely to include the signatories, their agents (e.g., attorneys, accountants, and employees), subsequent users (e.g., banks or union stewards), affected third parties (e.g., children in a divorce settlement agreement), and those involved in any future disputes (e.g., judges, attorneys, and litigants). You should review the proposed contract to see if it addresses the needs of each audience.

First, you need to consider the parties. Go over the contract with your client to see if it is accurate or if it omits any parts of the negotiated agreement. Your client's view of the contract probably is formed by the oral understanding he reached with the other party. He may have paid less attention to the language of the document than to the negotiations. If a dispute arises later, however, he may not be able to rely on the oral statements and may be bound by the terms of the written contract.[12] Therefore, you must be sure that the language reflects the client's understanding of the agreement.

Second, you should think about the audience that will use the document. Will they be able to understand it? Does it clearly define the scope of their duties and authority? Is it written in language that they can easily comprehend? Does it have clear headings that will help the users find the relevant parts of the contract?

Third, you should think about those who may never read the contract but are nevertheless affected by it. Does the contract anticipate the needs of affected third parties? For example, a settlement agreement in a divorce might provide for a parent to pay for a child's college costs. What happens if the nonpaying parent dies? The child did not sign the agreement. Does the agreement give the child a right to enforce the agreement for her own benefit? You should carefully review the draft to see how it impacts third parties.

Finally, you should think about how audiences involved in a future dispute will view the contract. Does the contract give enough facts for a judge to resolve a dispute? Does the contract specify where or how the dispute is to be resolved? Could a hostile audience successfully claim that any part of the contract is ambiguous? Be sure that the draft can stand up to hostile review.

In summary then, for each contract you must try to identify each prospective audience who will rely on the contract. Ask yourself:

1.   Who will read or use this contract?
2.   How will this audience use this contract?
3.   Is this audience hostile, friendly, or both?
4.   When will the audience use the contract?
5.   What is the audience's background or experience?

Exercise 5-1

a.   You have been asked to draft a settlement agreement to resolve all pending issues in a divorce case. The divorcing couple have three children, two of whom are minors. Identify each of the possible audiences, how you might expect these audiences to use the agreement, whether each audience is hostile or friendly, when you think the audiences will use the contract, and what the audiences' level of sophistication is. Also, identify how the answers to these questions might affect how you draft the agreement.

b.   You represent Imogene B. Smart. She wants you to review the following draft of an employment contract written by her future employer's attorney.

EMPLOYMENT CONTRACT

This agreement is made August 10, 1992, between The Inventive Company, Inc. ("TIC") and Imogene B. Smart ("Smart"). TIC invents and manufactures kitchen equipment. Employees have access to a number of inventions prior to patenting and to other trade secrets, which TIC wishes to protect. Smart is a designer who wishes to become a TIC employee.

Accordingly, TIC and Smart mutually agree:

1. EMPLOYMENT: TIC agrees to employ Smart according to the terms and conditions of this employment contract.

2. DUTIES AND INVENTIONS: Smart is employed as a designer to design kitchen equipment for TIC. All inventions, discoveries, and improvements ("discoveries") Smart discovers while in TIC's employ shall be TIC's exclusive property, regardless of whether such discoveries were made at work or elsewhere, during or after regular working hours.

3. PATENT RIGHTS: Smart shall promptly deliver a written report on all her discoveries to her supervisor. Smart assigns to TIC all her rights to such discoveries including any domestic and foreign patent rights or renewals. Smart shall sign any instruments necessary to protect TIC's rights to such discoveries, including, but not limited to, patent applications and assignments. TIC agrees to pay all costs associated with acquiring any necessary patents.

4. TRADE SECRETS: Smart agrees not to divulge any information concerning any TIC product or discovery to anyone, either during or after the termination of her employment. Smart agrees to deliver to TIC all notes and other data relating to her research when she leaves TIC's employ.

5. FULL TIME: Smart agrees to devote her full and exclusive time to TIC's business.

6. ANNUAL REVIEW: Smart's performance and salary shall be reviewed annually at the end of TIC's fiscal year.

7. TIC'S RIGHT TO TRANSFER SMART: TIC reserves the right to change the nature of Smart's duties and to transfer Smart to any other TIC department, branch, or subsidiary. If such a transfer requires Smart to relocate, TIC will pay Smart's moving expenses.

8. NONCOMPETITION COVENANT: Because Smart will acquire confidential information in the course of her employment; and because Smart will be performing special and unique services for TIC, Smart agrees that she will not engage in any business in competition with TIC within two years after she leaves TIC's employ.

9. TERMINATION: Either Smart or TIC may terminate this agreement on three weeks written notice.

10. GOVERNING LAW: This Contract shall be governed by the laws of the State of Illinois.

                                              THE INVENTIVE COMPANY, INC.

_____   _____
IMOGENE B. SMART   BY: PRESIDENT

Who are the prospective audiences for this contract? Will the agreement meet the needs of each audience? What items need to be changed to account for all the audiences?

c. You have been asked to draft a sexual harassment policy for a major public university. Who are the prospective audiences for this document? How will each audience use the policy? Describe each audience: Are they hostile or friendly, knowledgeable or unknowledgeable, sophisticated or unsophisticated?

2. Gather the Facts

When you analyzed the audiences, you should have discovered some of the underlying purposes of the contract. Now you must gather the facts so that you can draft the substance of the agreement. Recall the six simple questions that guide your inquiry: who? what? where? when? why? and how?

a. Who?

Start with the audiences you already have identified. Your primary audience will be the parties to the contract and their attorneys. Who are they? This question includes more than a mere inquiry into their names and addresses. You also have to identify their legal status. For example, if a dentist asks you to draft an employment contract with a dental hygienist, you need to know whether the dentist is in partnership with anyone else, and if so, whether the employee is to work for the individual dentist or the partnership. You need to know the precise legal name of the person or entity that is signing the contract.

Identifying contracting parties is more than merely getting the name right, however. You must assure yourself that they have the legal capacity to contract.[13] Capacity actually raises two different questions: whether the party is authorized, and whether the party is capable (old enough or has sufficient mental ability).[14] What is the role of the person signing the contract? Is he an agent for another? If so, the principal should be identified in the contract,[15] and you should satisfy yourself that the agent is sufficiently authorized to execute the contract. Be especially careful to verify the authority of those who sign on behalf of corporations.[16] Whenever possible, get written evidence of the agent's authority for your files.[17]

It is more difficult to protect your client from the claim that the other party lacked sufficient mental capacity to enter the contract. Self-serving statements are to no avail. However, if the other party was represented by counsel, be sure to mention it in the agreement. Minors' contracts typically are voidable, but if the minor lies about her age, she may be unable to avoid the contract.[18] Consequently, you may want to include a specific representation that the signatory is an adult in appropriate cases.

Next, you need to find out who will use the contract. Who is going to follow up to see that the promises in the contract are kept? Is it a known individual (e.g., John Smith) or an unknown member of a class (e.g., attorney for the purchaser, purchasing agent)? Who will need to look back at the contract for instructions on how to proceed? How much authority is given to this individual?

When you ask "who?" you must inquire further than the audiences for the contract, however. Often you need to think about who will be affected by the contract even if they never read it. For example, in the employment contract with the dental hygienist, if you ask who else might be affected, you might think about the patients. Are these patients going to continue to be the dentist's patients, or are they now the hygienist's patients? That sort of a question suggests substantive provisions like a covenant not to compete and a clear statement of who will be responsible for any malpractice claims. Accordingly, in gathering facts, you should ask not only who the audiences for the contract are, but also who else might be affected by the contract.

When you determine who else might be affected by the contract, you must anticipate future participants as well as current ones. For example, if the hygienist is hired to work for a dental partnership that currently consists of two dentists, what happens if the partnership is sold to a new group of dentists? Thus, asking the question "who?" can help you envision future contingencies. In summary, you must ask who will sign the contract, who will use it, and who will be affected by it.

b.   What?

After you have identified who is affected by the contract, you should consider *what* is covered. This question is both the most important and the most difficult to formulate. The answers to the "what?" question form the basis for the substantive provisions of the contract. However, the facts are almost infinitely varied. Although no simple formula exists for gathering these facts, a few strategies may help. Begin with general questions, which give your client an opportunity to educate you on the facts.[19] If you begin to question your client too closely on the details at first, you may give your client the impression that the other facts are irrelevant or already known. Once you have heard your client's description of the facts, you will need to inquire further to elicit facts your client may not have considered.

Although each contract is unique, some factual categories are relevant to most contracts: descriptions, money, duties, enforcement, and changed circumstances. First, you must determine what the contract is about: get crucial descriptions. For a purchase contract, for example, you would need a complete description of the item to be purchased. The description could include both physical characteristics and the underlying purpose of the item. For example, a contract to purchase computer equipment might list the equipment by make and serial number, or it might describe the equipment in terms of its expected use: a computer that would meet the needs of the purchaser.[20] Although you need not choose the final wording of your descriptions yet, you should discover all the different ways your client describes the crucial parts of the contract.

Most contracts call for the exchange of money or something else of value. Hence, you should ask about the financial provisions. Although a price term is not required for commercial sales contracts,[21] this provision may be the most important element for your client. You need to learn the amount, the manner of payment (e.g., check, cash, note, money order), the currency (e.g., U.S. funds), the time (e.g., at delivery, in advance, in installments), the payor, the payee, what the price includes (e.g., shipping, taxes, duties, licensing fees, attached fixtures, bonuses), and what changes may occur (e.g., interest, late fees, prepayment bonus, attorney's fees). If a specific sum cannot be named, try to define precisely

how it will be calculated later. Sometimes this will require asking relatively specific questions. For example, if a supplier is going to charge $10 per cubic yard
for clay fill, how will the purchaser verify the total yardage supplied? Will it be
based on the number of truck loads with an agreed upon yardage per truck? Will
it be based on the measure of the fill once it is deposited in place? Or, will it be
based on measurements of the excavation hole? Whatever the price terms are,
you should be sure that both you and your client fully understand them.

Most contracts also impose certain duties on the parties. You must find out
both what needs to be done and specifically who is going to do it. Be sure to find
out what preliminary steps are necessary. Is your client assuming certain conditions that will enable her or the other party to perform? What changes could occur
that would make it difficult or impossible to perform (e.g., bad weather, war,
inflation, transportation problems, supply shortages, changed interest rates,
bankruptcy, labor strikes, natural disaster)? You need to compile a complete list
of every step that must be taken to achieve the goals of the contract.

Now it is time to predict doom: What can go wrong? Gathering these facts will
help you plan for enforcement and changed circumstances. What are the likely
consequences of each missed step, failed condition, or unperformed duty? What
could be done to correct each problem? How much would it cost? How could it
be prevented? What are the limits your client is willing to accept on the other
party's duty to perform? If the other party fails to perform, what would protect
your client? What limits would your client like to put on her own duty to perform?
What events would excuse performance? If, for some reason, your client fails to
perform, what would she like the consequences to be?

In order to predict likely changes, you should be asking what the customs are
in the industry. Understanding broadly how the contract fits into the way your
client's business works helps you identify possible problems and highlights un-
conscious assumptions and preconditions that your client may take for granted.
Moreover, such industry customs may be used to define any missing or ambiguous terms.[22]

c. Where?

By now you have a substantial list of facts. For each entity, item, or duty you
have identified, you need to ask the question, "where?" Recall, for example, the
employment contract for the dental hygienist. You might want to find out where
he is obligated to work. Does the partnership have offices in different locations?
Would he be required to travel between the locations? If so, who provides and
pays for the transportation? Similarly, you would need his address to reach him
at home if necessary.

It is equally important to think about the location of items. For example, if a
party is agreeing to provide a computer to meet your client's needs, you might
ask where the computer will be located. Will it remain on the supplier's premises
and be connected by phone lines and modems to the user's premises? Will it be
physically moved onto your client's premises? Where will it fit? How big is it?
Will it need special hardware, electrical supply, or phone connections to work?

Similarly, you need to ask where duties are to be performed. For example, if
you are drafting a service contract for some office equipment, you need to know

whether the machines will be serviced on site or elsewhere. As always, when you ask one question, it frequently leads to others.

d. When?

Some "when?" questions are global and apply to the entire contract. Others are narrower and apply to specifics. For example, globally, you may want to know the duration of the contract, when it terminates, when it becomes effective, and how important timing is to the overall contract. Generally, minor delays in performance have little or no legal effect. So if parties want to cancel a contract because of a minor delay, they should expressly say so. Often that idea is expressed by saying that timing is "of the essence of the contract."[23] However, courts are increasingly reluctant to vitiate agreements for minor delays where one party has not sustained substantial damages.[24] Similarly, the failure to state that timing is the essence of the contract will not excuse major delays.[25] Accordingly, explicit statements about the impact of timing are wiser than generalized statements that timing is the essence of the contract.

Similarly, you often need to know about the timing of many details. For example, in a real estate contract you need to find out how long the buyer has to get an inspection, when the closing is, and when the buyer is entitled to possession.

In order to cover as many of the contingencies as possible, review your list of entities, items, and duties. For each one, ask how time affects it. In the case of the dental partnership hiring the dental hygienist, the partners and the hygienist are the primary people involved. What happens to partners over time? Some may become disabled or die; some may retire; some may quit; and some may be ousted. How would each of those contingencies affect the employment contract? If the partnership splits up, are any of the dentists still bound by the terms of the employment contract? Similarly, the hygienist might become ill or disabled. What then?

Review duties one by one as well. As to each duty, consider timing. When is each duty supposed to be performed? What if performance is delayed? What if performance is early? Ask your client what the specific impact would be, so that you can think about what appropriate remedies to build into the contract.

e. Why?

In order to write a contract, you must understand both the purpose of the contract and the intent of each of the parties. You may find it hard to identify the purpose because contracts often have multiple and conflicting purposes. Indeed each provision may serve its own purposes, and the parties may have differing reasons for each provision.

When you think about the purpose of the contract as a whole, the question is largely a matter of tone. Sometimes your client wants a contract that seems airtight in order to deter others from even considering a breach. For example, leases are often written in this almost adversary way in order to intimidate lessees into compliance. Other times your client may want a contract that seems more objective and flexible in order to nurture a valued relationship and induce compliance out of friendship.[26] Your client may want both: an airtight, one-sided contract that seems objective and flexible.

At the most general level, the purpose of most contracts is to create a legally enforceable agreement.[27] However, many contracts also are designed to record an agreement for future reference. For example, when a lease lists the address where rent is to be paid, its primary purpose is to provide necessary information rather than to bind the parties.

Many times parties are willing to sacrifice one purpose of a document for another. For example, when parties have to deal with each other repeatedly over a long period of time, they may be prepared to sacrifice the most favorable deal in order to maintain the relationship.[28] Similarly, they may decide to sacrifice price to timely completion, or speed to quality. Only your client can determine her own priorities. Of course those priorities must be meshed with those of the other contracting parties as well. One way to explore priorities is to push for explanations of every entity, item, or duty that you are contemplating for the contract. Why is this person or item important? Could it be served by a different one? Always ask "why?"

You should be especially careful to consider why a provision should be included when you are reviewing forms. All too often young lawyers "cut and paste" forms together without carefully thinking about the underlying purpose of either the particular provision or the contract as a whole. Never add a provision from a form unless you have a clear reason for doing so. When you are adding form language to fill a gap you had not considered, scrutinize the provision carefully. Can you tell from the way it is written what its initial purpose was? Language frequently favors one party or another. Whose perspective is reflected? Also consider how such a new provision fits with the overall purpose of the document.

The purposes of a contract or any given provision may be either explicit or implicit. Explicit purposes are included in the contract itself, while implicit purposes are not.[29] While you are gathering the facts, you need not worry whether a purpose will be written into the contract. Instead, concentrate on determining what all the various purposes and cross-purposes may be both for the contract as a whole and for each provision. If you do not know why you are drafting a provision, you will not know how to write it, nor will you be able to test it to see if it meets its purposes.

f. How?

Now that you have a good idea of what the parties want, you must determine how to achieve their goals. This issue raises three related questions: (1) How is the contract going to be implemented?; (2) how is the contract going to induce compliance?; and (3) how is the contract going to deal with noncompliance? Answering these questions provides you and your client with an opportunity to be very creative.

i. How Will the Contract be Implemented?

When you consider how to implement the agreement, the parties have the opportunity to structure the deal in many different ways. For example, if two entrepreneurs want to start a business with one supplying the capital and the other supplying the labor, they have a number of choices. They could form a partnership, a corporation, or a joint venture. They could also have one person operate a sole proprietorship and hire the other. They could even combine the various approaches: They could each incorporate and then form a partnership between the corporations. Usually, there are several routes to the same result. In order to discover all the possibilities, you need to consult many different sources, including clients and experts, as well as the industry and legal literature. Try to discover as many distinct possibilities as you can, and then discuss them with your client to see if some routes are preferable. For example, in the contract to purchase clay fill at $10 a cubic yard, you should first determine how the yardage can be measured (in place at source, in place at delivery, by estimated truckload, and so forth). Once you have identified the possibilities, find out what the advantages and disadvantages of each method may be. Is one faster, cheaper, more accurate, customary, more acceptable to the other party, or taxed more favorably? You should follow this process of identifying and evaluating the options for each provision in the contract. For each duty listed, ask how it is to be done, how else it might be done, and what the advantages and disadvantages of each approach are.

ii. How Will the Contract Induce Compliance?

Use a Carrot.   After you have figured out how the contract is to be implemented, you have to consider how to induce compliance. Your basic tools here are the carrot and the stick. The carrot acts as an incentive to induce compliance. Examples of such incentives are discounts for prompt payment or bonuses for better job performance. Such incentives have costs, so be sure to have your client identify both what items are worth offering incentives for and how much the extra compliance is worth.

Use a Stick.   The opposite of the carrot is the stick. Sometimes you can induce compliance by making noncompliance too costly. For example, many employment contracts have noncompete clauses that prohibit an employee from working in the same field in the same area for a period of time. The threat of forcing employees either to be unemployed or to move may be sufficient to induce them to remain on the job. However, using a stick may be risky. If the stick carries too big a threat it may kill the deal. Moreover, big sticks tend to undermine relationships built on trust and confidence. Of course, some enforcement mechanisms are more onerous than others. Penalties are harsher than graduated payment plans, for example. Once again, your goal is to go through the list of duties and to ask what would induce a party to comply. Consider how each and every obligation is to be enforced. Then you need to identify the advantages and disadvantages of each mechanism.

iii. How Will the Contract Deal with Noncompliance?

No matter how carefully you try to induce compliance, there is always a risk that some of the parties will fail to perform their duties. That risk raises two related questions. What are valid excuses or limits on liability? What are the appropriate remedies?

Create Excuses. Contracts frequently contain clauses that limit liability for nonperformance.[30] First try to envision every possible contingency that could prevent a party from complying with the contract. Then have your client try to decide which of those events should excuse a party from performing. Be sure to consider not only other parties' duties, but your client's duties as well.

Limits on liability need not be complete excuses. For example, a natural disaster might justify a delay without being an excuse to cancel the contract altogether. Similarly, the parties can agree to limit other kinds of liabilities in liquidated damage clauses or in clauses that waive the right to claim lost profits. The key is to ask what would be necessary to fix the problems caused by noncompliance.

Create Remedies. Limits on liability are closely related to provisions that specify what the remedy is for breach. Remember that not all breaches need to be treated the same way. Accordingly, delays can be treated differently from defective products or refusals to perform. Similarly, parties may elect to have more than one remedy for a single kind of breach. For instance, a landlord might be entitled both to evict a tenant for nonpayment of rent and recover a judgment for the amount owed. Review each duty and list every possible remedy for noncompliance. Then have your client evaluate the advantages and disadvantages of each.

This process of asking who, what, where, when, why, and how will help you gather the facts you need to write the contract. You need to ask these questions about the contract in general and about each item you think might turn up in the contract. Thus, the process is recursive. The more questions you ask, the more you need to ask.

Sometimes you may have an interview form that will help you gather the facts. You can find such forms in some practice manuals[31] and office form files. Although such interview forms can be very helpful, you must not rely on them exclusively. They cannot be tailored to the particular contract your client wants and they often omit creative questions that could lead to innovative contractual provisions. Nevertheless, forms may be a good checklist to see if you have forgotten anything. Be sure to evaluate the form critically. Does it ask all of the relevant questions: who, what, when, where, why, and how? Remember that you can individualize the form to ask questions you think are relevant.

In summary, you have to use creativity and judgment in gathering facts. You need to focus your inquiry so that you get both the broad background information and the specific details you may need. Finally, remember that gathering facts is not a single self-contained step. You may need to go back to ask questions about who, what, where, when, why, and how while you research the law, organize, write, test, and edit the contract.

Exercise 5-2

a. A man has made an appointment with you to discuss a possible divorce settlement agreement. What facts do you need?

b. Imogene B. Smart has asked you to review the employment agreement set forth in Exercise 5-1b. What additional facts do you need in order to evaluate the agreement?

c.   You have been retained by a state university to draft a sexual harassment policy that will cover students, staff, faculty, and administration. What facts do you need to know?

3.   Know the Law

Gathering facts and researching the law are closely related. Unless you understand the legal rules that may govern your contract, you may not know what facts you need. Conversely, unless you know what the facts are, you may not be able to predict the impact of the legal rules. For example, if you did not know the legal rule that minors could void their contracts, you might not think to ask how old the contracting parties are. Similarly, if you were unaware that one of the parties was a corporation, you might not think to look up the legal rules about how corporations must authorize agents to sign contracts. Because researching the law and gathering the facts are so closely related, you may perform these steps simultaneously, or move back and forth between them. Indeed, you often will return to look up legal questions that arise throughout the drafting process.

As you recall from Chapter 2, you need to understand four different categories of law in order to draft a contract: substantive law, procedural law, interpretive law, and ethical law.

a.   Know the Substantive Law

You probably already know a lot of substantive contract law, but you may not have thought about how it applies to drafting agreements. For example, you know the adage that a contract must be supported by adequate "consideration."[32] Accordingly, it may be wise to include a clause that specifies what the consideration is. However, you cannot blithely rest on this general knowledge. Some kinds of consideration may invalidate a contract. For example, in some states, a settlement agreement could not be made to encourage a divorce.[33] Hence, it would invalidate the agreement to include a clause like, "In consideration of Jane Doe's willingness to consent to a no-fault divorce. . . ." Therefore, you must research how your state applies the general precepts of contract law to the particular kind of contract you are writing.

You will not be able to confine yourself to applying broad contract principles, however. You also need to know the substantive law that governs a variety of specific issues. First, you need to discover what these issues are. That task is like issue-spotting on a law school exam. Review the facts that you have gathered. For each entity, item, and duty you have listed, think about the possible legal questions. If you do not have a good general background in the area covered by the contract, you should try to do some general reading first, so you have some idea of the kinds of legal issues that might arise. The more familiar you are with the field, the easier it will be to spot the issues.

Another way to spot issues is to look at practice manuals, checklists, and form books to see what provisions they discuss in contracts similar to the one you are drafting. Many bar associations, continuing legal education organizations and other groups publish practice manuals, which discuss legal issues that may arise in particular kinds of contracts. Although these books become dated quickly, they provide a way to double-check your own list of legal issues.

Once you have spotted an issue, you need to ask three questions: (1) If the contract is silent on this point, what will happen?; (2) can the parties change the result by the terms of the contract?; and (3) what are the limits of the changes the parties can make?

To illustrate how these three inquiries work, consider the following facts. Your client, a New York company, manufactures farm equipment, which it usually sells to distributors. Unfortunately, most of its distributors have gone out of business. A farmer in Iowa wants to buy a large piece of equipment directly from your client and pay for it in installments over time. Your client is worried that if the farmer defaults on the contract, the farmer will have to be personally served with a summons in order to give him notice of the suit. That might mean that your client would have to either hire an out-of-state lawyer or pay for its New York counsel to travel to Iowa. Your client is only willing to sell the equipment directly to the farmer if it can be assured that it will not have to personally serve the farmer notice in the event of litigation.

i. If the Contract Is Silent, What Will Happen?

The first question to ask when you begin your legal research on this point is what happens if the contract is silent? What is the law about how an individual must receive notice of an out-of-state suit? In order to answer that question, you may need to look at New York law, Iowa law, and even federal law, if you anticipate filing in federal court. Is it sufficient if a party receives actual notice by registered mail, or must the party be served personally? If the party must be served personally, who is authorized to serve the summons? Could the notice/summons be prepared out of state and mailed to the appropriate officer for service?

ii. Can Parties Change the Result by the Terms of the Contract?

Once you know what would happen if the contract is silent, consider whether the parties could change the result by contract. Can a party waive his right to receive notice of a suit?

iii. What Are the Limits of Changes Parties Can Make?

Assuming that a party can waive notice, then what are the limits on the ways that a party can waive his right? Could he simply agree in the contract to allow the other party to appear on his behalf and enter a default judgment against him without notice?[34] Could he appoint someone in New York to be his agent to receive the summons on his behalf?[35] As this illustration shows, for each legal issue you spot, you should ask yourself what the result would be if the contract were silent, whether the result can be changed by the terms of the contract, and what the limits on such changes are.

As the example with the farm equipment suggests, the way you structure a deal may change the legal issues involved. You must know the legal consequences of each approach. First, you must identify each different way to structure the deal.

For example, if two people want to start a business together, they might want to create a partnership, an employment contract, or a corporation. After you have considered the various ways to structure the deal, you must be sure you know the law concerning each structure. You may want to compare how each different approach affects a particular legal issue like taxes, or liability for debts. Only after you understand the advantages and disadvantages of each possible structure can you advise your client.

You also have a choice about the way you structure individual provisions. One of the most common choices you face is whether to create a representation, a promise, or a condition. A representation simply states a fact: "The roof does not leak." A promise commits one or both parties to act or to refrain from acting. Hence, promises create legal duties. For instance, the promise, "The seller will fix the roof," creates a legal duty. In contrast, a condition is an event that can trigger legal duties. For example consider, "If the roof leaks, the seller will fix it." The condition (the roof leaking) triggers the legal duty (fixing the roof). Again, once you have identified the different ways to structure the provision, you need to be familiar with the legal consequences of each choice. Are there different remedies for broken promises than unfulfilled conditions or misrepresentations? Are there special rules for some kinds of promises or representations (like warranties)?[36]

You cannot decide how to structure the deal unless you know the law about each of the possibilities. For each structure remember to ask the three questions: (1) What if the contract is silent? (2) Can the contract change any implied duties? (3) If the contract can change implied duties, what are the limits? If a contract is silent about the condition of the roof, what happens if the roof leaks?[37] Is there an implied warranty of habitability? If such an implied warranty exists, can the parties contract to change it?[38] What are the limits on such disclaimers?[39] Is it enough to restructure the implied warranty as a condition or an express promise? You can use this three-question method for each substantive provision in your contract including issues of time, money, enforcement, duties, modification, and cancellation.

b.   Know the Procedural Law

Clients often focus on the substance of the contract, without thinking about the process of contracting. You, as the lawyer, must know the procedural law that assures the contract is valid. For example, if you learn that one of the parties is a corporation, you must consider how a corporation can sign a binding agreement. First, you need to determine the technical requirements. Who can sign on behalf of a corporation?[40] That raises the question of corporate authority. If you research the issue, you are likely to find that it will be easier to enforce the contract if the signing officer had actual authority as opposed to apparent authority. Then you would need to discover what kinds of documentation establish such actual authority. Do you need a resolution of the board of directors?[41] Would the signature of two officers be enough?

Sometimes the law requires specific forms or formats for agreements. For example, some states require that health care powers of attorney be written in a particular form.[42] Such specific, formal requirements may be limited to a single clause or provision. For instance, some disclaimers in consumer contracts must be "conspicuous"[43] or displayed in a certain size type.[44]

Researching the procedural law may require you to think about provisions that are not legally required but are wise. To illustrate, in some states prenuptial contracts are only enforceable if both parties have independent counsel.[45] Although these states may not require the contract to explicitly list the names and addresses of the lawyers, if you do so, you make it easier to enforce the contract later.

c. Know the Interpretive Law

So far you have been thinking about law that limits either the content or the form of your contract. You should also consider law that will determine how your contract will be interpreted. Once again, there may be one set of rules that governs contracts in general, another set that governs specific kinds of contracts, and a third that governs individual provisions in contracts.

You are probably familiar with a number of the general interpretive rules of construction, such as: a contract will be construed against the drafter;[46] words will be given their plain meaning;[47] the contract will be read as a whole;[48] and the contract will be construed to create an enforceable agreement.[49] Additional rules govern how to interpret individual provisions of the contract. For example, when a general description follows specific terms, the general description is limited to items of the same general class as those listed in the specific terms.[50] Similarly, words take their meanings from the context.[51] However, particular clauses of the contract are subordinate to its general intent.[52]

Indeed, knowing the interpretive law may require you to research how courts have defined specific words or terms to be used in your contract. For example, the parties may agree that the defaulting party is responsible for "costs." Before you include that term in your contract, you should find out how the courts define "costs." Would they include attorneys fees? You can find such definitions of specific words in computerized research sources or the "Words and Phrases" sections of digests. Whatever the source, you must look up how courts will interpret the words you use.

Once again, this step is recursive. You may not know what specific terms you need to look up until you start drafting the contract. Similarly, you may not be able to evaluate how the contract will be read as a whole until you begin to test it. Accordingly, you will have to reconsider interpretive law during various other steps in the drafting process. However, if you discover the relevant interpretive law for contracts general, your particular kind of contract, and particular terms or provisions, you may be able to avoid some pitfalls in the drafting process.

d. Know the Ethical Law

Finally, you should know the ethical law that governs your transaction. Once again, ethical rules can be general, specific to the contract, or even specific to the provision. An example of a general ethical principle is the rule that lawyers must avoid conflicts of interest.[53] That rule can be tricky when you draft contracts because multiple parties may ask you to draft a contract for them, with each party considering you her lawyer. Although the parties may not perceive any current conflict of interest, such future conflicts may be inherent. Once again, you ask the three familiar questions. What happens if the contract is silent on the issue of conflict of interest? Can the parties contract around a conflict of interest? If so, what are the risks and limits?

Ethical problems also arise in specific kinds of contracts. For example, in some states, parties are ethically required to fully disclose all assets when negotiating either a prenuptial contract[54] or a divorce settlement agreement.[55] Nevertheless, lawyers are ethically bound to keep other facts completely confidential.[56] These particularized ethical rules may be found in cases, statutes, or compilations of ethical rules. Therefore, you need to discover the specific ethical rules that govern the particular kind of contract you are writing.

Finally, specific provisions also can raise ethical problems. For example, a client may want to include in the contract a provision that is not legally enforceable, such as a confession of judgment clause[57] or a forfeiture clause.[58] Sometimes clients purposefully include such clauses to frighten the other party into compliance.[59] If you know that a provision is legally unenforceable, can you ethically include it?

In summary, you should know the substantive, procedural, interpretive, and ethical law that governs contracts in general, your particular kind of contract, and the specific provisions you intend to include. For each, you should ask three questions: (1) What is the legal result if the contract is silent? (2) Can the parties change that result by agreement? (3) What are the limits on such private ordering?

Exercise 5-3

a. A client has made an appointment with you to discuss a potential divorce settlement agreement. Get an overview of the relevant substantive, procedural, interpretive, and ethical law so that you are prepared to discuss the agreement with him.

b. Review the contract set out in Exercise 5-2b. What issues of substantive, procedural, interpretive, and ethical law are raised by this contract? For each issue, determine what happens if the contract is silent, whether that result can be changed by agreement, and what the limits on such changes are.

c. A state university has retained you to draft a sexual harassment policy that will become part of its employee manual and its student handbook. The policy is to govern the behavior of students, staff, faculty, and administrators at the university. Faculty members include graduate students who act as teaching assistants, adjunct professors who teach a single course, lecturers who do not hold permanent positions, untenured faculty, and tenured faculty. The university wants the policy to be a strong one that protects potential victims, but the university also wants to be fair to alleged perpetrators. Most importantly, the university wants to avoid liability either for sexual harassment or for violating the rights of any students or employees. What issues of substantive, procedural, interpretive, and ethical law are raised in drafting such a policy? For each issue, identify what would happen if the policy is silent, whether that result can be changed by the terms of the policy, and what the limits are on such changes. Identify as many different ways to structure the policy as you can. What are the strengths and weaknesses of each approach?

4. Classify, Organize, and Outline

Once you have a list of the facts, and a list of the legal issues that could arise, you should be ready to classify, organize, and outline your contract.

a. Globally Divide Contract into Parts

Recall that most contracts are divided into six parts: identification, recitals, consideration, body, signatures, and acknowledgments. At this point, you may want to review the material about the parts of the contract at the beginning of this chapter.

All six of these parts are not always required for each contract. For example, if your research on procedural law reveals that the document need not be acknowledged, you may choose to omit the acknowledgment section. Similarly, in some circumstances you might elect to omit recitals as redundant. In any event, you need to review your facts and law to create a broad outline of the parts of the contract. Then you are ready to organize the most important part of the contract: the body.

b. Organize the Body of the Contract

Unfortunately, contracts are too varied to have a typical organization within the body. You will have to create this structure yourself. Although you may get some hints from forms or other contracts, you should think carefully about how to organize the body of the agreement.

You may recall the general process of organization from Chapter 2. Because this step is so important, it is broken down into minute detail:

1. list the facts,
2. list the categories,
3. rank the categories,
4. create an outline with subheadings,
5. integrate the facts into the outline,
6. reorganize to account for omitted facts, and
7. discover omitted categories and correct empty ones.

To illustrate this process, consider a proposed contract between a national inventory company, Business Inventory Systems, Inc. ("BIS") and a Mom and Pop inventory business run as a joint venture in Ohio called "Simpsons." Mr. and Mrs. Simpson want to retire and sell their customer list to BIS. They have worked for years developing this list and have always kept it in strictest confidence. It is the only marketable part of their business because the only other assets are some obsolete computers. They are willing to sell the customer list to BIS for $50,000. BIS is willing to pay $20,000 when the contract is signed and the balance within three months. The Simpsons want to be sure they will be paid, and BIS wants to be sure that they will not be liable for any obligations of the Simpsons' business. BIS also wants some assurance that if it purchases the customer list, the Simpsons will not compete with them or sell the list to others.

i.   List the Facts

The first step in organizing this material is to create a list of facts:

FACT LIST:

BIS = Illinois corporation
Simpsons operated business as joint venturers in Ohio
Only customer list being sold
Price = $50,000
No warranties
Effective on signing
Simpsons currently operate throughout Ohio
BIS operates nationally
Simpsons want to be sure they are paid
BIS wants to be sure that Simpsons don't compete
Customer list is the only salable asset of the business
Simpsons worked for five years developing the customer list and have always kept it in strictest confidence
Payment = $20,000 when contract signed, $30,000 within three months

In answering the questions of who, what, when, where, why, and how, you already have gathered facts about necessary descriptions, financial provisions, duties, enforcement, changed circumstances, timing, locations, purposes, and procedures.

ii.   List the Categories

The facts may suggest categories for the contract. For example, your fact list notes that BIS wants to be sure that the Simpsons will not compete with it. Accordingly, you know you will need a category for noncompetition in your agreement. For each item on your list of facts, decide what general category it might fit into. Add that category to your new list of categories. This list of facts suggests some categories:

Fact List:	Possible Category:
BIS = Illinois corporation	Parties
Simpsons operated business as joint venturers in Ohio	Parties
Only customer list being sold	Purpose
Price = $50,000	Price

No warranties	Warranty disclaimer
Effective on signing	
Simpsons currently operate throughout Ohio	
BIS operates nationally	
Simpsons want to be sure they are paid	Enforcement
BIS wants to be sure that Simpsons don't compete	Noncompete clause
Customer list is the only salable asset of the business	Customer list
Simpsons worked for five years developing the customer list and have always kept it in strictest confidence	
Payment = $20,000 when contract signed, $30,000 within three months	Payment terms

Your legal research may suggest yet other categories. You have reviewed the substantive, procedural, interpretive, and ethical law. Now you need to translate that abstract knowledge of the law into categories that may appear in a contract. For example, if you knew that the law implied warranties unless they were expressly disclaimed or limited, you should include categories for warranties and disclaimers. Similarly, procedural law may suggest relevant categories such as acknowledgments. Interpretative law may also suggest categories for the contract, like provisions as to what state's law governs, or mechanisms for resolving disputes. Even ethical law suggests contract categories. For example, in order to demonstrate that there was no conflict of interest you may want a provision stating that all parties were represented by their own counsel, or that an unrepresented party chose to represent herself. Review your legal research and identify a category for each legal issue you expect the contract to resolve. In case you missed any legal issues, you might want to check either form books or legal checklists to see if you have omitted any provisions. As a result of your research, you may decide to include categories for acknowledgments, governing law, dispute resolution, and representation by counsel. Your new list of categories would look like this (new categories are highlighted):

Price
Customer list
Noncompete clause
Enforcement
Payment terms
Signatures
Parties
Purpose
Warranty disclaimer
Acknowledgments
Governing law
Resolution of disputes
Representation by counsel

Exercise 5-4

a.   A client has made an appointment with you to discuss a potential divorce settlement. Review your list of factual questions from Exercise 5-2a and your legal research from Exercise 5-3a to generate a list of possible categories to be included in any divorce settlement agreement.

b.   Review the employment contract in Exercise 5-1b in light of the list of facts and legal issues you generated in Exercises 5-2b and 5-3b. What categories, if any are omitted from the contract? Now check form books and checklists to see if you have omitted any other categories.

c.   After reviewing the information you gathered for Exercise 5-2c and any available forms or checklists, make a list of categories to be included in a university sexual harassment policy.

d.   You have agreed to write a real estate sales contract for Nancy R. Denison, the seller. She is selling her house to Alice B. Tucker for $235,000. They hope to close the deal on August 6, 1994. Nancy has agreed that Alice can have five days to get the contract approved by her lawyer. Nancy also agreed that she would move out on or before closing or else pay $200 per day in rent. Alice is putting up $23,500 as earnest money. The taxes will be prorated at 110 percent of the prior year's bill up to the day of closing. Alice has seven days to get a home inspection. A microwave oven, a washer, a dryer, a stove, a refrigerator, and wall-to-wall carpeting are included in the purchase price. Nancy will provide a warranty deed at closing. She will also provide title insurance establishing clear title seven days before closing. If anything happens to the property before closing, Nancy will refund any money Alice has paid. The earnest money will be kept in an interest bearing account, with the interest to be credited to the purchase price at closing. Make a list of categories to be included in this residential real estate sales contract.

iii.   Rank the Categories

Once you have a preliminary list of categories, you must decide how to order them. Your reader expects the categories to follow some sort of logical progression. Various theories of organization are available, including general to specific, first to last, most important to least important, most used to least used, or familiar to unfamiliar. You may choose to start with general background information (the identification section) and move to more specific categories. You also may want to organize the document chronologically to state duties in the sequence in which they must be performed. Thus, the price should come before the payment terms. Alternatively, you can arrange your categories in order of importance, from the most important to the least important. Hence, the noncompete clause may precede the disclaimer of warranties. You also may want to place commonly used categories before more infrequently used ones. For example, the description of the customer list is more likely to be used than the category covering enforcement. A corollary of this principle is that you must move from familiar to unfamiliar material. For example, if you have to define a term, define it before you use it. Moving from familiar to unfamiliar material also suggests that you should place closely related categories together. Hence, the category covering price should immediately precede the category for payment terms. A multitude of orders are possible. Whatever order you choose, you should have a rationale that considers how the various audiences actually will use the contract. Now you should rank your categories in some sort of meaningful order:

RANK CATEGORIES

5	Price	(Ordered chronologically to move from
4	Customer list	familiar to unfamiliar ideas and to
7	Noncompete clause	group similar ideas)
9	Indemnification	
10	Enforcement	
2	Parties	
1	Purpose	
6	Payment terms	
13	Signatures	
8	Warranty disclaimer	
14	Acknowledgments	
11	Governing law	
12	Dispute resolution	
3	Representation by counsel	

Exercise 5-5

a.   For the list of categories you created for the divorce settlement agreement in Exercise 5-4a, identify appropriate principles of order (levels of generality, chronology, importance, likely use, or familiarity). Then list the categories in the appropriate order.

b.   Add your list of new categories for the employment contract in Exercise 5-4b to the existing list from the contract. Then evaluate the list to see if the provisions move in a logical sequence. Make a new list that creates a sensible sequence that is easy for the reader to follow.

c.   For the list of categories you created for the sexual harassment policy in Exercise 5-4c, identify appropriate principles of order (levels of generality, chronology, importance, likely use, or familiarity). Then list the categories in the appropriate order.

d.   For the list of categories you created for the real estate contract in Exercise 5-4d, identify appropriate principles of order (levels of generality, chronology, importance, likely use, or familiarity). Then list the categories in the appropriate order.

iv.   Create an Outline with Subheadings

Once you have generated an ordered list of categories, you must critically examine the list to see how each category fits into the overall contract. In order for your reader to be able to use the contract, your categories or headings must be mutually exclusive. If they overlap, the reader will not know where to look for necessary information. Even worse, you may give conflicting information in each section. For example, in preparing a real estate sales contract, a list of headings might include overlapping titles such as these: "Condition of Real Estate"; "Condition of Systems, Equipment, and Appliances"; "Warranties"; and "Inspections."[60] All four headings deal with the condition of the property.

When you find such overlapping categories, you should figure out how they relate to each other. Perhaps they are all subcategories of a more general topic like "Condition of the Property." Perhaps they really constitute two separate categories: "Condition of the Property" and "Inspections." If you decide to combine the topics into a more general one, then you should choose proper subcategories. For example, if you decide to include all four titles in "Condition of the Property," you might want to subdivide it into "Condition of the Land," "Condition of the Building," "Condition of Fixtures," and "Condition of the Contents/Personal Property." Thinking about how your topics fit together will help you create a topic outline that includes subcategories as well as general topics.

When you divide a main category into subtopics, think about the principle you are using to create the subtopics. Choose a principle that reflects the underlying purpose of your contract. To illustrate, if you were drafting the sexual harassment policy for a state university, you might have a main category such as "Individuals Governed." You can divide this group in several different ways: by age, by sex, by employment, or by rank. In prohibiting sexual harassment, the university wants to protect individuals from an abuse of power. Hence it makes sense to divide the group along power lines: students, staff, teachers, and administrators.

Once you have chosen a way to divide your topic, stick to it. Don't switch to a different principle of division within a given topic. For example, it would be confusing if you divided the section on "Individuals Governed" into students, staff, teachers, administrators, men, and women. This list of subtopics is divided both by power and by sex. The result is that the categories overlap. Individuals will fall into more than one category. To avoid that result, you must consciously choose how you are going to divide your topics and use the same principle for each subtopic.

Sometimes you will combine separately listed topics into subsections of a larger section. In the BIS contract you might decide to combine price and payment terms into a single category with subcategories for price and terms. Similarly, you might decide it makes more sense to include the corporate acknowledgment in the signature section rather than in a separate part of the contract. Once you have ranked your main topics and divided them into subcategories, you will have created a topic outline for your contract. A topic outline for the BIS contract follows:

I.   Purpose
II.   Parties
III. Representation by counsel
IV.   Customer list
V.   Payment
      A. Price
      B. Terms
VI.   Noncompete clause
      A. How long valid?
      B. Over entire state?
      C. Binding whom?
VII. No warranties
VIII. Indemnification against future liabilities
IX.   Enforcement
X.   Signatures

Notice that you have raised some unanswered questions that may require you to gather more facts or further research the law. For example, you will need to know how broad a noncompete clause your clients want, and you will have to do legal research to see what the legal limits are on such clauses. Similarly, you have not figured out how you intend to enforce the contract if BIS does not pay the balance due on time.

Exercise 5-6

a.   Using your ranked list of topics from Exercise 5-5a, decide which topics overlap. How can you eliminate the overlaps? Think of as many ways as possible. Given the purposes of the divorce settlement agreement, what are the best ways to subdivide it? Subdivide your topics to eliminate any overlapping categories. Identify the principle of division you are using for each main topic. Be sure that you follow that principle for each subtopic.

b.   Take the ranked list of topics for your employment agreement from Exercise 5-5b. Subdivide it so that no provisions overlap. Check to be sure that the main topics use the same principle of division for each of the subtopics. Compare the outline of the contract you just generated to the outline of the original contract you were given in Exercise 5-1b. Which is a better outline? Why?

c.   Subdivide the list of topics from Exercise 5-5c for the sexual harassment policy. Check to be sure that no topics or subtopics overlap and that appropriate principles of division have been chosen.

d.   Organize your list of topics for a real estate sales contract from Exercise 5-5b into an appropriately divided list of topics and subtopics.

v.   Integrate Facts into the Outline

The next step is to add the facts to the outline of categories. Often the facts require new subheadings. The BIS outline would like this after the facts are added:

I.   Purpose: complete sale & protect parties
II.   Parties
        A.   BIS, an Illinois corporation
        B.   Simpsons, former joint venturers
III.   Representation by counsel
        A.   BIS represented by Sarah Dixon
        B.   Simpsons represented by Jane Anderson
IV.   Customer list
V.   Price & payment terms
        A.   Price = $50,000
        B.   Terms =
             i. $20,000 when contract signed
             ii. $30,000 w/in 3 mos.
VI.   Noncompete clause
        A.   How long valid?
        B.   Over entire state?
        C.   Binding whom?
             i.   Only Simpsons?
             ii.   Simpsons' employees?

VII.   No warranties
VIII.   Indemnification against future liabilities
IX.   Enforcement
X.   Signatures
    A.   BIS
        i.   by president
        ii.   acknowledged by secretary
        iii.   with corporate seal
    B.   Simpsons

Exercise 5-7

a.   Integrate the facts for your divorce settlement agreement into the ranked list of categories you generated for Exercise 5-5a. Circle any facts you did not use.

b.   Integrate the facts for your real estate contract into the ranked list of categories you generated for Exercise 5-5d.

vi. Reorganize to Account for Omitted Facts

The BIS outline omits some of the facts that you had in your original fact list:

Omitted facts:

1.   Customer list is Simpsons' only major asset because the equipment consists of outdated computers

2.   Simpsons worked for 5 years to generate the customer list and always kept it confidential

Are these facts necessary? If the list is the only major asset of the business, this transaction might be considered a bulk sale. Hence, thinking about the omitted facts helps you spot a legal issue you may have missed. Similarly, if the customer list must continue to be kept confidential, some protection should be given against disclosure. These omitted facts suggest two new categories: Bulk Sales and Trade Secrets.

Where should these new categories go in your outline? In the case of bulk sales, you are trying to protect BIS from the claims of the Simpsons' creditors. Logically, then it would seem to be a subcategory of indemnification: one more thing the Simpsons will indemnify BIS against. The trade secret seems most closely related to the noncompete clause, so it should go either before or after that provision. Your new outline might look like this (new provisions are highlighted):

I.   Purpose: complete sale & protect parties
II.   Parties
    A.   BIS, an Illinois corporation
    B.   Simpsons, former joint venturers

III.   Representation by counsel
     A.   BIS represented by Sarah Dixon
     B.   Simpsons represented by Jane Anderson
IV.   Customer list
V.   Price & payment terms
     A.   Price = $50,000
     B.   Terms =
         i. $20,000 when K signed
         ii. $30,000 w/in 3 mos.
VI.   Trade Secret: promise not to disclose
VII.   Noncompete clause
     A.   How long valid?
     B.   Over entire state?
     C.   Binding whom?
         i.   Only Simpsons?
         ii.   Simpsons' employees?
VIII.   No warranties
IX.   Indemnification
     A.   Against claims of Simpsons' creditors
     B.   For any liabilities under the Bulk Sales Act
X.   Enforcement
XI.   Signatures
     A.   BIS
         i.   by president
         ii.   acknowledged by secretary
         iii.   with corporate seal
     B.   Simpsons

Thus the list of omitted facts will enable you to spot categories you may have left out of your outline of the contract. Then you will have to rethink the way you organized the topics. You may have to add, delete, expand, or contract various headings to accommodate the omitted information. The end result will be a more complete outline.

vii.   Discover Omitted Categories and Correct Empty Ones

Similarly, your outline may include topics with no supporting facts. In the case of the BIS contract, you know that the Simpsons want to be sure that they will be paid the balance owed. However, your clients may not have thought about how they intend to assure that. Should BIS execute a note for the balance due? Should it bear interest? Should there be a penalty for late payment? You will have to change your outline to accommodate any new facts.

Once you have an outline of your contract, you must double-check to make sure you haven't omitted anything crucial. First, compare your outline to sample contracts you get from form books, practice manuals, office files, or elsewhere. If possible, have a colleague look over the outline for omissions. Finally, review the outline with your client to see if she can think of anything to add. As always, any additions may require you to rethink the organization of that particular section.

In summary, you should organize your contract into a thorough outline. In general the steps are:

1. Create a list of topics from your knowledge of the facts and law.
2. Rank those topics into a meaningful sequence by levels of generality, chronology, likely use, importance, or familiarity. Be sure to keep related topics close together.
3. Subdivide that list into non-overlapping subtopics.
4. Integrate the facts into the outline.
5. Double-check with your client and form books or checklists to be certain that you haven't omitted anything.

5. Write Carefully

At long last, you are ready to write your contract according to the principles set forth in Chapter 3. You will need to think about how to write the contract as a whole, each heading, each paragraph, each sentence, and even each word. Your agreement will be well written if it uses the proper tone, is clear, and is concise.

a. Use the Proper Tone

Before you plunge into the details, you should consider the tone you want to take in the contract. In order to strike the right tone, recall the different perspectives of each of your audiences. For example, if you are drafting a contract to consummate a deal, your client probably wants the tone of the document to be cooperative and neutral. Clients hate to see lawyers destroy deals with adversary language. However, you know that if the contract is later breached, your client will want the contract to be either a sword or a shield. The key to balancing these conflicting perspectives is choosing the right tone.

To illustrate the importance of tone, consider these two breach provisions, each of which seeks to limit damages to repair or refund without consequential damages:

> MORE HOSTILE: Seller's obligations shall be limited, at Seller's option, to replace the goods or to credit the Buyer with an amount not to exceed the selling price. No allowance shall be made for any expenses incurred by the Buyer. If the Seller replaces a defective item, the Buyer shall bear the cost of shipping and handling. In no event shall the Seller have any liability for payment of any consequential damages of any kind, including, but not limited to, any loss of profits.

> FRIENDLIER: If any portion of the goods delivered are defective, Seller may choose to either replace such defective goods or to refund a proportionate amount of the sales price. The Seller shall not be liable for lost profits, handling costs, or any other consequential damages.

Both provisions permit the seller to choose whether to replace the goods or give a refund, and limit the seller's liability for handling costs, lost profits, or other consequential damages. The first provision, however, takes a more hostile tone by using words that provide the buyer "no allowance." Similarly, it suggests that the seller may not fully cooperate in remedying problems when it says, "If the Seller replaces a defective item. . . ." The second version offers a more cooperative view and tries not to set up the seller and the buyer as clear adversaries.

Sometimes your client wants a document that sounds tough so the other party will not even think of breaching it. You frequently see this stance in divorce settlement agreements or leases. However, the contract cannot seem too one-sided or the other party will not sign it.

If you are drafting a consumer contract, use a tone that will make the contract more accessible. For instance, you might want to make the contract more conversational by using personal pronouns such as "I" and "you." Similarly, you may be required to write your contract in "plain English."[61] To comply, you should avoid legal jargon, use short sentences, avoid archaic words, avoid vampires,[62] and avoid passives.[63]

You also can use tone to emphasize important material or to bury difficult material. Your readers will remember the words you repeat throughout your contract. Consciously choose which words or themes to repeat. Similarly, stress important information by placing it first or last; bury less important information in the middle; and consciously select what you want to emphasize.

Tone can be used to camouflage harmful information too. For example, you can bury damaging data in the middle of a long document. Similarly, you can use vampires to take the teeth out of nasty information. To illustrate, compare these two warnings drafted for a lawnmower:

> Under certain circumstances, when operated in excessive heat, or while not properly cleaned, or in some other instances, the mechanical parts of this equipment may become overheated and cause the unexpected ignition of combustible materials.
>
> WARNING! If this lawnmower overheats or is dirty, it may explode.

Whatever tone you select, you should consciously choose it. Before drafting any particular provision, think of the general tone you want the entire document to have. Realistically you will have to write several different drafts, so you will have an opportunity to edit for the proper tone after you have finished your first draft.

b. Be Clear

i. Focus Accurately

Your highest priority is to be clear. Your contract will be clear if it is well focused and ordered. First, choose your focus. If your focus is too narrow, you omit necessary information. If your focus is scattered, the document may be inconsistent. A reader cannot supply missing information or reconcile inconsistencies. Accordingly, if you focus your contract well, it will be complete and consistent.

By the time you begin drafting the contract, you probably have already chosen the proper focus for the transaction. For example, you and your client have decided whether you are going to structure the deal as a partnership, a closely held corporation, or a sole proprietorship with employees. You will still have to choose the proper focus for the contract as a whole, various sections, sentences, and even words, however. These choices turn on how open-ended you want the particular provision to be without creating any ambiguities.

How open-ended a provision is depends on whether it is general or specific, or abstract or concrete. Considering the differing perspectives of the parties to the contract enables you to consider how to focus the document. Is the contract supposed to be general articles of agreement that leave room for flexibility later, or is the contract meant to be a detailed enumeration of specific rights and duties? Sometimes the contract needs to serve both functions.

Choose How General or Specific to Be.   Once you have a sense of the overall focus of the document, you may be ready to convert your topic outline into prose. Although you may want to retain the outline format and use your major topics as headings, most of the provisions should be spelled out carefully in well-written sentences and paragraphs. As you write, you must consider how to focus your paragraphs to make sure the contract is clear. You must choose both how general or specific to be and also how abstract or concrete to be.

Even though most contracts are broken down into small sections called paragraphs, they are not the sort of paragraphs you may be used to writing in memoranda or briefs. The typical contract paragraph is short, numbered, and confined to a single subject. At the very least, you will need a separate paragraph for each part of the bargain. Try not to cram too many items into the same paragraph. If you over-stuff your paragraphs, you will have a hard time writing accurate headings and your readers will find it difficult to locate relevant information. To illustrate, read this provision of a real estate sales contract:

> The closing date and the date of possession is of the essence of this contract because the Buyer will incur substantial expenses if she does not receive possession on or before March 22, 1995. Seller agrees to vacate and surrender possession on or before March 22, 1995, or closing, whichever occurs first. Until possession is tendered, Seller shall pay for all fuel, water, and other utilities consumed in or about the property. If possession is not delivered on or before March 22, 1995, or closing, whichever occurs first, the sum of $2,500 will be withheld at closing from the Seller's proceeds of this sale and shall be held in escrow by the same party named in this contract to hold the earnest money. Escrowee shall pay the Buyer as liquidated damages the sum of $100 per day from any escrow established for each day that possession is not so surrendered and will pay the balance of such escrow fund, if any, to the Seller. If possession is not delivered on or before March 22, 1995, or closing, whichever occurs first, and no escrow funds are available, then Seller shall pay Buyer as liquidated damages the sum of $100 per day for each day that possession is not so surrendered.

Although this paragraph covers a single topic, it is long and difficult to read. The problem is that the paragraph is over-stuffed. To simplify it, break the paragraph down into smaller sections and draft appropriate headings to help the reader find the crucial information:

1. POSSESSION

a. <u>Importance of the Date of Possession</u>: The closing date and the date of possession is of the essence of this contract because the Buyer will incur substantial expenses if she does not receive possession on or before March 22, 1995.

b. <u>Date of Possession</u>: Seller agrees to vacate and surrender possession on or before March 22, 1995, or closing, whichever occurs first.

c. <u>Payment of Utilities until Possession</u>: Until possession is tendered, Seller shall pay for all fuel, water, and other utilities consumed in or about the property.

d. <u>Escrow Payment for Late Possession</u>: If possession is not delivered on or before March 22, 1995, or closing, whichever occurs first, the sum of $2,500 will be withheld at closing from the Seller's proceeds of this sale and shall be held in escrow by the same party named in this contract to hold the earnest money. Escrowee shall pay the Buyer as liquidated damages the sum of $100 per day from any escrow for each day that possession is not so surrendered and will pay the balance of such escrow fund, if any, to the Seller.

e. <u>Liquidated Damages for Late Possession</u>: If possession is not delivered on or before March 22, 1995, or closing, whichever occurs first, and no escrow funds are available, then Seller shall pay Buyer as liquidated damages the sum of $100 per day for each day that possession is not so surrendered.

By breaking the longer paragraph down into smaller components and writing descriptive headings, you make the identical language easier to read. This process is called "enumeration and tabulation."[64]

Notice however, that some of your "paragraphs" are only one sentence long. Although that practice would be unacceptable in most other forms of writing, it helps in some contracts. Not every paragraph, however, is a single sentence. The length of the paragraph is determined by the scope of the heading.

Indeed, it is crucial that your headings accurately reflect the content of the paragraph. Under-inclusive headings fail to flag important information for readers. As a result, courts may be reluctant to enforce provisions that have not been identified adequately in headings. For example, courts have refused to enforce disclaimers of warranties that were included in paragraphs labeled "Factory Warranty," or "Warranty."[65]

Over-inclusive headings can also be misleading. For example, one form of a real estate sales contract has a section labeled, "Provisions." The section includes subparts without headings that include real estate taxes, building code violations, and rules of interpretation.[66] If the headings are too broad, courts may refuse to enforce the underlying provisions.[67]

These problems reflect a failure to properly focus on the correct level of generality. "Factory Warranty" is too specific a heading and "Provisions" is too general a heading. For each provision you write, you must choose how general or specific to be.

General language is often preferable to detailed lists in providing for unforseen circumstances. A list is almost inevitably incomplete, and the omitted items will not be governed by the contract.[68] For example if a real estate sales contract includes "furnaces, boilers, and heating systems," it may not cover air conditioning. The more general term, "fixtures,"[69] includes them all.

EDITING TIP: If you list specific items, ask yourself how all those items are similar. The similarity may suggest a general term that will make the provision more flexible.

However, general language may be difficult for readers to apply. Consequently disputes may arise about what constitutes a "fixture." Do "fixtures" include window-unit air conditioners? General language also may create some enforcement problems. Unless the real estate contract lists the items found in the house, it may be difficult to prove that a seller has removed an item. Hence, it is often wise to combine a general term with specific examples: "all fixtures such as furnaces, boilers, heating systems, central cooling systems, and permanently installed air conditioners."

A reader construing this provision might assume that it only covered temperature control systems. Hence a dispute could arise over whether tacked down carpeting is included. The general word (for example, "fixtures"), is often defined by any associated specific lists.[70] In order to make the provision more inclusive, you should add language that explains how the general word and the specific list are related. Use appropriate connecting words like, "including, but not limited to."

EDITING TIP: If you combine general terms with specific items or lists, state how the general language relates to the specific terms. Are the specific terms illustrations, explanations, exclusive lists, or inclusive lists?

Many drafters prefer to worry about these problems after they have completed the first draft. That way they can focus on getting their ideas down and then spend time later refining the wording. Others prefer to write and rewrite a single provision over and over until they are satisfied before moving to a new provision. Either way, whether in the first draft or the last draft, you must consider the problem of how specific or general to be.

Choose How Abstract or Concrete to Be. You also must choose how abstract or concrete to make your language. Concrete language conveys images rooted in the real world, while abstract language conveys more mental images. You may recall the example from Chapter 3: "Ball" is a concrete word, while "sphere" is an abstract word. Abstractions focus on a more theoretical level. As a result, abstractions are useful to convey underlying purposes.

Generally, you should try to avoid abstract language because it may be harder for your readers to understand or apply. However, on occasion, abstract language can help you anticipate unforeseen consequences. To illustrate, compare these two provisions from condominium bylaws meant to regulate dog owners:

> CONCRETE: No unit owner will be permitted to maintain a dog who bites, is not fully house broken, is dirty, or barks uncontrollably.

> ABSTRACT: No unit owner will be permitted to maintain a dog who is a nuisance.

Although the concrete language is easy to understand, it is both over- and under-inclusive. It is over-inclusive because it limits owners from keeping dogs who are "dirty." Most dogs are occasionally "dirty." Similarly, it is under-inclusive because many dogs could make nuisances of themselves without violating any of the specific prohibitions. Thus, a dog on a leash who chewed up other people's lawn furniture would be permitted to remain. The abstract language solves those problems by prohibiting owners from keeping dogs who are "a nuisance." The abstract word, "nuisance," covers unforeseen ways that dogs can misbehave.

Unfortunately, however, the abstract word, "nuisance," also makes the provision harder to apply. Is a single incident of a puppy chewing a piece of furniture a "nuisance"? Who decides whether a given action constitutes a "nuisance"? Just as adding specific language can clarify a general provision, adding concrete language can clarify an abstract provision. For example:

> ABSTRACT & CONCRETE: No unit owner will be permitted to maintain a dog who is a nuisance. A dog shall be deemed a nuisance if it bites, is not fully house broken, is dirty, barks uncontrollably, or otherwise misbehaves.

This combination of abstract and concrete language provides concrete limits, while it also covers unforeseen circumstances.

EDITING TIP: If you use abstract language, think about whether you need to add concrete language to make it clear.

Although the concrete language helps to define a "nuisance," it also limits the scope of the word. Note the phrase "or otherwise misbehaves." This phrase creates a category of actions that constitute a nuisance. A dog is a nuisance when it misbehaves. Thus, arguably, a dog might not be a nuisance if it is merely sick, such as a dog with distemper or rabies. Courts limit the category to the class created by the specific lists.[71]

One way to avoid this problem is to delegate the authority to construe the language. Accordingly, the provision might read:

> No unit owner will be permitted to maintain any animal that the Condominium Board deems to be a nuisance.

Note that this language not only avoids the problem of defining a nuisance, but also expands the group to include other animals. Substituting the more general word "animal" for "dog" also makes the language more flexible to include unforeseen circumstances. Hence, the improved version uses both abstract and general language to focus the provision so it provides for unforeseen circumstances.

As you write your contract, you should think about how your various readers may use your document. Consciously choose the focus of each provision so that it meets as many needs as possible. Different provisions will require different levels of generality and abstraction.

Avoid Ambiguities Caused by Omissions and Inconsistencies. One of the primary risks in choosing an abstract or generalized focus, is that you may create ambiguities. If language gets too broad or abstract, it becomes amorphous. A provision is ambiguous if it is susceptible to two or more inconsistent meanings.

Ambiguities often arise from either omissions or inconsistencies. When you omit necessary information, your readers must supply the missing data from the context. Different readers are likely to supply different data, and therefore read the contract differently. Consequently, you create ambiguity when you omit necessary items at any level.

Occasionally entire documents are omitted, so that a necessary item is missing from a transaction. For example, an attorney preparing the documents for a real estate closing might forget to draft the Bill of Sale for personal property that is to be transferred with the house. Such omissions are easy to catch if you follow a checklist for your transaction. You can avoid losing documents you have already prepared by keeping all the necessary documents together.

Omissions within a contract are both more common and more difficult to spot. You are more likely to omit necessary provisions if you write without an outline or a checklist. Often drafters get so involved in phrasing one section that they forget to include another. If you have a good outline of your contract, it can serve as a checklist of provisions to be included. After you finish your first draft, go back to your outline and check to see if you have included all the necessary items. You can use forms as checklists too.

Finally test your first draft carefully by asking: who? what? when? where? why? and how? You should test your language even at the sentence level. All too often contract sentences create duties without specifying *who* must act: "The earnest money shall be deposited in an interest bearing account." Who has the duty to deposit the money: the listing broker, the selling broker, the buyer, or the seller?

EDITING TIP: Look for the passive voice.[72] Sentences written in the passive voice often omit the actor.

Ambiguities also arise from inconsistencies. Sometimes different documents that are part of the same transaction conflict.[73] For example, a seller may sign an agreement hiring a real estate broker weeks or even months before he signs a contract to sell his house. If the broker's listing agreement calls for the seller to pay the commission, but the real estate sales contract calls for the buyer to pay the commission, an ambiguity arises. If you write both the listing agreement and the sales contract, you can assure that they are consistent. Similarly, if you read the listing agreement before you write the sales contract, then you can make them consistent. In order to avoid conflicting documents, you either need to draft all the documents yourself or be familiar with the previously signed documents when you draft a new one.

Unfortunately, your client may arrive with inconsistent documents that already have been signed. Then your job is to resolve the ambiguity. Sometimes the contract will provide for attorney approval or modifications. Many residential real estate contracts have such clauses. Then you should confer with your client to see if you can work out a satisfactory way to resolve the ambiguity. You must be tactful in negotiating these changes so you don't destroy the deal. These kinds of transactional ambiguities are especially common in commercial settings where telephone negotiations are confirmed with documents that cross in the mail. The Uniform Commercial Code devotes a section to resolving this "battle of the forms."[74] Typically you have a limited amount of time within which to resolve any transactional ambiguities.[75]

Inconsistencies within a contract are even more common. Often, two or more provisions seem to contradict each other. For example, consider these two provisions from the same Condominium Declaration:

DUTY TO MAINTAIN UNIT

The unit owner shall maintain her unit in good condition and repair at her own expense. This duty to maintain the unit shall include the duty to keep all electrical wiring and plumbing in good working order.

RESTRICTIONS ON USE OF THE COMMON ELEMENTS

Unit owners may not construct, repair, demolish, or damage any part of the common elements including, but not limited to exterior surfaces or the roof. No unit owner may paint or decorate the outside of her unit, or install any fixtures outside her unit. All repairs to the common elements shall be the responsibility of the Board and shall be paid for from common funds.

What happens if a leak develops in a unit owner's apartment that requires access to pipes through an exterior wall? Who has authority to authorize the repair? Who is responsible for the costs? The provision on the duty to maintain seems to require the unit owner to fix the leak and pay for the costs. In contrast, the section on restrictions seems to prohibit the unit owner from fixing the leak, vests the responsibility in the Board, and treats the cost as a common expense.

In order to avoid such inconsistencies, you must draft your contract as an integrated whole, rather than as a group of unrelated parts. If you simply "cut and paste" together provisions from form books and other contracts, they are likely to be inconsistent. Although you need not reinvent every provision each time you draft a contract, you must scrutinize every provision you use to be certain that it suits your purposes and is consistent with the rest of the document.

Inconsistencies may even occur at the sentence level. Misplaced modifiers may permit two conflicting interpretations of the same sentence. If necessary, review the information on sentence level ambiguity in Chapter 3.[76]

Finally, you should be aware of the inconsistent interpretations of individual words. The worst problems arise with the conjunctions, "or" and "and." Each of these words is ambiguous. Consider the use of "or" in this provision:

> AMBIGUOUS USE OF "OR": An employee who is wrongfully discharged may be reinstated *or* receive back pay.

It is unclear whether the employee must choose between these two remedies, or whether the employee could be both reinstated and receive back pay. Sometimes "or" means a limited choice between two alternatives: either reinstatement or back pay, *but not both.* If you intend to use "or" in its exclusive sense, you should add language that indicates exclusivity. If the choice is limited to two alternatives you add the words like, "either," and "but not both" to the sentence:

> "EITHER . . . OR": An employee who is wrongfully discharged may *either* be reinstated *or* receive back pay, *but not both.*

When you want to express an exclusive meaning to "or," but you have more than two alternatives, you still should add language that explains that you intend to use "or" to limit the choices:

> "OR" USED TO LIMIT MORE THAN TWO OPTIONS: An employee who is wrongfully discharged may elect *one of* the following remedies: (1) reinstatement, (2) back pay, *or* (3) damages for emotional distress.

Sometimes, however, you want to create several choices that are not mutually exclusive. Then you should add inclusive language:

> INCLUSIVE USE OF "OR": An employee who is wrongfully discharged may elect *one or more* of the following remedies: (1) reinstatement, (2) back pay, *or* (3) damages for emotional distress.

"And" is also ambiguous:

> AMBIGUOUS USE OF "AND": Cash *and* payments within 30 days qualify for a 5% discount.

In order to qualify for the discount, must a payment be *both* in cash *and* paid within 30 days, or will it be sufficient if the payment is *either* cash *or* paid in 30 days? Again, you can make the statement clearer by adding appropriate language:

> "AND" MEANING "ALL": Payments qualify for a 5% discount if they are *both* in cash *and* paid within 30 days.

Do not use "and" unless you mean to include *all* items on the list as a single unit. If you mean "some, but not all," you should use *"either . . . or":*

> MEANING "SOME, BUT NOT ALL": Payments qualify for a 5% discount if they are *either* in cash *or* are paid within 30 days.

EDITING TIP: When you use "and" or "or," ask yourself two questions:

1. Are the items on the list mutually exclusive? If so, add words that specify exclusivity such as, "one" or "only."
2. Are the items on the list all inclusive? If so, add words that specify unity such as, "all," "both," or "together."

Other words also have inconsistent meanings. Pay particular attention to the words "shall," "may," and "will." These words all express the future tense and give directives. If you phrase your contract in the present tense, you can use these words precisely to convey three separate meanings:

Word:	Impact:	Example:
"Shall"	Issues an order (must)	Seller *shall* furnish a title insurance policy.
"May"	Grants discretion (may, but need not)	Buyer *may* inspect the property.
"Will"	States agreement (agrees to)	Seller *will* keep the property in good repair.

Contracts must be precise. You can eliminate ambiguities if you avoid omissions and inconsistencies at all levels. Checklists, outlines, and forms can help you catch omissions. Careful editing at the document, paragraph, sentence, and word levels can help you avoid inconsistencies.

ii. Order Carefully

No matter how well focused and precise your document is, it must also be well ordered if it is to be clear. You already have considered the global organization of your contract in step four of the drafting process. Now, as you write the first draft, you should concentrate on the internal organization of your paragraphs and sentences. Your contract will be well ordered if it (1) uses parallel structure, (2) moves from familiar material to unfamiliar material, and (3) is visually clear.

Use Parallel Structure.   You should express similar ideas in similar language. Hence, if you were listing contractual duties, you would phrase the duties the same way and use the same verb to express it:

> The seller *shall* convey the property with a warranty deed.

> The buyer *shall* pay the balance due at closing with a cashier's check.

These two provisions are parallel both grammatically and functionally. Grammatically, they both follow the same structure:

Noun	Verb	Object	Prepositional Phrase
"seller"	"shall convey"	"property"	"with . . . warranty deed"
"buyer"	"shall pay"	"balance due"	"with . . . cashier's check"

More importantly, both sentences are functionally parallel. They use similar language to express similar ideas:

Person	Duty	How Performed
seller	convey property	warranty deed
buyer	pay balance	cashier's check

Two related rules emerge: (1) Use similar language and structures to express similar ideas, and (2) use different language and structures to express different ideas. If you use similar language to express different ideas, the reader may miss the contrast. Recall this example from Chapter 3:

>   1. *The seller agrees to*[77] furnish the purchaser with a warranty deed to the property at the closing.
>   2. *The purchaser agrees to* apply for financing immediately and to use her best efforts to procure such financing.
>   3. *The parties agree to* reprorate the taxes when the next tax bill is issued.
>   4. *The parties agree to* include all personal property in the seller's bill of sale.

In the above example, the grammar is quite parallel. Each sentence begins with "The (noun) agrees to. . . ." However, the provisions are not functionally parallel as the following chart illustrates:

Who agrees:	What Agreed:	Who Performs:
1. **Seller**	furnish deed	**Seller**
2. **Purchaser**	apply for financing	**Purchaser**
3. **Parties**	reprorate taxes	**Parties** jointly
4. **Parties**	include in bill of sale	**Seller**

In the first three sentences, the individuals who agree are the ones who must perform. The seller must furnish the deed; the purchaser must apply for the financing; and both parties must reprorate the taxes. In the fourth sentence, however, both parties agree, but only the seller must furnish the bill of sale.

After reading the first three sentences, the reader would expect that all of the seller's obligations would begin with, "The seller agrees to. . . ." Accordingly, the reader may be confused by the fourth sentence and fail to see that it creates an obligation on the seller. Because the faulty parallelism in this example affects the meaning of the document, it is functional rather than grammatical.

When you repeat or vary language, you create patterns for your readers. Repeated language suggests similarities, and varied language suggests differences. If you adopt language from a variety of forms, different words may be used to express the same idea. Such unnecessary variation will confuse your readers. Therefore, you should always use the same words to describe the same ideas.

Move from Familiar Material to Unfamiliar Material.   "Start at the very beginning. It's a very good place to start."[78] Readers find it difficult to follow texts that skip around. You should lead your reader from familiar information to unfamiliar information, so that the reader can follow each step of the way. Most contracts are organized to reflect this precept. They begin by identifying the parties, move on to a background section (recitals), state the consideration, set forth the body of the agreement, and finish with signatures and acknowledgments. This organization moves the reader from familiar information to new information.

The same principles apply to writing each provision. Once you have established a familiar starting place, you should introduce each new idea by connecting it to a familiar one. You won't startle your readers with misplaced information if you:

1. identify your topics;
2. define your terms;
3. use transitions; and
4. order your sentences carefully.

Identify Your Topics.   Readers know what to expect if you identify your topics in advance. Accordingly, if your contract is more than a page long, you should create an index or table of contents to familiarize your readers with the overall organization and content of the contract. Indices and tables also help your reader find the relevant portion of the contract when they are looking for a particular provision.

For similar reasons, you should always use headings for each section. Headings serve three functions: They notify the reader of what to expect; they help the reader find relevant information; and they tie the contents of the section together with a common theme. As you know, you need to concentrate on the scope of the headings so they are neither too broad, nor too narrow.

EDITING TIP: If you have difficulty writing a good heading, perhaps your provision contains too many unrelated ideas.

Define Your Terms.   If you have identified your topics in appropriate head-ings, your readers may have a general idea of what to expect. However, they will not be able to follow the contract unless they can understand the terms you use. Your goal is to develop a shared vocabulary with your reader. Accordingly, you should define your terms.

You have to exercise judgment in deciding which terms to define. Don't assume that the reader shares your vocabulary, and remember that you are writing your contract for several different audiences, each of whom may have different areas of expertise. Whenever you use a term that may be unfamiliar to *any* of your readers, you should define it. Hence, most legal terms should be defined.

Even familiar terms may require definitions. When familiar words are likely to be the subject of later disputes, you should define them. Consider the word "price." Readers generally know what "price" means, but later disputes may arise about whether it includes items like shipping costs. Similarly, when you use familiar terms in unfamiliar ways, you should define the terms. For example, al-though most consumers understand the word "liquidated," they probably cannot make sense of the phrase "liquidated damages."[79] Accordingly, you should define key terms precisely.

Your definitions should be clear too. You should not define a word with jargon. Nor should you define a word in terms of itself. For example, if you are concerned that parties may dispute the meaning of the word, "profits," don't use "profits" as part of your definition. Similarly, you should not substitute a cross reference for a definition. You should use cross references to help readers find other rele-vant provisions only after you have defined the term itself.

Examples pose special problems for definitions.[80] They can be invaluable tools to help readers understand what you mean, but examples can also limit the scope of the definition and, hence, the contract itself. Be careful to define the term first, before you add examples. Otherwise, the example becomes the definition and your term has a very limited meaning. Even if you add examples to an adequate definition, you must be careful to explain exactly how the example relates to the more general definition. If you intend the example merely to illustrate, but not to limit your definition, you should introduce your example with transition words like:

> For example, . . .
> For instance, . . .
> . . . including, but not limited to . . .

In contrast, if you want your example to limit your definition, you should intro-duce it with words of limitation like:

> . . . only if . . .
> . . . provided that . . .

Once you have an adequate definition, you have to decide where to place it in your contract. You can either define a word in the text the first time you use it, or you can create a separate definitions section early in the contract that defines all the unfamiliar terms in the entire contract. Contextual definitions are easy for readers and work well in short contracts. Then the reader can remember the def-inition long enough to finish reading the rest of the contract or provision. In long contracts, you may introduce a term and not use it again for several pages. By then, the reader may have forgotten what the term means. If the reader returns to try to find the original definition, she may have trouble finding it in the text. In this situation, you should use a glossary section at the beginning of the contract so the reader knows exactly where to find the necessary definitions.

Wherever you place them, definitions are crucial. You must create a shared vocabulary with your readers to create common understandings of the contract. Definitions allow you to introduce unfamiliar material to your readers.

Use Transitions.   Transitions are another crucial way to link familiar and unfamiliar material. You already are aware of a number of transition words like "although," "including," "however," and "only if," which can connect new ideas to old ones.[81] Some words are better than others. "And" is often ambiguous. Try to make your transition words as precise as possible so your reader will understand exactly how the provisions relate.

The way you write your sentences also gives your readers clues about how various provisions are related. Thus, sentence structure can be a silent transition. Readers expect sentences to begin with familiar material and end with new material.[82]

<u>familiar</u>   UNFAMILIAR

The <u>owner</u> shall provide MAINTENANCE SERVICE.

Once material has been identified, it becomes familiar and can move to the beginning of the sentence:

<u>familiar</u>   UNFAMILIAR

<u>Maintenance service</u> includes PERIODIC CLEANING AND
                              REPLACEMENT OF WORN PARTS.

You have three choices in the way you create these silent transitions: a sequential pattern, a centered pattern, or a mixed pattern[83]:

Sequential Pattern
A → B   B → C   C → D

[The familiar material is underlined and the unfamiliar material
is in capitals.]

The <u>owner</u> shall provide MAINTENANCE SERVICE. <u>Maintenance service</u> includes PERIODIC CLEANING AND REPLACEMENT PARTS. <u>Replacement parts</u> shall only be provided for ORDINARY WEAR AND TEAR ON THE EQUIPMENT.

Centered Pattern
A → B   A → C   A → D

[The familiar material is underlined and the unfamiliar material
is in capitals.]

<u>Maintenance service</u> includes PERIODIC CLEANING AND REPLACEMENT PARTS. <u>Maintenance service</u> excludes DAMAGE CAUSED BY MISUSE OF THE

EQUIPMENT. <u>Maintenance service</u> shall be FREE OF CHARGE FOR A PERIOD OF ONE YEAR.

Mixed Pattern
A → B   A → C   C → D
or
A → B   B → C   B → D

[The familiar material is underlined and the unfamiliar material is in capitals.]

<u>Maintenance service</u> includes PERIODIC CLEANING AND REPLACEMENT PARTS. <u>Maintenance service</u> excludes DAMAGE CAUSED BY MISUSE OF THE EQUIPMENT. <u>The equipment may be damaged</u> by EXPOSING IT TO EXTREME TEMPERATURES.

Each pattern operates as a silent transition to the reader explaining how the provisions relate. The sequential pattern suggests that one idea leads directly to the next. As a result, you should use the sequential pattern to express sequence, causation, and interrelated conditions.

In contrast, the centered pattern suggests that all of the new material relates in the same way to the familiar topic. Hence, in the centered pattern example above, each different piece of new information (inclusions, exclusions, and cost) described the attributes of the central topic (the maintenance service). The centered pattern emphasizes the importance of the central topic and helps a reader through a section that shares a single topic. All too often, however, the centered pattern is used by default because the drafter has not figured out how the various provisions relate to each other. If you carelessly use the wrong pattern, you may confuse your reader.

The mixed pattern blends the sequential pattern and the centered pattern. You can combine the various patterns in any useful order. Each provides a precise structural transition that helps your reader understand how the contract parts fit together. Connectors and silent transitions help make your contract clearer.

Order Your Sentences Carefully.   Even your sentences should be carefully ordered to help your reader. Accordingly, you should follow the seven rules developed in Chapter 3 for writing carefully ordered sentences: (1) Identify the actors; (2) make the actors the subject of the sentence; (3) make the topic the grammatical subject of the sentence; (4) express the action as a verb (avoid vampires); (5) keep the subject and the verb together; (6) keep the subject and the verb close to the beginning of the sentence; and (7) keep modifiers close to the words they modify. You might want to review the discussion of these rules and the examples in Chapter 3. Well-written sentences will be clear.[84]

c. Be Concise

If your contract is well focused and ordered, it will be clear. Now you must make it concise. Readers have limited attention spans. The techniques for concise writing are simple: (1) control redundancy; (2) trim lists; (3) eliminate unnecessary descriptions; (4) eliminate unnecessary clauses; and (5) avoid long sentences. Although you want your contract to be lean, you do not want to omit crucial items. Accordingly, you must exercise your judgment about what is necessary. Clarity is your highest priority, though, so if conciseness and accuracy conflict, err on the side of accuracy.

i. Control Redundancy

Contracts have a tendency to be very repetitive. Every word, sentence, paragraph, and section of your contract should serve a specific purpose.[85] Accordingly, you should not repeat introductory phrases. Tabulate the provisions instead:

BAD:
1. *The seller shall provide* a title insurance policy insuring that the seller has clear title.
2. *The seller shall provide* a current survey of the property showing no encroachments.
3. *The seller shall provide* a current certificate of inspection for termites demonstrating that the property is free from termite infestation.

BETTER: *The seller shall provide:*
1. a title insurance policy insuring that the seller has clear title,
2. a current survey of the property showing no encroachments, and
3. a current certificate of inspection for termites demonstrating that the property is free from termite infestation.

However, you can't eliminate all repetition from contracts. Some repetition helps your reader recall necessary information buried elsewhere in the contract. For instance, if you have not referred to a provision for several pages, you may need to repeat it. You can minimize the need to repeat material by keeping related sections close together. Then your reader is more likely to be able to remember the material from section to section.

EDITING TIP: Look for repeated language. Will the reader be burdened or helped by the repetition?

You also should edit out redundant words; never use two words when one will suffice.

EDITING TIP: Look for the word "and." Can one of the words or provisions joined by "and" be eliminated without changing your meaning?

---

ii. Trim Lists

Most form contracts contain long lists. Often you can shorten the list by eliminating redundant words, or by substituting a more general word for an entire portion of the list. If you cut a redundant word, verify that it is synonymous with the word you retain. Similarly, if you substitute a more general word, think about whether a reader will be able to use the document as easily.

iii. Eliminate Unnecessary Descriptions

Although you sometimes need to use descriptive words like "willful" or "reasonable," lawyers tend to overuse such modifiers. Readers tend to discount embellishments. Try to replace weak adjectives and adverbs with more forceful nouns and verbs. For example, replace "clearly see" with "focus."

EDITING TIP: Look for words ending in "-ly." They may be extraneous modifiers that can be eliminated.

---

iv. Eliminate Unnecessary Clauses

Try to use a single word instead of a longer clause. If you overuse vampires, you may substitute clauses for single words:

> BAD: The seller shall provide the buyer with *notification* of any *cancellation* of the insurance policy.

> BETTER: The seller shall *notify* the buyer if the insurance policy is *canceled.*

Avoid other unnecessary clauses as well. For example, say "although" instead of "notwithstanding the fact that. . . ."

v. Avoid Long Sentences

Lawyers have a tendency to write sentences that go on for pages. Wordy sentences are confusing for three reasons: (1) They force the reader to concentrate on too much information at once; (2) they are likely to have misplaced modifiers; and (3) they are likely to have misplaced clauses. Break long sentences into parts, tabulating and enumerating them, if necessary. Whenever possible, eliminate modifiers and intrusive clauses. To be concise you need to control redundancy, trim lists, eliminate unnecessary descriptions, eliminate unnecessary clauses, and avoid long sentences.

Some lawyers pore over every detail of the first draft as they write it. Others jot their ideas down quickly and revise repeatedly. Whatever your strategy, you will need to write several drafts to get a contract that has the right tone, is well focused and ordered, and is concise.

Exercise 5-8

a.   Rewrite the following provision paying special attention to tone, clarity, and conciseness:

> If this contract is terminated without the Buyer's fault, the earnest money shall be returned to the Buyer, but such refund shall not release the Seller from the Seller's duties according to this contract. If the termination is the

Buyer's fault, then, the earnest money shall be forfeited and applied first to payment of Broker's commission and any expenses incurred, and the balance paid to the Seller. In the event of default, the Escrowee may give written notice to both the Buyer and the Seller of how the Escrowee intends to disburse the earnest money. If neither the Buyer nor the Seller objects in writing within 15 days, the Escrowee will disburse the earnest money as previously indicated by the Escrowee. If either the Buyer or the Seller objects to the intended disposition, then the parties agree that the escrowee may deposit the earnest money, less costs, with the Clerk of the Circuit Court by filing an action in the nature of interpleader.

   b.   Write a divorce settlement using the following facts. You represent Kathleen Miller, a 42-year-old homemaker, who is returning to college to become an accountant. She was married on July 17, 1975, to Steven Miller, an attorney. They have three children, Alex, who is 19, David, who is 13, and Sarah, who is 10. Both spouses plan to remarry once the divorce is final. They agree that they should share the cost of the childrens' college expenses. Because Steven earns more, he should pay more. They want the divorce to be as peaceful as possible for the children. Accordingly, they want joint custody, but they assume that the children will continue to live with Kathleen. They want the children to move freely between their homes, with the children controlling the visitation schedule as much as possible. However, Steven wants to be assured that he will see the children at least two weekends a month and every other school holiday.
   Steven and Kathleen own a house together and expect that Kathleen and the children will continue living there until Sarah graduates from high school. Then they intend to sell the house and split the proceeds. Steven will contribute more to major household repairs because of his higher income, but Kathleen will be responsible for minor problems. Although Steven will pay the real estate taxes, Kathleen will pay the mortgage.
   Steven will provide the children with life insurance on himself and health insurance for the children until they turn 22. He will pay child support now in the amount of $300 per month per child. He is willing to consider some formula to increase child support to reflect any increases in the cost of living. Steven will also pay Kathleen a lump sum of $75,000 payable over three years. All other assets already have been divided by the couple.
   c.   Write a sexual harassment policy that will become a part of the employee handbook for a state university using the information from prior exercises in this chapter and these additional facts. The university wants to protect potential victims of sexual harassment. It wants to define sexual harassment, create appropriate remedies, and provide minimal due process for those accused. The university is concerned that some instances of sexual harassment get "lost" in the system. For example, one student might complain to his faculty advisor about a harasser and decide not to proceed. A year later a different student might complain to a different advisor about the same harasser. In a large university, it might take years for the university to act, and the university might be liable for its failure to act. On the other hand, the university is worried about suits by disciplined employees.
   d.   Mary Clay and her husband, David Harper, run an inventory service out of the basement of their home. They perform inventories for stores during off-hours, while the stores are closed. They call their partnership "Counters Unlim-

ited." Although the work is variable, they make a comfortable living and control their own hours.

Mary and Dave want to buy a new laptop computer from Orange Computers, Inc., a California corporation. Having a portable computer along when they take inventories will increase their productivity significantly. Although they can't afford to pay the $4,000 purchase price in a single payment, they can make monthly payments of $100 toward the computer. The computer company won't sell the computer to them on time because they do not have a large enough down payment.

Mary's uncle, Stephen Babcock, has agreed to lend them the money to buy the computer. Although Stephen is generous, he wants to be sure that they repay the loan because he is counting on having the money and the interest it earns when he retires in five years. If Steve lends them the money, they will pay him $100 per month for five years. Stephen is also worried that the inventory business will fail and that Mary and Dave will be unable to repay him. Accordingly, he wants to use the computer as collateral for the loan.

You represent Stephen Babcock. Stephen wants to be legally protected, but he wants to remain on friendly terms with his niece and her husband. Draft all necessary documents to complete this deal.

e.   Draft the contract outlined in section C.4, pages 223 through 232 of this chapter.

6.   Test the Contract for Consequences

Once you have a draft of your contract, you must test it to see if you have predicted future circumstances adequately. Review each of the previous five steps of the drafting process, playing the "what if . . . ?" game.

a.   Test the Contract for Each Expected Audience

As you recall, you can expect to have two kinds of readers: friendly ones and hostile ones. Put yourself in the place of each person who might use the contract. Begin with your client. Does the contract provide the necessary information? Does it tell the client who is going to do what, when, where, why, and how? Can the client find crucial data using appropriate headings and indices? Is each step outlined for the client? Repeat this process for each reader who might use the contract. It should help you spot any omissions.

Next, pretend you are a party hostile to the contract. Try to pick the contract apart. Look for ambiguities to construe in your favor. Identify weaknesses, especially enforcement terms. Try to figure every possible way to weasel out of the contract.

b.   Test the Contract for Each Expected Fact

Return to your list of facts. For each fact on the list, imagine how it might change in the future. To illustrate, if your list of facts contains a price, imagine what circumstances might cause the price to change — for example, inflation, recession, war, natural disaster, and strikes. Play this "what if . . . ?" game for each fact. Then consider what changes you should make in the contract to provide for such changed facts.

For each substantive provision in your contract, ask the familiar questions: who? what? where? when? why? and how? You should be able to answer each question for every provision. If you can't, then you probably have omitted crucial information. For example, if your contract provides for the payment of money, it should identify who will pay it, what it will be paying for, where it will be paid, when it will be paid, why it will be paid, and how it will be paid (e.g., check, cash, money order, or credit). Playing this "what if . . . ?" game helps you spot omissions.

c. Test the Contract for Possible Changes in the Law

Students tend to think of the law as an immutable body of rules. Statutes and common law actually change rather quickly, however. Review your legal research. What if some of the legal rules changed after the contract was signed? For example, suppose your divorce settlement agreement provided for the spouse paying child support to get the tax exemptions for the children. What if the tax law changed by eliminating such exemptions? Would the payor be entitled to pay proportionately less child support? For each rule of law you identified, you should consider how it would affect the contract if the law changed.

On a broader level you should also consider the possibility that a court might disagree with your analysis of the law and hold some part of your contract to be illegal. If so, should the rest of the contract be enforced, or should the entire contract be voided? Always consider the possibility of illegality.

d. Test the Contract for Organization

Can each individual who might use the contract find the necessary information? Can you outline the contract with a clear organizational structure? What principles of subdivision did you use? Did you use them consistently? Does the outline of the existing contract correspond to the outline you wrote before you began drafting the contract? Are the provisions of the contract internally consistent?

e. Test the Contract for Language

Is the tone of the contract appropriate? Is the language friendly enough to facilitate the deal? Is the language strong enough to protect your client? Is important information emphasized? Is damaging information minimized? Is the contract well focused? Is the language general enough to include unforeseen circumstances but specific enough to be enforceable? Is the language abstract enough to cover future contingencies but concrete enough to be applicable? Does the contract move from familiar to unfamiliar material? Does the contract ramble on, or is it concise? Is the contract visually accessible with adequate size print, enumeration, and tabulation?

Testing each phase of the drafting process enables you to find omissions, ambiguities, and unforeseen circumstances. Be sure to keep a list of provisions to be changed as a result of the testing process.

Exercise 5-9

a.   Using all the information from prior exercises in this chapter, test the divorce settlement agreement you wrote for Exercise 5-8b. How would you change the agreement after testing it?

b.   Using all the information from prior exercises in this chapter, test the sexual harassment policy you wrote for Exercise 5-8c. How would you change the policy after testing it?

c.   Using all the information from prior exercises in this chapter, test the loan documents you wrote for Exercise 5-8d. How would you change the documents after testing them?

7. Edit and Rewrite

a. Revise the Contract in Light of Testing

First you should revise the contract to account for any problems you found while testing it. This process can be more complex than it sounds because your testing may have revealed organizational errors as well as omissions and ambiguities. You may need to rethink entire provisions of the contract and where they fit in overall scheme. Often, this step will require you to go back and repeat prior steps. For example, if you discover that you haven't specified how the contract price is to be paid, you may have to go back to your client to gather more facts. Would your client prefer cash, checks, money orders, or credit? What interest rates, if any, would apply? Similarly, you may find yourself researching law, reorganizing, or rewriting.

b. Proofread the Contract Carefully

Next, you should proofread the contract carefully for spelling, punctuation, and grammar. Although "spell-check" functions on computers can help you catch typographical errors, they are not substitutes for careful proofreading since they do not recognize errors that are actual words (e.g., "here" versus "hear"). Small errors can alter the entire meaning of the contract and diminish you in your client's eyes. Try not to be too enamored of your own flowing prose. Read the contract critically, preferably after a few hours or even a day or two. Such distance enables you to be more critical. Perhaps a colleague could proofread the contract as well.

c. Review Seven-Step Drafting Process

Finally, you need to review your notes from the drafting process. Make sure you have used the relevant facts you gathered. Check the contract to be sure it reflects the law you researched. Re-evaluate the organization, comparing it to other similar documents. Re-read the contract, scrutinizing each word to see if it is the best choice. This process of critical evaluation will produce both a better contract and a better lawyer.

Exercise 5-10

a.   Using all the information from prior exercises in this chapter, edit and rewrite the divorce settlement agreement you wrote for Exercise 5-8b.

b.   Using all the information from prior exercises in this chapter, edit and rewrite the sexual harassment policy you wrote for Exercise 5-8c.

c.   Using all the information from prior exercises in this chapter, edit and rewrite the loan documents you wrote for Exercise 5-8d.

D. Conclusion

Contracts are far more varied than wills or pleadings. Accordingly, you have more room to exercise creativity in structuring a deal, negotiating provisions, and drafting the contract. Nevertheless, drafting contracts, like other documents, involves the same seven-step process: (1) understand the audiences; (2) gather the facts; (3) know the law; (4) classify, organize, and outline; (5) write carefully; (6) test for consequences; and (7) edit and rewrite.

SAMPLE DOCUMENT
Settlement Agreement for Dissolution of Marriage

A sample contract written by students is attached with editorial comments. When you read it, think about whether you would have drafted it differently. Can you spot any errors in addition to the ones noted in the editorial comments?

SETTLEMENT AGREEMENT FOR DISSOLUTION OF
MARRIAGE OF DAVE AND MARY JO CASS
April 28, 1992

[1]The parties were married in Chicago, Illinois on January 2, 1980, and have 3 minor children, Rachel, born on January 26, 1981, Stephanie, born on February 17, 1983, and Jack, born on March 17, 1989.

As a result of disputes and serious differences that have caused the marriage of the parties to breakdown irretrievably, the parties separated on October 26, 1991, and are now living apart. They intend to continue to remain permanently apart.

The parties want to settle by agreement their affairs, including custody and support of their minor children, spousal support and maintenance, the division of their joint and separate property, and any other claims and demands each might have against the other by reason of their marriage.

Each party has fully disclosed[2] the extent of their estate, income, and financial prospects and has been fully informed concerning the extent of the estate, income, and financial prospects of the other, as appears in the sworn financial statements attached as Exhibits[3] to this agreement. Each party has been represented in the preparation of this agreement by independent counsel. Each has been fully advised of his or her rights by such counsel. Each party considers the terms of this agreement to be fair and reasonable.

The parties agree to dissolve the marriage in an action pending in court that bears docket number 12345678. [4]

[1] *Write Carefully:* Headings
Edit and Rewrite: Punctuation?

[2] *Know the Law:* Effect of undisclosed items?

[3] *Edit and Rewrite/Test for Consequences:* Exhibits attached?

[4] *Know the Law:* Defense of collusion?

NOW THEREFORE, the parties agree to the following:

1. Separation

Each party shall live separately from the
other for the remainder of his or her life at
any place or places that he or she may choose.
Neither party shall annoy, harass, molest,
threaten, injure, or interfere⑤ with the
other party in any manner whatsoever, or seek
to induce the other to cohabit or reside with
him or her by any legal or other proceedings or
by any manner whatsoever. ⑥ Each party shall
have the right to engage in any employment,
business, profession, or any other activity
without interference from the other party, in
any manner he or she considers advisable for
his or her sole use and benefit. ⑦

2. Custody, Visitation Rights, Visitation Schedule ⑧

The Wife shall have sole custody of the three
minor children of the parties.
The Husband shall have reasonable visitation rights set forth as follows:
  A. The Husband shall have the right to
visit the children:
    (1) Two weekends a month. [The weekend
  begins Friday at 5:00 p.m. continues until
  Sunday at 5:00 p.m. If the weekend is a
  three-day weekend,⑨ the Husband shall
  have visitation rights for the full extra

---

⑤ *Know the Interpretive Law:* Effect of list?

⑥ *Test for Consequences:* Enforcement? Can they remarry each other?

⑦ *Know the Law:* Duty to work to support children?

⑧ *Write Carefully:* Add subheadings for paragraph 2.

⑨ *Write Carefully:* Define 3-day weekend (legal holidays? work holidays? school holidays?).

day (either Friday, beginning at 9:00 a.m. or Monday, until 5:00 p.m.).]

(2) Half of every Christmas school recess. [The school recess is usually 10 days long. The Husband will alternate with Wife so that every other year Husband will have the children for the first half of the recess (the first five days, including Christmas) and half of the second part of the recess (the last five days, including New Year's Day).[10] Children will be returned to the home by 12 noon on the day before school begins.]

(3) Every Spring school recess, commencing at 9:00 a.m. on Monday after school lets out and ending at noon the day before school begins.

(4) Three weeks during every summer.

(5) Every other holiday for those not covered above.

(6) Other times as the parties may agree.

B. The Husband's visitation rights shall be paramount to any plans the Wife may make that might infringe on such rights, except the scheduling of activities for the child, such as attending friends' birthday parties or participation in extra-curricular activities,[11] provided the Husband is given at least 7 days notice of such activity and further provided that it is the Husband's choice as to whether or not he wants to incorporate these activities into his visitation schedule.[12]

[10] *Write Carefully:* Does the husband get 1/2 of the recess or 3/4?

[11] *Write Carefully*: Is a list of activities an illustration or a limitation? How will it be read?

[12] *Write Carefully and Test for Consequences:* One sentence? Who gives notice? What happens if notice is not given or less than 7 days is given?

3. Child Support

The Husband shall pay to the Wife for the support of each child of the parties, the sum of $1100. per month until the first child reaches her 18th birthday. Then the Husband shall pay the Wife $747. per month until the second child reaches her 18th birthday. Then the Husband shall pay the Wife $598. per month until the third child reaches his 18th birthday. At that time, child support payments shall cease. [13]

Child support payments may[14] cease with regard to any individual child upon the occurrence of the earliest of the following events:

(1) the child's death;
(2) the child's marriage;
(3) the child's entry into the armed forces of the U.S.
(4) judicial recognition of the child's emancipation.
(5) the child's 18th birthday, unless the child is still in high school, in which case payments shall continue until the child finish 12th grade.

4. College Education Expenses

The Husband and the Wife agree that they are obligated to pay for the college educations of their children so long as the child is a full-time student in good standing. [15] The Husband and Wife will[16] be responsible for up to four years of college education unless a child is prevented from attending school because of disability or illness. The two parties will confer to decide how to pay college

[13] *Edit and Rewrite:* Punctuation for dollar amounts?

[14] *Test for Consequences/Write Carefully:* Is the use of the word "may" accurate? Who decides?

[15] *Write Carefully:* What does "good standing" mean?

[16] *Write Carefully:* Use of the word, "will"?

expenses. [17] Each will contribute to the college education of the children according to their ability to pay. [18]

5. Maintenance [19]

The Husband shall pay to the Wife for support and maintenance, [20] the sum of $2300/month. Payment shall be made in advance on the first day of each month commencing the first day of May 1992. [21]

Payments shall terminate on the death of either party or the remarriage of the Wife, whichever event occurs first. The payments under this agreement have been established in light of the fact that the Wife is not employed and does not have any source of income other than the payments to be received from the Husband. On January 2, 1997, [22] the parties agree to review this award in light of additional factors according to the statutory factors (Ill. Rev. Stat. ch. 40, par. 504). As stated in the statute (Ill. Rev. Stat. ch. 40, sec. 502(b)), [23] the parties agree not to seek modification of maintenance until January 2, 1997.

In the event that the Wife secures employment or acquires an independant [24] income, or if there are any other favorable changes in the

[17] *Know the Law:* Agreement to agree?

[18] *Test for Consequences:* What if a parent dies? Is the estate liable for college costs? What if they cannot agree about how much each will pay?

[19] *Write Carefully:* Subheadings, pictorial clarity of the entire maintenance section.
Classify, Organize, and Outline: Should the maintenance section be reorganized?

[20] *Write Carefully:* Redundant word pair.

[21] *Test for Consequences:* Duration?

[22] *Write Carefully:* Sentence structure: modifier, January 2, 1997.

[23] *Test for Consequences:* What if statute numbers change or the statute is substantively amended?

[24] *Edit and Rewrite:* Spelling.

Wife's financial condition, [25] the parties shall confer for the purposes of determining a reduction in the maintenance payments. [26]

In the event that the parties are unable to arrive at a mutually agreeable adjustment, the matter shall be arbitrated. [27] Pending the decision of the arbitrator, the Husband shall pay to the Wife the sum provided under this agreement.

If the Wife loses her employment or other source of independent income after an adjustment is made by agreement or by arbitration, or if there is any other unfavorable change in her condition, the parties shall confer with regard to the restoration of all or part of the reduction that occurred. In the event that the parties are unable to agree, the matter may be arbitrated in the same manner and under the same terms described above. [28]

Any payments made by the Husband in excess of, or in addition to the payments he agrees to make here for the support and maintenance shall neither alter his obligations hereunder nor create any precedent for the future. In particular, they shall not be construed as proof of this ability to make increased support payments nor shall they be evidence of the Wife's need for increased amounts. [29]

[25] *Write Carefully:* What constitutes "any other favorable change in the wife's financial condition?" How are those words read with preceding, more specific examples?

[26] *Know the Law:* Agreement to agree?

[27] *Test for Consequences/Gather the Facts:* How is the arbitrator chosen? Who pays the costs?

[28] *Test for Consequences/Write Carefully:* Use of the words, "shall" and "may." Are they accurate? What if the parties are unable to agree but do not submit the matter to arbitration? What constitutes "any other unfavorable change"? How are those words read with the preceding, more specific list of examples?

[29] *Write Carefully:* Simplify language; sentence structure.

6. Property Settlement

The Husband agrees to pay the Wife the sum of $200,000 in five equal payments of $40,000 per year for five years. These payments are made as equalizing payments in light of the property distribution of marital assets cash in lieu of property. (See Exhibit A.) The first payment will be made on May 1, 1992. The next four payments will be made on January 1st of each new year. These payments are not deductible by the Husband, nor are they inductible [30] by the Wife. [31]

The Husband shall take out a five-year term insurance policy to cover the costs of the $200,000 maintenance payment. [32] The policy will pay out $200,000 if the Husband dies before the first payment of $40,000 is made on May 1, 1992. It will pay out $160,000 if the Husband dies before the second payment of $40,000 is made on January 1, 1993. It will pay out $120,000 if the Husband dies before the third payment of $40,000 is made on January 1, 1994. It will pay out $80,000 if the Husband dies before the third payment of $40,000 is made on January 1, 1994. It will pay out $80,000 if the Husband dies before the fourth payment on January 1, 1995. It will pay out $40,000 if the Husband dies before the last payment is made on January 1, 1996. [33] [34]

If the Wife should die before payments are complete, the payments will go to the wife's estate.

[30] *Edit and Rewrite:* Spelling.

[31] *Know the Law/Test for Consequences:* What if the tax law changes?

[32] *Edit and Rewrite*: Is the insurance policy to cover property settlement or maintenance?

[33] *Write Carefully:* Pictorial clarity.

[34] *Test for Consequences:* What if husband defaults?

7. Medical Insurance for the Children

The Husband currently has medical and dental insurance coverage for the minor children. He shall continue to provide coverage for each child until each one reaches his or her 18th birthday. The plan is provided by The New England Insurance Company and is known as The Family Health Plan bearing the plan number G5678. The Husband's identification number is C1234. [35]

All claims shall be submitted to the insurer for payment in accordance with the requirements of the plan. The Husband will provide the Wife with appropriately executed forms for submission to the health care provider. The Husband will arrange for the Wife to be the approved signatory on all claim forms so that the Wife can deal directly with the insurer. [36]

The parties will equally divide the costs of all uninsured medical and dental care for the children. The Husband will pay the appropriate amount due to the Wife within 7 calendar days of receipt by him of proof that such payment is due.

"Medical and Dental Care" of children includes any care given to a child by a medical doctor, dentist, orthodontist, or psychologist. It also includes the costs of all prescription drugs.

8. Medical Insurance for the Wife

The Husband currently maintains medical insurance coverage for the Wife and will con-

---

[35] *Test for Consequences:* What if the insurer cancels the policy or if it is replaced with a different one?
Classify, Organize, and Outline: Should the medical insurance for the children be reorganized?

[36] *Write Carefully:* Subheadings, pictorial clarity, and sentence structure.

tinue to provide such coverage until Wife finds full-time employment that provides medical insurance or until the Wife is fully economically independent and can purchase her own insurance. 37 If the Husband must make any additional premium payments in order to comply with this provision, such payments will be made at Husband's own cost and expenses. Husband shall not be entitled to any offset or reimbursement from the Wife for such payments. If and when the wife obtains full-time employment that provides health insurance, she shall notify Husband that she no longer needs his insurance coverage.

9. Life Insurance

The Husband's life is presently insured under a Mutual of Omaha life insurance policy. The children have been designated irrevocable beneficiaries of the Policies, in equal amounts of $100,000 each. 38

The Husband shall pay the premiums on the policy and keep them in force until his death.

10. Personal and Real Property Division 39

The parties make the following disposition and settlement with respect to their remaining marital property:

(1) All furniture, furnishings, household goods and appliances, fixtures and appurtenances, books and works of art, and other items of personal property located in

---

37 *Write Carefully:* Use of the word "will"; define "independent"; pictorial clarity for entire paragraph 8.

38 *Test for Consequences:* Mandatory insurance after children are adults? What if insurance company is replaced by a different one? *Write Carefully:* How many policies?

39 *Write Carefully:* Inaccurate heading.

the former marital residence at 18 Magnolia, City of Chicago, State of Illinois, shall constitute the sole and exclusive separate personal property of the Wife.

(2) In the future, except as otherwise provided, each of the parties shall own, have, and enjoy, independently of any claim or right of the other party, all items of tangible personal property now or in the future belonging to him or to her as if he or she were unmarried.

11. Occupation of the House

The parties acknowledge that they are joint owners of the real property[40] located at 18 Magnolia Lane, in the City of Chicago, State of Illinois. The parties agree that the Wife shall have exclusive occupancy of the residence over a period of 15 years, or until the first of the following events occurs:

1. The Wife remarries;
2. The Wife cohabits with an unrelated adult male;
3. The Wife permanently ceases to reside in the residence;
4. The youngest child becomes emancipated;
5. The Wife chooses to sell the residence;

12. Maintenance of the House[41]

The Husband has purchased a home shield insurance policy, which covers all the major systems of the house including repair or replacement of existing major appliances, the heating system, the air conditioning system, the plumbing system, the electrical system, and the sanitary sewage system. Husband agrees

---

[40] *Classify, Organize, and Outline:* Several different sections cover real property: paragraphs 6, 10, 11, 12, 13, and 14. How do they fit together?

[41] *Write Carefully:* Add subheadings.

to maintain this policy while the Wife and children are living in the house. [42]

The Wife shall be responsible for all expenses regarding the premises and its maintenance including but not limited to mortgage payments, real property taxes, appropriate insurance, normal maintenance, gardening, and repairs.

The Husband and the Wife agree to split the costs of any major structural changes or repairs to the house. ''Major repairs'' are defined as any expense over $1500.

13. Sale of the House [43]

On the occurrence of the first of any of the above events [44] the Property shall be placed on the market for sale and sold as quickly as is reasonably possible. The Property shall be available at reasonable times for inspection by brokers and by prospective purchasers. Both parties shall cooperate and use their best efforts to produce the highest sale price then available in the market. The parties shall agree in a prior writing on the minimum gross selling price and the brokerage commission to be incurred in consummating the sale. If the parties do not agree on a minimum selling price, the price shall be fixed by an independent real estate appraiser designated by the parties. [45] The determination of that appraiser shall be binding on the parties and the cost of the appraisal shall be shared equally by the parties.

The Husband and the Wife agree that they will split the net proceeds from the sale of the house. ''Net proceeds'' are defined as the gross receipts resulting from the sale of the Property less the usual expenses of the sale.

[42] *Test for Consequences:* Who is entitled to the insurance benefits?

[43] *Write Carefully:* Subheadings, pictorial clarity for the entire Sale of the House section; sentence structure.

[44] *Write Carefully*: What "above events"?

[45] *Test for Consequences:* Can't sell for less than appraised value?

The expenses of the sale include broker's commission, attorneys' fees for the representation of each party on the sale, costs of satisfying the existing first mortgage, termite expenses, agreed estimate or allowance for repairs to the purchaser and any other similar expenses incidental to the sale of the property and the closing of title. 46

It is agreed that the Wife, who is currently making all payments due on the mortgage on the Property, shall receive a credit at closing equal to the sum of all the mortgage payments she has made from the time of the execution of this document to the sale of the house. Thereafter, any balance remaining of the net proceeds shall be divided equally between the parties. 47

Each party agrees that he or she has done nothing and will do nothing to encumber the title to the Property, except for the lien of the existing mortgage. 48

14. Option to Purchase the House

The Wife shall have the first option to purchase the interest of the Husband in the marital home. The purchase price shall be calculated in accordance with the provisions set forth below. If at the time the marital home is listed for sale, the Wife does not exercise her option to purchase the Husband's interest, then the Husband shall have a second option to purchase the Wife's interest in the marital home on the same terms and conditions provided for the Wife's purchase. 49

---

46 *Write Carefully:* Define "split." What is the relationship between "Any other similar expenses incidental . . ." and the specific list that precedes it? Sentence structure.

47 *Test for Consequences:* What if total payments exceed the sales price (sold at a loss)?

48 *Know the Law:* Will routine maintenance work create liens? *Edit and Rewrite:* Does duty to maintain in paragraph 12 conflict with duty not to create liens?

49 *Edit and Rewrite:* "Below"? *Write Carefully:* Rewrite last sentence to be clear.

15. Failure of Wife to Make Prompt Mortgage Payments

In the event that the Wife shall fail to make prompt payment of the mortgage installments, insurance premiums and realty taxes when due, the Husband, at his option, shall have the right to make the payments on five days' notice to the Wife and to seek immediate reimbursement from Her. The Wife agrees to indemnify and hold the Husband harmless for all losses, expenses (including reasonable attorneys' fees and accountants' expenses), and damages in the event that she defaults in any of her obligations to the house.

The Husband and Wife shall split the allowable Federal and State tax deductions for the mortgage interests and real property taxes relating to the marital home.[50]

16. Bank Accounts, Credit Cards

The Husband transfers and assigns to the Wife the right title and interest in and to the following:

a.   Savings Account #: *555-1212-0*
b.   Checking Account #: *886-442-0*
c.   Credit Cards
      Bank of America Mastercard
      Bank of America Visa
      Sears
      J. C. Penny

The Wife agrees to request that the name of the Husband be removed from these accounts so that they will be sole the responsibility of the Wife.

17. Businesses as a Marital Asset

The Husband and Wife jointly own a closely held corporations, ABC Inventories, Inc. Due

[50] *Know the Law:* Will the IRS allow split deductions?

to the fact that there is no real market for these companies and because the stock cannot be sold publicly, the Wife agrees to sign over her share of these marital assets to the Husband.

In return, the Husband agrees to assume all debts and liabilities associated with the business and to forever discharge the Wife from any and all debts, sums of money, agreements, promises, damages, judgments, executions and demands that may arise from the business. 51

18.   Income Taxes 52

The Husband and the Wife agree to file separate income tax returns for the year in which the dissolution of the marriage takes place, and thereafter.

The Wife agrees that the Husband may deduct all maintenance payments from his taxes. The Wife understands that she must declare all maintenance payments she receives as income.

The Husband and the Wife agree to split the exemptions for the dependents. The Wife will take two exemptions. The Husband will take one. When the first child reaches the age of 18, the wife agrees that she will give up one exemption. When the second child reaches the age of 18, the Husband agrees that he will give up his exemption. Husband must be 100% current in child support payments in the year in which he claims the dependent exemption. 53

19.   Temporary Arrangements

The Husband and the Wife have been living separate and apart since October 26, 1991. The

---

51 *Edit and Rewrite/Gather the Facts:* How many corporations and which ones?
Write Carefully: Are all items in the list necesssary?

52 *Write Carefully:* Subheadings for Income Taxes section?

53 *Test for Consequences:* If not, can the wife claim the exemptions?

Husband has taken care of all living expenses of the Wife and children during the last six months. The Husband agrees to assume all outstanding debts incurred during the period between October 26, 1991 and April 28, 1992. The Wife agrees to assume all debts of the family following the execution of this agreement. [54]

20. Attorney's Fees

The Husband agrees to pay one-half of the Wife's attorney's fees for the execution of this agreement.

21. Arbitration

Any controversy or claim that arises out of this settlement agreement, including (1) a problem concerning the payment or nonpayment of maintenance or other items, (2) custody of the minor children of the parties, including any modifications; (3) visitation rights of the Husband, or (4) any other terms or conditions of this agreement shall be settled in accordance with the Rules of the American Arbitration Association. [55]

22. Modification

No modification, rescission, termination, or amendment of this agreement shall be valid, unless in writing and executed with the same formality as this agreement. If parties cannot agree on modification terms, either party can request arbitration as mentioned in paragraph 18 of this agreement. [56]

23. Remedies for Breach

If either party fails in the performance of his or her obligation under the Agreement, the

[54] *Edit and Rewrite:* Consistency? Family debts = living expenses?

[55] *Test for Consequences/Gather the Facts:* Costs? Selection of arbitrator?

Write Carefully: How does item (4) relate to the specific list, (1)-(3), that precedes it?

[56] *Write Carefully:* Watch for vampires.

aggrieved party shall have the right to pursue the remedies that are available, including a rescission of the agreement, an action for damages resulting from the breach, or specific performance as stated in the statute. 57

The party prevailing in such an action shall have the right to recover his or her costs and reasonable attorney's fees that result from the proceedings.

Neither party shall be entitled to pursue any remedy under this Agreement unless he or she has given notice of the claimed breach to the other party and allowed 30 days to pass between such notice and the exercise of any remedial claim.

24. Law Applicable

The validity, effect, and operation of this agreement shall be determined according to the law of the State of Illinois.

25. Mutual Drafting

This Agreement was drafted cooperatively by the parties counsels in consultation with the parties. Neither party shall be entitled to claim the benefit of any ambiguity resulting from the drafting therein. 58

26. Partial Invalidity; Severability

The Agreement shall not be invalid as a whole because any or more of its provisions is or are hereafter declared illegal. 59

---

57 *Write Carefully:* Watch for vampires.
Edit and Rewrite: Consistency? OK to litigate or must they arbitrate? (Problem of combining forms?) Any relationship to or inconsistency with arbitration provision in the maintenance section?
Know the Law: Are there other remedies, e.g., contempt?

58 *Edit and Rewrite:* Possessive?
Know the Interpretive Law: What does "claim the benefit of any ambiguity" mean?

59 *Edit and Rewrite:* Missing word? Double negative?

----

27.   Notices

All notices given pursuant to this Agreement shall be certified or registered mail directed to the parties at the following addresses 60 :

Dave Cass

Mary Jo Cass

28.   Binding Effect

This Agreement shall bind the parties.

29.   Execution and Delivery

This agreement has been executed in sextuplet. Each copy is considered an original. One original has been delivered to each of the following people: The Husband, The Wife, the Husband's Attorney, the Wife's attorney, two are being held for filing with the court at the time of the dissolution of the parties' marriage. 61

IN WITNESS WHEREOF, the partied sign this document on this _____ day of _____, 1992.

_____   _____   62

----

60 *Edit and Rewrite:* Missing information?

61 *Know the Law:* Contract incorporated into the divorce judgment?

62 *Edit and Rewrite:* Missing exhibits?

Notes

1. Form contracts for consumers often are not negotiated. Non-negotiated contracts may be called "adhesion" contracts and may be subjected to stricter scrutiny than freely negotiated contracts. *See, e.g.,* Restatement (Second) of Contracts §211 (providing that adhesion contracts will only be enforced if they fall within the consumer's reasonable expectations).

2. Uniform Partnership Act §18(a), 6 U.L.A. 213 (1969).

3. Be careful not to postdate an agreement that already has occurred. If the parties have been operating under the terms of the agreement before the written contract is signed, make sure that fact is clear from the contract.

4. Ludwig Mandel, The Preparation of Commercial Agreements 23 (1978).

5. *E.g.,* Ohio Valley Gas, Inc. v. Blackburn, 445 N.E.2d 1378, 1383 (Ind. Ct. App. 1983) (holding that where a loan receipt agreement was ambiguous, recitals could be used to determine the intent of the parties in the making of the loan); Stech v. Panel Mart, Inc., 434 N.E.2d 97, 101 (Ind. Ct. App. 1982) (holding that where a stock purchase agreement was ambiguous, the recitals could properly be admitted to show the parties' intent for disposal of stock upon death); State By Crow Wing Environment Protection Assn. v. Breezy Point, 394 N.W.2d 592, 595 (Minn. Ct. App. 1986) (holding that ambiguous language in a settlement contract between the EPA and the owner of a campsite as to sale on time-share basis could be supplemented with consistent terms used in the recitals to show the parties' intent at the time of contracting); Erickson Hardwood Co. v. North Pac. Lumber Co., 690 P.2d 1071, 1076-1077 (Or. Ct. App. 1984) (holding that recitals could properly be used to indicate intent as to exclusivity of agency in an ambiguous sale contract).

6. Wilson v. Towers, 55 F.2d 199, 200 (4th Cir. 1932); Coca Cola Bottling Co. v. Coca Cola Co., 164 F. Supp. 293, 301 (D. Minn. 1957); Ohio Valley Gas, Inc. v. Blackburn, 445 N.E.2d 1378, 1383 (Ind. Ct. App. 1983); Great W. Oil Co. v. Lewiston Oil & Ref. Co., 6 P.2d 863, 866 (Mont. 1932); McKinnon v. Baker, 370 N.W.2d 492, 494 (Neb. 1985); Neal D. Ivey Co. v. Franklin Assocs., Inc., 87 A.2d 236, 239 (Pa. 1952).

7. Restatement (Second) of Contracts §218(1) (1979). *See also* Fugate v. Town of Payson, 791 P.2d 1092, 1094 (Ariz. Ct. App. 1990); Illinois House Dev. Auth. v. M-Z Constr. Corp., 441 N.E.2d 1179, 1189 (Ill. App. Ct. 1982).

8. Restatement (Second) of Contracts §71 (1979).

9. *Id.*

10. *See, e.g.,* Hackworth v. Flinchum, 475 S.W.2d 140, 143 (Ky. Ct. App. 1971); Lawson v. Lawson, 362 S.E.2d 269, 271 (N.C. 1987).

11. Restatement (Second) of Contracts §131 (1979). *See also* N.J. Stat. Ann. §2A: 82-17 (West 1992); N.Y. Civ. Prac. L. & R. §4538 (McKinney 1993); Pa. Stat. Ann. tit. 21, §46 (1992).

12. For a fuller discussion of the parol evidence rule, *see* 3 Arthur L. Corbin, Contracts 583 (Supp. 1992). *See also* U.C.C. §2-202 (1992) for the parol evidence rule that applies to the sale of goods.

13. Mandel, *supra* note 4, at 20-23.

14. Scott J. Burnham, Drafting Contracts 56-57 (1987).

15. *See, e.g.,* Restatement (Second) of Agency §322 (1984) (both agent and principal are liable when principal is not disclosed).

16. Do not rely on the fact that you are dealing with a corporate officer or director. Depending on how your transaction is classified (ordinary course of business?; sale of

assets?), it may require approval of the board of directors, or even shareholders in some instances. *See, e.g.*, People v. Jasman, 284 N.W.2d 496, 499 (Mich. Ct. App. 1979) (holding that a corporation president has no presumed power to act on behalf of the corporation without an express grant from the board of directors); American Bank & Trust Co. v Freeman, 560 S.W.2d 444, 446 (Tex. Civ. App. 1977) (holding a corporation not liable for the act of the Board chairman when acting individually, without authorization of the duly assembled Board). *See also* Hardy v. International Paper Realty Corp., 716 F.2d 1044, 1046 (4th Cir. 1983) (holding that the corporation was not bound by the agent's offer where the agent had neither actual authority to bind the corporation nor corporate consent to give the appearance of such authority); Scientific Holding Co. v. Plessy, Inc., 510 F.2d 15, 21 (2d Cir. 1974) (holding that a corporate officer or director is not an agent for purposes of the Statute of Frauds); Marsh Inv. Corp. v. Langford, 490 F. Supp. 1320, 1324-1325 (E.D. La. 1980) (holding that a mortgage company dealing with an agent had the duty to discover if the agent had actual authority to act before relying on agent), *aff'd*, 1652 F.2d 583 (5th Cir. 1981).

17.   It is particularly important to keep a copy of written authorization for an agent to act if written authorization is required by law. For example, some states require written authorization for agents to deal with real estate transactions. *See, e.g.*, Cal. Civ. Code §2485, 2486 (West Supp. 1992); 765 ILCS 35/67 (1993); [At the time of this writing, the statutory compilations in Illinois have been changed from "Ill. Rev. Stat." to "ILCS." Since there is not yet an official Uniform System of Citation style for this new compilation, we have used "ILCS" consistently throughout this book. — Eds.] N.J. Stat. Ann. §25:1-2 (West 1992); N.Y. Gen. Oblig. Law §§15-301, 15-501, 15-503, 15-703 (McKinney 1993); Ohio Rev. Code Ann. §1337.01 (Anderson 1991).

18.   *See, e.g.*, Mossler Acceptance Co. v. Perlman, 47 So. 2d 296, 298 (Fla. 1950) (holding that a minor who falsely and knowingly represented his age as 21 and provided a drivers license stating his age as 21 was estopped from voiding based on minority a contract to purchase an automobile); Johnson v. McAdory, 88 So. 2d 106, 108 (Miss. 1956) (holding that a minor who represented himself as an adult was liable for the balance due on the purchase of a car); Manasquan Sav. & Loan Assn. v. Mayer, 236 A.2d 407, 407 (N.J. Super. Ct. App. Div. 1949) (holding that a minor is liable in a foreclosure when the lender reasonably relied on the minor's misrepresentation of her age in gaining the mortgage); R.J. Goerke Co. v. Nicolson, 69 A.2d 326, 328 (N.J. Super. Ct. App. Div. 1949) (stating that when a minor appears of age and falsely represents her age, she is estopped from bringing the defense of infancy in an action for the balance due on a charge account).

19.   For a general discussion of the forms of questions, *see* David A. Binder & Susan C. Price, Legal Interviewing and Counseling: A Client-Centered Approach 38-52 (1977).

20.   *See* Chapter 3, pages 67-69, on the choice between general and specific language.

21.   U.C.C. §2-201 (1992).

22.   *See, e.g.*, Kenner Indus., Inc. v. Sewell Plastics, Inc., 451 So. 2d 557, 560 (La. 1984) (holding industry pricing of sand applicable when deviation from industry standards was not expressly stated); Henry v. Ballard & Cordell Corp., 418 So. 2d 1334, 1340 (La. 1982) (holding the market value of gas to be the industry standard of value over the entire contract period when "market value" was not expressly defined); National Union Fire Ins. Co. v. Caesar's Palace Hotel & Casino, 792 P.2d 1129, 1130 (Nev. 1990) (stating that industry custom and usage in issuing special event insurance was relevant when the parties' intent as to coverage was ambiguous); Leslie v. Pennco, Inc., 470 A.2d 110, 113-114 (Pa. Super. Ct. 1983) (stating that industry custom and usage must be notorious, well established, and reasonable to show intent in an ambiguous contract); Fisher v. Congregation B'Nai Yitzhok, 110 A.2d 881, 883 (Pa. Super. Ct. 1955) (holding that established customs of orthodox Jewish synagogue were presumed part of the contract with a Rabbi in the absence of an express provision to the contrary); Luling Oil & Gas Co. v. Humble Oil &

Ref. Co. 191 S.W.2d 716, 724 (Tex. 1945) (holding that where no specific manner of measurement was given in the contract, oil industry and Railroad Commission standards of measurement of crude oil applied).

23. *See, e.g.,* Dikeman v. Sunday Creek Coal Co., 56 N.E. 864, 865 (Ill. 1900) (holding that parties have the right to make time of the essence and that a court of equity is bound to uphold such an agreement).

24. *See, e.g.,* Sahadi v. Continental Ill. Natl. Bank & Trust Co., 706 F.2d 193, 197 (7th Cir. 1983) (holding that a few-hour delay in payment of interest on a loan created only de minimis prejudice to the lender and was not a material breach when the contract did not state that "time was of the essence"); Tanenbaum v. Sears Roebuck & Co., 401 A.2d 809, 813 (Pa. 1979) (holding that a mere six-business-day delay in closing caused little or no injury because the contract did not expressly state or necessarily imply that time was of the essence and the contract was substantially performed); Carsek Corp. v. Stephen Schefler, Inc., 246 A.2d 365, 369 (Pa. 1968) (holding that no breach of contract occurred when the appellee suffered little or no harm from a 45-day delay in payment on a contract that did not expressly state that "time was of the essence").

25. *See, e.g.,* Ramesbotham v. Farmers Elevator Co., 428 N.W.2d 542, 544 (S.D. 1988) (holding that a five-year delay in payment for performance was unreasonable, even though the contract did not state that "time was of the essence").

26. *See infra* note 29.

27. Some agreements are ceremonial and not intended to be legally enforceable. For example, some Jewish couples sign a marriage agreement, or Ketubbah, when they get married. Often the Ketubbah is written in Aramaic or Hebrew, and the couple does not really intend to be bound by its terms. Other couples intend the Ketubbah to be enforceable. *See* Menachem Elon, The Principles of Jewish Law 388 (1975).

28. Ian Macneil has referred to this phenomenon as "relational contracts." *See generally* Ian R. Macneil, The New Social Contract: An Inquiry into Modern Contractual Relations (1980), and Ian R. Macneil, *Relational Contracts: What We Do and Do Not Know,* 1985 Wis. L. Rev. 483.

29. For a discussion of how to include explicit purposes, *see supra* page 205 on recitals.

30. These clauses are sometimes referred to as *Force Majeure* clauses. Black's Law Dictionary 645 (6th ed. 1990).

31. *See generally* West's Legal Forms (2d ed. 1983) and Current Legal Forms (Matthew Bender 1993).

32. "Consideration" may be defined as "[t]he reason or material cause of a contract. Some right, interest, profit or benefit accruing to one party or some forbearance, detriment, loss, or responsibility, given, suffered, or undertaken by the other." Black's Law Dictionary 306 (6th ed. 1990).

33. *See, e.g.,* Clark v. Clark, 425 S.W.2d 745, 747 (Ky. 1968) (holding a separation agreement based on future separation void and against public policy); Maynard v. Maynard, 45 N.W.2d 56, 58 (Mich. 1950) (holding a separation agreement between spouses void because it sought to bring about a future separation).

34. These clauses are called "cognovit" or "confession of judgment" clauses and are unenforceable in most states. *See infra* note 56.

35. *See, e.g.,* National Equip. Rental, Ltd. v. Szukhent, 375 U.S. 311 (1964) (holding that such a contractual waiver did not violate due process as long as the defendant received actual notice).

36. *See* U.C.C. §2-314 (1992) et seq.

37. *See, e.g.*, the requirements for compliance with implied warranties of merchantability under U.C.C. §2-314 (1992).

38. *See, e.g.*, the rules for disclaiming implied warranties of merchantability under U.C.C. §2-316 (1992).

39. *See* U.C.C. §2-316(2) (1992) (requiring disclaimers of implied warranties of merchantability to mention merchantability and to be conspicuous).

40. *See supra* notes 7 and 8.

41. Such a resolution might be required for substantial acts outside of the ordinary course of business. *See supra* note 7.

42. *See, e.g.*, Cal. Civ. Code §2432 (West 1992); 755 ILCS 45/4-10 (1993); Nev. Rev. Stat. §449.830 (1989); N.Y. Pub. Health Law §2981 (McKinney 1991); Tex. Civ. Prac. & Rem. Code Ann. §135.016 (West 1992).

43. *See, e.g.*, Lisi v. Alitalia-Linee Aeree Italiane, S.p.A., 370 F.2d 508, 514 (2d Cir. 1966) (holding that limitations on liability "artfully camouflaged" on the ticket did not give passengers sufficient notice to take additional precautions), *aff'd*, 390 U.S. 455 (1968); Egan v. Kollsman Instrument Corp., 234 N.E.2d 199, 202 (N.Y. 1967) (holding that conditions of contract containing Warsaw Convention disclaimer placed on the outside back cover and merely referenced on the face of the ticket was not conspicuous enough to give passengers notice), *cert. denied*, 390 U.S. 1039 (1968).

44. *See, e.g.*, Truth in Lending Regulations, 12 C.F.R. §226.2 (1992). *See* Chapter 2, note 10.

45. Potter v. Collin, 321 So. 2d 128, 131 (Fla. Ct. App. 1975); Britven v. Britven, 145 N.W.2d 450, 454 (Iowa 1966); Rudbeck v. Rudbeck, 365 N.W.2d 330, 332 (Minn. Ct. App. 1985).

46. *See, e.g.*, McGregor v. Board of Commrs., 956 F.2d 1017, 1022 (11th Cir. 1992); Forest Oil Corp. v. Strata Energy, Inc., 929 F.2d 1039, 1043 (5th Cir. 1991); Bicknell Minerals, Inc. v. Tilly, 570 N.E.2d 1307, 1313 (Ind. Ct. App. 1991); Cal. Civ. Code §1654 (West 1992).

47. *See, e.g.*, Boston Helicopter Charter, Inc. v. Augusta Aviation Corp., 767 F. Supp. 363, 369-370 (D. Mass. 1991); Glenview v. Northfield Wood Water & Util., 576 N.E.2d 238, 244 (Ill. App. Ct. 1991); Phillips v. Union Bankers Ins. Co., 812 S.W.2d 616, 618 (Tex. Ct. App. 1991); Cal. Civ. Code §1644 (West 1992).

48. *See, e.g.*, Bankier v. First Fed. Sav. & Loan Assn., 588 N.E.2d 391, 394 (Ill. App. Ct. 1992); Bicknell Minerals, Inc. v. Tilly, 570 N.E.2d 1307, 1313 (Ind. Ct. App. 1991); Massachusetts Mun. Wholesale Elec. Co. v. Danvers, 577 N.E.2d 283, 288 (Mass. 1991); Perkins v. Great-West Live Assurance Co., 814 P.2d 1125, 1128 (Utah Ct. App. 1991); Cal. Civ. Code §1641 (West 1992).

49. This rule has a particularly long Latin name: *interpretatio fienda est ut res magis quam pereat*, which means, "such an interpretation is to be made that the thing may rather stand than fall." *See, e.g.*, Karsh v. Carr, 807 S.W.2d 96, 99 (Mo. Ct. App. 1990); Cal. Civ. Code §1641 (West 1992).

50. This rule is often called *ejusdem generis*, or "of the same kind." *See, e.g.*, Samuels, Dramer & Co. v. Commissioner, 930 F.2d 975, 980 (2d Cir. 1991); Eastern Air Lines, Inc. v. McDonnell Douglas Corp., 532 F.2d 957, 988 (5th Cir. 1976); Colorado Milling & Elevator Co. v. Chicago, R.I. & P.R., 382 F.2d 834, 836-837 (10th Cir. 1967); Austin Co. v. United States, 314 F.2d 518, 520 (Ct. Cl. 1963), *cert. denied*, 375 U.S. 830 (1963). *See* Chapter 2, note 13.

51. This rule is referred to as *noscitur a sociis*, literally, "it is known from associates." *See, e.g.*, In re Lemmer, 477 N.W.2d 503, 505 (Mich. Ct. App. 1991); State v. Young, 818 P.2d 1375, 1380 (Wash. Ct. App. 1991); Cal. Civ. Code §3534 (West 1992).

52. *See, e.g.,* Boesl v. Suburban Trust & Sav. Bank, 642 F. Supp. 1503, 1511 (N.D. Ill. 1986); Jackson v. Donovan, 30 Cal. Rptr. 755, 758 (1963); In re Marriage of Sherrick, 573 N.E.2d 335, 338 (Ill. App. Ct. 1991); Cal. Civ. Code §1650 (West 1985).

53. Glover v. Libman, 578 F. Supp. 748, 760-761 (N.D. Ga. 1983) (stating that representation of multiple clients can create a conflict of interest if done without consent); Swope v. Bratton, 541 F. Supp. 99, 110-111 (W.D. Ark. 1982) (holding that a city attorney who had an ongoing attorney-client relationship with a police officer, the plaintiff in the present case against the city, must be dismissed for conflict of interest); Smallwood v. Overseas Storage Co., 33 N.Y.S.2d 876, 880-881 (1942) (holding that there was a conflict of interest by the attorney for the guardian of minors' estate when the attorney negotiated a loan for a corporation client from the estate without disclosing his interest to the guardian).

54. *E.g.,* Faver v. Faver, 583 S.W.2d 44, 48-49 (Ark. Ct. App. 1979) (holding that the husband's failure to disclose the value of his property made the antenuptial contract invalid); Osborne v. Osborne, 428 N.E.2d 810, 816 (Mass. 1981) (holding that antenuptial agreements are subject to the rules of full disclosure).

55. *E.g.,* In re Marriage of Modnick, 663 P.2d 187, 191-92 (Cal. 1983) (holding that by failing to disclose the existence of community property and taking deliberate steps to conceal the asset, the husband's conduct amounted to extrinsic fraud); Dodd v. Estate of Yanan, 587 N.E.2d 1348, 1352 (Ind. Ct. App. 1992) (holding that husband had a duty to disclose all of his financial holdings to wife when the property settlement agreement was negotiated and executed, and failure to provide full disclosure tolled the statute of limitations until wife discovered concealment). *Cf.* American Academy of Matrimonial Lawyers, Bounds of Advocacy: Standards of Conduct § 2.13 (1991) ("An attorney should never encourage a client to hide or dissipate assets").

56. Evans v. Artek Sys. Corp., 715 F.2d 788, 791 (2d Cir. 1983) (stating that using a confidence of a client to the client's disadvantage can disqualify an attorney from representing the client); Skokie Gold Standard Liquors, Inc. v. Joe E. Seagram & Sons, Inc., 452 N.E.2d 804, 813-814 (Ill. App. Ct. 1983) (holding an attorney disqualified from representing the plaintiff when the attorney had previously represented the defendant on a related matter and was the recipient of the defendant's confidences); Washington v. State, 441 N.E.2d 1355, 1358-1359 (Ind. 1982) (holding that an attorney must maintain confidences and secrets of a former client in subsequent criminal cases but may testify as to facts, such as the existence, nature, and dates of prior offenses).

57. *See* Underwood Farmers Elevator v. Leidholm, 460 N.W.2d 711, 713 (N.D. 1990) (judgment by confession clauses that fail to provide adequate notice violate due process); Mancine v. Concord-Liberty Sav. & Loan Assn., 445 A.2d 744, 745 (Pa. Super. Ct. 1982) (judgment by confession against a dead person is void); Dyer v. Johnson, 19 S.W.2d 421, 422-423 (Tex. Civ. App. 1929) (a judgment by confession obtained by fraud in another state is not entitled to full faith and credit). *But see* United Pac. Ins. Co. v. Lamanna's Estate, 436 A.2d 965, 968 (N.J. Super. Ct. Law Div. 1981) (foreign judgment by confession clauses are entitled to full faith and credit).

58. *E.g.,* Mitchell v. Mitchell, 310 A.2d 837, 841 (D.C. 1973); Eule v. Eule, 320 N.E.2d 506, 510 (Ill. App. Ct. 1974); Mulford v. Mulford, 320 N.W.2d 470, 471 (Neb. 1982).

59. These clauses are often called *in terrorem* clauses; they are often unenforceable. Cherry, Bekaert, & Holland v. Brown, 582 So. 2d 502, 505-506 (Ala. 1991); Howard Schultz & Assoc. v. Broniec, 236 S.E.2d 265, 268 (Ga. 1977); Reddy v. Community Health Found. of Man, 298 S.E.2d 906, 915-916 (W. Va. 1982).

60. These headings were all included in the MAP Multiple Listing Service Contract to Purchase Real Estate used in Chicago in 1991.

61. *E.g.,* Conn. Gen. Stat. Ann. §§42-152 (West 1992).

62.   Vampires suck the action out of a sentence because they turn verbs into nouns. For example, the verb "modify" is turned into the noun "modification." You may be familiar with the more technical term for a vampire: "nominalizations." For a more complete discussion of vampires, including how to recognize and change them, *see* Chapter 3, pages 99-103. *See infra* page 233 for an example of when vampires may serve a useful purpose.

63.   For a more complete discussion, *see* Chapter 3, pages 95-98.

64.   For a fuller description of the process, *see* Chapter 3, pages 106-111.

65.   Seibel v. Layne & Bowler, Inc., 641 P.2d 668, 670 (Or. Ct. App. 1982) (holding that the heading "WARRANTIES" gave no indication of disclaimer and the disclaimer was, therefore, unenforceable); Hartman v. Jensen's Inc., 289 S.E.2d 648, 649 (S.C. 1982) (holding that the heading "Terms of Warranty" was ambiguous and failed to give notice of an exclusion of warranty); Cate v. Dover Corp., 790 S.W.2d 559, 561 (Tex. 1990) (holding that the heading "TERMS of WARRANTY" failed to give notice of disclaimer and, therefore, the disclaimer was unenforceable).

66.   North Side Real Estate Board Real Estate Sale Contract — Condominium.

67.   *See* St. John's Episcopal Hosp. v. McAdoo, 405 N.Y.S.2d 935, 937 (Civ. Ct. 1978) (holding that a long paragraph labeled "Procedure of insured in claim or suit" obscured the duty of the insured to notify the insurer of claims and was therefore unenforceable).

68.   This rule of construction is called *expressio unis est esclusio alterius*. It means that the expression of one is the exclusion of others. *See* Chapter 3, Section C.2.

69.   A fixture is an article that has been "so annexed to the realty that it is regarded as part of the real property" or "affixed to real property" by roots, becoming imbedded, permanently resting upon it, or being permanently attached to the real property. Black's Law Dictionary 638 (6th ed. 1990).

70.   This doctrine is called *ejusdem generis* and means "of the same kind." For a fuller discussion of *ejusdem generis, see* Chapter 2, note 13; *see also* Norman J. Singer, Sutherland Statutory Construction §47.17.

71.   *Id.*

72.   *See* Chapter 3, pages 95-98.

73.   For example, most insurance contracts consist of a large policy document and smaller endorsement that lists the particular items that are covered or excluded. Sometimes parties allege that the endorsement and the policy conflict. *See, e.g.,* Southern Sash of Columbia v. United States Fidelity & Guar. Co., 525 So. 2d 1388, 1390 (Ala. 1988) (holding that the policy and the endorsement were consistent); Simon v. Shelter Gen. Ins. Co., 842 P.2d 236, 240-241 (Col. 1992) (holding that the provisions were in conflict and the endorsement, as the last expression of intent, must prevail).

74.   U.C.C. §2-207 (1992).

75.   Consider, for example this language from a real estate sales contract: "Attorneys may approve or make modifications mutually acceptable to the parties within 3 days after the acceptance of the contract." *See, e.g.,* U.C.C. §2-207(2)(c) (1992) (permitting changes if they are made within a "reasonable" time).

76.   Chapter 3, pages 72-81.

77.   In addition to the problem of parallelism addressed in the text, some problems may arise from the use of the term "agree."

78.   Rodgers and Hammerstein, "Do, Re, Mi," from *Sound of Music* (Twentieth Century Fox, 1965).

79.   "Liquidated damages" are amounts fixed by a contract to limit the claims a party may have for a given breach.

80. For a fuller discussion of these problems with examples, *see* Chapter 3, pages 88-89.

81. *See* Chapter 3, pages 90-91, for a list of useful transition words.

82. Grammatically, familiar material should be in the subject of the sentence and unfamiliar material should be in the predicate.

83. For a fuller discussion of these patterns, *see* Chapter 3, pages 90-94.

84. *See* Chapter 3, pages 94-106.

85. *Cf. Expressio unis est exclusio alterius*: the expression of one is the exclusion of another. Hence each word has a meaning that excludes different words and their meanings. *See* Corbin *supra* note 12, at §552.

CHAPTER 6

Drafting Pleadings

A. *Introduction*

Drafting pleadings is unique for two reasons. First, unlike wills, contracts, and legislation, which try to provide for future events, pleadings recount the past. You are trying to tell a story to the opposing counsel, judge, and jury. Ultimately, you are trying to persuade.

Second, and more importantly, when you draft a pleading you primarily act as an adversary. Your opponents will scrutinize the pleading for any flaws. If they succeed in finding substantial defects, the pleading may be dismissed. Typical pleadings consist of a complaint filed by the plaintiff, an answer or motion filed by the defendant, and occasionally a reply filed by the plaintiff. In more complex cases, other parties may file various other pleadings such as counter-claims and cross-claims. This chapter begins with the basic building block of all lawsuits: the complaint.

The basic drafting steps you learned in Chapter 2 apply when drafting complaints. You need to:

1. understand the multiple audiences;
2. gather the facts;
3. know the law;
4. classify, organize, and outline;
5. write carefully;
6. test for consequences; and
7. edit and rewrite.

If you have never drafted a complaint before, you will need to learn the law governing complaints. Accordingly, you may want to start at step three of the drafting process: know the law. Begin with learning the procedural law that governs the form of the complaint. The specific form of a complaint varies from jurisdiction to jurisdiction. Complaints in the federal courts are governed by the Federal Rules of Civil Procedure,[1] and most federal district courts also have their own local rules. Similarly, complaints in state courts may be governed by state court rules, civil practice statutes, or local rules.

Some of the procedural law you learn will govern how you organize your complaint in step four of the drafting process: classify, organize, and outline. In spite of the variations, almost all complaints are comprised of the following parts: (1) caption, (2) title, (3) introduction, (4) body, (5) prayer for relief, (6) signatures, and (7) attorney identification.

B. Parts of a Complaint

1. Caption

The first several lines of a pleading are called the caption.

Example

IN THE UNITED STATES DISTRICT COURT FOR THE SOUTHERN
DISTRICT OF NEW YORK

PETER S. PALMER,   )
)
          Plaintiff,   )
)
     v.   )   No. 88 C 1234
)
DAVID R. DREW,   )
)
          Defendant.   )

The first line or two set forth the name of the court where the action is filed. This segment labels not only the court, but the appropriate division or district as well, such as:

IN THE CIRCUIT COURT OF COOK COUNTY, STATE OF ILLINOIS

DOMESTIC RELATIONS DIVISION

It is important to comply with the local labeling practice because cases that are misfiled can be caught in procedural mazes for years. Choosing the correct court is one of the most important procedural questions a litigator has to resolve.

The caption also identifies all the parties by name. Whenever possible, use full legal names so there can be no confusion. Be especially careful with corporations, not only to get the right name, but the right entity. Naming one subsidiary when another one is the actual party will inevitably delay, and possibly defeat, your claim.[2]

Usually you should list every plaintiff and every defendant in the initial complaint. Where there are an unusually large number of parties, you may want to list them in an attached exhibit. Use *et al.* after the name of the first plaintiff and the first defendant to indicate that other parties exist. In subsequent pleadings, you only need to name the first plaintiff and the first defendant so long as you use *et al.* to be clear.

2. Title

Next comes the title of the pleading. If there is only one cause of action,[3] it can be listed in the title: "COMPLAINT FOR BREACH OF CONTRACT." Otherwise, simply title it "COMPLAINT" and move on to the introduction of the document. Be sure, however, that if you do not label the cause of action in the title, that you label the causes of action in the appropriate sections of the body of the complaint.

Also be careful to check local law to see if there are any additional requirements for the title. Some states may require such items as jury demands, the amount sought, or the nature of the case to be included in the title.[4]

3. Introduction

The introduction to the complaint comes next. This paragraph identifies the parties and the plaintiff's attorneys. Many lawyers still use archaic form language, but simple language is preferable, such as, "Peter S. Palmer, by his attorney, Alice Jacobson, complains of the defendant, David R. Drew. . . ." No magic words are necessary.

4. Body

The body of the complaint comes next. It is organized into "counts" designated by Roman numerals. Each count sets forth a separate cause of action, or claim. A cause of action is a set of "facts which give a person a right to judicial relief."[5] For example, Count I might be for breach of contract and Count II might be for breach of fiduciary duty. It is helpful to label the counts for easy reference: "Count I, Breach of Contract." Even if your jurisdiction does not require separate counts for each cause of action,[6] it is still wise to separate the different theories of recovery. Otherwise, your pleading may seem confused, and you may inadvertently fail to allege some of the necessary elements.

In multi-party litigation, different counts can be used to separate the claims of the various parties. Hence, Count I might set forth Palmer's claim for breach of contract against Drew, while Count II sets forth Palmer's claim for breach of contract against Baker.

Each count should be divided into separate paragraphs. Since the answer will admit or deny the allegations of the complaint paragraph by paragraph, you should avoid alleging too many items in a single paragraph. For example, assume that paragraph 1 alleged both that Drew signed a contract and that he breached it. If Drew denied paragraph 1, you wouldn't know if Drew's denial meant that he didn't sign the contract, or merely that he didn't breach the contract. Indeed, the federal rules require that each paragraph be limited to "a single set of circumstances."[7]

Each separate paragraph should be sequentially numbered throughout the complaint.[8] If Count I ends with paragraph 14, then Count II should begin with paragraph 15. Thus, when subsequent references are made to a given numbered paragraph, there is no confusion.

Traditionally, federal pleadings are divided into sections with descriptive titles like "JURISDICTION, PARTIES, COMMON FACTS, and COUNT I BREACH OF CONTRACT." This format avoids realleging common elements. When you need to restate the same thing in two different counts, there is no need to repeat the material verbatim. Simply say, "Palmer realleges paragraph 12."

Notice that the plaintiff was referred to by name. It is much clearer and simpler than referring to the "plaintiff" or the "defendant," especially in complex litigation where there may be several different plaintiffs, defendants, counter-plaintiffs, and counter-defendants. Of course, on occasion, for persuasive reasons, you may want to keep referring to a party as the "defendant" or the "corporation."

5. Prayer for Relief

The prayer for relief states precisely what the plaintiff wants the court to do. You may ask for compensatory damages, punitive damages, costs, or attorney's fees in appropriate cases. Similarly, you may ask for specific injunctive relief or other equitable relief, such as a writ of mandamus or an accounting. Whether a given remedy is available is determined by the law of your jurisdiction, so you need to do some research to find what remedies are available. For example, many states will not compensate a plaintiff for negligent infliction of emotional distress unless the plaintiff was within the "zone of danger."[9] You must research not only what remedies are appropriate, but how to ask for them in your jurisdiction. In addition to the specific request, you should include a general request for whatever relief the court deems appropriate.

Different legal theories entitle plaintiffs to different relief. For example, a fraud claim may entitle a plaintiff to punitive damages, while a contract claim entitles a plaintiff to expectation damages. Therefore, generally you should include a separate prayer for relief at the end of each cause of action. However, in a simple complaint, you may use a single prayer for relief at the end of the pleading. Traditionally, the prayer is set off by the word "WHEREFORE" in capital letters. Although the "WHEREFORE" is mere surplus legal language, it is harmless.

Example

Peter S. Palmer prays this Court to enter its judgment against David R. Drew for:

> A. $75,000 in compensatory damages,
> B. $300,000 in punitive damages,
> C.   costs,
> D.   attorney's fees,
> E.   an injunction prohibiting Drew from disposing of any of Palmer's assets, and
> F.   such other relief as this Court deems appropriate.

Make your prayer for relief complete. In the event of a default, you may be limited to the recovery you sought.[10] Once again, the requirements for the prayer for relief vary from state to state. Some states require a specific monetary request, while others prohibit them.[11] Be sure to check the local rules carefully.

6.   Signatures

Next come the signatures. In federal court, the attorneys sign all the pleadings.[12] Some state courts give the plaintiff the option to sign the complaint personally or to "verify" the complaint.[13] Other state courts require verified complaints.[14] A verification is a sworn statement that the party has read the pleading and that its allegations are true. One advantage of a verified complaint is that if the defendant defaults, the complaint is self-proving and the client will not need to appear in court to testify in order to get a default judgment.

Although federal courts do not require a formal verification, attorneys must sign all court documents. Lawyers' signatures certify that they have made a reasonable inquiry and concluded: (1) the complaint is not presented to harass or delay; (2) the legal claims are warranted by existing law or a nonfrivolous argument for changing existing law; and (3) any facts alleged are supported by evidence or if specifically identified, likely to be supported by evidence.[15] Hence, by signing a complaint, you are certifying to the court that you have investigated the facts and have or expect to develop evidence to establish those facts. You also certify that you have investigated the law and have determined that you have a claim under existing law or a nonfrivolous argument for the extension of existing law.[16] Attorneys are personally liable for costs and fees if they violate this rule.[17] These costs frequently are enormous, as illustrated by a case in which the attorneys were assessed $294,141.10 in sanctions for failing to adequately investigate the facts before they filed suit.[18] Thus you should be sure to do your homework before pleading.

7.   Attorney Identification

Finally the name, address, telephone number, and identification number of the lawyer or firm who drafted the document must appear somewhere on the complaint.[19] Some jurisdictions put this information at the bottom, while others put it at the top of the complaint.[20] As always, be careful to follow local rules.

Merely understanding the form of the complaint is not sufficient, however. Before you can actually start to draft a complaint you must understand some of the basic differences in pleading requirements in the state and federal courts.

C. *Distinctions Between State and Federal Courts*

Although the basic structure of state and federal pleadings are the same, there are very important distinctions. This section will examine some of the general differences, but remember that each state and locality has its own rules. Be sure to consult local law before drafting any pleading.

Perhaps the most obvious distinction between state and federal courts is the scope of their jurisdiction. Although entire courses are devoted to this topic, a brief review is useful, since you must establish that the court has jurisdiction early in the complaint.

1. Jurisdiction of State and Federal Courts

There are two kinds of jurisdiction: subject matter jurisdiction and personal jurisdiction.[21] A court has subject matter jurisdiction if it has the legal power to decide the issues of the case.[22] It has personal jurisdiction if it has authority over the parties.[23] Many state courts are courts of "general" jurisdiction, meaning that they have the power to decide most cases.[24] In contrast, federal courts have "limited" jurisdiction, meaning that they only can hear the cases they have been constitutionally and statutorily authorized to decide.[25]

Generally, Congress has granted federal courts the power to hear two kinds of cases: 1) those involving diversity of citizenship (28 U.S.C. §1332 (1982)), and 2) those involving federal questions (28 U.S.C. §1331 (1982)). Diversity exists when the plaintiff and defendant are citizens of different states. Notice that it is citizenship, not residency, that is important.[26] A corporation is deemed to be a citizen both of the state of incorporation and the state where its principal place of business is located.[27]

For diversity jurisdiction in federal court, the parties must not only be from different states, but each plaintiff must have more than $50,000 at stake in the litigation.[28] For example, Plaintiff Palmer cannot add his $30,000 claim to Plaintiff McMullen's $20,000 to reach the jurisdictional minimum. However, a single plaintiff can combine two separate claims, neither of which amounts to $50,000 alone, to reach the minimum. Thus, Plaintiff Palmer can add his $40,000 tort claim to his $10,000 contract claim against Drew to reach the amount required.[29] Whether punitive damages can be included in the jurisdictional minimum depends on the availability of punitive damages under state law.[30] When you plead federal diversity jurisdiction, cite the statute that grants the court jurisdiction and provide enough facts to support it.

Example

1. Plaintiff, Maker, Inc. ("Maker"), is incorporated under the laws of Delaware, having its principal place of business in Boise, Idaho.
2. Defendant, Middleman Trading and Supply, Co. ("MTS"), is incorporated under the laws of the state of Washington, having its principal place of business in Seattle, Washington.
3. Defendant, Samuel Salesman ("Salesman"), is an individual citizen of the state of Washington.
4. This complaint concerns a sale that occurred in Boise, Idaho.
5. The matter in controversy exceeds, exclusive of interest and costs, $50,000.
6. This court has jurisdiction over this diversity action by virtue of 28 U.S.C. §1332(a)(2).

Notice that both defendants are citizens of the state of Washington. That fact does not defeat diversity. Diversity can be defeated only if a plaintiff and a defendant are citizens of the same state. Thus, if either MTS or Salesman were citizens of Idaho, there would not be diversity of citizenship. If any plaintiff and any defendant are citizens of the same state, diversity is no longer "complete."[31]

Federal courts also have jurisdiction over cases involving federal questions. A case involves a federal question if it arises under the U.S. Constitution or statutes.[32] Suits involving a federal question need not meet the $50,000 jurisdictional minimum. You should cite both the statute or the constitutional provision in question and the statute conferring jurisdiction on the court.

Example

1. This action arises under the National Labor Management Relations Act, 29 U.S.C. §185(5).
2. This court has jurisdiction over this federal question by virtue of 28 U.S.C. §1331.

In addition to these general requirements, there may be special requirements for the particular claim asserted. For example, in an equal employment claim under the Civil Rights Act of 1964, the plaintiff must specifically plead that she filed a claim with the Equal Employment Opportunity Commission (hereinafter EEOC) and received a notice of a right to sue.[33] Accordingly, you must carefully research the particular jurisdictional requirements for your cause of action.

Although some state courts do not have limited subject matter jurisdiction in the same way federal courts do, many state courts are divided into districts or divisions. These various divisions may hear only certain kinds of cases (e.g., divorces), or the various divisions may be made on the basis of the amount in controversy.[34] So, even in state courts, you must check to see if the court has authority to hear the particular claims you raise.

Up until now you have been considering the kinds of cases that a court is authorized to hear, or subject matter jurisdiction. But remember, there are two sorts of jurisdiction: subject matter jurisdiction and personal jurisdiction. A court has personal jurisdiction if it has authority over the individual defendant. Generally courts have personal jurisdiction whenever a defendant is present in the state[35] or has sufficient minimum contacts with a state.[36] For example, a state court will usually have jurisdiction over companies that do business within the state.

Be careful not to confuse personal jurisdiction with diversity of citizenship. Personal jurisdiction requires that the defendant have enough contact with the state for it to be fair to force the defendant to come to the state to defend the action. Diversity requires that the plaintiff and defendant be citizens of different states. Thus the crucial question for diversity jurisdiction is: Are the plaintiff and the defendant *citizens* of different states? In contrast, the crucial question for personal jurisdiction is: Has the defendant had sufficient *minimum contacts* such as residency, citizenship, the transaction of business, or the commission of a tort in the forum state for it to be fair to force the defendant to defend the action here? The following chart illustrates the difference between subject matter jurisdiction and personal jurisdiction:

Subject Matter Jurisdiction	*Personal Jurisdiction*
diversity or federal question	minimum state contacts

The following chart assumes three auto accidents resulting in damages in excess of $50,000.

Example

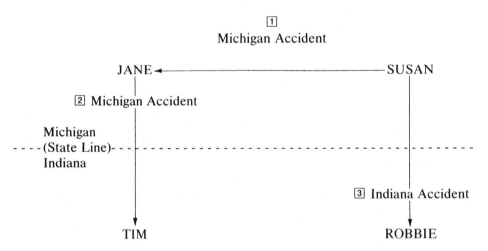

[1] Susan sues Jane over an automobile accident in Michigan: Only Michigan state courts have jurisdiction because there is no diversity of citizenship. Personal jurisdiction exists over Jane because she is a Michigan resident.

[2] Jane, a Michigan resident, sues Tim, an Indiana resident, over an automobile accident that occurred in Michigan. Jane may sue in:

    a.   Michigan state court because when Tim drove in Michigan he created a sufficient state contact for personal jurisdiction; or

b. Indiana state court because Tim's residence in Indiana is a sufficient contact; or

c. Federal court in either Michigan or Indiana because there is diversity of citizenship and Tim has sufficient state contacts with both states.

③ Susan, a Michigan resident, sues Robbie, an Indiana resident, over an automobile accident that occurred in Indiana. Susan may only sue in:

a. Indiana state court because Robbie has sufficient contact to Indiana; or

b. Indiana federal court because the parties are diverse; the amount in controversy exceeds $50,000; and Robbie, the defendant, has sufficient contacts with Indiana; but

c. not in Michigan in either state or federal court because Robbie does not have any contacts with Michigan, which would create personal jurisdiction.

You must establish personal jurisdiction early in the complaint. In both state and federal court, you should allege specific facts that establish the court's personal jurisdiction. In order to establish personal jurisdiction, you must allege that the defendant had some significant contact with the state such as residing there, signing or performing contracts there, committing torts there, or conducting business there.

The following chart might help you remember what you need to allege to establish jurisdiction:

	FEDERAL COURT	STATE COURT
Personal Jurisdiction (Same in both federal & state)	Particular facts that show that the defendant has sufficient minimum contacts with the forum state to make it fair to sue her there. Such contacts might include residency, commission of a tort, transaction of business within the state.	
Subject Matter Jurisdiction	1. Diversity of citizenship + claim in excess of $50,000 or 2. Federal question arising under the U.S. Constitution or federal statutes.	Although state courts vary, some courts are limited to certain kinds of claims like divorce, or to certain dollar values, like over $15,000.

One of the most important decisions you must make is where to file the suit. Of course, if your case involves neither diversity of citizenship, nor a federal question, you cannot file in federal court. When you do have a choice, you must make strategic decisions. You may want to file suit in the court in which the judges seem to have the greatest expertise. Sometimes practical concerns will guide you. Find out the backlog in both state and federal court. Usually, it will be in the plaintiff's interest to have the matter resolved as quickly as possible. Thus, you might choose the court that can resolve the issue the fastest. Once you have chosen the appropriate court, you must understand the kind of pleadings the court requires.

2. Fact and Notice Pleading Distinguished

Federal courts require only "notice" pleading[37] while many state courts require "fact" pleading.[38]

a. Federal Notice Pleading

Historically, there were four functions of pleadings:

1. providing notice to the defendant,
2. stating the facts,
3. narrowing the issues, and
4. quickly disposing of frivolous claims.[39]

In an effort to simplify the pleading process, the Federal Rules of Civil Procedure limited the pleadings to the notice function.[40] Other procedures such as discovery, pretrials, and motions perform the other functions.

Indeed, Rule 8 is very simple: "A pleading which sets forth a claim for relief, . . . shall . . . contain . . . a short and plain statement of the claim showing that the pleader is entitled to relief."[41] This notice pleading is intended to simplify the pleading process and move the case more quickly to a consideration of the merits. The U.S. Supreme Court has held:

> The Federal rules reject the approach that pleading is a game of skill in which one misstep by counsel may be decisive to the outcome and accept the principle that the purpose of pleading is to facilitate a proper decision on the merits.[42]

The chief characteristic of notice pleading is that the pleader is no longer required to plead facts in excruciating detail:

> [T]he Federal Rules of Civil Procedure do not require a claimant to set out in detail the facts upon which he bases his claim. To the contrary, all the Rules require is a "short and plain statement of the claim" that will give the defendant fair notice of what the plaintiff's claim is and the grounds upon which it rests.[43]

That is not to say that you never need to allege facts in notice pleadings, for "[t]he rule requires the pleader to disclose adequate information regarding the basis of his claim for relief as distinguished from a bare averment that he wants relief and is entitled to it."[44]

Thus, the test of notice pleading is whether you have given the defendant and the court enough information to understand the nature of the lawsuit. Your pleading should be relatively short and simple, but it should allege all the elements of your cause of action.

Although notice pleadings are generally sufficient in federal court, you should research your particular cause of action to be sure that it does not include an element that must be pleaded in more detail. For example, fraud, mistake, malice, intent, knowledge,[45] special damages,[46] and the futility of a demand in a derivative action suit[47] must all be pleaded in a much more detailed way, amounting to virtual fact pleading.

Example

COUNT I: BREACH OF CONTRACT

1. Palmer agreed to excavate Drew's drainage ditch for $55,000. A copy of the contract is attached as Exhibit A.
   - [a]
   - [b]
   - [c]
2. Palmer has fully performed all the terms of the contract.
   - [d]
3. Drew breached the contract by refusing to pay Palmer.
   - [e]

Notice that, although the example does not go into great factual detail, it does set forth each element of the cause of action: [a] mutual assent, [b] consideration, [c] contract terms, [d] plaintiff's performance, and [e] defendant's breach.

b. State Fact Pleading

Many state courts require much more detail than federal courts.[48] Fact pleading not only notifies the court and your opponent of the nature of your claim, but it also sets forth the facts that support your claim. You must plead the specific facts that establish each element of the cause of action. Thus, you must first decide what the elements of the cause of action are and then you must decide which facts prove those elements.

Example

COUNT I: BREACH OF CONTRACT

1. On April 1, 1990, Palmer and Drew signed a written construction contract. A copy of the contract is attached as Exhibit A.
2. According to the terms of the contract, Palmer agreed to excavate a drainage ditch on Drew's property located in Boise, Idaho.
3. According to the terms of the contract, in return for Palmer's agreement to excavate the drainage ditch, Drew agreed to pay Palmer $55,000, upon completion of the work.
4. Palmer completed the excavation of the drainage ditch on Drew's property on May 15, 1990.
5. On May 16, 1990, Palmer sent Drew a bill for $55,000, a copy of which is attached as Exhibit B.
6. Palmer has repeatedly telephoned Drew to demand payment, but Drew has consistently refused to pay.

Perhaps the easiest way to understand the difference between fact and notice pleading is to see how the same facts would be pleaded in each forum. The following chart enables you to compare the examples you just read:

Element	Notice Pleading (Federal Courts)	Fact Pleading (State Courts)
1. Mutual assent	1. Palmer agreed to excavate Drew's drainage ditch . . . A copy of the contract is attached as Exhibit A.	1. On April 1, 1990, Palmer and Drew signed a written construction contract. A copy of the contract is attached as Exhibit A.
2. Consideration	2. . . . for $55,000.	2. According to the terms of the contract, in return for Palmer's agreement to excavate the drainage ditch, Drew agreed to pay Palmer $55,000 upon completion of the work.
3. Contract terms	3. (included in mutual assent & consideration)	3. According to the terms of the contract, Palmer agreed to excavate a drainage ditch on Drew's property, located in Boise, Idaho.
4. Plaintiff's performance	4. Palmer has fully performed all terms of the contract.	4. Palmer completed the excavation of the drainage ditch on Drew's property on May 15, 1990.
5. Defendant's breach	5. Drew breached the contract by refusing to pay Palmer.	5. On May 16, 1990, Palmer sent Drew a bill for $55,000, a copy of which is attached as Exhibit B. Palmer has repeatedly telephoned Drew to demand payment, but Drew has consistently refused to pay.

As this illustration demonstrates, fact pleading must be much more detailed than notice pleading. Notice pleading allows you to state some legal conclusions like, "Drew breached the contract. . . ." In fact pleading, however, you cannot simply conclude that Drew breached the contract. Instead, you must plead all the facts that demonstrate the breach.

Now you understand some of the important differences between state and federal pleadings:

Federal Courts	*State Courts*
1. Notice pleading	1. Fact pleading
2. Limited subject matter jurisdiction	2. Subject matter jurisdiction varies by state. If limited, then limited by dollar amounts, or kinds of claims (e.g., divorce)
a. diversity	
b. federal question	
3. Personal jurisdiction	3. Personal jurisdiction

D.   *The Drafting Process for Complaints*

Now that you have familiarized yourself with the procedural law that governs complaints, you are ready to begin the more general drafting process. Recall the steps:

1.   understand the audiences;
2.   gather the facts;
3.   know the law;
4.   classify, organize, and outline;
5.   write carefully;
6.   test for consequences; and
7.   edit and rewrite.

1.   Understand the Audiences

Pleadings, like other documents, have multiple audiences. When you draft a pleading, you know that it will be read by at least three different groups: your client, your opponents, and the court. There may be other audiences as well. Other lawyers in your office may read the pleading. If you represent a corporation, either in-house or outside counsel will probably review pleadings. Similarly, in complex cases, various attorneys who represent other plaintiffs may review your complaint. In controversial cases, even the press may read the pleadings.

Each of these different audiences will be looking at the document differently. Many of these readers are lawyers or judges who are far more comfortable with certain forms of jargon than nonlawyers. However, at least two crucial audiences are unlikely to be lawyers: your client and possibly the jury.

Your client must be able to read and understand your pleading easily. Only your client can catch factual errors or omissions. If she cannot wade through the legalese, you have lost contact with the person who can help you the most. Accordingly, you must gear the pleading to the level of sophistication and legal knowledge of your client. One way to do that is to follow the plain English rules discussed in Chapter 3. Of course, you probably do not need to simplify your document quite as much as you would if you were writing a consumer contract, unless your client is particularly unsophisticated.

In trying to make your pleading accessible to the client, do not simply adopt the client's vocabulary. Frequently, when you are working closely with a client, you will learn a great deal about your client's business and its associated jargon. If you are not careful, you will begin to describe events using that jargon. This practice is very dangerous for two reasons. First, you may not clearly understand the meaning of the industry jargon and could inadvertently harm your client's case by misusing a term. Second, you run the risk of losing nonindustry audiences, such as a judge, when she reads the pleading. Thus, you need to simplify the language of the pleading to make it accessible to *all* your audiences.

The nature of your audience also affects the tone of your pleading. Since the primary audience of a pleading is the court, you know that your pleading is a formal document. Accordingly, you should avoid using contractions and slang expressions in pleadings. Tone is more than a matter of formality, however. Tone emerges from the way you describe facts. Compare these two examples:

> 1.   Defendant discarded debris and hot, combustible items into a disorderly burning refuse pile in the middle of the creek.
>
> 2.   Defendant recycled by-products into a dam constructed in the middle of the creek.

The first statement is dramatic and overstated. The second statement is quiet and understated. You want to plead your client's case forcefully but not alienate the court with inflamatory language. While persuading the court, you should sound as if you are a reasonable participant recounting your story even though you retain a strong advocate's position. Accordingly, you should omit most adjectives and adverbs and describe facts simply:

> The Defendant built a burning refuse pile in the middle of the creek.

This version eliminates the inflammatory words "discarded" and "disorderly," while retaining the description, "burning refuse pile," which suggests the defendant's culpability. Obviously, you must use your judgment in determining the proper tone to use. Remember, however, that judges often view emotional language as a mask for a weak case.

You also draft a complaint for hostile audiences as well. Your opposing counsel will be scrutinizing the complaint both for factual errors, which could result in sanctions against you,[49] and for grounds to dismiss the complaint. Thus, you must remember your hostile audiences when you gather the facts and research the law.

2.   Gather the Facts

The next step in writing a complaint may be the most important. You must gather all the facts. Since federal courts do not require you to plead all the facts in your complaint, you may think that this first step is less important in federal cases. On the contrary, you must have an evidentiary basis for your facts to avoid sanctions under Federal Rule of Civil Procedure 11. Furthermore, you cannot know whether you have a federal case or what the appropriate claims are unless you know all the facts.

Various fact-finding steps may be required depending on the nature of the suit, the reliability and knowledge of your client, and your own expertise. At a minimum, you must interview your client extensively and get copies of all documents. Remember to ask: who? what? where? when? why? and how?[50] Frequently, your client will forget something important, or you will discover a new question in the course of your research. Do not be reluctant to call your client to explore these matters.

Often, relying on your client will not be enough. Increasingly courts are holding attorneys liable for frivolous complaints.[51] Accordingly, you may need to take some steps to independently verify the facts that your client has presented. It is especially important for you to verify facts when your client lacks expertise. For example, in a personal injury action, you should obtain hospital and medical records before filing suit. Doing so will verify the client's perceptions, identify the appropriate defendants, and provide an accurate record of the facts that the client may not know.

Sometimes you are the one who does not fully understand the nature of the suit. In complex cases it may be wise to consult an expert who can explain exactly what happened. For example, in an action for breach of warranty on a piece of industrial equipment, hire an expert witness (an engineer or industrial designer) before you draft the complaint. Then the expert can educate you in time to draft an accurate complaint. If you do not fully understand exactly what happened, you will never be able to persuade a judge or jury.

When you are gathering facts, be sure to collect all the jurisdictional information, too. At a minimum get the residency, citizenship, principal place of business, and state of incorporation for every party. You will need specific addresses to write your clients and serve the defendants.

Once you have gathered all the facts, list them in chronological order. When you try to list the facts chronologically you may discover missing links you need to investigate further. You will use this fact list when you actually begin drafting the complaint and later when you prepare for motions for summary judgment or trial.

3.   Know the Law

Although you may have done some preliminary legal research to determine the form of the complaint and the requirements of the forum, you must have a thorough knowledge of your facts and the law of your jurisdiction. Such knowledge only comes from complete legal research of the ethical, procedural, and substantive law. Interpretive law may be subsumed in procedural law because courts intepret pleadings in light of procedural rules and statutes.

a.   Researching Ethics

All lawyers are constrained to act ethically in dealing with the court, their clients, and opposing counsel. The first step is to become familiar with all the relevant provisions of the ethical rules of your jurisdiction. At a minimum you must be honest, maintain confidentiality, and avoid conflicts of interest. You are personally responsible for both the truth and the legal sufficiency of your pleadings.[52] Although you may be allowed to file a pleading that tries to extend or modify existing law, if a court determines that your claim is frivolous you may be sanctioned. Thus, you should find out what steps your jurisdiction requires you to take in order to sufficiently investigate your client's claim.

Similarly, you should check to be sure that you do not have a conflict of interest. One common conflict occurs when you represent multiple parties to the same litigation. Even though your clients may start out sharing a common interest, later they may develop a conflict. These evolving conflicts frequently occur when the parties are related in some way. For example, two spouses may begin as plaintiffs suing a common insurer for their injuries in an auto accident. However, at some future time the passenger may end up suing the driver. Since the spouses really share an interest in recovering from the insurance company, they may not be concerned with the potential conflict. Nevertheless, you should be sure to research whether you can ethically represent them both, and if so under what conditions. Is disclosure of the conflict sufficient, or do you need a knowing waiver? If you cannot represent them both, do you have to recuse yourself from the entire case or can you continue to represent only one of them?

You need to research all the rules concerning attorney conduct, including ethical rules, court rules, and disciplinary rulings. Then you need to find the relevant cases construing those provisions.

b.   Researching Procedure

After you know that you can ethically represent your clients, you must discover how to do so. You need to research three different kinds of procedural requirements: (1) legal prerequisites, (2) technical requirements, and (3) more substantial procedural requirements, which affect the merits of the lawsuit. First, you must determine the legal prerequisites to filing your complaint. For example, in the earlier example, if you represented the ditch digger, Palmer, you might be wise to record a mechanic's lien[53] on the land before you filed suit. That way you could sell the land to enforce your judgment. Similarly, if the lawsuit you are filing affects land, you may need to record a notice of the suit to warn purchasers about the litigation.[54] In many other cases you must exhaust your administrative remedies before you can file suit. For example, in order to sue an employer for sexual or racial discrimination, you must get a right to sue letter from the EEOC. In order to get that letter you must first give any appropriate state administrative agency a chance to resolve the issue, and then give the EEOC a chance to rule.[55] Different claims have different procedural prerequisites.

It may be difficult to find these various procedural prerequisites. You will find some of the prerequisites in the process of researching the substantive law, either in statutes or in common law. You will find others in state or federal regulations. Frequently, materials published by local bar associations or continuing legal education groups will be a good introductory source for identifying the nature of such prerequisites and referring you to some of the appropriate cases, statutes, and regulations.

Once you have determined the prerequisites, you should determine the technical requirements for your pleading. As you remember from the previous discussion of jurisdiction, individual procedures may vary from court to court. The technical requirements for filing your pleadings, such as the size of paper used, the nature of the caption, the forms that must be used, the number of copies required, and the time limits for filing vary dramatically. Frequently these matters are governed by local rules, including in some cases municipal or county court rules. Even within a given court the procedures may vary from judge to judge.

Finally, you must research the more substantial procedural issues, which affect the merits of the suit. These procedural issues cover the wide range of topics typically covered in a Civil Procedure course, a task beyond the scope of this chapter. In order to understand the kind of procedural questions involved, consider a few examples including jurisdiction, statutes of limitations, preclusion, and remedies.

As you know, jurisdiction is crucial. You must research the specific jurisdictional requirements of each potential forum. As mentioned earlier, you must determine the appropriate rules for both personal and subject matter jurisdiction. Then you must research how those rules have been interpreted in cases with facts similar to yours. A court will not hear a case unless it has jurisdiction.

Similarly, courts will not hear stale claims. Thus, each different claim must be brought within certain time limits. The time limits vary according to the nature of the claim. For example, plaintiffs usually have longer to sue on a written contract than an oral one,[56] and longer to sue for a breach of contract than for a personal injury.[57] These time limits are established either by statutes of limitations, or by common law doctrines such as laches. Of course, these time limits vary from state to state.

Preclusion[58] is another example of a procedural issue that can affect the merits of your claim. Courts will not duplicate the work of other courts. Accordingly, you must determine if another court has ruled on either your claim[59] or a relevant issue.[60] If so, you are precluded from bringing your action. Even if the matters have not been presented to another court, you may be precluded from raising them if they could have been brought in another suit.[61] Thus preclusion requires two different kinds of research. First you must find out what the relevant rules of preclusion are for your issues in your jurisdiction. Then you must find out whether other litigation exists that might preclude you.

Similarly you must determine both what remedies you are entitled to seek and what you must allege in order to obtain those remedies. For example, are punitive damages available in your state for your claim? If so, must you plead willful misconduct or merely reckless conduct? Are you entitled to recover attorney's fees? How are your damages to be measured? Will damages make your client whole? Do you want additional equitable remedies such as an injunction or specific performance? If so, what must you plead to warrant the special relief? Are you entitled to a jury trial for any of these issues? If so, do you have to demand one in your complaint?

All these different procedures are closely tied to the nature of your substantive claim. You cannot decide on the proper measure of damages until you have chosen your legal theories of recovery.

c. Researching Substantive Law

Choosing your theories of recovery may be the most difficult part of drafting a complaint. Needless to say, you cannot do it in a vacuum. Not every grievance creates a legal remedy. For example, when a mother disciplines her child by sending him to his room, the child has no legal recourse against his mother. When a legal remedy exists for a grievance, the plaintiff has a "cause of action" or "claim." In essence, a claim is a legal theory that justifies recovery. Your complaint must state a claim. Each claim is comprised of certain necessary "elements." For example, the elements of a negligence claim might be: (1) defendant's duty to plaintiff, (2) defendant's breach of duty, (3) causation, and (4) plaintiff's injury. You must allege all the necessary elements or the complaint will be dismissed.

The defendant's conduct may create several different claims. For example, if a manufacturer sold a purchaser a defective product, there are several different possible claims depending on the precise facts: (1) breach of express warranty, (2) breach of implied warranty, (3) breach of contract, or (4) fraud. If you sue the manufacturer on one theory, but fail to raise other possible theories, you may be precluded from recovering on the other theories later.[62] As a result, you want to be certain that you have included all the relevant claims in your complaint.

Accordingly, your first job is to determine what claims are available for the particular facts of your case. Although there are no set rules for researching what claims are available, there are a few techniques that may help. Sometimes you may have no idea where to begin. Then you need to do some basic background reading just to get an overview of the general law in the field. Good sources for general background information are treatises, law review articles, and legal encyclopedias.

Once you have a general idea about the law in the area, start your research with general categories and then narrow it down. Has a contract been breached? If so, was it a written, oral, or implied contract? How was it breached? Has the defendant committed a tort? If so, which one? Were the defendant's actions negligent, intentional, or willful? Has the defendant violated any statutory provisions? Which ones?

Review your list of facts. Are there any key words that would help you find relevant cases and statutes? In the example in which Palmer agreed to dig Drew's ditch, such key words might be "construction," "contract," and "excavation."

Your substantive research will not be significantly different in a federal suit, since federal courts follow the local substantive law in diversity cases.[63] Of course, if your claim involves a federal question, you will have to become familiar with the federal statutes, constitutional provisions, and cases construing them.

Exercise 6-1

a.   Consider these facts: Paula Pedestrian was walking down the street with her husband, Patrick. When the "walk" signal came on, they started to cross the street. Daniel Driver disregarded a red light and struck Paula. Paula claims that Daniel was speeding at the time. Paula also states that she smelled liquor on Daniel's breath when he came to see if she was all right. Paula broke her leg and strained her back. Paula's husband, Patrick, jumped out of the way and was physically uninjured but was extremely upset watching his wife's plight. What are the available claims in your state?

b. Consider the facts alleged in the illustration of fact pleading on page 289. That pleading alleged a breach of contract. What other claims might be available to Palmer? [Answer: Mechanic's lien.]

Once you have a complete list of your theories of recovery, you are ready to move on to identify the elements of each claim. Every claim consists of certain necessary elements. You may remember the elements of a breach of contract claim: (1) mutual assent, (2) consideration, (3) contract terms, (4) plaintiff's performance, and (5) defendant's breach. In both state and federal courts, a complaint must set forth every one of these elements to establish a *prima facie* case. Once again, the essential elements will be the same in either state or federal court because a federal court adopts the law of the state in which it sits.

Nevertheless, various states define the claims differently. For instance, in some jurisdictions, the plaintiff must plead that he has fulfilled all conditions precedent to a contract, while in other jurisdictions, the defendant must allege which conditions were not performed. Accordingly, you will need to research your state's law. If you fail to allege any required element, your complaint can be dismissed.

Exercise 6-2

a. Reconsider the Pedestrians' claim against Driver from Exercise 6-1a. What are the elements of each available cause of action? What are the available remedies for each cause of action?

b. Reconsider Palmer's claim, see page 289, against Drew for digging the ditch. What are the elements of each available cause of action? What are the available remedies for each cause of action?

4. Classify, Organize, and Outline

Now that you know both the facts and the law, you must combine them coherently. Once you have identified all your claims and their respective elements, you are ready to insert the facts. You should sort the facts to supply support for each element. Although sorting facts may seem less important in notice pleading, it helps you to organize and highlight any missing information. Needless to say, sorting facts is absolutely crucial in fact pleading.

Sorting facts for a complaint is different from sorting facts for a contract or will. In a contract or a will, a given provision appears only once in the document. Hence, you can cross the fact off your list once you have used it. In a complaint, the same fact may be used to support several different propositions, so you may want to simply check off facts, but keep them on your list for later use.

Since you have already generated both a fact list and an element list, the sorting process is not too difficult. Start with the list of facts and the list of elements that you have already prepared. For each fact on your list, jot down which claim and element it establishes. Some facts will not support any given element. These facts may be irrelevant or they may be necessary background information. Other facts may support several different elements of different claims. Then go through your list of elements and be sure you can find facts to support each one. The following illustration demonstrates how to sort facts:

Example

Fact List

1. Plasco is a company that manufactures plastic packages from a raw material called resin.

2. Plasco hired Denise Devlin to be its president and chief executive officer on January 11, 1983. (I.A. & II.A.)

3. Without telling Plasco, Devlin formed her own wholly owned corporation, Risky Resin. (I.E. & II.C.)

4. Risky Resin began buying and selling resin. (I.E. & II.C.)

5. Devlin, acting through Risky Resin, bought 100,000 pounds of resin for $4.00 per pound. (I.E. & II.C.)

6. Devlin then caused Plasco to buy 100,000 pounds of resin from Risky Resin at $5.00 per pound. (I.E., I.F., II.C. & II.E.)

Element List

I. Breach of Employment Contract

  A. Mutual Assent (Fact 2)

  B. Consideration

  C. Contract terms

  D. Plaintiff's performance

  E. Defendant's breach (Facts 3, 4, 5 & 6)

  F. Plaintiff's damages (Facts 4, 5 & 6)

II. Breach of Fiduciary Duty

  A. Existence of Defendant's fiduciary duty to Plaintiff (Fact 2)

  B. Nature of fiduciary duty

  C. Breach of fiduciary duty (Facts 3-6)

  D. Proximate cause

  E. Plaintiff's damages (Facts 4-6)

This example illustrates how sorting facts helps you to find missing information. The client, like many, was so anxious to tell all the details about what Devlin did wrong, he omitted many crucial facts: (1) Consideration: Did Devlin get paid a salary, commission, bonus, or percentage of the profits? How much? (2) Contract terms: What were Devlin's duties? Was she expressly prohibited from engaging in other businesses? Was the contract oral or written? (3) Plaintiff's performance: Did Plasco pay Devlin?

Also notice that fact 1 does not specifically establish any element of either claim. Is it necessarily irrelevant then? In this case, it provides useful background information. You will have to judge for yourself whether facts that do not support any specific element are necessary background information or irrelevant detail.

There is another major flaw with this fact list. It does not contain any jurisdictional facts. Where does Devlin live and vote? Where is Plasco incorporated?

Where is its principal place of business? Jurisdictional facts must always be a part of your fact list too.

Exercise 6-3

a. Assume the following facts: Plasco is incorporated in Our State, with its principal place of business in Dickens, Our State. Elias McCawber, Plasco's vice president and chairman of the board, also lives in Our State. McCawber hired Devlin to be Plasco's president and chief executive officer but never reduced the agreement to writing. McCawber told Devlin she would be paid an annual salary of $75,000. It never occurred to McCawber that Devlin would set up her own dummy corporation to acquire resin and resell it to Plasco. Plasco paid Devlin her salary on a bimonthly basis until McCawber learned of Devlin's self-dealing. Then Plasco stopped paying Devlin. Risky Resins is incorporated in Delaware, but has its principal place of business in Idlewood, Other State, where Devlin lives. Add these facts to the fact list given in the previous example and sort them into the appropriate elements.

b. Using the list of elements you prepared for Exercise 6-1b, sort the facts into the element list. What additional facts do you need from your client?

Once you have made your lists of facts, claims, and sorted them into the appropriate elements you are ready to complete your final organization. When a document is not well organized, readers do not know what it says. Accordingly, a badly organized complaint is far more likely to be dismissed for failure to state a claim than a well-organized document. Although the material you are organizing differs in fact and notice pleading jurisdictions, the general rules of organization still apply. You may want to organize the material by order of importance, complexity, chronology, or persuasiveness.

As always, when you begin to outline, start with your most general categories, in this instance your various claims. Each claim will be assigned a Roman numeral and designated a "count" of the complaint. You have already identified the various claims. Now you must decide how to order these various counts.

Consider how each count relates to the others. If a given count contains information that will have to be realleged elsewhere in the complaint, then you may want to make that "Count I." If a breach of contract is your simplest theory of recovery and a breach of implied warranty your most complex count, then plead the breach of contract first. If you have a strong negligence case, but a weak one for intentional misconduct, plead negligence first. Remember, a claim need not be Count I just because it was the first theory of recovery you identified.

Exercise 6-4

a. How many counts would your complaint for Paula Pedestrian have? (See facts in Exercise 6-1a.) What counts are they? What order would you put them in your complaint?

b. How many counts would your complaint for Plasco have? (See page 298 for facts.) What counts are they? What order would you put them in your complaint?

Now that you have put the counts in logical order, you can begin to organize the supporting allegations. In a notice pleading forum, your supporting allegations may be simply elements of the cause of action. In contrast, in a fact pleading state, your supporting allegations include facts as well as elements. In either case, you should remember that a complaint tells a story and should therefore be organized in rough chronological order. When events are discussed out of time sequence, the reader becomes disoriented. If a judge cannot follow your story, he is more likely to dismiss your complaint.

Inexperienced lawyers frequently forget the time sequence when they simply adopt the organization of their research materials. There is no magic rule that says that the elements of each count must be presented in the same order as they appeared in a case, statute, or article. The previous illustrations listed consideration as the second element of a breach of contract case. Frequently, however, payment is one of the last things clients do. Thus, you might want to allege the existence of consideration after you have established the existence of the contract and the contract terms. There is no single organization that will work for all cases; you must tailor your organization to the particular story you are trying to tell.

However, do not get so enamored of chronological order that you forget to include any of the necessary elements. Indeed, after you have outlined your claim, review your fact list and your element list to be sure all the necessary allegations have been made. Some required elements may be difficult to fit into your smooth story. Nevertheless, every element must be pleaded or else the complaint may be dismissed. If you cannot find a logical place for an omitted element, try putting it either first or last. Do not stick the "leftovers" in the middle to break up your otherwise polished story.

Jurisdictional facts may be one such "leftover." As noted previously, you should allege the elements of jurisdiction first so the court will not have to search to find out if it has power to hear the case. Like all other allegations, jurisdictional facts must be organized. Generally, you will have two broad categories: subject matter jurisdiction and personal jurisdiction. Be sure to account for every plaintiff and every defendant.

Venue is another such "leftover." Some attorneys like to include a statement as to proper venue with an appropriate statutory reference. Whether venue should be raised in a complaint is a question of local law and strategy. In many jurisdictions, improper venue is a defense that is waived if not raised. Thus, a complaint is sufficient without any statement as to venue. If the defendant does not question it, the suit stays where it is. In those jurisdictions, it may be waving a red flag to the opponents to include a venue statement when venue is questionable. If you intend to omit a venue statement, check local law to be sure that the plaintiff is not required to plead proper venue.

Exercise 6-5

a. Using your sorted fact list that you created in Exercise 6-3b, make an outline of Paula Pedestrian's complaint against Daniel Driver.

b. Using your sorted fact list that you created in Exercise 6-3a, make an outline of Plasco's complaint against Devlin and Risky Resin.

5. Write Carefully

At last you are ready to put words on paper. If this is the first complaint that you have drafted, you may be concerned about the proper form. Generally, students and inexperienced lawyers exaggerate the importance of form. Of course, you want to research the local rules of your forum to be sure that you comply with any specific form requirements, but generally you should be far more concerned about the substance of your complaint.

Do not rely on form books. When novices use form books, they risk using the wrong form. The results can be catastrophic.[64] Many form books are old and outdated and, thus, are of very limited value. They can give an attorney an idea of what causes of action are available, but it is crucial to actually research the law of the local jurisdiction to see if any special requirements have been added or changed. The facts of each suit are different and the complaint your client needs to recover from the defendant has never been drafted before. Remember that if you fail to adequately research either the law or the facts you may be subject to sanctions.

Form books are also guilty of speaking in the worst type of legalese. They thrive on seventeenth century language and excess verbiage. There is no reason for a complaint to read like an exercise in Old English. If it does, judges, clients, and possibly juries are unlikely to understand it and are unlikely to read it all the way through. Therefore, refer to the parties by their proper names instead of their legal titles as plaintiff, defendant, counter-plaintiff, or cross-claimant. Similarly, do not start every paragraph of a complaint with the word "that" or use synonymous word pairs like "allege and state," or "by and through." The archaic words most frequently used in pleadings are:

by and through	thereby
foregoing	therein
hereof	to wit
in accordance with	true and correct
pursuant	true and exact
said	whereupon
thereafter	

One purpose of a complaint is to convince a court that the defendant is culpable. In order to do so, you must be very precise about who did what to whom. Accordingly, you must always use the active voice, which identifies the actor. For example, say: "Palmer excavated Drew's ditch." Never say: "The ditch was excavated." Similarly, say: "Daniel Driver, driving at high speed, struck Paula Pedestrian." Never say: "Paula Pedestrian was struck." If you are unsure about how to recognize the passive voice, pay particular attention to the rules on passives and the related exercises in Chapter 3.

Actually writing the complaint should now be fairly simple. Begin with the appropriate caption and list your chosen forum and parties. After the proper title and a short introduction, you should make your jurisdictional allegations and statement of venue. Now it is finally time to tell your story. Label your first count and begin.

In both fact and notice pleadings each count will be divided into separately numbered paragraphs. These paragraphs are not as broad as the paragraphs you use in standard prose. Since a defendant will admit or deny the allegations paragraph by paragraph, you do not want to put too much information in any one paragraph. If you include 12 statements and only one of them is inaccurate, the defendant may deny the entire paragraph. That is not to say that every sentence must be separately numbered. You do not want to distract your reader with a choppy style that obscures your meaning.

Your complaint concludes with a prayer for relief[65] and signatures. Now you have written your first draft. When you begin to revise your complaint, be sure to send your client a copy to see if any crucial information has been omitted or misconstrued.

Exercise 6-6

a.   Use the outline you prepared in Exercise 6-5a and your fact and element lists to draft Paula Pedestrian's complaint against Daniel Driver.

b.   Use the outline you prepared in Exercise 6-5b and your fact and element lists to draft Plasco's complaint against Devlin and Risky Resins.

6.   Test for Consequences

Now that you have completed a draft of your pleading, you are ready to test it. Remember that your pleading is written for several different audiences: the court, your opponent, and your client. Begin with the most hostile audience, your opponent. If you represented the defendant, how would you attack the pleading? You may assume that your opponent will try to have the pleading dismissed. Common grounds for dismissal include:

1.   lack of jurisdiction,[66]
2.   improper venue,[67]
3.   failure to state a claim,[68]
4.   failure to join a necessary party,[69] and
5.   failure to state facts in sufficient detail.[70]

a.   Jurisdiction

Look for all the elements of both personal and subject matter jurisdiction. Be sure that you have alleged specific facts that establish:

1.   the citizenship of all plaintiffs and defendants,
2.   the contacts of all defendants to the forum state, and
3.   the amount in controversy, where relevant.

Pretend you are the opposing counsel and try to outline a motion to dismiss your complaint.

b.   Venue

Have you alleged why the suit should be brought in this particular court? Have you stated the connections between the claim and the forum? Are there witnesses here? Did the claim arise here? Why? Find particular allegations that establish the facts to support venue. Is that part of the complaint labeled "Venue" to help the judge find it?

c.   Cause of Action

List all possible theories of recovery, for example: fraud, breach of contract, and violation of implied warranty. For each theory list each element you need to prove to establish a prima facie case. Now go back through your complaint and list the paragraph number that alleges the necessary element. Double-check each cause of action to make sure you have not omitted a single element. If possible, have another lawyer in your office read the complaint to be sure you have not missed an entire cause of action.

d.   Necessary Parties

You must be certain you have sued all the necessary parties, including those who may be only indirectly responsible for the problem. Make a flow chart of the problem, which traces it both forward and backward in time. For example, if you have a cause of action for a defective product that injured your client, trace the product all the way back through the chain of production. From whom did your client buy the product: a retailer, a distributer, a wholesaler, a warehouse, an assembler, or a manufacturer? Where did the seller get the product or its components? Who manufactured or sold the component parts? Then trace the product forward from your client to other possible parties: To whom did your client sell or give the product? Where is the product now? You may need to gather more facts to answer these questions. Once you are sure of the facts, be sure you know which of those parties may arguably be held liable legally. Double-check your complaint to be sure that you have included all necessary defendants and that you have specific allegations addressed to each one. A complaint that names a party as a defendant but fails to allege a claim against her will be dismissed.

e.   Necessary Detail

Identify which, if any, of your allegations must be alleged in detail. If you are in a fact pleading jurisdiction, all your allegations must plead specific facts. Otherwise, only some of your allegations, such as fraud or intent, may need to be pleaded specifically. Re-read those allegations that require factual pleading. Remove any words that generally describe other terms. (These descriptive words are often adjectives that describe people or things — e.g., "*negligent* driver" — or adverbs that describe actions — e.g., "drove *negligently*.") Imagine yourself being cross-examined by a hostile opponent about every statement in the pleading. Ask yourself: "How do I know that?" and "Why?" Answering such questions may give you the necessary facts, or at least alert you as to what facts are missing from the complaint. Thus, the answer to how you know the defendant was driving negligently may be that your client said the defendant ran a red light. These are the details that you need for a factual pleading.

After playing the hostile role of your opponent, you should take the more objective position of the trial judge reading the complaint for the first time. First, the judge will want to know whether she has jurisdiction to hear the case. Have you clearly labeled the jurisdictional section of the complaint so the judge can find it quickly and easily? Are all the jurisdictional facts organized so the judge can determine jurisdiction from reading a few sentences or paragraphs, rather than having to flip through and search the entire document? Remember, if the judge cannot find the jurisdictional information, she may presume that her court does not have jurisdiction.

Now that you have convinced yourself as a judge that you have the power to rule, you need to learn about the nature of the lawsuit. Are the different counts of the complaint labeled to let the judge know quickly what the appropriate legal theories are? Sit back and read the complaint straight through at one sitting. Does the complaint tell a story that is easy to follow? If not, you need to reorganize the document so that it flows as a believable story. Look for missing transitional information that will help the complaint make more sense. Double-check the chronology to be sure that the judge can follow the story. However, do not get so carried away in your story telling that you confuse the elements of different claims. If a judge cannot find a necessary tort element in the tort count, she may dismiss it.

Now evaluate the tone of the complaint. Does the story portray the plaintiff to be sympathetic without being melodramatic or maudlin? Does the complaint seem to be exaggerated like the story of a small child accusing a sibling of a misdeed? If so, the tone may be too overstated. The appearance of objectivity adds credibility. Does the complaint seem strident or whiny? If so, adjust the tone to be more formal and legal, but do not lose the story in legalese. You want the judge to read your story carefully, and so you make it interesting, not formulaic and boring.

Is the complaint consistent? Do you contradict yourself? Good advocates can and should plead in the alternative in appropriate circumstances, but they should not make sloppy errors in simple facts. Consider both the strategic risks and advantages before you plead in the alternative. If you decide to plead in the alternative, use language that makes it clear that you are making an alternative argument, not just contradicting yourself.

Finally, judges need to know exactly what it is you want them to do. Is your prayer for relief specific? Is it complete? Have you included post-judgment interest, attorney's fees, special damages, or equitable relief? Do you want the judge to retain jurisdiction after judgment for any reason? Be as specific as possible, but include a sentence that allows the judge to be creative in creating an appropriate remedy.

The last audience to consider is your client. Is the complaint written simply and clearly enough for your client to read and understand easily? All too many clients would prefer to rely on their attorneys without reading the complaint. That is a very dangerous practice. Only your client really knows what happened. He is in the best position to supply omitted information and correct misunderstandings of fact. If the complaint is too difficult to read, he either will not read it at all or will merely scan the document without catching any of the omissions or errors. After your client has read the complaint, you should have a conference with him to make sure that he understands the complaint and that it is accurate. Think about this conference when you evaluate the tone of your complaint. How have you portrayed your client? Will your client be pleased with that picture? If not, how can you soften the complaint to put your client in a better light while remaining completely honest?

Exercise 6-7

a.   Test the complaint you drafted for Paula Pedestrian in Exercise 6-6a from the perspectives of the opposing attorney, the judge, and the client. Pay particular attention to organization, tone, and content, including errors and omissions. Rather than try to rewrite each problem section, simply identify the problem in the margins or between lines on your first draft. This technique will let you concentrate on spotting problems without getting sidetracked on rewording. Pretend you are your own supervising attorney noting problem areas to be corrected without actually rewriting the pleading yourself.

b.   Test the complaint you drafted for Plasco in Exercise 6-6b from the perspectives of the opposing attorney, the judge, and the client. Pay particular attention to organization, tone, and content, including errors and omissions. Rather than try to rewrite each problem section, simply identify the problem in the margins or between lines on your first draft. This technique will let you concentrate on spotting problems without getting sidetracked on rewording. Pretend you are your own supervising attorney, noting problem areas to be corrected without actually rewriting the pleading yourself.

7.   Edit and Rewrite

Now that you have identified various problems in the complaint, you can begin the more detailed work of rewriting it. Concentrate first on reorganization. The way you organize a complaint may have an impact on your word choice and transitions. Move from information that is familiar to the judge to information that is unfamiliar. Start with what is most important to the court: jurisdiction. In the process of pleading jurisdiction you will have identified the parties. Order the various counts so that you begin and end on strong issues. Make sure that each count contains all the necessary elements, and that no necessary information is missing. Within the legal structure of the causes of action try to follow rough chronological order. Be careful to add any new information in its logical place in the complaint. Make sure you include such new information in each count in which it is relevant.

Once you are satisfied with the overall structure of the complaint, edit it for tone. Your goal is to appear objective while still zealously representing your client. This tone is difficult to achieve and may take several different rewrites to get the correct word choice. Write in short active sentences, eliminating adjectives and adverbs wherever possible. Edit out legalese.

Finally, proofread the complaint very carefully. Clients pay high rates for precision, so sloppy errors irritate them. Even worse, you lose credibility with the court, which is likely to assume that careless editing may reflect equally careless legal and factual research. If you are working on a computer, the first step is to spell-check your document. That will not only catch some spelling errors, it will also find some typographical errors as well. You cannot rely on the computer to proofread for you, however. For example, a computer will not catch the substitution of "hear" for "here" because both are recognized words. Allow some time between the time you draft the complaint and the time you proofread it. Otherwise you will read what you meant, not what you wrote. Always allow time to read the pleading "cold" and revise it.

Exercise 6-8

  a. Rewrite and edit your draft complaint for Paula Pedestrian.
  b. Rewrite and edit your draft complaint for Plasco.

SAMPLE DOCUMENT
Complaint

The following complaint illustrates how the drafting steps work. The complaint was drafted by first year law students who took their facts from some actual litigation involving a dam failure in 1972.[71] Note that the students chose to include detailed facts in order to be persuasive, even though the federal rules require only notice pleading. Margin notes identify various mistakes and problems.

IN THE UNITED STATES DISTRICT COURT FOR
THE SOUTHERN DISTRICT OF WEST VIRGINIA

DENNIS PRINCE, et al.,   )
)
            Plaintiffs,   )
      v.   )
)
PITTSTON MINING CO.,   )
)
            Defendant   )

                Complaint

DENNIS PRINCE et al. by the law firm, [1] Student and Student, complains of the Defendant, PITTSTON MINING COMPANY:

---

[1] *Know the Law:* Attorneys are responsible under Rule 11.

<u>Jurisdiction</u>

1. Plaintiffs are residents[2] of West Virginia.

2. Defendant is a Delaware corporation[3] and the sole stockholder of its subsidiary, Buffalo Creek Mining Company ("BMC").[4]

3. This complaint concerns the failure of a dam, owned by Pittston's division[5] of BMC, to contain sludge refuse from the mining process.

4. This failure occurred in West Virginia.[6]

5. The total amount in controversy exceeds $50,000.[7]

6. This court has diversity jurisdiction by virtue of 28 U.S.C. §1332(a)(2).[8]

<u>Count I</u>
<u>Negligence</u> [9]

7. BMC, a division of Pittston, erected massive coal waste refuge[10] piles, which dammed up a stream in Middle Fork Hollow in the

---

[2] *Know the Law:* Diversity requires *citizenship* not residency.

[3] *Write Carefully:* Ambiguous: state of incorporation or place of business?

[4] *Classify, Organize, and Outline:* Sort facts: BMC not a party, so necessary background fact or irrelevant detail?

[5] *Edit and Rewrite:* Inconsistent with paragraph 2.

[6] *Edit and Rewrite:* Purpose? Venue? Then should be labeled "venue." Meant to establish Pittston's contacts with the forum for personal jurisdiction? Then Pittston's connection to the forum needs to be clearer.

[7] *Know the Law:* Jurisdictional minimum must be alleged for each plaintiff.

[8] *Test for Consequences:* Omission: Only grounds for jurisdiction? Federal question too? See Count I, paragraph 9.

[9] *Test for Consequences:* All elements included? *Classify, Organize, and Outline:* Facts linked to necessary elements?

[10] *Edit and Rewrite:* Typo that spell check cannot catch.

mountains of West Virginia. Behind the dam was a huge coal washing operation containing around 130 million gallons of water and waste. [11]

8. In the valley below the dammed stream were sixteen communities consisting mostly of miners and their families.

9. §77.215 of the Federal Safety Standards prohibits the use of refuse piles to impound water. BMC by erecting the dams failed to comply with this safety standard. [12]

10. Customary engineering practice is the building of a spillway to divert excess water behind a dam. This practice was not used[13] in the construction of this dam.

11. In February 1972 the dam broke, releasing a wall of water and sludge 20 to 30 feet high, travelling at speeds of 30 miles per hour, which devastated[14] Buffalo Creek's sixteen communities. [15]

<u>Count II</u>
<u>Negligent Infliction of Emotional</u>
<u>Distress</u>

12. When the dam collapsed and flooded the valley, over 125 people were killed[16] and 4,000 more were affected. [17]

[11] *Write Carefully:* "Operation" = general noun that leaves reader unclear on the facts.

[12] *Write Carefully:* Unclear whether claiming (1) a mining act violation or (2) a breach of a *per se* duty?
Classify, Organize, and Outline: Alleges multiple elements: both breach and duty

[13] *Write Carefully:* Passive voice makes it unclear who was at fault.

[14] *Write Carefully:* Emotional and imprecise term.

[15] *Write Carefully:* Communities are not the plaintiffs.

[16] *Write Carefully:* Are "people" the plaintiffs? Passive omits Defendant's role.

[17] *Write Carefully:* "Affected" is too vague.
Classify, Organize, and Outline: Injury should have been pleaded in Count I too. Do you want to begin with injury in Count II?

13. The construction and consequential breaking[18] of the dam constitutes reckless and intentional[19] conduct by the defendants because:

    a. A reasonably prudent person would have recognized the dam's flawed construction as observed by expert engineers. [20]

    b. No engineers were consulted as to how the dam could be built safely.

    c. The dam was built in flagrant[21] disregard for established industry safety standards.

14. Defendant's behavior in the construction of the dam was extreme and outrageous[21] in light of history's strong suggestion of the probability of such an accident.

    a. Defendant had a similarly constructed dam collapse with like consequences in Virginia in 1955.

    b. Dams which had previously been constructed on this site had broken.

    c. A similar disaster had occurred in Aberfam, Ireland in 1966. [22]

15. A causal relation exists between the defendant's conduct and the severe emotional distress[23] suffered by the plaintiffs.

    a. Plaintiffs would have suffered no emotional distress if the dam had not broken.

---

[18] *Write Carefully:* "Construction" and "breaking" = vampires, which distance the defendant from culpability.

[19] *Write Carefully:* It's acceptable to plead in the alternative, but you need different counts.

[20] *Know the Law:* What = duty? Duty to inspect or duty to listen to engineers?

[21] *Write Carefully:* Emotional labels without supporting facts.

[22] *Test for Consequences:* Does the reader know what elements of the claim subparagraphs (a), (b), and (c) establish?

[23] *Write Carefully:* Distress never mentioned before. Remember to move from familiar material to unfamiliar material.
Edit and Rewrite: Eliminate vampires.

b.   Prior to the dam's breaking, plaintiffs had expressed distress[24] over the
dam's safety and were pacified by agents of
the defendant.

c.   A reasonably prudent person could
have been substantially certain that severe
emotional distress would result to a reasonable person following such an occurrence. [25]

16.   As a result of defendant's conduct and
the ensuing disaster, plaintiffs suffered severe emotional distress as evidenced by such
symptoms as:

1.   the death imprint,
2.   the death guilt,
3.   psychic numbing,
4.   impaired human relationships,
5.   attempt to give death encounter signif-
     icance. [26]

17.   The plaintiffs were closely related to
the victims of the disaster. The people who
died were the plaintiffs' family members,
close friends, and fellow community and church
members. [27] Damages $50,000 per plaintiff[28]

[24]   *Write Carefully:* Uses the word, "distress" to describe both injury and pre-disaster concern. Undermines the extent of injury and inconsistent with subparagraph a.
Classify, Organize, and Outline: If purpose = establish knowledge or malice, then misplaced in count for "negligent. . . ."

[25]   *Test for Consequences:* Is this meant to establish malice, recklessness, or plaintiffs' reasonable behavior?

[26]   *Test for Consequences:* Does the reader know what these terms mean?

[27]   *Write Carefully:* Suggests plaintiffs are not victims! *Know the Law:* Need the plaintiffs be closely related to the physically injured to recover?

[28]   *Write Carefully:* Not a sentence! *Know the Law:* How are these damages calculated or apportioned?

```
┌ ─ ─ ─ ─ ─ ─ ─ ─ ─ ─ ─ ─ ─ ─ ─ ─ ─ ─ ─ ─ ─ ┐
│              Prayer for Relief              │
│    WHEREFORE, Dennis Prince et al. pray this│
│ court to enter its judgment against Pittston│
│ for:                                        │
│       A.  $31,000,000  in  compensatory dam-│
│ ages,                                       │
│       B.  $21,000,000 in punitive damages,  │
│       C.  Costs,                            │
│       D.  An  injunction29 prohibiting Pitts-│
│ ton from constructing any further dams on   │
│ Buffalo Creek.                              │
│       E.  Such other and further relief as this│
│ Court deems appropriate.                    │
│                                             │
│                                             │
│                          Signed:            │
│                                             │
│                                             │
│                                             │
│                          ─────────────────  │
│                          Attorney for       │
│                          Plaintiffs         │
│                                             │
└─────────────────────────────────────────────┘
```

[29] *Know the Law:* Hasn't pled irreparable injury which is not compensable at law. Therefore not entitled to an injunction.

E.   *Other Pleadings*

So far, we have been considering how to draft complaints. The same guidelines would apply to counterclaims because counterclaims merely are complaints filed by defendants. Answers, replies, and, in some circumstances, motions to dismiss also serve pleading functions. These documents are much easier to draft than complaints because they are responses to other pleadings.

In an answer a defendant only has four legally recognized responses to any allegation of the complaint:

1.   she can admit it;
2.   she can deny it;
3.   she can claim she does not know; or
4.   she can avoid it by pleading other facts, typically in the form of an affirmative defense.[72]

Answers simply adopt the organization and numbering of the complaint and respond to each allegation in order. Any new matter may either be included with an answering allegation or set forth separately as an affirmative defense. The following presents a sample answer to Count I of the preceding complaint.

SAMPLE DOCUMENT
Answer

IN THE UNITED STATES DISTRICT COURT FOR THE SOUTHERN DISTRICT OF WEST VIRGINIA

DENNIS PRINCE, et al.,   )
)
              Plaintiffs,   )
    v.   )   No. 13698
)
PITTSTON MINING CO.,   )
)
              Defendant   )

Answer

PITTSTON MINING CO. ("Pittston") by its attorneys, Susan Student, answers the complaint of DENNIS PRINCE et al. as follows:

  1. Pittston is without knowledge as to paragraph 1.

  2. Pittston admits paragraph 2.

  3. Pittston denies that Buffalo Mining Co. ("BMC") is a division of Pittston, but otherwise admits paragraph 3.

  4. Pittston admits paragraph 4.

  5. Pittston denies that each plaintiff has more than $50,000 in controversy.

  6. Pittston denies that this court has diversity jurisdiction and affirmatively states:

     a. Each plaintiff does not have $50,000 at stake;

     b. BMC is a necessary party to this litigation under Rule 19 of the Federal Rules of Civil Procedure.

     c. BMC has its principal place of business in West Virginia, so the neces—

sary parties to this litigation are not
completely diverse.

Count I

7. Pittston admits that BMC constructed
some sort of refuse pile in Middle Fork Hollow. Pittston has no knowledge of the quantity of water in the coal washing operation.

8. Pittston denies that the stream was
"dammed" and has no knowledge of the demographic patterns of the valley.

9. Pittston denies paragraph 9 and affirmatively states that it is not legally responsible for the actions of its subsidiary BMC. Pittston further affirmatively states that BMC constructed this pile before Pittston purchased BMC's stock.

10. Pittston denies paragraph 10.

Signed:

_____

Attorney for
Defendant

Note that the answer addressed each paragraph of the complaint individually in order, rather than skipping through the document. By following this format, you can be sure that you have responded to every allegation of the complaint. The court will also be able to tell at a glance precisely what your response is to any issue.

If a paragraph of the complaint contains multiple facts, some of which are true and others which are untrue, you should specifically state which facts you admit and which ones you deny.[73] As always, you are personally responsible for the truth and accuracy of the statements you make in the answer, including admissions, denials, and denials of knowledge.[74] Thus, you have a duty to investigate the facts and the law when you draft an answer or any other court document.[75]

One of the legal questions you will need to research is what matters must be raised as affirmative defenses. An affirmative defense is "new matter which, assuming the complaint to be true, constitutes a defense to it."[76] Some matters are defined as affirmative defenses as a matter of statute, such as assumption of risk, fraud, or illegality.[77] Others, such as the existence of an easement, are defined to be affirmative defenses by common law.[78]

If you fail to raise an affirmative defense in your answer, you may waive it, even if you deny all the allegations of the complaint.[79] However, you should remember that the defendant carries the burden to prove affirmative defenses, while the plaintiff must prove the elements of the prima facie case alleged in the complaint.

Exercise 6-9

a.   Draft an answer for Daniel Driver to the complaint you prepared for Paula Pedestrian in Exercise 6-6a.

b.   Draft an answer for Denise Devlin and Risky Resins to the complaint you prepared for Plasco in Exercise 6-6b.

F.   Conclusion

Drafting pleadings follow the same basic steps of drafting any document. You must:

1.   understand the audiences;
2.   gather the facts;
3.   know the law;
4.   classify, organize, and outline;
5.   write carefully;
6.   test for consequences; and
7.   edit and rewrite.

Notes

1. Fed. R. Civ. P. 1 *et seq.*

2. *See, e.g.*, Schiavone v. Fortune, 477 U.S. 21 (1986). In *Schiavone*, the plaintiff tried to sue Fortune Magazine for libel. Plaintiff named "Fortune" as the defendant rather than "Time, Inc.," the publisher, which merely used "Fortune" as a trade name. The failure to timely name Time, Inc. as the defendant defeated the suit.

3. A cause of action, or claim, is a set of "facts which give a person a right to judicial relief." Black's Law Dictionary 221 (6th ed. 1990). For example, negligence or a breach of contract are causes of action. For further descriptions of causes of action or claims, *see infra* pages 296-297.

4. For example, in the District of Columbia, if the adjudication of the case may affect real property interests, the complaint must state: "Action Involving Real Property." D.C. Super. Ct. R. Civ. P. 3-1. In Illinois, complaints must state whether they are in the law division, in the chancery division, in the probate division, or in small claims court. Ill. S. Ct. Rule 132 (1993). Similarly, the Pennsylvania Rules of Civil Procedure mandate that all civil actions must state either: "Civil Action — Law" or "Civil Action — Equity." Pa. R. Civ. P. 1018.

5. Black's Law Dictionary 221 (6th ed. 1990).

6. For example, the Federal Rules of Civil Procedure do not require that the complaint be divided into separate counts reflecting various theories of recovery. Fed. R. Civ. P. 8(e)(2). However, some states require that separate counts reflecting various theories of recovery be pleaded in separate counts. *See, e.g.*, Md. R. Civ. P. 2-305; Mo. R. Civ. P. 55.11; N.Y. Civ. Prac. L. & R. 3014 (McKinney 1974); Okla. Stat. tit. 12, §2010(b) (Supp. 1985); Pa. R. Civ. P. 1020(d).

7. Fed. R. Civ. P. 10(b).

8. *See id.* As always, check local practice.

9. *E.g.*, Tebutt v. Virostek, 483 N.E.2d 1142 (N.Y. Ct. App. 1985).

10. *See, e.g.*, 735 ILCS 5/2-1301 (1993). [At the time of this writing, the statutory compilations in Illinois have been changed from "Ill. Rev. Stat." to "ILCS." Since there is not yet an official Uniform System of Citation style for this new compilation, we have used "ILCS" consistently throughout this book. — Eds.]

11. In Kansas, a plaintiff may not request a specific dollar sum unless it is less than $10,000. Kan. Stat. Ann. §60-208 (Supp. 1986-1987). For larger amounts, the plaintiff must simply state that the amount sought is in excess of $10,000. *Id.* On the other hand, in Illinois, a plaintiff must request specific damages unless the action is a personal injury claim. 735 ILCS 5/2-604 (1993). For personal injury actions, Illinois law simply requires the plaintiff to state whether the amount is more or less than the required jurisdictional amount. *Id.* In New York, a plaintiff does not need to demand a monetary amount in medical malpractice actions or in suits against municipalities. N.Y. Civ. Prac. L. & R. 3017 (McKinney 1974). A pleader may request general relief, but if the defendant requests that the monetary amount be specified, the plaintiff may file a supplementary demand for relief. In Florida, each complaint is construed to pray for general relief in addition to the pleader's specific request. Fla. R. Civ. P. 1.110(b). Generally, you should include a separate prayer for relief at the end of each cause of action.

12. Fed. R. Civ. P. 11.

13. For example, in Colorado and Florida, most pleadings do not have to be verified. Colo. R. Civ. P. 11; Fla. R. Civ. P. 1.030. In Illinois, plaintiffs are not required to verify

their pleadings in most actions. However, if plantiffs choose to verify their pleadings, all subsequent pleadings must also be verified. 735 ILCS 5/2-605 (1993).

14.   Oregon requires verified pleadings. Or. R. Civ. P. 17. New Mexico requires verified pleadings for adoption (N.M. Stat. Ann. §40-7-42 (Michie 1986)), habeas corpus (*id.* §44-1-3), support (*id.* §40-6-11)), and divorce (*id.* §40-4-6). Although Colorado does not generally require verified pleadings, complaints alleging contempt or seeking a temporary restraining order must be verified.

15.   Fed. R. Civ. P. 11.

16.   *E.g.,* In re T.C.I., Ltd., 769 F.2d 411 (7th Cir. 1985).

17.   *Id.*

18.   Unioil, Inc. v. E.F. Hutton & Co., 809 F.2d 548 (9th Cir. 1986).

19.   *E.g.,* Rules for United States District Court for the Northern District of Illinois, Rule 9B.

20.   Some states require strict caption and title requirements. For example, in California, the top eight lines of the complaint must follow the approved format: line 1, left of center, is the name, address, and phone number of the filing attorney. Lines 1-7, right of center, are to be left blank for the clerk's exclusive use. The title of the court is then centered on line 8. Below the title, left of center, is the title of the case, while opposite the title is the case number. Below this is the nature of the pleading and the action's character (probate, civil, etc.). Cal. Super. Ct. R. Civ. P. 201(c). Idaho has similar strict requirements. Idaho R. Civ. P. 10(a)(1).

Other jurisdictions are far more flexible in matters of form. *See, e.g.,* 735 ILCS 5/2-603 (1993), which merely requires a "plain and concise statement" of the cause of action, which should be divided appropriately into counts for each cause of action.

21.   *See* Charles Wright, The Law of Federal Courts 25-26 (4th ed. 1983).

22.   *Id.*

23.   David Currie, Federal Courts: Cases and Materials 369 (3d ed. 1982).

24.   Wright, *supra* note 21, at 22-26.

25.   *Id. See also* U.S. Const. art. III; 28 U.S.C. §1330-1364 (1982).

26.   *See, e.g.,* Nadler v. American Motor Sales, 764 F.2d 409 (5th Cir. 1985); Jagiella v. Jagiella, 647 F.2d 561 (5th Cir. 1981). *See also* Fed. R. Civ. P. 8(a)(1). Although citizenship is important, note that citizenship is often equated with domicile. *E.g.,* Prakash v. American Univ., 727 F.2d 1174 (D.C. Cir. 1984).

27.   28 U.S.C. §1332(c) (1966). If the corporation is an insurer, it is also considered a citizen of the state of its insured. *Id.*

28.   28 U.S.C. §1332(a) (1966).

29.   Crawford v. Neal, 144 U.S. 585 (1892). *See also* Fed. R. Civ. P. 18.

30.   *See* Erie Railroad Co. v. Tompkins, 304 U.S. 64 (1938).

31.   Wright, *supra* note 21, at 141.

32.   28 U.S.C. §1331 (1982).

33.   *E.g.,* Ludington v. Sambo's Restaurant, 474 F. Supp. 480 (E.D. Wis. 1979).

34.   For example, it is common for state courts to divide the general jurisdiction into separate courts depending on the amount in controversy. In Michigan, the Circuit Courts hear cases over $10,000, while the District Courts hear cases involving amounts in controversy under $10,000. Mich. Comp. Laws §600.601, §600.8301 (Supp. 1961). Virginia has a similar division, except the cutoff is $1,000. Va. Code §16.1-77, §17-123 (Supp. 1985). Under the Texas Constitution, three courts are created: district, county, and justice courts.

Tex. Const. art. V, §§8, 16, and 18. *See also* Tex. Stat. Ann. art. 41, §1970(a) (Vernon Supp. 1986).

35.   Burnham v. Superior Court of Cal., 495 U.S. 604 (1990).

36.   International Shoe Co. v. Washington, 326 U.S. 310 (1945).

37.   Fed. R. Civ. P. 8. *See also* Mitchell v. E-Z Way Towers, Inc., 269 F.2d 126 (5th Cir. 1959).

38.   There are currently 24 states that are fact pleading states. *Arkansas:* Ratliff v. Moss, 678 S.W.2d 369 (Ark. 1984), Ark. R. Civ. P. 8(a); *California:* Signal Hill Aviation Co. v. Stroppe, 158 Cal. Rptr. 178 (Ct. App. 1979); *Connecticut:* Francis v. Hollauer, 475 A.2d 326 (Conn. App. Ct. 1984); *Florida:* Rishel v. Eastern Airlines, 466 So. 2d 1136 (Fla. Dist. Ct. App. 1985); *Illinois:* Doyle v. Schlensky, 458 N.E.2d 1120 (Ill. App. Ct. 1983), *see also* 735 ILCS 5/2-613 (1993); *Louisiana:* Erath Sugar Co. v. Broussard, 125 So. 2d 776 (La. 1961); *Maryland:* Continental Masonry v. Verdel Constr., 369 A.2d 566 (Md. 1977); *Missouri:* Romanus v. American Triad Land Co., 675 S.W.2d 122 (Mo. Ct. App. 1984); *Nebraska:* Russell v. First York Sav., 352 N.W.2d 871 (Neb. 1981); *New Jersey:* Miltz v. Borroughs-Shelving, 497 A.2d 516 (N.J. Super. Ct. 1985); *North Dakota:* Mitchell v. Barnes, 354 N.W.2d 680 (N.D. 1980); *Oklahoma:* Birchfield v. Harrod, 640 P.2d 1003 (Okla. Ct. App. 1982); *Oregon:* Davis v. Tyee Indus., 688 P.2d 1186 (Or. 1983); *Pennsylvania:* Alpha Tau Omega Fraternity v. University of Pa., 464 A.2d 1349 (Pa. Super. Ct. 1983); *South Carolina:* Dale v. South Carolina Tax Commn., 276 S.E.2d 293 (S.C. 1981); *South Dakota:* Oesterling v. Oesterling, 354 N.W.2d 735 (S.D. 1984); *Tennessee:* W & O Constr. v. City of Smithville, 557 S.W.2d 920 (Tenn. 1977); *Virginia:* Ted Lansing Supply v. Royal Aluminum & Constr., 277 S.E.2d 228 (Va. 1981).

The rest of the states are notice pleading states. *Alabama:* Harvell v. Ireland Elec. Co., 444 So. 2d 852 (Ala. 1984); *Alaska:* Chaible v. Fairbanks Medical & Surgical Clinic, Inc., 531 P.2d 1252 (Alaska 1975); *Arizona:* Arizona Dept. of Revenue v. Transamerica Title Ins. Co., 604 P.2d 1128 (Ariz. 1979); *Colorado:* Davidson v. Dill, 503 P.2d 157 (Colo. 1972); *Georgia:* Mills v. Bing, 352 S.E.2d 798 (Ga. Ct. App. 1987); *Hawaii:* Hupp v. Accessory Distrib., Inc., 616 P.2d 233 (Haw. Ct. App. 1980); *Idaho:* Dursteler v. Dursteler, 697 P.2d 1244 (Idaho Ct. App. 1985); *Indiana:* Houin v. Bremen State Bank, 495 N.E.2d 753 (Ind. Ct. App. 1986); *Iowa:* I.G.L. Racquet Club v. Midstates Builders, Inc., 323 N.W.2d 214 (Iowa 1982); *Kansas:* Matter of Estate of Moe, 719 P.2d 7 (Kan. Ct. App. 1986); *Kentucky:* United States v. Commonwealth, Cabinet for Human Resources, 706 S.W.2d 420 (Ky. Ct. App. 1986); *Maine:* Travelers Indem. Co. v. Dingwell, 414 A.2d 220 (Me. 1980); *Michigan:* City of Auburn v. Brown, 230 N.W.2d 385 (Mich. Ct. App. 1975); *Minnesota:* Hutton v. Bosiger, 366 N.W.2d 358 (Minn. Ct. App. 1986); *Mississippi:* Miller v. Miller, 512 So. 2d 1286 (Miss. 1987), Miss. R. Civ. P. 8(b); *Montana:* R.H. Schwartz Constr. Specialties, Inc. v. Hanrahan, 672 P.2d 1116 (Mont. 1983), Mont. R. Civ. P. 8; *Nevada:* Hay v. Hay, 678 P.2d 672 (Nev. 1984); *New Hampshire:* Robbins v. Seekamp, 444 A.2d 537 (N.H. 1982); *New Mexico:* Foundation Reserve Ins. Co. v. Mullenix, 642 P.2d 604 (N.M. 1982); *North Carolina:* Smith v. City of Charlotte, 339 S.E.2d 844 (N.C. Ct. App. 1986); *North Dakota:* Production Credit Assn. of Mandan v. Olson, 280 N.W.2d 216 (N.D. 1980); *Ohio:* Wilson v. Riverside Hosp., 479 N.E.2d 275 (Ohio 1985); *Rhode Island:* Placido v. Mello, 492 A.2d 1226 (R.I. 1985); *South Dakota:* Wilson v. Great N. Ry. Co., 157 N.W.2d 19 (S.D. 1968); *Tennessee:* Vythoulkas v. Vanderbilt Univ. Hosp., 693 S.W.2d 350, 359 (Tenn. Ct. App. 1985); *Utah:* Sears v. Riemersma, 655 P.2d 1105 (Utah 1982); *Vermont:* Lemnah v. American Breeders Serv., Inc., 482 A.2d 700 (Vt. 1984); *Washington:* Parks v. Western Washington Fair Assn., 553 P.2d 642 (Wash. Ct. App. 1975); *West Virginia:* Sticklen v. Kittle, 287 S.E.2d 148 (W. Va. 1981); *Wisconsin:* Wagner v. Dissing, 416 N.W.2d 655 (Wis. Ct. App. 1987); *Wyoming:* Ogle v. Caterpillar Tractor, 716 P.2d 334 (Wyo. 1986).

39.   Charles Wright & Arthur Miller, 5 Federal Practice And Procedure §1202 (1990).

40. Fed. R. Civ. P. 8.

41. *Id.*

42. Conley v. Gibson, 355 U.S. 41, 48 (1957).

43. *Id.* at 47.

44. Wright & Miller, *supra* note 39, at 64.

45. Fed. R. Civ. P. 9(b).

46. *Id.* at 9(g).

47. *Id.* at 23.1(2).

48. *See supra* note 38 (for a list of the states that require fact pleadings).

49. Fed. R. Civ. P. 11.

50. If a complaint fails to answer the following questions, it may be dismissed: "Plaintiff's allegations do not disclose *what* occurred, *when* it occurred, *where* it occurred, *who* did *what*. . . ." Gillespie v. Goodyear Serv. Stores, 128 S.E.2d 762 (N.C. 1963).

51. *Id.*

52. Fed. R. Civ. P. 11.

53. Contractors and subcontractors who furnish materials, work on buildings, or repair buildings are entitled to place a lien on the real estate they work on in order to secure the payment of their bill. These liens are called "mechanic's liens." *See, e.g.,* In re Louisville Daily News & Enquirer, 20 F. Supp. 465, 466 (W.D. Ky. 1937).

54. This notice is called a *lis pendens* notice.

55. *See* Kremer v. Chemical Constr. Co., 456 U.S. 461 (1982); Bray v. N.Y. Life Ins., 851 F.2d 60 (2d Cir. 1988).

56. *See* McMahon v. Pennsylvania Life Ins. Co., 891 F.2d 1251 (7th Cir. 1989).

57. *See* Hahn v. Atlantic Richfield Co., 625 F.2d 1095 (3d Cir. 1980).

58. Prior litigation may preclude a party from relitigating a given issue or claim. *See, e.g.,* Martino v. McDonald's Sys., Inc. 598 F.2d 1079 (7th Cir. 1979).

59. Claim preclusion is often called *res judicata* and bars all claims that a litigant either raised or should have raised in prior litigation. *Id.*

60. Issue preclusion is sometimes called "collateral estoppel" and prevents necessary issues from being relitigated even if the issues arose in different claims. *See, e.g.,* Halpern v. Schwartz, 426 F.2d 102 (2d Cir. 1970).

61. *See, e.g.,* Roach v. Teamsters Local Union No. 608, 595 F.2d 446 (8th Cir. 1979).

62. This is referred to as "claim preclusion" or "*res judicata.*" A party is precluded from relitigating all matters that could have been raised in a prior suit. *Id.*

63. Erie R.R. Co. v. Tompkins, 304 U.S. 64 (1938).

64. *See, e.g.,* Ross v. Mather, 51 N.Y. 108 (1872). In *Ross,* a plaintiff used the wrong form from a form book. *Id.* The selected form alleged fraud instead of a breach of warranty. *Id.* This pleading error caused the plaintiff's judgment to be reversed on appeal. *Id.*

65. For a fuller description of the Prayer for Relief, *see supra* page 283.

66. *E.g.,* Fed. R. Civ. P. 12(b).

67. *E.g., id.*

68. *E.g., id.*

69. *Id.*

70. *E.g., id.* at 9, 23.1.

71. For a complete description of the facts and the litigation, *see generally* Gerald Stern, The Buffalo Creek Disaster (1977).

72. *See, e.g.,* Fed. R. Civ. P. 8(c).

73. "When a pleader intends in good faith to deny only a part or qualification of an averment, he shall specify so much of it as is true and material and shall deny only the remainder." Fed. R. Civ. P. 8(b).

74. *Id.* at 11.

75. *Id.*

76. Black's Law Dictionary 60 (6th ed. 1990).

77. *See, e.g.,* Fed. R. Civ. P. 8(c).

78. *See, e.g.,* Layman v. Southwestern Bell Tel. Co., 554 S.W.2d 477 (Mo. Ct. App. 1977).

79. *Id.*

CHAPTER **7**

Drafting Legislation

A. *Introduction*

Every practicing attorney should know how to draft legislation. The reason is simple: Virtually any legal problem can require consideration of a legislative solution at some point.

In a legal world that is increasingly dominated by statutes,[1] most legal disputes turn on the meaning of legislation. Attorneys file lawsuits, negotiate settlements, try cases, and file briefs with appellate courts based more and more on statutes. Win or lose, however, the court's decision is not necessarily final. If an appellate court interprets an existing statute in a manner that is adverse to your client, for example, it may be appropriate to amend the statute. Similarly, cases won in the courts are often lost in the legislature.[2] For that reason, legislative drafting may simply be another means of furthering the interests of your client. In some cases, particularly when no other means exist or when those means that do exist have proven futile, legislation may be the only way to help your client.

At the local government level, legislative drafting becomes particularly significant. Local ordinances, including zoning ordinances, are amended frequently. Helping your client could easily involve drafting proposed changes to a local ordinance or code.

Learning to draft statutes and ordinances also will deepen your understanding of legislation, even if you do not draft such documents as a lawyer. You will have greater insight into reading and interpreting a statute, applying a statute to specific legal problems, and writing precisely. Putting yourself in the position of the drafter gives you a feel for legislation and statutory construction that you can never get by simply reading and applying legislation that someone else wrote.

Legislative drafting requires a real world understanding of the underlying problem, the utility of various potential solutions, and the likely results of different
alternatives. Legislative drafting requires participation — directly or indirectly —
in the legislative process. Legislative drafting is more than the sum of various
discrete rules; it is an exciting and intellectually challenging process.[3]

1. Attorney and Client

Legislative drafting is standard practice for some attorneys. These attorneys
include the professional drafters in legislative service agencies who assist legislators and their staffs in preparing bills for introduction and in amending bills.
They include attorneys for government agencies who prepare legislation that they
hope to have introduced. Lawyers for trade associations, corporations, and individuals who might be affected by, or who would like to influence, legislation are
also included in this group. Attorneys who are skilled in legislative drafting nonetheless have the direct ability to help clients when a problem may require legislative change, regardless of whether such drafting is a standard part of their
practice.

In any legislative drafting situation, your client is the individual who would like
a bill drafted to solve her problem. This client might be a legislator, but it could
be anyone, from private citizens to corporations. Regardless of who your client
is, you should also consider the legislature as a kind of client because you are
performing work for the legislature. As a practical matter, no legislature does all
of its own drafting. Bills and amendments to bills are often drafted by persons
outside the legislature.

2. The Legislative Process

Statutes are categorical rules creating rights or duties, establishing procedures
to resolve questions or disputes, or prohibiting certain actions. Statutes are passed
by Congress and state legislatures. Ordinances, which are equivalent to statutes,
are passed by boards or councils, the lawmaking bodies for cities, townships,
counties, boroughs, and other local governments.

Legislative drafting is different from other drafting because every sentence in
a statute is public law — law that applies or can apply to anyone. Unlike contracts, wills, or pleadings, moreover, statutes result from a democratic process.
These two facts profoundly affect your role and responsibility as a lawyer.

Bills become law in a way that is relatively straightforward in theory but is
often more complex and circuitous in practice. You need to understand the legislative process to be effective. In Congress, and in all states except Nebraska,
the legislature is bicameral, which means there are two houses (in Congress, the
House of Representatives and the Senate). A bicameral legislature is supposed to
ensure that proposed bills are fully and independently considered before they become law.

Individuals are elected to each house from districts. In Congress, each state
elects two members to the Senate. Representation in the House depends on the

relative population of each state. In the 1990s, Alaska, Delaware, South Dakota, Vermont, and Wyoming each send only one member to the House, while California sends 52.[4] State legislatures are divided into somewhat similar districts. The purpose of such representation is to ensure that the interests of each state, part of a state, or district are represented. Legislators typically represent their districts by following their constituents on some issues and voting their conscience or the views of their party on other issues.

Each legislator can introduce bills, which means that he can have them drafted, printed, and submitted to the house for consideration. Committees in each house are responsible for reviewing bills pertaining to particular subjects (e.g., agriculture; urban affairs; and conservation and natural resources). Each committee has expertise in its particular area. When a legislator introduces a bill, the bill is automatically referred to the appropriate committee for consideration.[5] Bills are referred to committee by the house leadership, which is composed of members representing the majority political party in the house.

If the committee holds a hearing on the bill, persons may testify for or against the bill, or may recommend amendments to it. Hearings are a relatively visible part of the legislative process since they are routinely covered by the media. But most of the important work usually goes on behind the scenes, as legislators confer with one another, their staffs, lobbyists, and constituents. If the committee then brings the bill to vote, it will debate and often amend the bill, and then vote for or against it. If the committee votes in favor of the bill, it is sent to the entire house for a vote. Once again, the bill will be debated, and frequently amended, before there is a vote for or against it. If one house votes in favor of the bill, it is referred to the other house, where the process usually starts again. If the bill is passed by the other house, but in a different form, a conference committee is created to work out the differences. Each house then votes on the compromise version worked out by the conference committee. Once the same version of the bill has been passed by both houses, it is sent for signature to the president, governor, or other executive. Upon signature, the bill becomes law. A bill that is vetoed by the president may become law only if each house passes the bill by a two-thirds majority.[6]

Because legislators make law, the process has a free-wheeling and open-ended style that contrasts sharply with adjudication. Although interested persons are frequently given an opportunity to argue their positions, no requirement exists that this occur in all cases. Legislators are not required to be impartial, but most try to be fair. Legislative decisions are based more on policy — a sense of what is right or appropriate — than on the niceties of legal method.

The legislative process thus has two sides. Much of it occurs — or can occur — in public. The public side often is described as the "civics class" version of how legislation is made. The legislative drafter often finds her work discussed in newspapers, magazines, newsletters, or on television or radio. Political campaigns often win or lose based on legislation that has passed or failed to pass. Obviously, wills, contracts, and pleadings are usually prepared and executed in much greater privacy.

The process also has a private and unofficial side. Some see this side of the process as necessary for the efficient management of legislative business, and others see it as seamy or even corrupt. The process is more complex than the civics class version would suggest: there are exceptions to most rules, what is said at public hearings often matters less than what is said privately, major decisions are often made with virtually no media coverage, and more. To a great extent, the private side represents the real face of the legislative process. You need to be aware that both sides exist.

3. Legislation as a Problem Solver

As important as legislative drafting can be, it is not an all-purpose way of solving problems. Some problems lend themselves to a legislative solution, and some do not. At the state and federal level in particular, legislation tends to address broad categories of persons, places, or things. As a result, legislation is usually not appropriate for problems that are unique. Legislators are generally unwilling to create exceptions to existing laws for individual persons or situations,[7] unless they are examples of more general problems. This is somewhat less true on a local level where, for example, zoning ordinances are constantly being amended in response to requests from individuals.

Even when a client's problem falls into a broader category, legislation tends to be appropriate if a problem cannot be addressed, or properly addressed, through existing laws, and if litigation or administrative interpretation is unable to solve the problem. Legislation should be a strategy of last resort because it requires a time consuming process that may yield nothing. Most bills, once introduced, die in the committee to which they have been assigned. Bills die because hundreds, perhaps thousands, of other bills are competing for legislative attention. However necessary a bill may be, it will go nowhere unless legislators are willing to give it priority over other bills. In an important sense, the purpose of the legislature is to kill bills, not to pass them.[8]

B. The Drafting Process for Legislation

There are still many times when the problem is broad enough, and when other avenues have been exhausted, that a legislative solution is appropriate. The following seven steps, which were described generally in Chapter 2, should then be followed. These steps are not necessarily sequential, and it may be necessary to repeat some or all of them during the drafting process.

1. Understand the Audiences

Legislation generally has much broader and more numerous audiences than other drafted documents. In fact, legislation has two kinds of audiences, one in the bill phase and the other in the statute phase.

In the bill phase, the audience is legislators and their staff, lobbyists representing those who would be affected, government agencies, and interested citizens and editorial writers. Many of these people are lawyers but probably more are not. The most important of these groups are the legislators themselves, because they ultimately decide the fate of proposed legislation.[9]

You should keep in mind several important points about this audience. First, while individual legislators are sometimes interested in details, most are primarily concerned with general concepts and policies. This suggests that legislation should be drafted in relatively general terms, although the appropriate level of detail may vary from issue to issue.

Second, many legislators are primarily interested in how general concepts in a bill would affect specific situations, particularly those involving their constituents. In other words, the overall structure of the legislation may be less important to a legislator than its impact on specific people or organizations.

Third, some legislators are far more important to the passage of legislation than others. These include the chair of the committee to which the bill is assigned, the ranking minority party member of the committee, and the legislative leadership. These people exercise much influence on other members because of their apparent expertise or their leadership position. You should draft with their views, or potential views, in mind.

Fourth, some legislators are likely to be supportive, and others are likely to be hostile. Knowing why legislators may be supportive could lead you to frame a bill in a way that is more likely to gain their support. Similarly, knowing why legislators could be hostile could lead you to draft the legislation to avoid their opposition.

Finally, and more broadly, different legislators approach problems in different ways. Some tend to see problems in fairly simple and practical ways, but others understand issues in more complex terms. Many legislators give less attention than they should to how the bill will actually work, and others care deeply about implementation. Legislators are influenced by their staffs, lobbyists, constituents, the media, and others. Many of these people are interested in the potential effect of legislation. Because these people play an important role in educating legislators — for better or for worse — you must craft legislation that will maximize results that are generally understood as fair or positive. You must also avoid unnecessary and undesirable consequences.

The audience shifts if a bill becomes law. Many of those who supported and opposed the bill will continue to be involved. Invariably, many persons who are affected by legislation become aware of its provisions only after it becomes law. Those affected by legislation tend to be more interested in how details and specific applications of a bill relate to their situation and less interested in the underlying policies. Although many nonlawyers read and apply statutes, attorneys are asked to interpret difficult provisions or provisions that seem to produce harsh results. The legislature may continue to have some involvement, through oversight or requests for amendment or repeal of the legislation, but its role is diminished. When a government department is required to administer the statute, that department is an important part of the audience. And at this point another actor enters the scene: the court, which will be asked to interpret or apply the statute.

These audiences create a tension for you, the drafter, although this tension can be used constructively. In general, you should be interested in legislation that is well crafted, tailored to the particular problem in question, likely to achieve the desired result, internally coherent and logical, and relatively easy to understand and use. Many legislators and many of those that may be affected by the legislation, however, are likely to have a more narrow and somewhat different agenda. They will be interested in how the legislation affects a particular constituent and, perhaps, in amending the bill to help or protect constituents or advance their own policy goals. Of course, most legislators also are interested in re-election. These interests are not necessarily improper, but people advancing them may not care about whether the legislation is coherent and logical. Legislators sometimes propose bills or amendments that work like a machete when a scalpel would do. As a result, you may find yourself drafting or redrafting to incorporate these concerns into the legislation without unnecessarily compromising it — redrafting machete language or ideas into scalpel language.

In addition, your interest in clearly resolving a question, one way or the other, may be trumped by political concerns. Sometimes, the more precisely a bill addresses a certain point, the less likely it is to garner sufficient support to be passed. Certain portions of bills are therefore made general, with the understanding that courts or agencies will be required to interpret them.

Finally, many bills are drafted simply to satisfy a constituent or raise general issues that can be more specifically addressed in committee, with little concern about the language or mechanics of the bill itself. Quick and dirty drafting is commonplace.

You must therefore recognize the hurly-burly of the process that approves, changes, or rejects your work. You also must be sensitive to the different views that various legislators will bring to the process, as well as the opinions and perspectives of others. Your "professional" role and the legislator's "political" role are different but not necessarily incompatible. These role differences can lead to different views about what is important. In the final analysis, however, the legislature (not you) is responsible for legislation and may be held accountable through the election process for its decisions.

Exercise 7-1

a. Your client, the Shady Grove Homeowners' Association, has just learned that the Johnson Quarry Co. is seeking to operate a limestone quarry adjacent to the village of Shady Grove. The Homeowners' Association is made up of low- to middle-income people and is racially and ethnically diverse. The Homeowners' Association is worried about the potential effect of this possible quarry on property values, a Native American archeological site, and the quality of a nearby stream. The Homeowners' Association wants you to draft legislation that would prevent the quarry from operating.

What potential audiences would be important in the state legislature? What potential audiences would be important if the bill becomes law? How will the scope of the legislation affect those audiences? What will those audiences want to know about this legislation? Which audiences are likely to be friendly, and which are likely to be hostile?

b. Your client, Rebecca Zosia, operates Becky's Bed and Breakfast, a large Victorian home in which up to nine rooms are rented to overnight guests who are served breakfast. Ms. Zosia was just visited by an inspector from your state's health department, who told her she had to make numerous mechanical and electrical changes in her kitchen to comply with the Restaurant Health and Safety Act. She wants the statute repealed.

What potential audiences would be important in the state legislature? What potential audiences would be important if the bill becomes law? How will the scope of the legislation affect those audiences? What will those audiences want to know about this legislation?

2.   Gather the Facts

Fact gathering has two meanings. First, you must obtain basic data about the problem that a given piece of legislation would address, and about whether legislation is even an appropriate solution to the problem. Second, and usually at the same time, you must understand your client's preferences. How would your client have this problem addressed? As a practical matter, these two meanings work together. Your client's preferences will help direct your fact gathering, and the information you obtain may influence your client's preferences.

a.   Data

Legislation is almost always motivated by concrete, real world problems, not abstractions. Your client may complain about the manner in which a utility cut off her electricity. A business may find that an old statute prevents a planned expansion. Understanding your client's problem enables you to determine whether a problem really exists and whether the problem merits legislation. It also enables you to proceed with confidence that the legislation you draft may actually solve it. Put another way, data gathering is both a way of testing whether legislation is appropriate and a method for drafting on a firm foundation.

As obvious as it may sound, clearly and thoroughly understanding your client's problem is an essential but sometimes overlooked step in the drafting process. It involves obtaining information about the problem from your client and others through interviews, file searches, and other means. This data may not simply be historical; it may include information about what will happen if legislation is or is not adopted.

A related step is to determine whether your client's problem typifies the real world, or whether it is isolated. This is important because, as already indicated, problems usually are not the proper subject of legislation unless they are significant or widespread.

You must therefore determine whether a general or overall problem exists that would justify a legislative solution. That is, you must learn who shares your client's problems, in what manner, and to what extent. Are other people experiencing problems with electricity cutoffs, for example? If so, how many? Why? Factual information is frequently available in studies, reports, periodicals, and books, but often the best information is not published. It is thus important to interview people and travel to places where the problem has occurred. Such research obviously is necessary to explain and justify a decision to proceed, or not to proceed, with legislation. But it also provides insight into important questions. When and if drafting begins, you will have a better idea of who or what is affected, and what the implications are.

You also should review any previously drafted bills in the jurisdiction on the same subject. This step is in addition to knowing the law, because it involves looking at proposed laws. Such research helps you determine whether the problem has previously been recognized and, if so, what solutions have been suggested. It also enables you to understand the history of previous legislative discussions, including the issues that were raised, the legislators who sponsored the bills, and the interest groups that were involved. These bills may also contain useful ideas for legislatively solving your client's problem.

Finally, testimony from any legislative hearings on these bills can be an extremely useful source of information and ideas, not to mention a source of individuals who can be contacted. Be sensitive to proposals at other government levels. If you are thinking about state legislation, for example, you should know about any proposed federal or local legislation.

b. Preferences

You must understand what your client wants, and make sure those preferences are accurately reflected in the legislation. Every sentence in a statute stands for a different proposition, and each sentence must be discussed with your client to be sure it reflects what your client wants.

Your client's preferences can be understood in two different but related ways: What your client says he wants, and what his real interests are. Understanding your client's goals may be complicated by your client's statement of the means he would use to achieve particular goals. Because your client may not know all of the available methods, you must concentrate on finding out your client's real interests.[10]

You should interview your client to be sure you understand what he wants. Putting your client's ideas in legislative form requires that the interview cover those points that will form the essential elements of the statute. You should take detailed notes during an interview and use those notes when you write your initial draft. Each preference your client expresses represents a point that may not be deducible from the others, and a draft that leaves out points made by your client in an interview may cause your client to lose confidence in you. You will frequently find, as part of the writing process, that some questions come up that were not previously discussed. You can leave those issues unresolved until the next interview or suggest a resolution to your client in the draft. In either case, you should discuss these issues with your client. You should not be surprised or frustrated if it takes several drafts to obtain a meeting of the minds.

Throughout the process, you should give your client every opportunity to state and restate what he wants. You should listen carefully to be sure that your client's formulation is the same as yours. Restate in your own words what you think your client said. Ask him whether your understanding is correct. Be alert for clues that you and your client are not communicating. Are you using different words for what you think is the same idea? Are you ignoring something your client says because you don't understand it? When you believe there might be misunderstanding, say so, explain the reason, and ask how your client wants the matter resolved.

In the following case, for example, an attorney has heard her client say two seemingly inconsistent things:

Attorney: Let me see if I understand. You don't think anyone should build a hazardous waste incinerator within 1,000 feet of a wetland.

Client: That's right.

Attorney: But you said just a minute ago that you weren't worried about certain wetlands.

Client: Yes. This prohibition should apply only to significant wetlands.

Attorney: What do you mean by a significant wetland?

Resolution of this inconsistency leads to a distinction between two types of wetlands, and a discussion of how that distinction should be made.

Exercise 7-2

Consider again the Shade Grove Homeowners' Association in Exercise 7-1a.

a. What do you need to learn before you conclude that a legislative solution is appropriate?

b. What would you want to learn about quarries to assist your client? What information sources would you use?

c. What questions would you ask your client to determine its preferences?

d. Ask a classmate to play the role of the executive director of the Homeowners' Association. Interview the executive director on the Homeowners' Association's preferences for legislation.

Exercise 7-3

Consider again Becky's Bed and Breakfast in Exercise 7-1b.

a. What do you need to learn before you conclude that a legislative solution is appropriate?

b. What would you want to learn about restaurants to assist your client? What would you want to learn about bed and breakfast houses? What information sources would you use?

c. What questions would you ask your client to determine her preferences?

d. Ask a classmate to play the role of Rebecca Zosia. Interview her to determine her preferences for legislation.

c. Questions

Fact gathering — for both data and your client's preferences — should cover the following questions.

i. Who?

It is extremely important to be able to identify the class of persons, places, things, or activities that will be covered by the legislation. The scope, meaning, and effect of the bill all depend on this question, which also determines the audience.

Assume, for example, that a huge pile of waste tires recently caught fire in your state. It took dozens of fire fighters four days to put out the fire, which created a noxious smoke that was visible for miles. Liquid from melted tires has polluted a nearby stream and significantly contaminated groundwater. The clean-up is proving costly and difficult, and those individuals responsible for the blaze cannot be found. Your client wants you to draft legislation to make sure this doesn't happen again.

Such legislation clearly will be directed at piles of waste tires and will likely require people who own land on which such piles are located to take certain actions to prevent fires and other problems. An important question will be the size of those piles. You should learn as much as you can about the category of persons, places, things, or activities that would be affected, and which parts of that category really matter to your client. Your client clearly is interested in large tire piles and agrees that a homeowner with five old tires piled near his garage should not be covered by the legislation. What about the gas station or tire dealer that collects hundreds of waste tires before they are hauled away? Your client says she doesn't want to affect these people either, but wants to discourage them from letting large numbers of tires pile up.

In cases like this, the category your client wants to affect does not lend itself to words that can be found in the dictionary, or that are defined in the dictionary as you want them to be used in the legislation. You therefore will draft specialized definitions for terms that do not lend themselves to dictionary meanings. For example, you and your client may decide to use the term "waste tire site" to mean "a site that is used for the storage or disposal of 1,000 or more waste tires." Only persons who own such sites would be affected by the legislation. As described below, most statutes contain such definitions.

ii. What?

Once your client has identified who will be covered, your client must be asked what it means to be covered. You must ask your client what she wants to allow, prohibit, restrict, or otherwise affect. Your client will frequently have a general idea of what she wants. These wants must be translated into legal categories. Implementing a particular choice may require a series of minor decisions that your client previously has not made. In this case, your client has told you that she doesn't want any more tire pile fires, period. Is it enough to write a law stating that people with "waste tire sites" may not cause or allow the tires to burn? To answer this question, you need to learn what people who have such sites actually do with the tires, and what legislative rules would influence their behavior. Assume you find that some of these people are storing waste tires as part of a genuine recycling operation and that other people are simply being paid to have tires dumped on their property. Your research may lead you to conclude that lightning could start fires at either kind of site and that there is some risk of an intentional fire at the latter kind of site. You and your client might conclude that the risk of large fires is reduced if people who operate these sites store tires in smaller piles that are located far enough apart so that a fire at one pile doesn't spread to other piles. You and your client also might conclude that a good market for recycled waste tires would discourage these piles in the first place.

That leaves at least three means to accomplish your client's goals: a simple prohibition against tire fires, limitations on how waste tires may be stored, and mechanisms to improve the market for recycled waste tires. Some of these choices, in turn, require additional choices. Your task is to help your client decide which of these options, or which combination of these options, will best achieve her goals. Answers to these questions may form the heart of the bill. It is therefore important to be sensitive to your client's overall language skills, to educate your client about the legal meaning and likely effect of these options, and to ask additional questions if there is doubt about whether ideas are mutually understood.

The imposition of waste tire storage limitations, for example, raises numerous questions. Your client says she believes that waste tires should be stored in small piles that are far enough apart to prevent the spread of any fire. That's a start. But you must always be sensitive to how the legislation will actually work. Simply throwing a law at the problem won't do. Will anyone who has a waste tire site know exactly how big the piles should be or exactly how far apart they should be? Will complying with the law, or taking enforcement action, be easier or harder without more detail? More basically, who will enforce these rules? Perhaps the state Department of Environmental Quality could be required to enforce the statute and regulations, and to provide the details of enforcement of the legislation by regulation.

Improving the recycling market raises other questions. Perhaps your client believes that subsidies and grants for tire recyclers, coupled with regulatory incentives, would help the market for recycled tires. Again, that's a good start, but where will the money come from? Who will decide where the money goes? Will subsidies or grants do any good? What regulatory incentives will be offered? Your client may decide that a one dollar fee should be charged for each new tire sold, and that this fee money should be deposited in a special fund that will be used for the subsidies and grants. Your client also may decide that the state Department of Environmental Quality should administer the subsidy and grant program and should develop the regulatory incentives.

iii. Where?

For most legislation, the answer to this question will be the jurisdiction covered by the legislative body. State legislation on waste tire sites will probably cover the entire state. In other cases, it is appropriate to target legislation to specific parts of the jurisdiction. Legislation that protects specific rivers would be an example. Specific sections of legislation also may require answers to "where?" For instance, where are appeals of government decisions under the waste tire legislation to be taken?

iv. When?

You must ask your client whether the bill should go into effect as soon as it is signed into law, or whether the effective date should be later. If it will take some time for affected persons to respond to new requirements, as perhaps it might for the tire legislation, delaying the effective date for 60 days may be appropriate.

This question also is important to triggering events in legislation. Statutes are often structured so that something happens, or is allowed to happen, only when something else occurs. You and your client may decide that the waste tire legislation should allow citizens to bring actions to force people with waste tire sites to comply with the statute. A citizen suit is an action brought by a person other than the government to enforce a statute. The citizen suit provision could encourage out-of-court solutions by requiring that 60 days' written notice be given to the alleged violator before suit can be brought.

v. Why?

You already should have an answer to this question if your client has decided to seek a legislative solution. Answers to this question will provide specific ideas for purposes, goals, or findings in the legislation. As discussed below, purposes, goals, or findings usually are stated in a statute and provide the general rationale for the statute. Your client's answers also will suggest how well your client understands specific problems that crop up and the solutions being proposed. If your client believes that citizen suits will help ensure that tire pile fires do not occur again, she is more likely to want a citizen suit provision in the statute. The quality of your client's answers will indicate how much guidance she needs throughout the legislative process. Some clients have a clear and highly developed sense of what they want, while others have only a general sense of what they want.

vi. How?

You must be ever alert to the virtual certainty that some persons will ignore or violate the requirements of the legislation. Ask your client what penalties should be imposed. Your client may defer to your expertise because enforcement and penalties are understood as more "legal" in nature. Nonetheless, you should discuss the issue with your client. It is essential that provisions to ensure compliance and to punish violators are drafted to actually achieve those outcomes. You may also want to consider incentives to ensure compliance.

The enforcement provisions in the waste tire legislation will depend on how the legislation is written. For example, if there is a simple prohibition against fires at waste tire sites, your client may want a fine of up to $25,000 or one year in jail. If the state is required to develop market incentives for recycling waste tires, other mechanisms are probably more appropriate. These may include public reporting by the state or citizen suits.

Gathering facts about the problem and your client's preferences is not a straightforward process. You must ask who? what? where? when? why? and how? over and over in various contexts.

Exercise 7-4

a. Consider again the Shady Grove Homeowners' Association in Exercise 7-1a. What are the who? what? where? when? why? and how? for this problem? Where choices exist in responding to any one of these questions, identify the two best options.

b.   Consider again Becky's Bed and Breakfast in Exercise 7-1b. What are the who? what? where? when? why? and how? for this problem? Where choices exist in responding to any one of these questions, identify the two best options.

3.   Know the Law

At all stages in the drafting process, the law presents both obstacles and opportunities. Knowing the law is not only a way to avoid mistakes but also a way to find creative ideas, particularly as your knowledge and experience with the law grow. For example, your state may have a law that requires sellers of automobile batteries to accept an old automobile battery for each one they sell and that prohibits anyone from discarding old automobile batteries. This law encourages the recycling of these batteries. Perhaps your client would be interested in applying that concept to tire purchases. Requiring tire merchants to accept an old tire for each new tire they sell and prohibiting the disposal of old tires would make tire manufacturers and retailers responsible for waste tires and encourage tire recycling.

Do not limit your research to the governmental level at which you are working. If you are considering federal legislation, for example, you may find significant state or local laws. These laws may provide useful ideas and may even show that a potential solution is already available.

a.   Know the Substantive Law

You should research and review existing substantive law to discover whether a statute, regulation, constitutional provision, or judicial decision provides a potential answer to your client's problem. Perhaps administrative regulations already exist governing storage of waste tires, and your client is not aware of them. Using an existing law is easier and less expensive than asking the legislature to enact a new law. Moreover, if you don't research, you may be embarrassed later if it becomes apparent that legislation is not necessary. Even when the research reveals only another opportunity for a solution, such as an administrative procedure or litigation based on an ambiguity in the law, it usually is better to attempt that route before going to the legislature.

You also may find that a statute already covers the subject but fails to address your client's problem or conflicts with what your client wants. In that case, your research will suggest that an existing statute should be amended.

Sometimes, research may raise state or federal constitutional provisions that prevent your client from obtaining what he wants or force your client to respond in a different way.[11] It is also possible that the research will disclose no alternatives. In that case, the research will help you explain why other solutions are unavailable.

Basic research is not limited to the early stages in the process. Very often your client will raise issues that will require additional research. Once a bill is introduced, proposed amendments will likely raise still more issues.

Exercise 7-5

Consider again the Shady Grove Homeowners' Association in Exercise 7-1a. What substantive laws exist in your state that may give your client the relief it seeks? In light of these laws, how would you counsel your client to proceed?

b.   Know the Procedural Law

You should also be aware of rules, often contained in statutes, ordinances, or state constitutions, that may affect the drafting process. These rules may affect the validity of legislation, but they are directed to the drafting process rather than the substantive law in question. For example, some state constitutions prohibit a bill from having more than one object.[12] Assume that your client, a nonprofit foundation concerned with juvenile delinquency, would like you to draft a bill that amends the criminal code for certain juvenile crimes and also establishes a state Conservation Corps to provide work for juvenile delinquents. If you draft a single bill, the constitutional error may prevent its introduction, create major problems during the legislative process, or give someone a perfect opportunity for judicial challenge if the bill becomes law.

Exercise 7-6

Consider again the Shady Grove Homeowners' Association in Exercise 7-1a. Does your state constitution contain any provisions that may affect the drafting of legislation?

c.   Know the Interpretative Law

In addition, you must be familiar with and adhere to the statutory construction rules that would be used by attorneys and the courts to interpret the legislation you are drafting. These interpretative rules are important because they affect the meaning of legislation. Many statutory construction rules, including the requirement that a statute be read for its "plain meaning," simply require adherence to ordinary rules of grammar, word use, and sentence structure.

Other rules are similar to those used when drafting other documents. As discussed more generally in Chapter 3, every time a particular concept is expressed, it should be expressed with the same words; otherwise, a reviewing court will conclude that the legislature meant several different things even if you had only a single concept in mind. In nonlegal writing, this repetition would be considered monotonous.

Statutory construction rules also include specific conventions that are unique to statutory construction. For example, in the event of conflict between two provisions, the provision prevails that is placed closest to the end of the statute. Rules such as this one generally are not necessary if a statute is drafted properly. In the federal system, and in many states, statutory construction rules are embodied in case law.[13] In other states, there is a statutory construction law that sets out the essential rules.[14]

d. Know the Ethical Law

It should go without saying that you need to be familiar with the Rules of Professional Conduct, including those concerning competence, communication, confidentiality, and conflicts of interest.[15] For example, you must be sure that the legislation accurately and completely reflects what your client wants. To the extent that you substitute your judgment for that of your client or fail to discuss parts of the legislation with your client, you have shirked a basic responsibility.[16] You must help your client think fully and clearly about the meaning and implications of her ideas. The extent to which you play this role will depend on the interest and abilities of your client, but it is extremely important to ensure that the ideas contained in a bill have been thoroughly discussed and understood.

You should give your client the opportunity to read the text of successive drafts. Some clients will want to do that carefully, and others will not. In the latter case, you should tell your client what is in the draft and inform him that a meeting of the minds would be better assured if he read the draft.

You should be aware of numerous ethical considerations. Most basically, you should not draft statutes that are clearly unconstitutional. Although various lawyers and clients have different views about what risks are worth taking, a point exists beyond which virtually all lawyers would agree that a proposal is not constitutional. For example, no one should draft a law that imposes a penalty on an owner of a waste tire site without giving that person an opportunity to appeal the penalty. Otherwise, the person would be deprived of property without due process of law, in violation of the Fourteenth Amendment to the U.S. Constitution. It is also important to be sensitive to your own moral or religious views, as well as those of your client. Some ethical constraints, moreover, are based on prudence and good sense.

You also have a duty as a participant in the democratic process to be sure that the legislation is drafted as clearly as possible. Legislation that conceals its purpose or effect makes it hard for the public and the media to understand what is happening, makes it impossible for legislators to know the meaning of what they are voting for or against, and ultimately means that the legislation, if passed, may operate in a manner contrary to everyone's expectations. Apart from all other considerations, such deceptive drafting tarnishes your reputation and lowers others' confidence in you.

Exercise 7-7

Consider again the Shady Grove Homeowners' Association in Exercise 7-1a. How would your representation of the Homeowners' Association be affected if:

a. Your firm routinely handles worker's compensation claims for Johnson Quarry Company?

b. You were asked to defend a lawful position in which you did not personally believe?

Knowing the substantive, procedural, constitutional, and ethical rules that govern your drafting work is thus essential to your effectiveness.

4. Classify, Organize, and Outline

You should be thinking about organization long before you begin to do any drafting. Each statute addresses one general subject, and all of the parts of the statute should be related to that subject. In legislative drafting, there is a hierarchy from the general to the specific. Because organization involves the relationship between different concepts, thinking about organization enables you to explore with your client how different ideas are related and forces you to see how well she understands the concepts. Although there are differences from jurisdiction to jurisdiction, statutes tend to follow a relatively consistent organizational scheme:

Title — This is the name of the statute. It should state the subject (or subjects) of the legislation as simply as possible.

Findings and Purposes — These statements of legislative intent are not strictly necessary, but they often provide some assistance to courts in reviewing and interpreting legislation. As suggested earlier, they also give your client an opportunity to say something about the need for the legislation that he might not be able to say as effectively anywhere else.

Definitions — These are reserved for those words or phrases that are used as "terms of art" in the legislation. As discussed earlier, they either have no dictionary meaning, or they are not used in their ordinary dictionary meaning. They are important only insofar as they are used in the substantive, procedural, and enforcement provisions of the text.

Substantive and Procedural Provisions — These rules are the heart of the legislation and express most directly what your client wants from a statute. These rules prohibit or allow certain things, require persons to obtain a license or permit before conducting certain activities, or establish procedures that govern other activities. They also may provide incentives to ensure compliance.

Enforcement Provisions — These provisions describe what happens, or can happen, to persons who do not comply with the statute. Such provisions may include penalties, as well as procedures for setting penalties. Enforcement provisions need not be penalties, however. For example, child support statutes generally require that child support payments be automatically withheld by the supporter's employer. Other statutes authorize individuals to have access to information so they can enforce the statute through private litigation or public pressure. Such provisions may or may not be located separately from the substantive and procedural provisions. Whatever the enforcement mechanism, you should specifically grant jurisdiction to the appropriate court or administrative tribunal.

Repealers (if any) — A repealer is a statement in legislation that all or part of a previous statute is hereby repealed. Repealers are necessary when legislation amends or repeals prior legislation.

Effective Date — Legislation does not necessarily become effective on the date it is signed by the executive. Therefore, it is usually necessary to specify an effective date.[17]

This organizational scheme, however, resolves only the most basic questions about what should go where, because most of the statute will be contained in its substantive and procedural provisions. Although statutes vary in length and complexity, from a simple concept stated in several sentences to complex interwoven systems expressed in several hundred pages, drafting bills of any length requires an understanding of the basic principles of statutory organization.

For statutory drafting, the organizational steps set forth in Chapter 2 apply as follows.

a.   List the Facts

These facts will generally be your client's preferences. They may also include factual information about the problem, which is helpful in the findings and purposes section of the legislation. If you have taken notes so that all of these preferences are located in one place, you already have your list. For the waste tire legislation, the list might include the following:

- Fires at large waste tire piles can cause significant environmental problems.
- The legislation should prevent future waste tire pile fires.
- The legislation should only apply to owners of sites that are used for the storage or disposal of 1,000 or more waste tires.
- At least three means should be used:
  1. prohibiting tire fires.
  2. limiting how waste tires may be stored. The state Department of Environmental Quality should promulgate regulations on waste tire storage and should enforce the regulations.
  3. improving the market for waste tires through subsidies, grants, and regulatory incentives. A one dollar fee should be charged for each new tire sold, and this fee money should be deposited in a special fund that will be used for the subsidies and grants. The state Department of Environmental Quality should administer the subsidy and grant program and should develop the regulatory incentives.
- The legislation should take effect 60 days after it is signed into law.
- Citizens should be allowed to bring actions to force owners of waste tire sites to comply with the statute after giving 60 days' written notice to the alleged violator.
- People who cause or allow fires at waste tire sites should be subject to a fine of up to $25,000 or one year in jail.
- The state should be required to make public reports on its progress in developing market incentives for waste tires and should be subject to citizen suits.
- Tire merchants should be required to accept an old tire for each new tire they sell, and the disposal of waste tires should be prohibited.

Exercise 7-8

Consider again the Shady Grove Homeowners' Association in Exercise 7-1a. Make a list of the facts you would use in drafting legislation. Assume there is no alternative to a legislative solution.

b.   List the Categories, or Classifications, for the Sections of the Document

At a minimum, a category should be established for each of the basic parts of the organizational scheme described above. You also may find, based on your legal research, that some additional categories need to be created. For the most part, these categories will depend on the facts you have listed.

The initial organization would look like this:

Title

Findings and Purposes

- Fires at large waste tire piles can cause significant environmental problems.
- The legislation should prevent future waste tire pile fires.

Definitions

- The legislation should only apply to owners (and others) of sites that are used for the storage or disposal of 1,000 or more waste tires. This will require a definition for "waste tire site" and perhaps also a definition for "owner" and "waste tire."

Substantive and procedural provisions

- At least three means should be used:
  1. prohibiting tire fires.
  2. limiting how waste tires may be stored. The state Department of Environmental Quality should promulgate regulations on waste tire storage and should enforce the regulations.
  3. improving the market for waste tires through subsidies, grants, and regulatory incentives. A one dollar fee should be charged for each new tire sold, and this fee money should be deposited in a special fund that will be used for the subsidies and grants. The state Department of Environmental Quality should administer the subsidy and grant program and should develop the regulatory incentives.
- Tire merchants should be required to accept an old tire for each new tire they sell, and the disposal of waste tires should be prohibited.

Enforcement provisions

- Citizens should be allowed to bring actions to force owners of waste tire sites to comply with the statute after giving 60 days' written notice to the alleged violator.
- People who cause or allow fires at waste tire sites should be subject to a fine of up to $25,000 or one year in jail.
- The state should be required to make public reports on its progress in developing market incentives for waste tires, and should be subject to citizen suits.

Effective date

- The legislation should take effect 60 days after it is signed into law.

In parts of this outline, however, further organization and clarity is needed. The substantive requirements could be consolidated a little, particularly on recycling markets. The reporting requirement under enforcement provisions is more appropriately a substantive requirement. The bill needs a title. The citizen suit provision appears to be directed at both people who have waste tire sites and the government and could be consolidated under the enforcement provisions. Finally, the sentence under the definitions heading should be translated into a statement of the terms that need to be defined. The outline, after this reorganization, would look like this:

Title: Waste Tire Recycling and Control Act

Purposes, goals, or findings

- Fires at large waste tire piles can cause significant environmental problems.
- The legislation should prevent future waste tire pile fires.

Definitions

- Waste tire — a tire that can no longer be used for its original purpose.
- Waste tire sites — sites that are used for the storage or disposal of 1,000 or more waste tires.
- Owner — a person who own a waste tire site in fee simple.

Substantive and procedural provisions

1. Prohibition against tire fires.
2. Limitations on how waste tires may be stored. The state Department of Environmental Quality should promulgate regulations on waste tire storage and should enforce the regulations.
3. Improvements in the market for waste tires through subsidies, grants, and regulatory incentives. A one dollar fee should be charged for each new tire sold, and this fee money should be deposited in a special fund that will be used for the subsidies and grants. The state Department of Environmental Quality should administer the subsidy and grant program and should develop the regulatory incentives. The state also should be required to make public reports on its progress in developing market incentives for waste tires.
4. Tire merchants should be required to accept an old tire for each new tire they sell, and the disposal of waste tires should be prohibited.

Enforcement provisions

1. Citizens should be allowed to bring actions to force owners of waste tire sites to comply with the statute and to force the state to develop market incentives, after giving 60 days' advance written notice to the alleged violator.
2. People who cause or allow fires at waste tire sites should be subject to a fine of up to $25,000 or one year in jail.

<u>Effective date</u>

- The legislation should take effect 60 days after it is signed into law.

Exercise 7-9

Reconsider the Shady Grove Homeowners' Association in Exercise 7-1a. Using the facts you listed in Exercise 7-8, list the categories or classifications you would use for presenting sections of the legislation.

c. Rank the Categories in Logical Order

This is the most important and difficult step in legislative drafting and thus will be described in some detail. Most of the important organizational issues occur in the substantive and procedural provisions, and to some extent the enforcement provisions. These issues require you to understand the relationship between the large parts of the legislation, as well as the organization within each part. While there is no simple formula for ranking categories, it is helpful first to cluster the categories, as follows:

Place closely related provisions together. A key to effective organization is understanding the relationship between the various ideas proposed by your client. The more closely related the ideas, the more they should be located in the same place. Because all of the ideas in a bill should be related in some way, you need to organize in the same location provisions that are immediately dependent on one another, provisions that are part of the same procedure, and provisions that relate to the same topic or subtopic.

Our notes show two places in the draft waste tire legislation where tire fires are addressed: in the substantive and procedural provisions and in the enforcement provisions. They should be consolidated and can logically be placed in the enforcement provisions. Consolidation helps you better understand how the various parts of the legislation fit together and also helps the reader find related provisions.

When the bill addresses two or more concepts or issues, each should be expressed in distinctly separate places in the bill. This rule applies to all levels of organization within a statute, including chapters, sections, and subsections. A clear separation of material helps both you and the reader understand the meaning of the bill and provides an easy way to locate provisions in the bill or to determine where to place new amendments. For example, the storage, marketing, and mandatory tire return concepts are sufficiently different to warrant separate treatment in the legislation.

Once categories are clustered or divided in specific subjects, some parts of a specific subject need to be addressed before others.

Place the core provisions — those on which others depend — first. This placement ensures that both you and the reader fully understand what a particular provision says and ensures that such an understanding occurs with as little difficulty as possible. For example, the general rule should be stated before the exceptions to the rule.

Place substantive requirements before procedural requirements. In the tire legislation, the availability of a grant should be stated before the grant application procedures are explained. The procedural requirements do not make sense without the prior statement of the substantive rule.

Place provisions in the chronological order in which they will be used. If the waste tire legislation allows the state Department of Environmental Quality to make certain decisions, and then allows aggrieved parties to appeal the Department's decision before a board of appeals, organize the statute chronologically in this process. You should state the Department's responsibility for making the decision before stating the provision allowing appeals.

Difficult organizational problems sometimes occur when there are competing organizational principles — that is, when there are two or more ways of dividing and organizing the material in the bill. When that occurs, choose the organizational principle that most closely corresponds to the way in which the bill, if enacted, will actually be used.

In this case, for example, the provisions for tire recycling markets require a fee for the sale of new tires. A separate requirement provides that those individuals who sell new tires must accept an old tire for each new tire they sell. This lends itself to two possible organizational schemes for the fee requirement. Under the first, the fee requirement is included with provisions on recycling markets. Under the second, the fee provision is included with the requirement that tire sellers accept old tires.

The second scheme is better because it corresponds to the way the legislation will actually be used. If a person sells automobile tires, the person will charge a one dollar fee for each tire and also will be obliged to accept one old tire for each new tire sold. The provisions for tire recycling markets are not likely to be applied at the time of this transaction. Moreover, provisions of the second scheme have the same audience — those who buy and sell new tires. The second scheme also is better because, if the bill becomes law, it is more likely that it will be applied as intended, since all relevant provisions can be found in one place. Finally, the second scheme is better because it forces you to focus on how the system will actually operate. In this case, it ought to raise the question of whether the tire seller should be allowed to charge an extra fee to cover any extra costs that the tire seller might incur for receiving old tires.

The first scheme, by contrast, makes it harder for you and the reader to understand how the statute will work. It is harder to think clearly about how a particular system will work when its various pieces are scattered about the bill. The first scheme also makes it less likely that you will think clearly about whether tire retailers should be allowed to charge an extra fee to cover their costs.

The second scheme raises an additional organizational question, though. Should the prohibition against tire disposal be located with provisions concerning the retail sale of tires? The answer, again, depends largely on the audience. After this legislation is passed, tire retailers may be the only significant class of people who need to get rid of old tires. But in the meantime, other people may dispose of old tires as well, and this disposal may continue after the legislation goes into effect. This prohibition probably deserves a separate section, although it makes sense to locate it close to the provisions concerning the retail sale of tires.

Once you have sorted the various pieces of the legislation into larger groupings, it is time to look at the logical order for stating these larger groupings. We are left with four basic categories under the substantive and procedural provisions: storage limitations, market development incentives, requirements for retailers, and a prohibition against disposal. The retailer requirements could logically come first because they include a funding mechanism for waste tire recycling and because they effectively direct most waste tires back to the tire retailer. The prohibition against disposal could then follow. Market development incentives could easily come next, since they explain how the fee money will be spent. The storage requirements would come last because they explain how waste tires should be stored before they are recycled into other products.

Organizing the enforcement provisions is a little easier. Ordinarily, citizen suits are considered a supplement to government enforcement. Thus, it is logical to place the government's penalty provisions for waste tire fires ahead of the citizen suit provision.

This kind of analysis, coupled with some additional thinking about the details of the legislation, suggests the following refinements for the substantive and procedural provisions and the following ranking for the major sections:

Substantive and Procedural Provisions

4. Limitations on how waste tires may be stored. The tires must be in relatively small piles far enough apart to prevent the spread of fires. The state Department of Environmental Quality must promulgate and enforce regulations.
3. Improvements in market for recycled waste tires. The state Department of Environmental Quality should administer a special fund based on the fee for the sale of new tires. The fund should be used for subsidies and grants for tire recyclers. Grant provisions should include availability and application procedures. The department should develop regulatory incentives for tire recycling. The state also should be required to make public reports on its progress in developing market incentives for waste tires.
1. Requirements for tire retailers. A one dollar fee should be charged for each new tire sold, and tire merchants should be required to accept an old tire for each new tire they sell.
2. Disposal of waste tires: Such disposal should be prohibited.

Enforcement Provisions

2. Citizens should be allowed to bring actions to force owners of waste tire sites to comply with the statute, and to force the state to develop market incentives, after giving 60 days' advance written notice to the alleged violator.
1. People who cause or allow fires at waste tire sites should be subject to a fine of up to $25,000 or one year in jail.

Obviously, cases exist where the formal logic of these ordering principles will lead to inconsistent conclusions about what should be first, but these principles, taken together, provide a useful way of organizing material in a bill. These principles, moreover, are all subsidiary to the central organizational principle of drafting: The best organizational system presents the material in the most functional and easily understood manner.

Exercise 7-10

Rank in a logical order the categories or classifications you set out in Exercise 7-9.

d.   Convert the Ranked Categories into an Ordered List of Headings

This step formalizes and reorganizes the work of the previous step. When you have done this, you should inspect the result to be sure that the organization appears satisfactory.

In this case, the result looks like this:

Substantive and Procedural Provisions

1. Requirements for tire retailers. A one dollar fee should be charged for each new tire sold, and tire merchants should be required to accept an old tire for each new tire they sell.
2. Disposal of waste tires: Such disposal should be prohibited.
3. Improvements in market for recycled waste tires. The state Department of Environmental Quality should administer a special fund based on the fee for the sale of new tires. The fund should be used for subsidies for tire recyclers, which will be developed by the department, and for grants for tire recyclers. Grant provisions should include availability and application procedures. The department should develop regulatory incentives for tire recycling. The state also should be required to make public reports on its progress in developing market incentives for waste tires.
4. Limitations on how waste tires may be stored. The tires must be in relatively small piles far enough apart to prevent the spread of fires. The state Department of Environmental Quality must promulgate and enforce regulations.

Enforcement Provisions

1. People who cause or allow fires at waste tire sites should be subject to a fine of up to $25,000 or one year in jail.
2. Citizens should be allowed to bring actions to force owners of waste tire sites to comply with the statute and to force the state to develop market incentives after giving 60 days' advance written notice to the alleged violator.

Exercise 7-11

Convert your ranked categories from Exercise 7-10 into an ordered list of headings.

e. Convert the Ordered List into a Preliminary Topic Outline

This step requires you to organize the material within each of the large group-ings and allows you to discard two category names — "substantive and proce-dural provisions" and "enforcement provisions." As stated in Chapter 2, you may revisit this step later. In fact, this step requires you to revisit the principles in step three of the drafting process — know the law. Your outline of the entire statute might look like this:

I.   Title: Waste Tire Recycling and Control Act
II.   Findings and purposes.
        A.   Fires at large waste tire piles can cause significant environmental problems.
        B.   The legislation should prevent future waste tire pile fires.
III.   Definitions.
        A.   Waste tire — a tire that can no longer be used for its original purpose.
        B.   Waste tire sites — sites that are used for the storage or disposal of 1,000 or more waste tires.
        C.   Owner — owner of waste tire site in fee simple.
IV.   Requirements for tire retailers.
        A.   A one dollar fee should be charged for each new tire sold.
        B.   Tire merchants should be required to accept an old tire for each new tire they sell.
V.   The disposal of waste tires should be prohibited.
VI.   Improvements in market for recycled waste tires.
        A.   The state Department of Environmental Quality should admin-ister a special fund based on the fee for the sale of new tires.
        B.   The fund should be used for:
              1.   Subsidies for tire recyclers.
              2.   Grants for tire recyclers. Grant provisions should include availability and application procedures.
        C.   The department should develop additional regulatory incen-tives for tire recycling.
        D.   The department also should be required to make public reports on its progress in developing market incentives for waste tires.
VII.   Limitations on how waste tires may be stored.
        A.   The piles must be relatively small and far enough apart to pre-vent the spread of fires.
        B.   The state Department of Environmental Quality must promul-gate and enforce regulations.
VIII.   Tire fires. People who cause or allow fires at waste tire sites should be subject to a fine of up to $25,000 or one year in jail.
IX.   Citizen suits.
        A.   Citizens should be allowed to bring actions to:
              1.   Force owners of waste tire sites to comply with the statute and regulations.
              2.   Force the state to develop market incentives.

          B.   Suit can be brought only after giving 60 days' advance written notice to the alleged violator.

   X.   Effective date. The legislation should take effect 60 days after it is signed into law.

Exercise 7-12

Convert your ordered list of headings from Exercise 7-11 into a preliminary topic outline.

f.   Integrate the Facts into an Outline

For legislative drafting, this step requires more than a review of your notes to see if your client's wishes are reflected in the draft. You must think about whether the legal requirements and procedures set out in the draft will give your client what she actually wants. This requires you to think about how various parts of the legislation will actually work and whether it all fits together.

The Department is expressly allowed to punish people for tire fires under the current outline but is not given clear authority to do anything else. If a person stores waste tires unlawfully, the outline says only that the agency can take enforcement action. After discussing this issue with your client, you learn that she wants the agency to be able to enforce the various provisions of this legislation. The legislation therefore needs to provide the agency with clear authority to enforce the entire act and the regulations adopted pursuant to the act. These enforcement provisions may include administrative orders, civil penalties and court actions.

The outline distinguishes between grants and subsidies. If the purpose of the grant is to subsidize certain costs to tire recyclers, however, the distinction is meaningless and confusing. You may want to limit the use of the fund to grants. At the same time, your client may want to consider the possibility of loans.

g.   Reorganize and Reclassify the Categories to Account for Omitted Facts

This step requires you to find a place for any facts that do not fit in the outline. Look for the place in the outline where such facts would most plausibly fit. If there is no particular place, you might consider creating separate places in the outline for them.

In this case, you may want to add the following after Item VIII:

   IX.   Enforcement authority for Department of Environmental Quality. Whenever any person violates this act or a regulation promulgated under this act, the department may:
      A.   Issue an administrative order.
      B.   Seek an injunction.
      C.   Assess a civil penalty.

You may also want to revise the grants and subsidies language so that it reads as follows:

B.   The fund should be used for grants for tire recyclers. Grant provisions should include availability and application procedures.

Exercise 7-13

Reorganize and reclassify your topics from Exercise 7-12 to account for any omitted facts.

h.   Consult Your Client and Review the Law and Forms to Discover Any Omitted Categories

The outline now contains only three definitions. You should check to be sure you and your client fully understand the meaning of each word that is used in the draft and add or refine definitions when appropriate. For example, what is a tire recycling facility? Your client is probably thinking of a manufacturing facility where tires are turned into usable products. But what about a power plant where tires are used for fuel?

There are no form books for legislation, but other laws often can be used as a checklist or even as a drafting guide. These laws might be from other jurisdictions, or they might be from your jurisdiction concerning a closely related or parallel subject. These laws often can identify issues that need to be addressed in your legislation. For example, you may find that other laws also authorize the government to go to court to enforce the law, and you would probably want to add that to the department's enforcement authority. Be very careful not to blindly follow the exact language of other laws, however. These laws often rely on different terms, procedures, and substantive rules than your client wants and sometimes contain drafting errors.

Exercise 7-14

Review your answer to Exercise 7-13 with the classmate who portrayed the executive director of the Homeowners' Association in Exercise 7-2. Modify your outline as appropriate.

i.   Convert the Outline into a Draft of the Legislation

This conversion translates the outline format into the basic organizational system for legislation. This also anticipates, and to some extent overlaps with, the "write carefully" rule stated below.

Statutes generally are organized in the form of sections and subsections. These terms correspond to the outline you have created. Sections include a discrete piece of the legislation. For waste tires, the legislation could properly have 11 sections, one for each Roman numeral in the outline. Subsections are needed when a section's topic has discrete components; many sections have no subsections at all. Each subsection (or section, if there are no subsections) is comprised of one or more sentences. In general, the headings that begin with a capital letter in the outline would each correspond to a subsection. Although breaking subsections into smaller divisions is often necessary, you should try to use such divisions infrequently. Elaborately divided legislation tends to confuse both you and the reader.

Chapters or subchapters, which are necessary only for lengthy statutes, are comprised of a group of sections relating to a specific topic. The waste tire legislation would not require subchapters. The federal Surface Mining Control and Reclamation Act,[18] however, has separate subchapters for abandoned mine reclamation (13 sections) and regulation of active mining (29 sections).[19]

The number and length of sections, subsections, and chapters or subchapters should ensure that the statute can be easily read and that its specific provisions can readily be found. There are no hard and fast rules, but you should carefully scrutinize subsections that are more than three or four sentences long, sections that contain more than six to eight subsections, and chapters or subchapters that have more than 25 or 30 sections. Nor are there any hard and fast rules about when a subsection is necessary; it depends on the level of detail in the legislation.

The language in the outline also needs to be translated into legislative form. That means that every single sentence (other than findings, goals, or purposes) must be translated into a rule. In general, statutory rules prohibit, require, or authorize activities. That means that each sentence should contain a word such as "shall," "may," or "may not." Some rules are conditional (if X, then Y) and some rules are unconditional. Legislation does not describe, endorse, argue, analyze, or evaluate the law. It *is* the law.

In the examples that follow, several issues arise in translating ordinary English into drafting English. These issues are the use of action words like "shall" or "may," the use of more precise language, and the development of additional questions that must be discussed with your client. Again, these issues may be solved, in part, by the rules set forth under step five of the drafting process, "write carefully." Invariably, however, the actual drafting of legislation raises new questions about how to create rules.

i. Rules Prohibiting an Activity

In their simplest form, these rules state that something may not be done. In this case, "should be" is translated into language that actually prohibits:

BEFORE: The disposal of waste tires should be prohibited.

AFTER: No person may dispose of waste tires.

Some rules prohibit an activity by attaching a penalty to it. This is a common practice in the drafting of criminal statutes. The rule concerning waste tire fires is an example:

BEFORE: People who cause or allow fires at waste tire sites should be subject to a fine of up to $25,000 or one year in jail.

AFTER: A person who causes or allows a fire at a waste tire site shall, upon conviction, be sentenced to pay a fine of not more than $25,000 per day for each violation or to imprisonment for a period of not more than one year, or both.

Redrafting this rule requires an understanding of the difference between conviction and sentencing in a criminal proceeding. It also required an answer to still another question — whether the penalty should be imposed on a "per day" basis.

ii.   Rules Requiring an Activity

In their simplest form, such rules should be drafted as follows:

BEFORE: Tire merchants should be required to accept an old tire for each new tire they sell.

AFTER: A person selling new tires at retail shall accept, at the point of sale, used tires from customers in a quantity at least equal to the number purchased.

Changing "should" to "shall" is the most basic part of drafting mandatory rules. But note two other kinds of changes. First, the language of the redrafted sentence is more formal. "An old tire for each new tire they sell" has been replaced by "a quantity (of tires) at least equal to the number purchased." Statutory language tends to be more formal than the words we speak — partly to make sure that it is clear and precise and partly to make sure that it can be understood by a wide audience. Second, the term "tire merchants" has been replaced by "a person selling new tires at retail," a more precise but narrower term. This change avoids the need to define another term. The new language also makes it clear that we are not discussing tire wholesalers, but you wouldn't want to make that change without first discussing it with your client. Translating an outline into legislative language often raises new issues. Consider another example:

BEFORE: Grants for tire recyclers. Grant provisions should include availability and application procedures.

AFTER: The department shall award grants and loans for the development and implementation of tire recycling programs, upon application from any tire recycler that meets the requirements of this section. The application shall describe the program, the number of tires to be recycled, and the method of recycling.

In this example, grant "availability and application procedures" had to be fleshed out. Once again, this additional detail needs to be discussed with your client. Should the legislation address any other grant application issues?

iii.   Rules Authorizing an Activity

These rules authorize things that otherwise may not be lawful or possible. For example:

> BEFORE: Whenever any person violates this act or a regulation promul-
>   gated under this act, the department may issue a civil penalty.
>
> AFTER: The department may assess a civil penalty upon a person who
>   violates this act or a regulation promulgated under this act.

The only significant difference between these two versions is that the "after" draft makes it clear that the civil penalty is to be assessed upon the violator. Be very careful to spell out precisely who can do what to whom; leaving such matters open-ended can create significant interpretative problems or, worse still, lead to interpretations that your client does not want.

Some drafting problems are more complicated:

> BEFORE: A. Citizens should be allowed to bring actions to 1) force own-
>   ers of waste tire sites to comply with the statute and regu-
>   lations, and 2) force the state to develop market incentives.
>   B. Suit can be brought only after giving 60 days' advance writ-
>   ten notice to the alleged violator.
>
> AFTER: A. Any person may commence a civil action on his own behalf:
>   1. against an owner of a waste tire site who is alleged to
>   be in violation of this act or a regulation promulgated
>   thereunder, or
>   2. against the department when there is alleged a failure
>   to develop market incentives as required by this act.
>   B. No action may be commenced prior to 60 days after the
>   plaintiff has given written notice of the alleged violation to
>   the person or department.

Note that the "should" language has been replaced by "may," but that the authorization has been limited to two circumstances. Authorizing language generally says that only specified persons can do specified things. Note, too, that the prohibiting language in subsection (b) conditions the authority granted in subsection (a).

j. Amendments

Drafting amendments to existing statutes presents a variation of these basic organizational problems. Instead of determining how the entire statute should be organized, you must determine where the amendment should be placed. The general rule to apply is this: Place the amendment where it would have been located if it had been part of the original statute. In other words, place the amendment into the existing organizational scheme. That requires application of the principles stated here to an already existing statute. If the organizational scheme of this statute is significantly different than what is described here, you should usually defer to the existing organization unless doing so would make the amendment difficult to find or understand.

k. Drafting Conventions

The format suggested in this chapter contains the basic elements needed for legislative drafting. But every jurisdiction has drafting conventions — styles of drafting particular legislative provisions. Here, for example, are two ways of stating some of the definitions in the waste tire legislation:

FEDERAL: For the purposes of this act, the term —
    (1) "waste tire" means a tire that is no longer suitable for its intended purpose because of wear, damage or defect.
    (2) "waste tire site" means a site that is used for the storage or disposal of 1,000 or more waste tires.

PENNSYLVANIA: The following words and phrases when used in this act shall have, unless the context clearly indicates otherwise, the meanings given to them in this section:
    (1) "Waste tire." A tire that is no longer suitable for its intended purpose because of wear, damage, or defect.
    (2) "Waste tire site." A site that is used for the storage or disposal of 1,000 or more waste tires.

You would use the first format if you were drafting this legislation for Congress, and you would use the second format in Pennsylvania. Drafting conventions represent the accepted practice among the drafters in a particular jurisdiction; they may or may not be found in practice manuals, but you can learn many of the conventions by going through recently passed legislation. Drafting that does not follow these conventions will be seen as wrong. Although you won't want to blindly follow such conventions, it is best to use them unless they are obviously wordy or convey the wrong meaning.

Exercise 7-15

Convert your outline from Exercise 7-14 into a draft of the legislation.

5. Write Carefully

The basic rules for good writing discussed in Chapter 3 apply to statutory drafting. In addition to the rules stated above for converting the outline into a draft of the legislation, several points are worth emphasizing.

a. Clarity

Clarity of expression is particularly important. For the democratic process to work properly, the essential meaning of the bill must be plain from its language. You should therefore draft the bill in as simple a manner as the subject matter will allow. For example, the best sentences are relatively short, express only one idea, and contain few if any clauses. Simple and clear writing tends to force clarity of thought in drafting, which makes it more likely that the legislation will work as intended. Complicated sentences with multiple clauses can frequently be interpreted in more than one way and also can obscure ideas that you should specifically address.

Set out everything that is important. The kind of informal, unwritten understandings that often embroider the meaning of other drafted documents, such as contracts in which a course of dealings may affect the expectations of the parties, are not available to legislative drafters. What is written becomes law, and informal unwritten understandings vanish upon enactment. Therefore, nothing essential to the effective, fair, and constitutional operation of the system should be left to inference or implication. Omissions often give rise to expensive and time consuming lawsuits that cast a cloud over the implementation of new statutes. It is possible that a court will fill in, or allow a department to fill in, missing pieces, but it is also possible that a court will do so in an undesirable manner. Courts usually are not asked to interpret the most important parts of statutes; they are asked to interpret the most confusing parts of statutes.[20]

Because statutory construction is extremely sensitive to word choice, it is important to be sure, in drafting and reviewing each sentence, that each word clearly reflects the intended meaning. Statutory construction rules presume that words are used in their ordinary and common meaning unless they are defined differently in the legislation. Words that connote or imply other meanings should be changed. One way of ensuring this, as will be discussed below, is to apply the drafted rule to various problems that are likely to arise. Simulating real life problems is a good way of assuring that the words being used convey the correct meaning. Asking someone (not necessarily an attorney) to read particular provisions is another way of checking whether the meaning intended is the meaning received. If not, and if the term is important and used several times, it needs to be defined in the legislation.

The choice of precision or generality raises other important questions. The legislative expertise in general policy rather than details means that there is a limit to how detailed legislation should be. The less detailed a bill is, the shorter it will be. This kind of conciseness has several advantages. First, it helps ensure that the legislature writes rules at a level that it understands and therefore does not make mistakes. Second, it is a way of managing the problem of foreseeability; the more general that legislation is, the more likely it is to apply fairly in all cases. The more specifically a bill addresses certain things, the more likely a court is to find that it did not address other things, and the more likely the bill may be to produce harsh or unfair results in unanticipated situations.

The precision with which you craft a rule will depend on how well you can foresee all of the situations where the rule will be applied, how many factors are likely to play a role in making a decision under the rule, who will be applying the rule in the first instance, how litigation is likely to occur, and how often the rule will be applied. For example, general language may exist in a rarely used rule, the application of which depends on many factors and involves a wide variety of situations. A frequently used rule that will be used in a narrow range of situations where the decision depends on one factor will likely be more precise.[21]

The level of precision will also depend on what your client wants, and this will be answered differently by different clients. The government department that will administer a bill may want general language to maximize its own flexibility. If the bill allows an administrative department to promulgate regulations, many issues of detail can be resolved in that manner. Persons who will be affected may want some issues resolved at a very high level of detail in legislation because they do not trust the department, because they want to be certain about the outcome, or both.

Be sure, particularly in complex legislation, that all of the pieces fit together coherently. Sometimes several provisions located in different parts of a bill will cover the same subject or will come into play at the same time. To the extent this can occur, you should be sure that the different provisions work together smoothly, rather than contradict each other or create interpretative problems. As stated earlier, you may want to locate them in the same place.

Visual clarity is needed to enable the reader to find things quickly. A statute ultimately becomes a reference for lawyers and nonlawyers, most of whom are very busy. The document should therefore be as accessible as possible. Provisions that are hard to find are less likely to be used or will cause people to waste time finding them.

Visual clarity of legislation is most enhanced with the use of section titles, coupled with subsection headings. A subsection heading is simply a one-, two-, or perhaps three-word title that appears before each subsection. A table of contents at the beginning, showing each section number and title, also is very helpful. Managing the length of sections and subsections, which was discussed above, further enhances the visual clarity of legislation.

These titles and headings serve as a useful check on the organization of legislation. In more complicated drafting projects, it is relatively easy to "get lost" in the mass of material that you have drafted and lose track of where things are or ought to be placed. Scanning the table of contents, as well as section titles and subsection headings, can bring problems to light rather quickly.

The use of lists, which is discussed in Chapter 3, is also important in legislative drafting. Apart from making the material more readable, lists make legislation easier to amend later by adding to or deleting from the lists. Because legislation is likely to be amended sooner or later, such features are a service to future drafters.

b. Tone

As noted above, statutory language attempts to achieve two different goals: It must be sufficiently clear and precise to achieve its purposes, and it must be understood by a wide audience. The second goal is important because statutes address categories of persons, places, or activities. Most of the people who read statutes, in fact, are not lawyers. You should therefore draft in ordinary and understandable English. The examples shown above illustrate the basic tone of legislative drafting.

c. Conciseness

Saying what needs to be said in the fewest number of words, and without repetition, was emphasized in Chapter 3. In drafting legislation, remember that courts will presume every word is included for a reason, and that unnecessary language can cause delays, confusion, expensive litigation, and sometimes judicial decisions that conflict with the intent of the legislation.

Exercise 7-16

Consider again your draft legislation for the Shady Grove Homeowners' Association from Exercise 7-15. Redraft that legislation to conform to the rules stated above.

Exercise 7-17

a.   Your client, the Environmental Resources Committee in the state House of Representatives, has decided to develop legislation to prevent anyone from selling detergents containing phosphorus. Phosphorus leads to rapid algae growth in rivers and lakes, which blocks light needed for other plants. When the algae die, they decompose and draw oxygen that is needed by other aquatic life.
Redraft the following:

1.   No one should sell detergents that contain any phosphorus.
2.   The act should not apply to cleaning agents that are to be used outside the state. Nor should it apply to detergents used in hospitals and similar facilities. Detergents used in agricultural production should be excluded, too.
3.   The state Department of Environmental Quality should be able to create additional exceptions. These exceptions should be in the form of regulations. Even with an exception, the cleaning agent should not exceed 8.7 percent phosphorus. The Department should not be able to create an exception unless there would otherwise be an unreasonable hardship to the user based on the lack of an adequate substitute.

b.   Redraft the following:

Notwithstanding any provision in the bonds, the ordinance, or in the bond resolution, if the city shall default in the payment of the principal or of the interest on any series of bonds after the same shall become due, whether at the stated maturity or upon call or prior redemption, and such default shall continue for 30 days, or if the city shall fail to comply with any provision of the bonds, the ordinance or in any bond resolution, the holders of 25% of the aggregate principal amount of the bonds of such series then outstanding, by an instrument or instruments filed in the department of records in a city signed and acknowledged in the same manner as a deed to be recorded, may appoint a trustee, who may be the sinking fund depository, to represent the holders of all such bonds and such representation shall be exclusive for such purposes herein provided.

6.   Test for Consequences

Legislative drafting is much more than a set of mechanical skills. It involves practical judgment about what will work in the real world. The broad applicability of statutes makes testing for consequences a central problem — perhaps *the* central problem — in legislative drafting.

Chapter 2 describes the importance of walking through the document step by step to see it if it is internally coherent and legally valid and to determine whether the classification and organization of the document are logical. This kind of testing is important in legislative drafting. Chapter 2 also describes a testing process that involves review of the audience and facts, altering them to see whether predicted outcomes actually occur. This section of the chapter will concentrate on this part of the process because of the broad scope of legislation.

As already stated, statutes establish rules that apply to entire classes of persons, actions, or things, rather than rules that apply to specific individuals or corporations. In general, wills, contracts, and pleadings involve a smaller number of persons, actions, and things, and these are readily identifiable. As important as it is to test for consequences in drafting such documents, the relatively small size of the affected universe makes the problem more manageable and more certain. In legislative drafting, however, assessing the potential effect of legislation on entire classes of persons, actions, or things is more complex and fraught with uncertainties. It is also more difficult to determine whether all of the specific cases embraced by a category really belong there.

You must constantly test the drafted language against the range of possible situations that it might cover. You must use your imagination to envision a world in which the bill has become law. Does the language give the desired result? Would other language be clearer? Does the language cover more than it should? Would other language work better? You must conduct this testing process, with real and hypothetical examples, as objectively as possible. Otherwise, you will be blinded to problems in the bill at the stage when they are most easily resolved. Testing for consequences, preferably, should be done with others, but not necessarily attorneys, to ensure its objectivity and completeness.

Use concrete examples throughout the testing process, starting with your client. Does the draft legislation lead to the outcome he wants? If so, you have a good start. If not, you have a problem right away. Be sure that the legislation clearly gives your client the outcome he wants; if ambiguity exists in the language, you should fix it. Then look at the language of the draft legislation and identify other people or situations it includes. Check to see how the legislation will affect them. This part of the review involves two questions: 1) Should these other people or situations be included at all?, and 2) if so, will the legislation, as drafted, lead to fair and appropriate results for them? As you look at other potentially included people or situations, be sure that similarly situated people or situations are treated the same as your client. You also should look carefully at who or what else the language might include, and whether the draft provides appropriate outcomes for them. Brainstorm for examples that fit the drafted language but do not belong there.

a.   Common Problems

The testing process should be especially directed against these common pitfalls:

i.   A Legislative Solution that Will Not Work

This occurs more often than you might think. It is often easier to learn about a problem than it is to develop an effective solution. Much of the current debate about the Great Society programs of the 1960s is about the effectiveness of legislation that was intended to address great social problems.

For example, assume that a number of people in your state have come down with giardiasis, an intestinal disease caused by a parasite that sometimes occurs in lakes and streams. Your client seeks legislation that will require monthly testing for giardiasis so that water supply operators will know whether the parasite exists in their source water. It sounds good, but it will not work. The giardia may exist in the source water for the supply, but will not necessarily be detected by the test. Solid research will tell you that.

ii.   Accidental Over-Inclusiveness or Under-Inclusiveness

The impulse to adopt a statute frequently comes from specific cases that reasonable people would agree had bad outcomes. As previously suggested, you must ensure that the language used to embrace those cases also does not include cases that should be let alone, or at least treated differently. One way of inspecting the inclusiveness of the categories is to identify the most varied cases that could reasonably fit the language describing these categories.

For example, you know that a person who has repeatedly violated some of the state's most important environmental laws is interested in tire recycling, and your client does not want that person to be able to obtain a tire recycling grant under the legislation. Your initial draft of that rule might look like this:

> No person who has violated the Air Pollution Control Act, the Water Quality Act or the Solid Waste Act is eligible to receive a tire recycling grant under this act.

That language clearly includes this person, but it also includes people who have had minor violations of these laws and who have subsequently corrected these violations. Does your client want to exclude them? In this case, your client's sense of fairness, and the likelihood that others reading the legislation will oppose or seek to amend the legislation because they believe that result to be unfair, have led your client to ask you to redraft the sentence. Your redraft might look like this:

> No person who has failed and continues to fail to comply with the Air Pollution Control Act, the Water Quality Act, or the Solid Waste Act is eligible to receive a tire recycling grant under this act.

It is also important to go through each use of a defined term in the legislation and determine whether the defined meaning is the meaning sought. Many mistakes of over-inclusiveness or under-inclusiveness are made in definitions. Here and elsewhere in legislative drafting, seemingly mundane tasks can spot and correct significant mistakes.

iii. Oversimplified Model of Problem

It is relatively easy to discuss one part of a problem as if it were the entire problem, and then to prepare legislation accordingly. Many hard interpretative questions and consequent litigation stem from legislation that failed to consider all aspects of the problem. This pitfall underscores the importance of basic factual research about the overall problem, not simply your client's problem.

The waste tire legislation will run into difficulty, for example, unless you and your client are aware that many companies now retread old tires and sell them for use as tires. Is this recycling? Should there be special storage rules for these people? The answer to these and other questions should be contained in the draft legislation. In short, if you do not have complete information about your topic — for example, if you do not understand the full range of things that happen to old tires — you risk creating significant problems with the legislation.

iv. Unstated Premises

It is possible to unintentionally omit important provisions of a bill. You can guard against this by attempting to find the textual basis for your explanation of how the legislation would work in specific cases. Use concrete examples to see if the legislation really addresses them. For example, this chapter has discussed waste tire piles primarily in terms of the potential for fires. You might draft a sentence from the outline as follows:

> The state Department of Environmental Quality shall promulgate and enforce regulations to prevent and control fires at waste tire sites.

But there are other problems as well, including the potential for disease transmission because these piles can be a breeding ground for rats and mosquitos. If your client has been talking about tire fires as a way of talking more generally about environmental problems from these sites, the sentence should read differently:

> The state Department of Environmental Quality shall promulgate and enforce regulations to prevent and control fires and other public nuisances at waste tire sites.

v. Hostile Audience

Simulating real life also involves being sensitive to an audience that, as indicated, is made of people who are both supportive and hostile. Hostile people, including lawyers and nonlawyers, are likely to be interested in avoiding all or part of the legislation and will be looking for a means of doing so. The federal homesteading laws of the nineteenth century often contained a requirement that a person establish a "domicile structure" on a parcel as a prerequisite to claiming the land. In many cases, people claimed that this requirement was satisfied by the temporary erection of a bird house![22] At the same time, larding up a statute with procedural or other requirements to prevent such ruses can defeat the purposes of the legislation.

vi. Unstated Legal Consequences

Legislation should spell out the legal consequences of actions that are taken under it. In the waste tire legislation, for example, your client may conclude that waste tire recycling facilities should obtain a permit from the state Department of Environmental Quality. You may draft provisions concerning the permit application and how the department is to decide whether to approve the permit. What if the department denies the application? For a variety of reasons, you need to consider what appeal rights the applicant will have. If that issue is not addressed, the legislation might even be found unconstitutional as not affording due process to the applicant. You might respond by inserting language providing the applicant a right of appeal or by referencing another statute that provides generally for appeals of department decisions. But then another question arises. What if the department issues the permit and someone other than the applicant — a citizen or municipality perhaps — is adversely affected? If the legislation states only that the applicant can appeal, then the legislation is unfair and perhaps unconstitutional.

b. Possible Solutions

When you find one of these pitfalls, you can change it either by clarifying the statutory language or by adding new provisions. Another common result of the testing process is the drafting of escape clauses, if the legislation might otherwise yield a harsh or unreasonable result in some cases. It is often said that good writing is free of unnecessary qualifications and hedging. While that also is true of drafting, it is important to recognize that exceptions, variances, and other escape provisions frequently ensure that a statute operates more fairly than it might otherwise. The need for such provisions will depend on how well you and your client understand what will fall within the categories being created.

It has become clear, for example, that the use of lead pipe, pipe fitting, solder, and flux in plumbing systems causes higher levels of lead in drinking water at the tap. A statute prohibiting this could be drafted as follows:

> No person shall use or authorize another to use any pipe, pipe fitting, solder, or flux that is not lead free in the construction, modification, or repair of any plumbing system.

Does that mean that no one may use existing plumbing systems that contain lead? If it does, a great many people would be subject to potential enforcement action for turning on their tap or shower. This problem could be solved by adding the following:

> This act does not apply to plumbing systems in existence on the effective date of this act, but does apply to modifications and repairs of such systems after the effective date of this act.

The additional sentence also ensures that existing systems are not excluded from the lead prohibition if they are repaired or modified.

c. Incentive and Enforcement Provisions

You especially must be careful in evaluating and testing the incentives and enforcement provisions because of the importance of compliance to most statutes
and because of the deference that you are likely to be given on compliance matters. Incentive provisions encourage or reward compliance. Enforcement provisions deter and punish violations. You must ensure that both types of provisions
will be effective.

On the one hand, incentive provisions actually must motivate people to comply
with the legislation. You should be open to a variety of economic and other incentives to ensure compliance with the legislation. For example, if the legislation
requires the payment of a fee, the amount of the fee could be discounted slightly
for early payment. Public utility legislation directed at increased energy conservation could be structured to give electric utilities more direct credit for energy
conservation. The only limits, apart from constitutional limits, are your imagination and what will actually work.

On the other hand, enforcement provisions must be strong enough to prevent,
deter, and punish those who violate its requirements, considering the discretion
those enforcing the law are likely to have. That means the bill should allow penalties that are high enough to be effective against the worst offenders but that are
adjustable for less significant offenses.

You also must insert those enforcement provisions that you know, based on
research or experience, are most likely to yield outcomes that your client wants.
These options are likely to be disclosed by research, including a review of com-
parable existing statutes. A statute enforced by a government agency, for
example, could authorize the issuance of administrative orders, civil penalty as-
sessments, civil and criminal actions, and citizen suits against the government or
against violators. Because enforcement in individual cases is ordinarily a discretionary activity, the basic questions are whether the enforcement department has
been given enough tools to do the job in all of the various cases that may come
before it and whether each tool can be effective at least some of the time.

You also must consider whether the enforcement system taken as a whole
would be fair to those affected and whether the enforcement provisions in the
legislation are proportionate to the kinds of violations that will occur. In addition,
you must consider who will enforce the legislation.

Drafting a statute is something like engineering: What is put on paper must
work in the real world. Putting your draft through a variety of concrete examples
before it becomes law is the best way to see whether it will actually work as
intended. At this stage mistakes are easily corrected and are less embarrassing
than after the legislation has been enacted.

Exercise 7-18

Reconsider, with the executive director of the Shady Grove Homeowners' Association, your draft from Exercise 7-17.

a. Explain precisely how this legislation will give your client what it wants.
What are the most likely ways of not getting this result? How does the legislation
address them?

b.   Using your analysis in Exercise 7-1a, critique your draft legislation from the standpoint of the most hostile audiences. What changes, if any, would you and your client make to avoid or minimize their opposition?

c.   What incentives does your legislation contain to help ensure compliance?

7.   Edit and Rewrite

Editing and rewriting are basic to legislative drafting. The late Professor Reed Dickerson wrote that it is not unusual to put legislation through between 5 and 20 drafts.[23] As you have no doubt discovered, the steps described here will frequently take you back to other steps for corrections as you proceed through the drafting process. Rewriting and reorganizing, editing, and reviewing the document as a whole are not chores you do at the end; they should be a continuing part of the drafting process.

Legislative drafting raises several unique editorial problems, though. First, the breadth of the categories being used means that your client's satisfaction with the document is never enough. The legislation will affect others, and these persons will undoubtedly have views about the way it affects them. Because of concern for potential hostile audiences, you must constantly be alert to ways that legislation could be crafted to avoid such hostility. At the same time, potential supportive audiences could suggest other amendments to expand the likelihood of a favorable outcome.

Second, legislation is hardly ever passed and signed into law in the form in which it was drafted. Amendments are proposed and adopted with frequency. Therefore, your chores do not end with the introduction of a bill because other people will be attempting to edit and rewrite the legislation by amendment. If asked to respond to amendments proposed by others, you have several responsibilities. One is to counsel your client about the effect that the amendment would have on the proposal. If your client is willing to accept the amendment or if the amendment is likely to be adopted regardless of your client's opposition, you must then be sure that it is in the proper form. The amendment must use the same terms, particularly definitions, and its meaning and effect must be clear. You may find yourself writing others' amendments to preserve the overall structure and purpose of the legislation. Although it usually takes months, even years, for a bill to emerge from the legislative process, this kind of counseling and redrafting often must be done with little advance notice, and in hours or even minutes, or the opportunity is lost.

Third, it is extremely difficult to correct mistakes once a bill has been signed into law. As indicated earlier, it is relatively difficult to get the legislature's attention on an issue. Then, having grappled with an issue and apparently resolved it, most legislators are anxious to proceed to other issues. As a general matter, it is hard to get the legislature to promptly correct mistakes, many of which will seem major to an attorney but technical to a policy-oriented legislator. This is a relatively significant departure from some kinds of drafting, such as wills or contracts, where there is often little to prevent attorneys and their clients from correcting mistakes that become clear over time.

You can respond effectively to these problems in several ways. An important method, alluded to earlier, is to share a draft with others. Depending on the subject, it may be better for at least some of these people not to be lawyers. Because of the breadth of legislation, a fresh look by someone else is often extremely helpful in highlighting potential problems.

Another method is to recognize that the research, interviews, drafting, and redrafting necessary for an effective document require time, and to plan accordingly. Hasty drafting may get quick legislation, but it may also result in difficult implementation. If time is available, it is far better to be sure that the legislation is prepared in a thorough and complete manner. This helps the editorial process because you will have enough time to set the document aside for a while and then review it from a fresh perspective.

Legislative drafting can seem tedious during this editing and rewriting process, but you have an exciting opportunity. You are not writing about the law or what the law should be; you are actually writing the law. Few people will know who drafted a particular statute, but the satisfaction of having done so can be immeasurable.

Exercise 7-19

Prepare a final draft of the legislation, using your answers to Exercise 7-18.

SAMPLE DOCUMENTS

The following section contains two bills. The first is a near-final draft of the waste tire legislation that has been described in this chapter. As you read it, think about the ways in which the outline has been translated into statutory language. The marginal notes identify issues or questions that must still be resolved. You will find that a bill may look good on first reading but, after careful study, you may discover the bill contains problems that must still be resolved. As suggested earlier, the drafting process is recursive.

The second sample bill is used oil recycling legislation that contains several major kinds of problems. As you study it, consider how you would resolve these problems. The oil recycling legislation takes a different approach than the waste tire legislation. As you read it, consider the similarities and differences between them. Which is more likely to achieve its intended purpose? How would you redraft this legislation to make it more effective?

WASTE TIRE RECYCLING AND CONTROL ACT
Section 1. Title.

This act shall be known and may be cited[1] as the Waste Tire Recycling and Control Act.

Section 2. Findings and Purposes.

(a) Findings. The legislature finds that fires at large waste tire piles can cause significant air and groundwater pollution. [2]
(b) Goals. It is the purpose of this act to:
(1) Prevent and control air and groundwater pollution from large waste tire piles.
(2) Encourage the recycling of waste tires.

Section 3. Definitions. [3]

The following words and phrases when used in this act shall have, unless the context clearly indicates otherwise, the meanings given to them in this section:
"Owner." The owner of a waste tire site in fee simple. [4]
"Waste tire." A tire that is no longer suitable for its intended purpose because of wear, damage, or defect.
"Waste tire site." A site that is used for the storage or disposal of 1,000 or more waste tires.

- -

[1] *Write Carefully:* Do we need "known" *and* "cited?"

[2] *Classify, Organize, and Outline:* Should there be a finding that piles are a breeding ground for mosquitos? Note that your answer affects subsections (a) *and* (b).

[3] *Edit and Rewrite:* Do other terms need to be defined? Note the repetition of Department of Environmental Quality throughout the text. It would be better to create a term called "Department."

[4] *Test for Consequences:* If owners are limited to fee simple owners, how does the legislation affect a person who dumps loads of tires on another person's property? Remember to test definitions by the way they are used in the rest of the legislation.

Section 4. Requirements for Tire Retailers.

(a) Fee. — There is hereby imposed a fee on each sale in this state of new tires for highway use ⑤ at the rate of one dollar per tire

(b) Collection of used tires. — A person selling new tires at retail ⑥ shall accept, at the point of sale, used tires from customers in a quantity at least equal to the number purchased.

Section 5. Disposal of Waste Tires.

No person may dispose of ⑦ waste tires.

Section 6. Tire Recycling.

(a) Tire recycling fund. — All fees received pursuant to Section 4 shall be paid into a special fund to be known as the Tire Recycling Fund, which is hereby established. The Fund shall be administered by the Department of Environmental Quality. ⑧

(b) Appropriation. — All moneys placed in the Tire Recycling Fund are hereby appropriated to the Department of Environmental Quality for the purposes set forth in this section. The Department of Environmental Quality shall annually submit to the Governor for his approval estimates of amounts to be expended under this act. ⑨

---

⑤ *Gather the Facts:* Limiting the legislation to tires used on highways will exclude tires used on agricultural and mining vehicles.

⑥ *Write Carefully:* Subsections (a) and (b) seem to refer to the tire seller in different ways; the language should be the same.

⑦ *Test for Consequences:* What about the person who says he is only storing tires until a market develops, and who has a five-year-old pile?

⑧ *Test for Consequences:* How does the money get from the tire seller to the fund? It won't happen unless the bill includes appropriate language.

⑨ *Know the Law:* In this jurisdiction, special funds can be used only with this language. It is especially important to use the right language on matters involving money.

(c) Expenditures. — The Department of
Environmental Quality shall expend the moneys
received by the Tire Recycling Fund for grants
and loans to persons who convert waste tires
into usable products⑩ or energy⑪.

(d) Grants and loans. — The department
shall award grants and loans for the development and implementation of tire recycling programs, upon application from any person who
meets the requirements of this section. The
application shall describe the program, the
number of tires to be recycled, and the method
of recycling⑫. A person engaged in the business of tire retreading is not eligible for a
grant or loan.

(e) Incentives. — The Department of Environmental Quality shall promulgate new regulations, and amend existing regulations if
appropriate, to provide additional incentives for tire recycling.

(f) Annual reports. — The Department of
Environmental Quality shall publish and make
available to the public an annual report on its
progress in developing market incentives for
waste tires.⑬

⑩ *Write Carefully:* We had previously discussed a possible definition for tire recycler. When the term is only used once, it is better to describe it in context or define it in the section in which it is used.

⑪ *Test for Consequences:* Does this language authorize grants and loans for persons who simply burn tires without recovering energy? Even if "usable" modifies "energy," it doesn't say that the energy must actually be used or recovered.

Do we know whether usable products will actually be used?

⑫ *Write Carefully:* A grant program gives money to people without any expectation that the money will be returned, while a loan program involves the repayment of money. Is it necessary to include different provisions for each in the bill?

⑬ *Edit and Rewrite:* There was discussion about tire recycling permits. But there is nothing in this section or elsewhere about that.

Section 7. Waste Tire Storage. [14]

(a)   Tire piles. — The owner of a waste tire site shall store tires in piles that are sufficiently small and far apart to prevent the spread of fire to other piles.

(b) Regulations. — The Department of Environmental Quality shall promulgate and enforce regulations to prevent and control fires and other public nuisances at waste tire sites. [15]

Section 8. Tire Fires.

A person who causes or allows a fire at a waste tire site shall, upon conviction, be sentenced to pay a fine of not more than $25,000 per day for each violation or to imprisonment for a period of not more than one year, or both[16] .

Section 9. Enforcement. [17]

(a)   Administrative orders. — The Department of Environmental Quality may issue such orders to persons as it deems necessary to aid in the enforcement of the provisions of this act and the regulations promulgated under the act.

(b) Restraining violations. — The Department of Environmental Quality may institute a suit in equity in the name of the state where unlawful conduct exists for an injunction to restrain a violation of the act and[18] the regulations promulgated under the act.

---

[14] *Classify, Organize, and Outline:* Should this be combined with Section 5?

[15] *Classify, Organize, and Outline:* This sentence overlaps with Section 9(d). *Write Carefully:* Are subsections (a) and (b) consistent?

[16] *Write Carefully:* Are there other violations for which this penalty might be appropriate?

[17] *Classify, Organize, and Outline:* Sections 8 and 9 both deal with enforcement. How would you solve this problem?

[18] *Write Carefully:* Use of the word "and" throughout this section suggests that there must be a violation of both the act and the regulations in order to take an enforcement action. Is that what your client wants?

(c) Civil penalties. — The Department of Environmental Quality may assess a civil penalty upon a person for a violation of the act and the regulations promulgated under the act. The maximum civil penalty that may be assessed under this section is $10,000 per violation. Each violation for each separate day and each violation of any provision of this act and any regulation adopted under the act shall constitute a separate offense under this section.

(d) Regulations. The Department of Environmental Quality shall promulgate such regulations as are necessary to carry out the provisions of this act[19].

Section 10. Citizen Suits.

(a) Authority to bring civil action. — Any person may commence a civil action [20] on his own behalf against one or more of the following:

(1) against an owner of a waste tire site who is alleged to be in violation of this act or a regulation promulgated under the act.

(2) against the Department of Environmental Quality where there is alleged a failure to develop market incentives as required by this act.

(b) Notice. — No action may be commenced under this section prior to 60 days after the plaintiff has given written notice of the alleged violation to the person or Department.

Section 11. Effective Date.

This act shall take effect in 60 days.

[19] *Classify, Organize, and Outline:* Does this subsection belong in this section? If not, where should it be placed?

[20] *Test for Consequences:* What court will have jurisdiction for such a suit?

Exercise 7-20

Redraft the tire legislation, using your answers to the questions raised above. Does the Used Oil Recycling Act, which is set out below, contain any helpful ideas?

USED OIL RECYCLING ACT
Section 1. Short Title.

This act may be cited as the ''Used Oil Recycling Act.''

Section 2. Legislative Findings and Purpose.

The Legislature finds that a substantial number of gallons of used oil are generated each year in this state, that used oil is a valuable petroleum resource which can be recycled and reused, and that in spite of the potential for recycling, significant quantities of used oil are wastefully disposed of or improperly used by means which pollute the water, land and air, and endanger the public health and welfare. Used oil should be collected, recycled and reused to the maximum extent possible, by means which are economically feasible and environmentally sound, in order to conserve irreplaceable petroleum resources, preserve and enhance the quality of natural and human environments, reduce our dependence on imported foreign oil and protect the public health and welfare. [1]

Section 3. Definitions. [2]

The following words and phrases when used in this act shall have, unless the context clearly indicates otherwise, the meanings given to them in this section:
    ''Department.'' The Department of Environmental Quality.

---

[1] *Edit and Rewrite:* What would you do to make this more readable?

[2] *Edit and Rewrite:* Do other terms need to be defined?

"Oil retailer." Any person who annually sells more than 500 gallons of lubricating oil in containers for use on the retailer's premises. ③

"Person." Any trust, firm, joint stock company, corporation (including a government corporation), partnership, association, State, municipality, commission, political subdivision of a state, or interstate body. ④

"Recycle." To prepare used oil for reuse as a petroleum product or petroleum product substitute by refining, re-refining, reclaiming, reprocessing, or other means, or to prepare used oil in a manner that substitutes for a petroleum product made from new oil, provided that the preparation or use is operationally safe, environmentally sound and complies with all laws and regulations.

"Used oil." A petroleum-based or synthetic oil that is used in an internal combustion engine as an engine lubricant, or as a product used for lubricating motor vehicle transmissions, gears, or axles, which through use, storage, or handling has become unsuitable for its original purpose due to the presence of chemical or physical impurities or loss of original properties.

"Used oil collection site." Any state inspection facility, oil retailer or retail service station, or any other site that accepts used oil for recycling with no charge to the public for the service⑤, and which has a used oil collection tank existing on the premises.

"Used oil storage facility." Any facility which receives more than 10,000 gallons of used oil annually⑥ not including a used oil collection site.

---

③ *Gather the Facts:* What kinds of operations are excluded from this definition?

④ *Write Carefully:* Is anything missing from this definition?

⑤ *Test for Consequences:* What happens if the site operator must charge a fee to avoid losing money for accepting used oil?

⑥ *Write Carefully:* Does this include used oil collection sites? Should it?

Section 4. Duties of the Department; Public Education Program; Registration.

(a) The department shall, in cooperation with any appropriate agency or instrumentality of the state or any of its political subdivisions, conduct a public education program to inform the public of the need for and the benefits of collecting, recycling, and reusing used oil in order to conserve resources, preserve the environment and decrease our dependence on imported foreign oil. As part of this program:

(1) Oil retailers shall be required to post and maintain at or near the point of display or sale durable and legible signs informing the public of the importance of proper collection and disposal of used oil and referring them to the appropriate agency to obtain information on the locations and hours of operation of conveniently located used oil collection sites. [7]

(2) A used oil information center shall be established by the department, in cooperation with any appropriate agency or instrumentality of the state or any of its political subdivisions, which will explain Federal, State, and local laws, ordinances and regulations governing used oil, as well as how and where and in what manner used oil may be properly disposed of. [8]

(b) A used oil collection site operator may register with the department the name, location and hours of operation of the used oil collection site. [9]

(c) The registration and subsequent recognition of a facility as a used oil collection site shall be contingent upon a determination by the department that the proposed means of

[7] *Write Carefully:* Can you make this more readable?

[8] *Write Carefully:* How many sentences should this be?

[9] *Edit and Rewrite:* Would subsection headings make this legislation easier to read? What headings would you use?

collection and storage are operationally safe, environmentally sound and consistent with the provisions of this act. [10]

Section 5. Used Oil Collection Site Operators. [11]

Each used oil collection site operator who registers with the department shall post and maintain a durable and legible sign, readily visible in an appropriate place, which indicates that the facility is an operating used oil collection site. [12]

Section 6. Collection, Storage, Transportation and Recycling.

It shall be unlawful for any person who collects, stores, transports, or recycles used oil to transfer such used oil to persons other than used oil collectors, used oil storage facilities, used oil transporters, or used oil recyclers who comply with the terms and conditions as set forth in this section. [13]

Section 7. Disposal.

(a) No person shall deposit, dispose of, or cause to be deposited or disposed of, any used oil into any sewers, drainage systems, surface

[10] *Test for Consequences; Write Carefully:* Does the act provide the Department with authority to conduct inspections? To revoke registrations when appropriate?

[11] *Test for Consequences:* Does the legislation do enough to encourage persons to become used oil collection site operators?

[12] *Classify, Organize, and Outline:* Would you combine this with the provision on signs in section 4(a)(1)?
Test for Consequences: What might happen if there are no specific requirements to prevent spills or other discharges of oil into the environment?

[13] *Test for Consequences:* Would the legislation work better if there were record keeping requirements? How would you draft them?

---

or ground waters, watercourses or marine
waters[14] in the state, or onto any public or
private land within this state unless a used
oil collection tank for such proper deposit is
located on said land. [15]

(b) No person shall discharge water, anti-
freeze, industrial waste, or any other contam-
inant into a used oil collection tank and used
oil storage facility.

(c) The provisions of this section do
not include the application of used oil to
roads for maintenance purposes or the use of
recycled or used oil for maintenance or lubri-
cation of agricultural equipment, unless
such application is specifically prohibited
through any Federal, State, or local law,
ordinance or regulation. [16]

(d) Any person who burns or incinerates
used oil must bear the burden of proof that
such burning or incineration is nontoxic and
free of any chemical or physical contaminants
that may endanger the public health, safety,
and welfare, or that may pose a threat to the
environment.

Section 8. Report to the Legislature.

The department shall prepare and submit an
annual report to the Legislature summarizing
information on used oil collection, storage,
transportation, recycling, and reuse, analyzing the effectiveness of the provisions of
this act and their implementation and making
recommendations for any necessary changes in
the provisions of their administration.

Section 9. Used Oil Products.

All officials of this state and any of its
agencies or any political subdivisions and
persons holding contracts with the State or
any of its political subdivisions shall

---

[14] *Edit and Rewrite:* Is it necessary to refer to surface waters, water courses, *and* Marine Waters? there a better way to refer to the land than as "said land"?

[15] *Write Carefully:* Would more than one sentence help here? Is

[16] *Write Carefully:* Can you think of a simpler way to state this?

encourage and to the extent possible require the procurement and purchase of recycled oil products represented as substantially equivalent to products made from new oil in accordance with rules prescribed by the Federal Trade Commission under section 383(d)(1)(a) of the Energy Policy and Conservation Act, Public Law 94-163, [17] whenever such products are available at prices competitive with those of new oil produced for the same purpose. [18]

Section 10. Enforcement and Penalty for Violation.

(a)(1) The department shall have the right to conduct inspections of the property of any person subject to the provisions of this act for the purpose of complying with the act.

(2) Should the department find any person in violation of the provisions of section 4(a)(1) or section 5 the department shall issue a written notice of violation of the act, which notice shall state the specific section and which shall require compliance within 30 days of receipt of notice. [19]

(3) Should said person fail to comply with the act within 30 days, said person shall be guilty of a misdemeanor. [20]

(b) Any person violating the provisions of section 7 shall, upon first conviction, be guilty of a misdemeanor. [21]

[17] *Know the Law:* How does this legislation affect the procurement of used oil products?

[18] *Test for Consequences:* How likely is this to stimulate the market for used oil products? What else can be done to stimulate that market?
Write Carefully: What rules for drafting clear sentences have been violated?

[19] *Write Carefully:* Is this merely a notice of violation, or is it an order?

[20] *Know the Law:* Is there another statute setting out penalties for a misdemeanor? If not, the penalties need to be set forth here.

[21] *Write Carefully:* Note which sections of the act can be enforced under subsections (a) and (b). How will section 6 be enforced?

(c) The department may, in lieu of, or in addition to, any criminal penalties herein prescribed, impose civil penalties for violations of this act of not more than $1,000 for each violation; each day of a continuing violation after notice requirements of subsection (a)(2) shall be deemed as a separate violation[22].

(d) Upon a violation of this act or any rules, regulations or orders issued under this act, the department may institute a civil action in the State District Court in the judicial district in which the violation occurs for injunctive relief to restrain the violation and for such other relief as the court shall deem proper. Neither the institution of this action nor any of the proceedings therein shall relieve any party to the proceedings from other fines or penalties prescribed for the violation of this act or any rule.

Section 11. Effective Date.

This act shall take effect immediately[23].

---

[22] *Write Carefully:* Can you write this more clearly?

[23] *Test for Consequences:* What effect will this have?

Notes

1. Guido Calabresi, A Common Law for the Age of Statutes 5-6 (1982). The drafting principles in this chapter also apply to regulations, although the administrative rulemaking process differs from the legislative process.

2. *See, e.g.,* Zygmunt Plater, *In the Wake of the Snail Darter: An Environmental Law Paradigm and Its Consequences,* 19 U. Mich. J.L. Ref. 805 (1986).

3. Drafting is not the same thing as lobbying, or attempting to persuade a legislator to favor or oppose a certain bill or amendment to a bill. Lobbyists and others use a variety of advocacy strategies, which are beyond the scope of this chapter but which anyone seriously interested in ensuring the passage of legislation should learn. For amusing but instructive "war stories" about lobbying in Congress, *see generally* Michael Pertschuk, The Giant Killers (1986).

4. U.S. Department of Commerce, Statistical Abstract of the United States 1992, at 255 (1992).

5. Referring a bill to committee is one of the many ways in which bills are helped or hindered in the process. A classic method for killing bills, particularly when their subject is encompassed by the jurisdiction of more than one committee is to have them assigned to a hostile committee. This is one of many ways in which seemingly neutral processes can be used to affect outcomes without ever having a vote on the legislation.

6. For an excellent case history of how a bill becomes a law, *see generally* Eric Redman, The Dance of Legislation (1974). The legislative process is different in a one house legislature or at the local government level primarily because a bill is sent to the executive for signature after lawmaking body passes it; there is no second house.

7. An exception occurs in the Internal Revenue Code. The "category of one" (or several ones) became part of the Tax Reform Act of 1986. For example, the Act contains transition rules for tax exempt bonds for certain facilities, including a convention center that "was initially approved in 1983 and is for San Jose, California." Pub. L. No. 99-514, §1317(7)(d), 100 Stat. 2085, 2684 (1986).

Congress can also pass private laws for the relief or benefit of particular individuals. For example, Congress adopted a law requiring that the survivor annuity paid to Mary E. Stokes under a particular federal statute be calculated to include her late husband's military service. Priv. L. No. 99-14, 100 Stat. 4318 (1986).

8. Richard Neely, Why Courts Don't Work 71-72 (1982).

9. The most important audiences for some bills are the constituents for which they are drafted. These are bills that are introduced primarily to show particular constituents that the legislator is sensitive to their concerns. The legislator introducing them usually recognizes that these bills have little or no chance of passing.

10. Roger Fisher & Scott Brown, Getting Together 143-145 (1988). In drafting, as in negotiation, it is important to be aware of the potential difference between a person's position and that person's interests.

11. State constitutions are increasingly important as state appellate courts interpret the substantive provisions of their own constitutions more broadly than the U.S. Supreme Court interprets the federal constitution.

12. Mich. Comp. Laws Const. of 1963, art. IV, §24 (1991).

13. *See, e.g.,* United States v. Gullickson, 981 F.2d 344 (8th Cir. 1992); Nationwide Ins. Co. v. Resseguie, 980 F.2d 226 (3d Cir. 1992); Schmidt v. Michigan, 490 N.W.2d 584 (Mich. 1992); Altman v. Charter Township of Meridian, 487 N.W.2d 155 (Mich. 1992).

14.   *E.g.,* Pennsylvania Statutory Construction Act of 1972, 1 Pa. C.S. §§1501-1991 (Supp. 1993).

15.   Model Rules of Professional Conduct Rules 1.1, 1.4, 1.6, 1.7-1.9, 3.1 (1992).

16.   *Id.* at Rules 1.2, 1.4.

17.   The effective date is more a matter of local and state law than of federal law. Federal statutes tend to take effect immediately upon the president's signature.

18.   30 U.S.C. §§1201-1328 (1993).

19.   Statutes are organized in the U.S. Code as chapters. For example, the Surface Mining Control and Reclamation Act is Chapter 25 of Title 30. Some states also consider each statute to be a chapter. In these jurisdictions, the large divisions within a statute are subchapters. In other states, the large divisions are called chapters. The name given these divisions, however, is less important than the organizational function they serve.

20.   For an example of a drafting problem that was significant, *see* Patrick Parenteau & Nancy Tauman, *The Effluent Limitations Controversy: Will Careless Draftsmanship Foil the Objectives of the Federal Water Pollution Control Act Amendments of 1972?*, 6 Ecology L.Q. 1 (1976). Ultimately, the U.S. Supreme Court resolved the ambiguity in E.I. du Pont de Nemours & Co. v. Train, 430 U.S. 112 (1977).

21.   Colin Diver, *The Optimal Precision of Administrative Rules,* 93 Yale L.J. 65 (1983). A law requiring airline pilots to retire at age 60 will involve a large number of people. Because it is simple and mechanical, it will be reasonably easy to administer. Other rules can be more complicated because they will be used only rarely, and thus the administrative burden of the rule will not be overwhelming. For example, a law might authorize the siting of hazardous waste disposal and treatment facilities based on conformance with a statewide plan, the impact of the facility on the health and safety of the surrounding area, consistency with local planning, consistency with applicable environmental laws, and meaningful public participation.

22.   Marc Reisner, Cadillac Desert: The American West and Its Disappearing Water 56 (1988).

23.   Reed Dickerson, The Fundamentals of Legal Drafting 62-63 (2d ed. 1986).

Index